To Dick,
with all my love,
Mamie

Rev. Richard E. Gregory
33 / 2 Ruen Rudee Lane, Soi 1
Bangkapi,
BANGKOK, THAILAND

Preaching Values

In New Translations of the
New Testament

HALFORD E. LUCCOCK

ABINGDON PRESS
NEW YORK ● NASHVILLE

PREACHING VALUES IN THE NEW TRANSLATIONS
OF THE NEW TESTAMENT

Copyright 1928 by Halford E. Luccock

P
SET UP, PRINTED, AND BOUND BY THE
PARTHENON PRESS, AT NASHVILLE,
TENNESSEE, UNITED STATES OF AMERICA

CONTENTS

FOREWORD

"Sure I am, that there commeth more knowlege and understandinge of the Scripture by their sondrie translacyons than by all the gloses of oure sophisticall doctours."

These are the words of Myles Coverdale in the Prologue to his translation of the Bible into English published in 1535.

This present volume is put forth in the hope that it may direct increased attention to the riches of "knowledge and understanding of the Scriptures," brought to light by "sondrie translacyons" of the New Testament made in our own time. In particular the aim of the book is to suggest, by presenting more than one hundred and fifty texts, the great values for preaching as well as private reading, to be found in three modern translations of the New Testament, those of Dr. James Moffatt, Dr. Richard Francis Weymouth, and Dr. Edgar J. Goodspeed.

The texts chosen are merely a few of the many renderings of these three notable translations which add a new, significant idea or a fresh insight, which does not so readily appear, if at all, in the more familiar language of the King James and Revised Versions.

With each text there are a few short paragraphs of comment. These comments are not sermons. Nor are they intended at all to serve as sermon outlines. They aim simply to afford, if possible, starting points for thought. They are indications of possible ways in which these fresh, gripping and vivid renderings of the words of the New Testament into the daily speech of our time may be put to the service of winning an eager hearing for New Testament truth.

Grateful acknowledgment is made to the publishers of the translations of the New Testament used in this volume.

To The Abingdon Press and to George H. Doran Company, New York, for permission to quote from *The New Testament—a New Translation*, by James Moffatt.

To James Clarke and Company, London, for permission to quote from *The New Testament in Modern Speech* (Fourth Edition), by Richard Francis Weymouth.

To The University of Chicago Press, Chicago, for permission to quote from *The New Testament, an American Translation*, by Edgar J. Goodspeed.

The italics, in the printing of selections from the foregoing translations, are in every case mine, and not the translators'.

HALFORD E. LUCCOCK.

PREACHING VALUES

THE INSIPID CHURCH

If salt becomes insipid, what can make it salt again?—
Matt. 5. 13 (Moffatt).

THIS word "insipid," which Doctor Moffatt uses
for salt which has lost its savor, is a new window
through which to view an old landscape. The
word speaks with great vividness to our time. It
represents the peculiar danger to a church. The
greatest danger which confronts the church is not
that it may die. The church will not die. The
ever-present danger which always lurks before a
church is that it may become *insipid*—that it may
stand for nothing in particular. Jesus was giving
expression to his fear that his truth and his cause
might be committed to those who would lose the
bitingly Christian flavor which characterized his
way of life.

When does a person become insipid? The dictionary tells us that an insipid thing is something
"without tang." That word "tang" is hard to
define, but what intensely real pictures, tastes,
feelings it suggests! The crisp air of a spring
morning, the blue smoke of burning wood, the
taste of a russet apple, what Browning calls "The
cool silver shock of a plunge in the pool's living
water"—all of these things have *tang*. You can
remember them thirty years without any effort.

In one of the most beautiful of all his poems
Rupert Brooke has listed with vividness a few of
the concrete things of earth which have this individual tang. The words take form and leap out
of the printed page:

"These I have loved:
   White plates and cups clean-gleaming,
 Ringed with blue lines; and feathery, faery dust;
 Wet roofs, beneath the lamplight; the strong crust
 Of friendly bread; and many-tasting food;
 Rainbows; and the blue bitter smoke of wood,
 And radiant raindrops couching in cool flowers;
 Shining and free; blue-massing clouds; the keen
 Unpassioned beauty of a great machine;
 The benison of hot water; furs to touch.[1]

Jesus was looking for people with tang; for those
who had a penetrating, peculiar flavor in act, in
viewpoint and in spirit. Jesus' way of life was
both a criticism of the life around him and a redeeming agency to lift it up. If we lose our tang, if we
become insipid, what good are we, as far as Jesus'
purpose in the world is concerned?

When the church's message loses its piercingly
Christian flavor it becomes a thin broth. We have
far more respect for a thing we hate than for a
thing so insipid that we need not dignify it even
by anger. A man was recently saying of another,
"He's as insipid as"—and then he paused, hunting
for an appropriate simile—"as insipid as the white
of an egg," he concluded. The simile was well
chosen. Most people would probably admit that
there is nothing which excites them less than the

---

[1] *The Collected Poems of Rupert Brooke.* Copyright by Dodd,
Mead & Company, Inc., publishers. Used by permission.

white of an egg. Yet the gospel of Jesus has frequently been denatured into such a neutral dish:

How many slippery ways there are of becoming insipid! "We have bleached all the color out of Jesus," declares Dr. W. R. Maltby, describing the way in which the rugged concreteness of the Master has been blurred. Jesus had a coat of many colors, blazingly bright positives. What a tragedy when they are toned down into thin pastels of platitude or the dull gray of generalities, as vague as a Newfoundland fog! Surely we have not so learned Christ. Philip Guedalla reports the French statesman Thiers' conjecture that the morning prayer of Napoleon III was, "Give us, this day, O Lord, our daily platitude." Does it not seem sometimes also to be the daily prayer of the preacher whose eloquence exhausts itself on bromidic generalities which have long since lost their power to arrest or pierce?

We can sidestep live questions or delve into antiquarian researches which are eminently safe. We can, and frequently do, straddle controversial issues and flee to the safety zone of the fervent reiteration of obvious platitudes. Or we can occupy ourselves with the mere cranking of ecclesiastical machinery and shrink from the more dangerous business of prophetic leadership. But, as Jesus asked long since, "If we become insipid, what good are we?"

John Kelman says: "It is not for the mere sake of adventure that the preacher of to-day must often go upon 'the dangerous edge of things.' It is for the souls of men and the love of Christ."[1]

---

[1] From *The War and Preaching*, Yale University Press. Used by permission.

The Church of Christ started in the world with a cutting edge to its truth. It came into the Roman life of the first century with a message so peculiarly different from the standards of life then current that it literally turned the world upside down. Then as it grew it became more reasonable, more sane, more strategic—in a word, insipid. The glory and the radiance had departed. So to-day if the church has nothing to give but a weak sevenfold "Amen" of blessing on the standards of the world, if it has no shrill reveille of alarm against the forces which prey on human life, it is a mere bankrupt. If it has nothing piercingly Christian to say about the issues of the day, if it merely echoes in resonant, pious tones the safe generalities to be heard everywhere throughout the land, what good is it?

"*Insipid*"—a good word to look at, with the question in our hearts, "Lord, is it I?"

THE VILLAGE AND THE PRINCE

From thee shall come a Prince.—*Matt. 2. 6* (Weymouth).

WHAT are the great cities of the world? Rome, Paris, London? Interesting, all of them. But in the very literal sense of the word, they are not *outlandish* enough to be in the first rank. "Princes," as a rule, come from the *out-lands*, the back districts, the despised small town, from the "sticks."

These words, spoken of Bethlehem, are the charter of the small village, its crown of fame, its immeasurable service to the world. The really great places of the world, in a vital sense, are its little Cinderella towns, despised through all the ages by the *intelligentsia* as the abode of "yokels" and "peasantry," yet the givers of princes to humanity.

With high truth we may parallel these words and say: "And thou, Hodgenville, art not least among the cities of America, for out of thee shall come a prince." Hodgenville, Kentucky—why, the very name is grotesque, almost barbaric! Yet what place could file a stronger claim as a Royal City?

"And thou, Epworth, art not least among the cities of England, for out of thee shall come a prince." Epworth? Why, you cannot even find the place on a railway map! Stuck in the mud in the northern moors! Outlandish! Exactly, from the outlands again came a Prince.

"And thou, Eisleben, art not least among the cities of Germany, for out of thee shall come a prince"—"The monk that shook the world."

The encyclopedia will list the towns of the world in the order of their importance this way: London, New York, Tokyo, Chicago, Berlin. Encyclopedias are useful but fallible.

Thousands of the world's children drew up a different list a few months ago. Many thousands of the school children of thirty countries participated in a voting contest to choose the twelve greatest characters in history. In choosing the twelve greatest servants of humanity the children also unconsciously made up a new list of the great towns of the world. And here is the list, the wierdest collection of impossible towns ever put in a row:

Dole	Florence
Hodgenville	Domremy
Genoa	Athens
Bridges Creek	Mainz
Boston	Blantyre
Staunton	Wylam

Yet they are authentic Royal Cities. For in
Dole, France, Louis Pasteur was born; Hodgen-
ville, Kentucky, Abraham Lincoln; Genoa, Italy,
Christopher Columbus; Bridges Creek, Virginia,
George Washington; Boston, Massachusetts, Ben-
jamin Franklin; Staunton, Virginia, Woodrow
Wilson; Florence, Italy, Florence Nightingale; Dom-
remy, France, Joan of Arc; Athens, Greece, Socrates;
Mainz, Germany, Johann Gutenberg; Blantyre,
Scotland, David Livingstone; Wylam, England,
George Stephenson.

The only true measure of any locality is the quality of the manhood which it produces. Any other
standard of greatness is impertinent. If we could
only learn that in these days of frenzied efforts to
swell the mass of cities, and slogans of "Greater
This" and "Greater That"!

It is the princes, the servants of mankind, the
lovers of humanity which justify a town's existence.
And the final and searching question for every
town is this: Are we furnishing the environment
that can produce a prince—a servant of God and
the world? Are the social forces at work which will
train, inspire, empower true princes?

THE ART OF MALIGNING

Whoever maligns his brother.—*Matt. 5. 22* (Moffatt).

WHAT subtle art it is—that of maligning! And what adepts men are in its practice! The Authorized Version translates the word "gets angry with his brother." But this word "malign" gives the deadly flavor of prussic acid to the boiling mixture of anger. Anger may clear itself like a running stream. When we malign we have venom.

Maligning is a branch of the art of murder. And it is here linked up with the punishment for murder. It murders reputation and influence, both of which are sacred, inseparable parts of personality. When men malign they may murder by *poison*, the most cowardly type of murder. Arsenic, before modern tests were discovered, used to be greatly favored by poisoners because its evidences passed away. We can malign by insinuations which are much like arsenic in that it is hard to establish positive guilt. This sort of murder has often been done by the mere lifting of the brow or a half-formed sneer. It is more often done in this manner than by direct assault and battery. The most deadly way of maligning is to misstate either carelessly or with malice another's position. He is rarely able to refute.

What a text this is for Christian controversialists! In contrast to this study in murder in the first degree set these principles of Christian controversy which come from the mind and heart of that rare Christian spirit, Dr. Henry T. Hodgkin:

I will always seek to discover the best and strongest points in my brother's position.

I will give him credit for sincerity.

I will try to avoid classifying him, and assuming that he has all the characteristics of the class to which he is supposed to belong.

I will emphasize our agreements.

When others criticize, I will try to bring out favorable points.

When there is misunderstanding, either I of him, or he of me, I will go to him direct.

I will seek opportunities to pray together.

I will try to remember that I may be mistaken and that God's truth is too big for any one mind.

I will never ridicule another's faith.

If I have been betrayed into criticizing another, I will seek the first opportunity of finding out if my criticism is just.

I will not listen to gossip and second-hand information.

I will pray for those from whom I differ.

YES OR NO

Let what you say be simply "yes" or "no."—*Matt. 5. 37* (Moffatt).

THIS is a timely word for the twentieth century, for we have fallen heir to a bewildering variety of ways of saying both *Yes* and *No* at the same time. Jesus' rule of alternatives seems to make life too meager for a rich age like ours. Our powers of expression run beyond the choice of little mono-syllables. Inclusiveness is more alluring.

Bishop Francis J. McConnell has recently satir-ized the eclectic skill of saying both Yes and No in one breath:

During the Boxer Rebellion, hundreds, yes, probably thousands, of Chinese Christians were martyred. There they knelt, with their heads on the blocks, and the knives trembling in the hands of the executioners. All they needed to do was to grunt out a Chinese word that meant "I recant" and their lives would be saved. Now, what should I have done under these circumstances? And I speak not simply personally, but in a representative capacity, for I think the rest of you are very much like myself. With my head on a block, I think I should have said, "Hold on! I think I can make a statement that will be satisfactory to all sides."

How well that fits so many noble resolutions adopted after prolonged laboring by ecclesiastical and other gatherings! How well it pictures the nimble compromises in personal life, the Yes-No disciples! Trying to locate them definitely on one side of a moral issue is like trying to tell time by the clock, with which the following directions were furnished: When the hour hand points to four and the minute hand to six, the thing strikes nine, and then you know it must be about seven o'clock.

One of the unforgettable characters in Bunyan's *Pilgrim's Progress* is Mr. Facing-Both-Ways. He had a most hospitable and catholic mind. The firm foundation of his philosophy was, "There is much to be said on both sides." And he always said it, charmingly, persuasively, *seriatim* and *in extenso*. He has left a large progeny. After all, there is something to be said for old Cyclops with his one eye. He had a definiteness of outlook that Argus with his thousand eyes missed. A little more of the Cyclops strain in our make-up and a little less

of the versatility of Argus would be a decided asset
to the kingdom of God.

For Mr. Facing-Both-Ways has the futility of a
long, complicated equation in algebra which cancels
out, one side against the other, till the net result
is beautifully simple, $X = O$.   Current styles in the
Yes and No designs, now popular, are the Wet-
Dry, the militaristic devotee of peace, and the
theological chameleon whose doctrinal coloring reflects accurately and successively his immediate
environment.

LIVING BY ROTE

Do not pray by idle rote like pagans.—*Matt. 6. 7*
(Moffatt).

DON'T live by it either!   For rote is the arch enemy
of the creative life as well as of creative prayer.
The abundant life which Jesus strives to open up
to men is essentially a creative life as opposed to
a mechanical or a petrified one.   His warning
against idle rote becomes increasingly timely, it
seems, as the processes of regimenting and standardizing life go on in our age of mass production and
mass thinking.   The forces making for conformity,
for making men march in the goose-step of thinking
and acting, are causing the minds of multitudes to
become as interchangeable as Ford parts.   Our
industrial paradise, with its vast machines for
standardizing thinking, glorifies *rote* as never before
in history.

A Syrian and an American were sitting together in the salon of a Mediterranean steamship, when the ship's orchestra began to play that lively little march tune, "The Parade of the Wooden Soldiers." The Syrian gravely and courteously rose and stood at attention. The American, quite puzzled, asked him why he did it. The Syrian answered, inquiringly, "Why, I thought it was your national anthem!" He was not joking. He had merely mistaken the tune. He honestly thought that the "Parade of the Wooden Soldiers" was the American national anthem.

Perhaps it is worth while to ask the question seriously: "Is it the national anthem?" Are the forces flattening out individuality and independent personality, the characteristic activities of our national life? Are we becoming standardized into living by rote? That frustration of creative living is deadly to the purposes of Jesus.

THE GENEROUS EYE

If your eye is generous.—*Matt. 6. 22* (Moffatt).

How penurious to have a stingy eye! Eyes are ungenerous when they refuse to *light up* and when they refuse to *see*. Miserly eyes that never glow, that never kindle with luster, fail to achieve one of the highest uses of the eye—that of being the outward and visible sign of a living soul. The human eye is an organ of sight but it is also an organ of speech, and it carries messages too deep, too

high for the voice to utter. The life-giving power
of a generous eye, flashing the quick movements
of a sympathetic heart, is well expressed in Browning's words, "We lived in his mild and magnificent
eye." Even the animals which have no equipment
of distinctively human muscles—those we use to
smile with—nevertheless have the gift of eyes which
speak. The human whose inert and stingy eye,
holding back like a miser its possible healing and
cheering radiance, never speaking the warm glow of
the spirit, descends even below the level of the
dog and horse.

Ungenerous eyes are also those which see only
a pitiful fraction of the human and divine scene.
Such stingy eyes do not swing on a pivot like a
searchlight; they are set solid like a lamppost.
They see only a groove running in one direction.
Edwin Arlington Robinson paints a memorable
picture of Aaron Stark, a miser, in his line, "With
eyes like little dollars in the dark." Little dollars
in the dark—what an equipment with which to
see God's world! And yet how many people have
traded eyes for little dollars! Goodspeed translates
it "if then your eye is sound"—if it can do all that
eyes should do—if it is whole, not fractional. Sound
eyes are generous eyes. Miserly eyes are diseased,
self-blinded.

Generous eyes see the *inside* of life as well as
the outside. We are told that man looketh on the
outward appearance but God looketh on the heart.
But the power to see into the heart is part of our
inheritance from our Father. That inheritance may
be increased and multiplied by use.

Generous eyes see the *top* as well as the bottom;

the sky as well as the earth; the high as well as the low; the Mount Everests of human nature and achievement as well as the Mammoth Caves of descent.

Generous eyes see the *light* as well as the dark. They see the *far* as well as the near.

But, "if your eye be selfish"—your portion is with the bats, in a night without a sunrise.

LIFE AMONG THE PAGANS

Pagans make all that their aim in life.—*Matt. 6. 32* (Moffatt).

HERE is Jesus' definition of paganism—it is the great preoccupation with *things*—with food, clothing, and drink. It is interesting to note that Jesus, at the very outset of his training of the disciples, threw up into their vision and warned chiefly against this toughest, deadliest, and everlasting enemy of his gospel and way of life. Paganism in a variety of forms flourished luxuriantly in the world in which Jesus moved. He did not bother about any of them except this, the essence of paganism, this practical denial of God by smothering the very thought of him with food and clothes. All the other first century paganisms have died; have been embalmed in a Dictionary of Classic Antiquities. We need to call in Bullfinch's Mythology for first aid when we are asked about them. But this Paganism still strides the earth like a Colossus, a hungry giant who leaps on men with a strangle hold.

What a commentary this sharply etched picture of the pagan aim in life is on Christendom, on its ruling motives, on what we call (with far less complacent pride than a generation ago) Western civilization! "What shall we drink?" There is the obsession of a host of Americans, frantically scurrying after the bootlegger, as though it were life's major question. "What shall we wear?" That preoccupation calls forth the empire of Paris and its gods of style and display; that paganism whose first article of faith is that life is a show window.

The struggle against that fundamental atheism of materialism seems to grow more intense—certainly it grows more complex—as the number of things to buy is multiplied by new industrial magic. J. George Frederick has put this intensity in our generation in a few sentences:

Statisticians have calculated that one hundred years ago the average person had just about 72 wants, of which 16 were necessities; whereas, the average person to-day has 484 wants, of which 94 are nowadays rated as necessities. Furthermore, one hundred years ago there were not more than 200 items urged upon the average man by the seller, whereas to-day there are something like 32,000. A home containing all the modern inventions and improvements available to-day would have a grand total of about 100 separate mechanisms. The total number of items sold to-day, including different brands of one-type of article, reaches the dizzy heights of approximately 365,000.

A state of civilization such as this gives very especial point to the phrase of Emerson, "To be simple is to be great," for, indeed, it requires a certain kind of greatness to be simple in days when complexity spins about one like a whirlpool drawing us toward a vortex of endless wants and mechanisms.

Especially do young people need to be guided when they come upon this vast bazaar of brilliantly illuminated merchandise. They almost literally never spend a moment beyond the range of the electric signs, printed advertisements, and seductively arranged window displays of merchandise, of our 365,000 material things. They are plainly bewildered and put at a disadvantage, whatever may be the air of nonchalant sophistication which they wear. The great numbers of young criminals and the preponderance of economic crimes by the young plainly demonstrate the intensity of the money-pressure which the young who start in life feel.[1]

We would bitterly resent being called a pagan. But let us dare to lay Jesus' definition of paganism down beside our own life and test it.

There is only one preoccupation that defeats this essential paganism—"Seek God's realm and his goodness."

This was Lesson One in Jesus' curriculum with his disciples. Unless it were learned there was no need of further lessons. For unless, empowered with God's help, we shake life free from the strangling of materialism, we shall never know either peace or power.

SPLINTERS AND PLANKS

Why do you note the splinter in your brother's eye and fail to see the plank in your own eye?—*Matt. 7. 3* (Moffatt).

THESE words, "splinter" and "plank," do not

---

[1] *The Christian Advocate*, March 31, 1926.

add anything to the meaning of the words "mote" and "beam" of the Authorized Version. But they make the meaning harder to get away from. We cannot duck it so readily. The question hits us right between the eyes. We know splinters; we run them into our fingers quite often enough. Sometimes we can hardly see them they are so small. And a plank is enough to stop a street car.

The contrast is so great that we think the parallel with our actions exaggerated. But if we stop to think of those actions, it does not seem half big enough.

A. D. 27 or A. D. 1927—how much fuss we make about minor infractions of laws that are or never were much more than customs, and complacently we ignore denials of the whole Christian ideal of life!

The splinters and planks of other days look grotesque to us. In colonial Virginia a man could be sent to jail for failing to attend church twice on Sunday. For a third offense he could be legally executed—while all the time the slave trade, "the sum of all human villanies," went on with the holy blessing of the church. That was a plank big enough to carve the Leviathan out of!

A century later in England many Victorian families were quite agitated over the monstrous impiety of playing the piano on Sunday. But many of these heads of families, noting the piano splinter, were drawing their income from the fat profits of child labor, during that orgy of child murder which the industrial revolution brought in England.

But why stay back in the last century? Has the splinter and plank scandal become history?

The irony of Jesus still comes to our own day with blistering truth. How many people fussed about the splinter of the omission of the name of God from the Peace Treaty of Versailles at the end of the Great War, and did not notice the violation of both Christian idealism and practical political wisdom by some of its harshness and blindness.

There has been great discussion over the correct keeping of the American cemeteries at Belleau Wood and other places in France. Rightly. But some concerned over that matter have given small care to the larger question of whether future wars shall be allowed to fill the earth with similar acres of white crosses.

Theological splinters have distressed many souls with a passion for regulating orthodoxy—while they have cared far less for the business of getting on with the task of making over the world after the mind of Christ.

Many parents who denounce the young people of to-day, including their own sons and daughters, are oblivious to the fact (as big as a California redwood tree in an open field) that they have failed to supply them an example of persuasive Christian living.

We all have enough planks to build an ark!

THE ART OF NOTICING

On entering the house of Peter, Jesus *noticed* his mother-in-law was down with fever.— *Matt. 8. 14* (**Mof. fatt**).

JESUS *noticed:* It was a habit with him. That
word "notice" gives a shade of meaning not found
in the more general word "saw." It pictures the
alert and sensitive sympathy of Jesus. You can
almost see his eyes take in the whole situation with
a keen, swift glance. No one had to shout it into
his ear. He noticed it; "so he touched her hand."
We have an instance of the play of that sympathetic eye, restlessly on the *qui vive*, in Luke 8. 47,
where the woman who touched the hem of Jesus'
garment "saw that she had not escaped *notice*"
(Goodspeed).

It was a trait of Jesus, this art of noticing every
detail that affected the lives about him, which was
close to the very center of his personality and message. It cannot be left out if we are to understand
him or imitate him. James Russell Lowell once
gave this wise advice to James T. Fields, concerning
writing: "Be sure and don't leave anything out
because it is trifling; for it is out of the trifles only
that it is possible to reconstruct character, sometimes, if not always." Jesus never missed "trifles"
where a person was concerned.

Nothing human was foreign to his eye. He
noticed the patched garments of children, the long
lines of men out of work. In the midst of his loftiest
discourse he noticed when people grew hungry.
He noticed the flushed anxiety of a woman at that
critical moment in a housekeeper's day of trans-
ferring a dinner from the fire to the table. When
his disciples were intent on the architecture of the
Temple he noticed a poor widow casting her mite
into the alms box.

What a high art it is—just noticing! Some people

never really notice anything. A fact has to hit
them in the face or they miss it. It must be shouted
through a megaphone. And life's deepest things
never come through megaphones. The deepest
needs of men and women must be noticed, or we
miss them. If we stalk through life with a glazed
eye and a blunted heart, we are barred out from
life's finer adventures in human relationships, those
in which we discern of ourselves the unspoken
aspirations, hopes, needs, frustrations of people
about us.

A Christlike eye notices so many things the
world in general misses. "How are you?" we ask
one another and rarely stop to see for ourselves.
The question is merely a routine exclamation. It
is a sadly rare thing to notice what another person
really wants, even when we have known them for
years! In *The Cathedral*, Hugh Walpole has drawn
a powerful and painful picture of Archdeacon
Brandon, who lived for twenty years with his wife,
a sensitive, gentle woman, without coming within
a thousand miles of ever learning what she really
was, how life seemed to her, what she wanted of
life. It was the tragedy of the man who never
noticed.

This art is one in which science and religion
unite in a perfect harmony. Science is just organized noticing. Science began when men ceased to
guess, and theorize from guesses; when they threw
over superstition and began to notice facts. Christian love, like science, is the genius of noticing.

Contrast the things which Jesus noticed with
what the eagle eyes of the scribes pounced upon.
Mark 7. 2—the scribes noticed "unwashed hands."

Aha! They were on the outlook for picayunish infractions of tradition, prospecting for quibbles. What kind of things do *you* notice?

FATHERS AND SONS

We have Abraham as our forefather.—*Matt. 3. 9* (Weymouth).

AND the answer was, What of it? God is not much interested in forefathers. He cares about *sons*.

BIGGER AND BETTER SALUTES

If you salute only your near relatives, what praise is due to you?—*Matt. 5. 47* (Weymouth).

THAT'S our long suit—saluting our near or fancied relatives. To those within the sacred circle, gathered round the same totem pole of race or nation or class privilege and profit, we are adepts at saluting. We "snap into" attention, the heels click smartly, and the hand goes briskly up and down.

We need some new salutes, but our minds and muscles are awkward at new gestures. We do them stiffly or not at all. Salutes across the barbed wire barriers of race are new tricks for old dogs. Millions of us have been accustomed to read our Bible in this fashion: "God so loved the Nordics that he gave his only begotten Son (also a Nordic) that whosoever believed on him might not perish but have everlasting life in a Nordic heaven."

Saluting the family only gets to be such tame stuff. It is an eternal variation of the chant, "We are it." We know it forward and backward and there isn't a bit of thrill in a whole year of it. W. S. Gilbert has put the whole rigmarole of such mutual saluting societies into classic words:

> "I am right and you are right,
> And we are right as right can be."

Walt Whitman is a wonderful drill master for leading bigger and better salutes. He does not waste his time on measly little salutes of twenty-one guns to ruling monarchs and other minor character. He salutes the whole horizon. His mind stretches the whole human octave:

"I see Africa and Asiatic towns,
  I see Algiers, Tripoli, Derne, Mogadore, Timbuctoo, Monrovia,
  I see the swarms of Pekin, Canton, Benares, Delhi, Calcutta, Tokyo;
  I see the Kruman in his hut, the Dahoman and Ashantee-man in their huts;
  I see the Turm smoking opium in Aleppo,
  I see the picturesque crowds at the fairs of Khiva and those of Herat;
  I see Teheran, I see Muscat and Medina, and the intervening sands;
  I see the caravans toiling onward.
    . . I mix,
  I see ranks, colors, barbarisms, civilizations; I go among them, indiscriminately,
And I salute all the inhabitants of the earth."

Frequently our salutes are confined to one sub-division of our own little tribe, with some such deforming result as that pictured in the creed of the Pendyce family, given in Galsworthy's novel, *The Country House:*

I believe in my father and his father and his father's father, the makers and keepers of my estate, and I believe in myself and my son and my son's son. And I believe that we have made the country, and shall keep the country what it is. And I believe in the Public Schools, and especially the Public School that I was at. And I believe in my social equals and the country house, and in things as they are, for ever and ever. Amen.[1]

Yet that pathetic credo would serve for millions of people.

Bigger and Better Salutes are Needed:

1. THE SALUTE ACROSS RACE DIVISIONS. The form of this salute is with the uplifted hand. It is the hand lifted up to one Father and stretches out in the grasp of brotherhood.

2. THE INTERNATIONAL SALUTE. Nations are learning better salutes. The world cannot go on if nations are to form merely a mutual irritation society. But the salute of good will and trust across national boundary lines demands the over-powering of selfcentered, egoistic, aggressive nationalism. The signs found on buses in large cities should be posted conspicuously in the world's parliaments, "Courtesy will prevent accident."

3. THE RELIGIOUS SALUTE. Across the lines of different religions must come the recognition of

---

[1] Charles Scribner's Sons, publishers. Used by permission.

the common pilgrimage of all men in search of the one God.

4. The Salute across *the picket fences of caste and class*.

IN THE WIDER STREETS

You must not be like the hypocrites. They are fond of standing and praying . . . at the corners of the wider streets.—*Matt. 6. 5* (Weymouth).

THEY had an instinct for the Boulevard. There is a very fine touch in Weymouth's phrase, "the wider streets." The back alleys were no place for a splurge. Side streets and narrow lanes might do very well for simple souls but only the wider streets gave proper scope for leaders of public opinion.

So the spiritual descendants of these first-century publicity experts gravitate to Broadway and Fifth Avenue, to Michigan Avenue and State Street, Trafalgar Square, the Rue de Rivoli, but always to the wider streets, the traffic centers.

It is a word with a sharp thrust for an age and a nation in which publicity is one of the major industries. The desire for splurge bulks so largely in our national mood at the moment that the instinct for wide streets very easily gets into even our labors for good causes. Without any conscious hypocrisy we easily lose our sense of proportion. The bright lights blind us. We forget that the bulk of the world's business is done in side streets and country roads and that "the streams which turn the machinery of the world take their rise in solitary places."

Look down one or two of the wider streets which have a very seductive appeal to the mind of our time.

Certain kinds of *public meetings* hold a will-o'-the-wisp promise of magical effectiveness, to the discount of more routine gatherings. Banquets hold forth to many a pastor a throne from which to orate to fascinated and applauding audiences. Compared to such wider streets, the Sunday morning service or the bedraggled midweek meeting seems a back lane indeed. Or the meeting of the Association for the Improvement of Statistics beckons as a surpassing street corner on which to do really big business.

Social work of every sort, tackling the problems of society wholesale, is the characteristic wider street of our day. In the recognition of the indispensable need of the social expression of the gospel, and its application to all of life, there has come also to many people a tendency to onesidedness, a delusion that the world can be saved by organization and public crusade and agitation alone. They regret such retail employments as dealing with individuals because that street does not seem wide enough.

A wide street of perennial appeal is that of *dealing with evils by public meetings and resolutions*. The native hue of resolution may be "sicklied over" with the pale cast of thought, but the crop of resolutions never fails in these days. They are turned out of meetings in quantity production like Ford machines from the factory. They give a fine thrill especially to the mover and seconder and the committee which has labored to bring them forth. They create the illusion of doing business in big waters. The snare is in the fact that they so easily become a substitute for real work.

What gloriously wide streets *railroad tracks are!* The joy of getting into such avenues of prominence was denied to the Pharisees of Jesus' day. And how they would have reveled in them! There is no more subtle way in which a man gets the delusion that he is doing a tremendously influential work than in the fact that he is always hopping a train to go somewhere. Now, of course, some of the most influential people living are continual travelers. But travel is no proof of influence. It is frequently an escape, a refuge from the hard, grinding work of concentration.

We read in the book of Acts the assertion of Peter, speaking of the crucifixion and resurrection of Jesus, that "this thing was not done in a corner." True. But nine tenths of Jesus' days were passed in obscure corners of earth. The Lord's Prayer was taught in a corner. The impact of his life on his disciples, those men who were to be the main channel of his influence on the world, was made in side lanes. It could not be made anywhere else. He spent much of his life in a steady effort to keep away from the wider streets, so that he could do his supreme work of shaping and training men in personal contact. And we suffer an irreparable loss if the current frenzy for publicity blinds us to the truth that the widest opportunity in the world is the quiet spot where one soul comes into contact with another with lasting influence.

WEAR AND TEAR

Where . . . wear-and-tear destroy.—*Matt. 6. 19* (Weymouth).

WEAR and tear are the chief destroyers of things, beyond all other calamities. It is a more inclusive phrase than the word "rust." The depreciation of property and possessions is usually a story of wear and tear. And the depreciation of spirit, of soul, is usually the same prosaic, but tragic story.

The deadliest war is always a war of attrition. It is not the thundering charge of temptation, not the onslaught of opposition or trial, which is most fatal to the life of the spirit. It is the incessant rubbing of the daily entanglements of life. Life is a war of attrition. It is the standing in the trenches, the fatigue duties, the route marches, which wear down the spirit as well as its clothing, the body. When the fine promise of a life becomes overcast, when the eager sensitiveness to moral values and achievement drops out, when the spiritual glow dwindles to a black ember, and we ask, What happened? the answer is not usually to be found in anything special. It is a case of not standing the wear and tear.

The morale of the spirit is broken by wearing down.

"To-morrow and to-morrow and to-morrow,
Creeps in this petty pace from day to day."

The sharpness of vision is lost in a dull mist. The need of repeated effort finds a lessening response. Bishop Francis J. McConnell, in *The Christlike God*, has put this deterioration from wear and tear very realistically:

The wear and tear of daily living is such that men tire out in the pursuit of the good life. With the best intentions men get discouraged by repeated failures. They do not definitely give up, it may be, but they loosen hold of the higher principles and cease to care. The chief tragedies of the moral life come of the moral weariness. The most deadening question one can ask as to the moral life is, "What is the use?" When life is young there is a tingle about the moral battle on its own account; but the years come on without fail. All sorts of compromises have to be made as practical adjustments to the world in which we live. Legitimate hopes are thwarted, griefs settle down upon us, power begins to slacken. The mockery of death is on every hand. Then comes the question, "What is the use?" This does not mean that a man who has fought a noble battle all his life is about to cease fighting. It does not mean that he will give himself up to selfish indulgence. It does mean that he has lost the zest of the moral struggle. He may hang on grimly to the end, but with the inner fire burning low.[1]

Hopeless, is it? Is life then necessarily a tragedy of degeneration?

The answer is furnished by the human body. When we realize what science has to tell us of the appalling tearing down that goes on in the body in the course of a day, we wonder how anyone can live a week. We die daily. Wear and tear are ceaselessly destroying at a rate that threatens every vital organ every day. The only reason we live five minutes is that a rebuilding process is going on as incessantly and relentlessly as destruction.

[1] The Abingdon Press, publishers. Used by permission.

Every breath is a new life, a rebuilding of worn tissue. We could live only a few days without constant rebuilding by food, air, water, exercise of the tissues worn out by the mere process of existence.

The soul must be restored by replenished strength to offset wear and tear, just as the body must be. Just as the body can be kept in abundant energy and vigor, by constant restoring, so the process may be as sure with the spirit.

❈ ❈ ❈

JESUS AND THE ADVERTISING PAGES

Do not worry and say, "What shall we have to eat?"
—*Matt. 6. 31* (Goodspeed).

WITH these words in mind and the verses which follow them, run through the advertising pages of any large popular magazine. You will come to the conclusion that one of the major obstructions to the Christian way of life in our day is the steady impact of the advertisements on our minds and hearts. With the cumulative force of endless repetition, with the persuasive power which an increasing employment of science, especially that of psychology, gives, there is an insistent bombardment of our eyes and ears with the gospel that life *does* consist in the abundance of things. Buy! Buy! Buy! We have it screamed at us from the newspaper, magazine, billboard, electric sign, street car. And even the sky is being annexed as advertising space.

The "sales resistance," even of the strongest, tends to weaken under the hypnotic suggestion.

But that is not all. Read the advertisements with care, particularly that large class of advertisements of luxuries, and you will find many aimed deliberately and with diabolical seductiveness at some of the most ignoble human traits, such as, for example, pride, envy, acquisitiveness, covetousness, the desire for ostentation, snobbery. "Do you want your neighbors to envy you?" inquires a recent automobile advertisement. The answer implied is, "Of course." The result of such appeals is not merely to sell goods. It is also to stir up in multitudes who react to the suggestions, attitudes and moods and qualities which are utterly unchristian. Right here is one of the often unnoticed but tremendously strong forces working against the establishment of the Christian way of life.

A correspondence school offers to teach a course for sales managers on "How to break down sales resistance." Stuart Chase comments that one of America's greatest needs at present is someone who can teach effectively "How to *build up* sales resistance!"

Jesus has the power to redeem life from the dominance of things. There is no other name given in heaven or earth which can save life from degenerating into a sordid scramble of covetousness and acquisitiveness.

THE BEWILDERED CROWD

As he saw the crowds he was moved with pity for
them; they were *harassed* and *dejected.—Matt. 9. 36*
(Moffatt).
They were *bewildered.*—(Goodspeed.)

No one else saw it but Jesus. His followers saw
the people, of course. But they were used to
crowds. Crowds were frequently a nuisance. They
did not see the soul of the crowd. Only Jesus saw
that. For him alone did the curtain of appearances
lift so that he had an overwhelming sense of the
pathos of the lives and hearts of men and women.
His imagination and sympathy both were stirred
with the vision of the human pilgrimage—harassed,
exploited, defrauded; dejected, with the gilt knocked
off of life, with empty places in the heart which
hope, now dead, had once filled; bewildered, wondering what it was all about.

That is just what the great portion of the human
parade has been and is to-day as well as in all the
yesterdays. Outwardly that crowd in Galilee is
centuries away from the crowd of the rush hour in
our great cities to-day. But disregarding the minor
accidents of clothes and setting, inwardly it is the
same heart beating, the same baffled aspiration,
the same burdened trudge, the same fumbling
bewilderment.

Many have looked at that crowd through the
centuries, that lost battalion of the human host.
Some have looked, like Thomas Hardy, with irony
and pity; some, as is the current fashion to-day,
with cynicism; some with dull, unseeing indifference,
and some with the eyes of Jesus, sharing in his

sympathy and dedication. John Masefield has caught marvelously this spirit of Jesus, looking out on the human scene, in one of his finest poems, "Consecration." He dedicates his song to "the slave with the pack on his shoulders," "the sailor," "the stoker of steamers." "Let others sing of princes," he cries, "but mine be the dirt and the dross, the dust and the scum." And of these, too, was Jesus' tale told.

These words hold a penetrating picture of our time. It is a *harassed* generation. Life has been smashed up for so many millions. Who can visualize the harassing of the hounds of war? See what modern war does to humanity: in round numbers, 10,000,000 known dead soldiers; 3,000,000 presumed dead soldiers; 13,000,000 dead civilians; 20,000,000 wounded; 3,000,000 prisoners; 9,000,000 war orphans; 5,000,000 war widows; 10,000,000 refugees.

It is a *confused* generation. Many are like sailors making for a port of which the very lighthouses seem themselves to move and blink unsteadily at times and the channel buoys float out to sea. An older simplicity has given way to a baffling complexity. In Baker Brownell's words: "Intellectually the modern world is a corral of wild horses. Each specialty kicks and bites at every other."

It is an age of *disillusion* to multitudes. Sometimes the disillusion is from the collapse of false gods, sometimes from the decay of a true faith.

Yet, now as then, the bewildered crowd is a wistful one, reaching out beyond the panorama of sense, "crying after lost desire;" and Rupert Brooke speaks for the hearts of many, an authentic voice of our generation.

> "O Thou
> God of all long desirous roaming,
> Our hearts are sick of fruitless homing,
> And crying after lost desire.
> Hearten us onward! as with fire
> Consuming dreams of other bliss.
> The best thou givest, giving this
> Sufficient thing—to travel still
> Over the plain, beyond the hill,
> Unhesitating through the shade,
> Amid the silence unafraid,
> Till, at some sudden turn, one sees
> Against the black and muttering trees
> Thine altar, wonderfully white
> Among the Forests of the Night."[2]

Jesus facing a bewildered world was never helpless. "He had for weary feet, the gift of rest;" for strayed minds a goal and a way.

IMPIOUS!

"Such language is *impious*," said some of the scribes among themselves.—*Matt. 9. 3* (Weymouth).

HORRORS! A new vocabulary! No wonder the scribes sputtered. The fear of a new word, a new idea, is the most terrifying fear a literalist and traditionalist can ever know. And the unfailing reception which every true word of prophecy has met through the centuries has been—"Such lan-

---

[2] *The Collected Poems of Rupert Brooke.* Dodd, Mead & Company, Inc., publishers. Used by permission.

guage is impious." "He does not speak the same
shibboleths; we don't hear the metallic click of the
worn counters of speech. He uses strange words
and we have to think. It is a nuisance to think.
It isn't pious."

Emerson pictures this hatred of a fresh vocabulary:

As soon as we hear a new vocabulary from our own, at
once we exaggerate the alarming differences, account the
man suspicious, a thief and a pagan and set no bounds
to our disgust or hatred, and late in life, perhaps too late,
we find he was loving, doing and thinking the same
things as we under his own vocabulary.

Jesus cared about *things;* the scribes cared about
words. We search the New Testament in vain for
any instance that they ever once made an effort
to understand what Jesus meant, what spirit was
his. They asked him scores of questions. Evidently, it was one of the popular sports of their
day to try to trip or snare Jesus in a verbal net.
But never did they ask Jesus a question for the
elementary and obvious purpose of finding out
something. Robert Lynd, in a very charming,
and thoughtful essay on *The Pleasures of Ignorance,*
points out that one of the finest delights of life is
that of asking questions. "The man who has
exchanged that pleasure," he says, "for the pleasure
of dogma, which is the pleasure of answering, has
already begun to stiffen."[1]

The scribes knew no "pleasure of ignorance."
They had long since stiffened. They cared only
for the sound of their stereotyped phrases. When
Jesus came, caring more for truth than for "bab-

[1] Charles Scribner's Sons, publishers. Used by permission.

bling repetitions," more for God than for phrase
books, more for man than for traditions, he was
"impious."

Which do we care most about, God's universe
or dictionaries? Things or words?

NEWS; NOT ADVICE

Proclaiming the *Good News* of the Kingdom.—*Matt. 9.
35* (Weymouth).

"CHRISTIANITY is good news, not good advice."
It was first preached as news. Wherever it has
been preached with power it has been preached as
news. Christianity is first and foremost a historical
religion. Something happened: The Word became
flesh and dwelt among us, full of grace and truth.
When the Christian evangel ceases to be good news
and dwindles down into mere advice it has ceased
to be itself and loses its power.

MAKE YOURSELF AT HOME!

While Jesus was *at home* at table, a number of tax
collectors and irreligious people came in.—*Matt. 9. 10*
(Goodspeed).

JESUS was at home everywhere. These words
from our daily life, "at home," give a touch which
illuminates Jesus' whole life, all his contacts with

men, women, and children. He set people at their
ease in circumstances which to another would have
been painful with embarrassment. He inspired
utter confidence in the most unlikely folks.

Try to imagine one of the Pharisees sitting down
at a hastily gathered dinner party of Matthew's
cronies—tax-collectors, ward politicians, and irreligious people. His very entrance would have
brought a December chill that would freeze the
genial current of the feast. He would have suffered himself and induced in all the rest a paralyzing
self-consciousness. A provocative sense of superiority would have charged the air with electric
antagonism and resentment.

But Jesus was *at home*. Without either compromise or patronage, with ease and naturalness,
he created the climate of home wherever he went.

It was no trick of manner. It was nothing put
on. It was an inevitable result of his conception
of God and man.

1. The world was his Father's House, all of it.
So he was literally and profoundly at home everywhere. How could it be otherwise? There is a
beautiful old proverb which says, "To him to whom
God is a Father every land is a fatherland." There
was no nook or corner of earth which was not
fatherland to Jesus.

2. To Jesus, everyone belonged to his Father's
family. The intensity of that truth literally made
every company a home circle for him. All folks
were "home folks," brothers and sisters. That
truth was the very air in which he moved. Go
through the gospel records carefully and you will
discover that he never met a stranger in his life.

He met only brothers. He was at home in his Father's family.

That was Jesus' secret. That may be the priceless faculty of anyone who really shares that tremendous faith of Jesus. The Christian religion says to man, "Make yourself at home." This world is not a battle ground of blind forces. It is not a machine shop. It is not an orphan asylum. It is your Father's house. At its center is

> "Immortal love, forever full,
> Forever flowing free."

This phrase "at home" raises an inescapable personal question: Where do we feel most at home? It was said of Henry Drummond, "He was more at home with Jesus Christ than with anyone else."

❧ ❧ ❧

JESUS' APPEAL TO THE IRRELIGIOUS

I did not come to invite the pious but the *irreligious*.—
Matt. 9. 13 (Goodspeed).

THESE words bring a new shade of meaning to the Authorized Version—"I am not come to call the righteous, but sinners." For the contrasted types of people, "the pious" and "the irreligious" represented not merely, or even chiefly, differences in ethical conduct but in temperament and disposition.

It is well worth pondering deeply that Jesus had a strong appeal for a class of people who are conspicuously absent from our churches to-day—the irreligious. They are people of whom we cannot say that the religious instinct is lacking in their make up. We cannot say that of any individual, and much less of any group. They are people who are much less susceptible to the moods and feelings of piety than others. Religious ceremonies and observances do not appeal to them or yield them the satisfaction which they do to the group Jesus called "the pious." Frequently they have little of the mystical temperament with which many seem to be endowed. Usually they are not by disposition either docile or credulous. Institutional religion has at all times found "the irreligious" a hard class to win, a hard class to hold. Perhaps part of the reason is that many within the church have found them a hard class to like.

Church people have often taken two lines of least resistance in dealing with the irreligious. They have tagged them with the label "sinners" and here left them alone. And in doing this they have been treacherous to the example of Jesus.

There is an unfailing attraction in men who possess large endowments of human energy and force. Their power may be undisciplined and misdirected, but the power attracts. No one can study Jesus' life without feeling that he would be attracted to that kind of men too. His fellowship with the irreligious was one of the major scandals of his life.

Marguerite Wilkinson, in her poem, "Black Sheep," has pictured with striking force these two contrasted groups, the pious and irreligious, and suggests the eager quest of Jesus for those whose temperaments make them hard to shepherd.

"The white sheep are placid
  And feed in quiet places;
Their fleeces are like silver
  That the moon has known.
But the black sheep have vigor
  In their ugly faces.
The Best of all the shepherds
  Wants them for his own.

"The white sheep are humble,
  And they will always follow
The soft call of leaders
  To the dear home fold.
But the black sheep are wayward
  In many a wintry hollow.
The Best of all the shepherds
  Would save them from the cold.

"The white sheep are gentle,
  And bend their necks together;
They crop in God's pasture
  Grasses sweet and mild.
But the black sheep are starving
  Alone in heavy weather.
Oh, Best of all the shepherds,
  Feed them in the wild!"[1]

Think of that phrase in the first verse—"But the black sheep have vigor." No wonder Jesus loved them! How he loved energy! Run through his parables and note how many of them extol energy—the talents, the importunate widow, the lost coin and the lost sheep. Look at the men he chose to be his disciples many were entirely outside of the inner circles of the professionally religious. Men of

[1] From The Ladies' Home Journal. Used by permission.

prodigious energy, whose chief virtues did not rank
high, if at all, on the regulation religious score
cards of the day.

Where have we lost this appeal of Jesus to the
irreligious, to those not pious in the conventional
sense? For, in losing it, the church has suffered an
immeasurable loss. This particular class of people
is growing in numbers to-day and seemingly destined
to increase in the future.

Some elements in this appeal of Jesus to the
irreligious, to be recovered in our time, may be
merely suggested.

1. Jesus had a tremendous liking for men—all
kinds of men, for the whole Noah's ark of the
human race. Let us use the word "liked" in this
connection. The more adequate word, "love," has
theological associations which are not stressed here.
We are thinking not in theological terms but in
terms of the personality of Jesus. He did not have
a pigeonhole mind or a synagogue-mind, which classified men by types. He never thought, what we so
often think of a person, "He is not our type." All men
were his type because they were God's children.

2. Jesus never underrated or disregarded any
fine human quality or virtue in the way his followers so frequently have. Magnificent human
virtues have even been discounted as pagan virtues
because they did not fit into a neat preconceived
schedule of ecclesiastical goodness. As Dr. W. R.
Maltby so well says:

Our theological coat was cut for the figure of total
depravity, but when it was tried on it was found not to
fit any kind of human nature. Accordingly, we let out a

seam in the back, and the margin thus gained, with the stitches still showing, we called prevenient grace. Still the coat does not fit, for it is not by any afterthought that we can do justice to that boundless patience and holiness of God which loves goodness everywhere, labors for it, and delights in it everywhere. . . . These vast tracts of the unbaptized human life we make over to poets and novelists and dramatists, who explore them with inexhaustible interest and sympathy. Yet that interest and sympathy come from God, who loves this human life of ours, not only as a novelist, approving where it is good, and disapproving where it is bad, but as a poet or an artist loves it because he cannot help loving a thing so strange, piteous, and enthralling as the story of every human soul must be. For the most part the church has only taken account of the baptized virtues. The other kind she did not deny, but she has often acknowledged them with uneasiness—much as the vicar allows the saintliness of a Dissenter within his faithful parish, or a squire concedes that there is a very savory smell in the poacher's kitchen.[1]

3. There is an immense appeal to the "irreligious," an appeal not used in anything like its full power, in Jesus' disregard of petty legalisms and formalisms of every sort.

4. We have held off men who might have been won, as Jesus' first disciples were won, because we have emphasized intricacies of opinion, and raised barbed wire entanglements in God's open lanes of invitation.

5. Jesus had a lasting appeal to people largely occupied with practical affairs in his emphasis on the expression of faith in practical conduct.

---

[1] From The Methodist Recorder, London.

CAN YOU DISMISS A CROWD?

When he had driven the people out.—*Matt. 9. 25*
(Goodspeed).

THESE words occur in the story of the healing
of a little girl. They bring to mind Jesus' attitude
toward crowds and furnish a fine theme for meditation in an age of crowds, such as ours is to-day.

Jesus lived amid crowds. Any moments of privacy—and he made many—were deliberate achievements. From Capernaum to Jerusalem he was
rarely outside of the hearing of tramping feet.
Yet the crowd never trampled him down. He
never seeks it. He is never dependent upon it.
Further, whenever he wants to do anything of first
importance, as a rule he dismisses the crowd. With
us, on the other hand, whenever we feel that any
prospect really big is on foot, the first question
usually is, "How shall the publicity be handled?"

Jesus' concern was to dismiss the crowd; ours is
to gather one.

Is it not probable that the reason we are able
to do so little with the crowd is that we do so little
apart from it? Does not a man's final and lasting
influence with a crowd depend on what he does
away from the crowd—alone?

That is a truth so easily forgotten in an age of
publicity. The glare of the crowd has the same
effect on a man and his message as the glare of
the desert. The streams dry up. There is often
deep irony in the phrase, "a public man." For
the man who revels in the crowd depends upon it. He
becomes more and more the public figure and less
and less the *man*. Many a preacher has allowed

his message to become a thin trickle of soothing syrup, because he could not dismiss the crowd and replenish life from deep inner springs. Without those springs the rôle of prophet is impossible; one must perforce become a showman.

Can you dismiss a crowd? It seems the last thing a modern man can do. The heady wine of publicity, the intoxication of print, the glare of the spotlight—all these rush upon our generation as upon no other that has preceded it. Without eternal vigilance they become meat and drink to us.

It is a strong verb used here. Jesus had to *drive* out the crowd. So do we, if we are not to be trampled down. Can you get along without the crowd, more eager for inner realities than market place notice, measuring life's significance by the eternal standards of God rather than by inches of newspaper space? What we can do in the crowd depends on what we become away from it. If we cannot dismiss a crowd, we will never be able to do much else with it.

CONTROLLED POWER

Wise like serpents and *guileless* like doves.—*Matt. 10. 16* (Goodspeed).

THE familiar phrase "harmless as doves" has a somewhat unfortunate sound in that it seems to suggest weakness. Who wants to be called "harmless"? As ordinarily used, the word has a contemptuous ring. "He could not do any harm if he wanted to," it seems to say. The phrase "harmless lunatic" is a frequent one, almost a technical expression to describe a person out of his right mind but of a mild disposition and so not dangerous.

Unfortunately, that phrase "harmless lunatic" describes exactly a common idea of Christian character. The Christian is thought of as a weakling, a gentle, sisterly, ineffectual type of being, perfectly harmless and, by so much, perfectly useless.

Doctor Goodspeed's word "guileless" corrects this distortion. It suggests not the absence of power but *controlled* power; not impotence but might in leash; not the absence of force but the domination of hatred and guile by the positive power of good will.

THE GREAT BETRAYAL

The father will *betray* his child.—*Matt. 10. 21* (Weymouth).

THESE words sketch a detail of the testing times which it is predicted that the disciples of Jesus will see. It is a crowning touch. The inference is that there could be nothing worse than to betray a child.

All will agree to that. Yet is not that a fairly common occurrence about us? Not in the literal sense the words contemplate—yet not in any remote metaphorical sense either. The child is not betrayed intentionally or even consciously, very often. But it is done continuously and effectively.

Of course the risks of such a preposterous adventure as parenthood are enormous. No insurance company, not even Lloyds, has ever issued a policy against the possibility of being a bad parent. The risks would be too great. Emerson has well expressed the seat of the trouble when he says: "Children are all foreigners. We treat them as such. We cannot understand their speech or mode of life and so our education is remote and accidental and not closely applied to the facts."

Yet the word "betrayal" is too strong to apply to the fumbling all parents do in trying to penetrate the mysteries of that baffling foreigner, their child. Betrayal implies "handing one over to the enemy," and that is exactly what sometimes happens—the child is handed over to the enemy.

How many children, for instance, have been betrayed into the hands of *fear*—to remain captives for life. Bondage to fear is not a natural state—the child is betrayed into it by the timidities, hesitations, and terrors of the parents, and the possibility of a victorious stride through life, buoyant and confident, is lost. What a wonderful parent Jesus was in his training of the disciples! "Fear not!" "Trust!" That was an early lesson. Unless it were mastered there was no use of going on to any other lesson.

Betrayed into *conventionality*—is the fate of others. That does not sound like a base betrayal perhaps. Look closer. No doubt a parent who deliberately set out to train his children to be rebels would be looked upon as a madman. Yet

he would come much nearer to saving their souls
alive than the parent who deliberately trains them
for "success," in the common vulgar meaning of
that term. For conventionality is an ogre which
transforms children into wax statues, fashion plates
and machines. It strips them of individuality, of
God-given spontaneity, robs them of the priceless
gifts of independence of thought and spirit of adventure, which are the world's chief hope of redemption from the tyranny of tradition and sanctified
stupidities.

A common betrayal of a child is to *keep him out
of a great inheritance.* A guardian who would de-
fraud a child from sharing in a large money inheritance would be sent to jail. A parent who defrauds
a child from sharing in his great religious heritage
is so common that he is not noticed. Yet the
betrayal in the first case is slight compared with
the other. A large company of parents subscribe
to the program of Charles Lamb, who once said
jokingly, "I am determined that my children shall
be brought up in their father's religion, *if they can
find out what it is.*" What Lamb proposed face-
tiously is acted upon seriously and the children,
being unable to discover what the father's religion
is, naturally adopt the same religion for themselves.

Miriam Van Waters, of the Los Angeles Juvenile
Court, has written entertainingly and effectively on
"Nineteen Ways of Being a Bad Parent." Probably to cite nineteen distinct yawning pitfalls would
be discouraging to the average amateur parent.
But the theme is one that greatly needs discussion
and is an admirable theme for timely and direct
preaching in these days.

Here are some ways of betrayal common enough ways of being a bad parent that are to be met with on nearly every block.

Half-Time parents are bad ones: parents who act as such only spasmodically and then frequently at the wrong time.

A Bad Parent is one who never lets a child grow up, who does all his thinking for him; the "mother-knows-best" type of parent.

A parent betrays a child who builds up in him a feeling of inferiority. He has crippled the child for life.

Many a parent, in demanding rigid obedience, succeeds only in arousing rebellion.

A parent betrays his child if he fails to distinguish between major and minor values. In a home where "manners" rank higher than moral values it is hard to expect any development in genuine Christian character.

※ ※ ※

THE REPELLENT CHRIST

Blessed is the man who finds nothing that *repels* him in me.—*Matt. 11. 6* (Goodspeed).

THERE is a shock in the very words—the repelling Christ. Christ repel men? We prefer to think of him as the universal magnet. And rightly. Yet we know only very superficially the life and spirit of our time if we do not realize that there is real meaning in the words—the repellent Christ. There are elements in Jesus distinctly repulsive to the spirit and ruling ideas of large numbers of people in our day. It was true in Jesus' day, as even the most cursory reading of the Gospels shows. It has always been true. It is true in many peculiar ways to-day.

1. The spirit of acquisition, so dominant a force in such wide areas of life, the love of power, the motive of profit, the measurement of life in material terms, the worship of success—these find much in Christ that repels them. Jesus' demand for humility and repentance, seems a strange language to-day. "How," asks Reinold Niebuhr, "can we get a gasoline-propelled, fur-coated congregation of prosperous Americans to share that uneasy sense over possessions that is so characteristic a note of the New Testament?" The feeling that there is anything fundamentally wrong with our whole way of life is repulsive to a materially successful industrial civilization.

2. The modern love of comfort, nursed by a thousand modern labor-saving and luxury-producing inventions, is repelled by the whole sacrificial character of Jesus' teaching and life. Consequently, Jesus is, as Dr. Bernard I. Bell declares, "an enigma to the mood of the moment." He thus describes the spirit that is reflected by Jesus.

As for comfort, we twentieth-century people are soothingly immersed in it. Ours is a steam-heated, well-lighted, cunningly upholstered, warm-bathed era. With almost incredible ingenuity we ward off the pumps, plane the sharp corners, "escalate" the heights. From twilight sleep birth to narcotized death we insist on ease. It is that without which all else is intolerable. Only to ex-

ceptional people has it yet occurred that the whole cult
is petty, ignoble, unworthy of human nature.[1]

"Let him take up his cross"—that repels children of comfort whose only contact with rough
roads is on balloon tires.

3. There is a moral austerity in Christ which
cannot be fitted into the spirit of multitudes of
pleasure-loving people with wavering moral standards. With all appreciation of Jesus as the bringer
of joy—yet there is a severity of personal discipline
in his demands which cannot be blinked even by
the loosest thinking. To the current mood of
many—that of obsession with sex—Jesus is a disturbing, a rebuking figure. Frankly—though it is
not often expressed frankly—he is repulsive.

4. To the cult of self-assertive nationalism Jesus
is repulsive. Here the repulsion is more outspoken.
It does not take the form of open reviling so often
as that of distortion. Militarism tries to twist
Christ into its own likeness. Blustering and aggressive nationalism substitutes itself for Christianity as
a religion. Jesus' disregard for boundaries of race
and tribe, his universal mission, his repudiation of
force all make him a dangerous enemy to that competitive nationalistic spirit which generates war.

WISE FOOLS

Hiding all this from the . . . *intelligent.*—Matt. *11. 25*
(Goodspeed).

---

[1] *The Atlantic Monthly*, 1927. Used by permission.

THAT word *intelligent* sort of "clicks" in our mind. It calls up that unlovely modern word— with such a deadly aroma of snobbishness—*intelligentsia*. And it would be rather hard to find a word which describes more exactly the kind of people Jesus had in mind—so grievously learned that they miss what is best worth learning. The *intelligentsia* are the consciously, the self-admittedly, intelligent. They are the "highbrows." They are so intent on complexities that they have forgotten the simplicities; so eager on the quest of the whims and the crazes that they have lost the "ancient, beautiful things."

The picture of some of these wise fools has perhaps never been sketched with more telling irony than by James M. Barrie in his play, "The Admirable Crichton." The characters are a family of society people and their butler wrecked on a desert island. They are possessed of an impressive variety of sophisticated learning and skill. They know Burke's Peerage by heart. They have a complete mastery of the technique of auction bridge. In the knowledge of good form for all occasions from a court reception to a hunt they are letter perfect. Yet they would have speedily starved to death had it not been for the butler. He alone had any knowledge of the common, elementary processes of sustaining life. Their crazy jumble of artificial learning had about as much connection with elementary human needs as if they had lived on the moon.

This titled family on their desert island were a fair picture of "the intelligent" Jesus had in mind, ignorant of life's most vital primary truth.

What a boisterous crew our self-styled *intelligentsia* are to-day! From the heights of sophistication they look down with Olympian contempt on the poor "morons" who make up the average run of the human race. They are the "civilized minority." Whatever the majority has valued and admired must necessarily be passé, outworn drivel, fit only for "yokels." To such emancipated minds Dickens is impossible, George Eliot hopelessly mid-Victorian—mere pygmies compared to James Joyce and Dreiser. Tennyson is food for babes, not to be mentioned in the same breath with Ezra Pound.

The suggestion that anything of worth could be hidden from the wise and learned would be intolerable. A study of what such intelligent minds miss is vastly rewarding.

"I thank thee, Father, Lord of heaven and earth, for hiding all *this* from the learned and intelligent"—

All *what?*

For one thing, any conception of the reality of *religious experience*. There has been a progressive emancipation of humanity from superstition in recent years. And many in throwing over superstition have thrown out all the precious and tested religious experience of millions of men and women throughout the centuries. They have been so painfully clever that this deepest, most vital of human quests and achievements has been hidden from them. One modern wise man—and a rare wisdom he has in many ways—George Santayana, grows positively gay over the prospect of unloading what he calls the "burden" of faith.

"Farewell, my burden! No more will I have
The foolish load of my fond faith's despair,
But try the idle race with careless feet.
The crown of olive let another wear;
It is my crown to mock the runner's heat
With gentle wonder and with laughter sweet."[1]

The learned and *intelligent*, in Jesus' use of the word, frequently miss the deep wisdom distilled from the experience of the race. The lasting, immemorial joys of family life, won and tested by the experience of the ages, are too naïve, and simple and "stuffy" for many of these learned. Traditional sex morality is too intolerable a repression for many of the truly emancipated. Listen to Bertrand Russell. Speaking of the sex education of his own children he declares, "I shall not teach that faithfulness to one partner through life is in any way desirable or that a permanent marriage should be regarded as excluding temporary episodes."

The *intelligentsia* frequently miss the wisdom of *sympathy*. "A loving heart," says Carlyle, "is the beginning of all knowledge." For a feeling of kinship with common humanity, a sympathetic understanding of and identification with the life and aspirations of all kinds and conditions of men, many have substituted the delights of a superior contempt and cynicism. And the price they always pay is blindness.

---

[1] Charles Scribner's Sons, publishers. Used by permission.

THE KINDLY YOKE

My yoke is *kindly.*—*Matt. 11. 30* (Moffatt).

A MUCH better word than "easy." Jesus' yoke is not always easy. It *is* always kindly. Just as a father's discipline of a child is not always easy—sometimes it is very grievous. Yet it may be kindly even when it rests heavily.

Some people find Jesus' way of life easy only because they have followed it very superficially. A congregation can sing lightly and absent-mindedly,

> "His yoke is easy;
> His burden is light.
> I've found it so—"

who have never felt the fellowship of his sufferings at all. No wonder they've found it easy! They've never tried it! The yoke of Jesus is *kindly.* He asks much. But he asks it from love, so that by bearing it our joy may be full and our life abundant.

THE WRANGLERS

He will not *wrangle* or *shout.*—*Matt. 12. 19* (Moffatt).

YET how much of it his disciples have done! These words occur in an Old Testament description of the Messiah. They are characteristics which Jesus supremely fulfilled. They should be out-standing marks of Jesus' disciples. Yet how little would an outsider in most any century have ever

guessed that the Christians were the followers of
One whose distinguishing mark was that he would
not wrangle! They have been the senior wranglers
of all history! Frequently they have been too
busy wrangling to do much of anything else. The
different things they have wrangled over would
fill pages in the dictionary with a catalogue of
"isms" all the way from gnosticism down to the
"isms" of our own day.

And many of the wrangles have been a fresh
crucifixion of Jesus. The greatest obstacles to the
establishment of the kingdom of God have not
been the outside oppositions but the inside wrangles.
Again and again the curtain has been rolled back
to disclose new opportunities of world winning,
only to find the forces of Christianity largely divided
into preoccupied debating societies. The call from
over the seas, "Come over and help us," has been
drowned out by the hoarse cries of debaters shriek-
ing rebuttals and invective.

Of course it should not be forgotten that Christianity has necessarily had to make its way against
competitive religions and intellectual opposition.
Argument has not only been a necessity; it has
been an indispensable means of evangelization in
many instances. Again and again has it been
necessary to state the Christian evangel in adequate
terms in the presence of very real dangers of movements toward fatal distortion or compromise.

But such argument is high above the level of
mere "wrangling and shouting." A wrangle is an
acrimonious, wordy warfare over secondary or incidental aspects of religious opinion or ecclesiastical
tradition. There is a fine insight in this matter in

Emerson's statement that "truth has already ceased to be truth when it is polemically said."

What a future would open out for the Christian forces of the world if it should ever become a major characteristic of them, as it was of their Master, that they shall not "wrangle"! Even so, come, Lord Jesus!

THE CARELESS WORD

For every *careless* word that men utter they will have to answer on the Day of Judgment.—*Matt. 12. 36* (Goodspeed).

THE meaning of "idle words" of the Authorized Version is much the same—but the word "careless" adds arresting suggestions. For careless words may be very busy words: in fact the busier our words the more careless they are liable to be.

One large class of careless words are those that run like the driftings of a leaky spigot. The person who is not "gifted with flashes of silence," or who does not acquire the gift by dint of self-control is bound to have most of his words careless words. Don Marquis has put into brisk, humorous verses this insidious process by which words just run on endlessly with hardly any oversight from the mind. He describes his task as being merely that of taking the words which Noah Webster has collected and arranging them in a row till a column has been filled. "It's so easy, it's a cinch," he cries. Niagara Falls seems to be the ideal which many have set up, con-

sciously or unconsciously, as a model for conversation.
It runs on with an endless continuance, with all the
resources of four great lakes and the clouds of an
infinite heaven behind it.   It is one of the natural
wonders of the world.   The Niagara Falls type of
conversationalist, however, is one of the *unnatural*
wonders of the world, an endless flow with negligible
supply.

This kind of mass production lays up an enormous liability for every Judgment Day.   And Judgment Day is to-day, to-morrow—not merely off in
some remote future.   For we are all in the same
position as the person under arrest—"everything
we say will be used against us"—in the determining
of the weight and quality of our influence.

Another class of careless words are all those that
do not have a bit of our real selves wrapped up
inside of them—just words, conventional rubber
stamps, that do not carry any flavor of our own
personality.   No matter how pompously we intone
them, words which are not really parts of our
selves are perniciously careless words.

❧ ❧ ❧

THE DULLED MIND

This nation's *mind has grown dull.*—*Matt. 13. 15*
(Goodspeed).

THESE words, first spoken by Isaiah of his own
nation, Judah, make a penetrating text for America

to-day. By that we do not imply that any blanket charge of dullness or slow-wittedness, uttered in a querulous spirit, should be made against the United States. But it is a very timely and rewarding inquiry to ask in what sense and over what areas of our life this judgment of Isaiah, quoted by Jesus and searchingly applied to his own nation, might be true of our nation to-day.

At the outset of every such inquiry it is well to bear in mind the weighty word of Henry James, "Most forms of contempt are unwise but one of them seems to us particularly ridiculous: contempt for the age one lives in." There is a vociferous brood of critics of America to-day whose chief stock in trade is contempt. Their only gesture is a leer, their only vocal utterance raucous laughter. Contempt is always sterile. It yields no desirable fruit. Any valuation of a nation's life and trends, if it is to have any valid worth, must issue from love and understanding of its virtues and strength as well as its liabilities.

On the face of it to say of America that "this nation's mind has grown dull" seems the height of the ridiculous. Nowhere has education been diffused over so large a proportion of the populace as here to-day. In every field there is the keenest competition of sharpened wits.

Yet the text has a deep meaning even for a nation living on its wits. For sharpened wits may easily go with a dull mind. Dullness has to do with perception of values; and a nation may gain a whole world of technical and intellectual agility and yet remain dull in the discernment of other and deeper life values.

It is in that sense that this text is a searchlight. We cannot look deeply into many characteristics of large areas of life without feeling the presence of a disconcerting dullness in the estimate of relative values.

A nation's mind is dull when it is dominated by *things*. Alcohol befuddles the judgment of a mind; proportions and perspectives are lost in an opaque haze. In just the same disastrous manner, materialism, the lust of acquisition, the measurement of life and definition of success in terms of outward possessions, clouds and dulls the mind. Disraeli diagnosed many years ago the malady that infects and threatens a large section of Western civilization to-day when he said: "The European talks of progress because by the aid of a few scientific discoveries he has established a society which has mistaken comfort for civilization." Oswald Spengler in *The Decline of the West* has put the results of this same dullness of mind which elevates material things over the life and achievements of the spirit in striking form:

The ossification and death of ancient civilizations occurred when they concentrated in great cities, as the classical civilization did in Rome and Alexandria, and the Arabic civilization did in Damascus and Bagdad; and when their creative and vital principle, which expressed itself in a living religion, true art, and the higher spiritual manifestations of the mind and soul, had spent its force and was replaced by absorption in material progress. That is the present stage of our Western civilization, which has now spread over the whole world.[1]

[1] Copyright, 1926, by Alfred A. Knopf, Inc., publishers. Used by permission.

Trial by market is the final test of a large multitude of people. An American traveled all over France recently using only one French word, "*Combien?*"—"How much?" He got along perfectly. That was all he wanted to know. He had only one measure of values. The tragedy of the man was not that he knew only one word of French but that he knew only one word of any language. He knew only one word of English. His mind had grown dull. His was not a unique case. His one word is a symbol for a large number of people. To be fair to them, it is not so often money they idolize but money as a symbol of success. Gamaliel Bradford has pointed out that the American has not the miser's passion for accumulating, as such. "He is just as ready to spend as he is to gain, to fling away dollars for amusement or benevolence as fast almost as they come in, unless retaining them is clearly necessary to get more." Success in money-making is the crude, obvious form that appeals to a nation which has not yet wholly grasped, or lost to some extent, the finer issues and interests of life.

Edwin Arlington Robinson has some searching verses, words which he puts into the mouth of a modern "Cassandra."

> "I heard one who said: 'Verily,
>   What word have I for children here?
> Your Dollar is your only Word,
>   The wrath of it your only fear.
>
> "'You build it altars tall enough
>   To make you see, but you are blind;
> You cannot leave it long enough
>   To look before you or behind.

"'Are you to pay for what you have
   With all you are?' No other word
We caught, but with a laughing crowd
   Moved on. None heeded, and few heard."[1]

"Are you to pay for what you have with all you
are?"—that question probes to the heart of a
prosperous industrial civilization.

Clinging to the outworn sophistries of militarism,
wallowing in a rising tide of vulgarity, are not
such things also symptoms of a nation's mind
grown dull?

THE MAN WHO SHOCKED PEOPLE

Do you know that the Pharisees were *shocked* to hear
you say that?—*Matt. 15. 12* (Goodspeed).
The Pharisees were *greatly shocked*.—(Weymouth.)

JESUS never *tried* to shock people.

He was never *afraid* of shocking people.

In both characteristics he is well worthy of study
and emulation.

Jesus never went out of his way to say shocking
things. That was a juvenile kind of thrill in which
he had no interest. Indeed, all through his ministry we can discern the care which he took to
prepare a pathway for his truth to the mind of the
people he was speaking to. He eagerly seized
whatever he could build on in their minds. All
his words were at the service of a positive, con-

---

[1] From "Cassandra," in *The Man Against the Sky*. The Macmillan Company, publishers. Used by permission.

structive purpose, "I am not come to destroy, but to fulfill."

Compared with this patient strategy of Jesus the sensationalism of people who find delight in shocking folks is not only pathetically childish but vicious. Such tactics on the part of those, whether in the pulpit or out of it, whose ostensible desire is to inculcate truth have aroused wholly avoidable opposition and resistance and have caused a world of futile bickering and unnecessary pain.

Sometimes this effort to shock people comes from a mere desire for notice. The English poet, Rogers, was once asked why he said so many malicious and scandalous things. "I have a weak voice," he confessed candidly, "and unless I say something shocking no one ever listens to me." His tribe is legion.

Sometimes this habit is from the domination of a mind by one idea. That becomes the universe, shutting out everything else. Such a state is always a form of fanaticism, which rides gayly and unconcernedly over the feelings and ideas of other people. Samuel McChord Crothers says very keenly, "When a new idea gets into an unfurnished mind it has the time of its life. There is nothing to oppose its autocratic rule."

Sometimes the effort to be shocking is merely the gratification of egotism. "I'll show these old fogies a thing or two" is the mood. Fortunately, this crass conceit is frequently only a disease of youth, like the measles, and is outgrown. But when it hangs on it is malignant.

The kingdom of God has suffered unmeasurable harm from such "shock troops."

The second truth which emerges from a study

of Jesus' teaching and preaching—that he was never afraid to shock people—may seem at first glance to be contradictory to what has just been said, but only on a superficial view.

Jesus never allowed his strategy in persuasion to cloud or tone down his message. When the truth would shock—let it shock. "To this end ... come I into the world, that I should bear witness unto the truth." Nothing else mattered. He put his message in a way that it would be heard. His words stuck like burrs to the mind. If they shocked and stung like burrs, let them sting! He was never deterred from his witness to God by asking, "What will people think about it?" or "How will it affect my safety or popularity?" These two questions trip us up again and again. When either becomes dominant in our thinking truth is muffled so that it is never effectively heard.

Imagine how a cautious adviser might have spoken words of prudence to Jesus in this instance. "Now, Master, of course your ideas of the importance of ceremonial cleansing are all right, but don't just say them out bluntly. There is a way of putting it so as not to offend the Pharisees. They are very excellent and influential people and you can't afford to shock them. Put it this way: 'You are greatly to be honored, dear friends, for your devotion to your tradition. May I suggest that there are other things also that will perhaps bear looking into?' "

If Jesus had spoken in that strain, he would have shocked nobody, and nobody either then or since would have remembered what he said. It would all have ended in an incoherent mumble. Jesus

never mumbled. He spoke so clearly and forcibly
that he shocked the world into a new way of life.
He came to make "a new and living way unto the
Father." It was a task of building a new road,
and road building requires blasting.

The church which never shocks anybody will
never save anybody. When his disciples told Jesus
he had shocked the Pharisees, it never occurred
to him to apologize. He merely said, "Let them
alone." His example and counsel always was to
get on with their message, to preach the kingdom
of God. The test of a message is frequently the
same as the test of an electric wire—its capacity
to shock is an indication of life. When nothing
happens, it is dead!

JESUS AND THE AVERAGE MAN

Are you *totally* ignorant?—*Matt. 15. 16* (Moffatt).

"DON'T you know *anything?*" There is a clear
note of exasperation in this question voiced by
Jesus. And it is very easy to understand. He
had just been stating a principle that seems to us
utterly elementary and axiomatic—that it is not
the things which go into a man's mouth which
defile him, but the things which come out of the
heart; evil thoughts, murders, adulteries, lies, theft.
He had stated it in words as clear as sunlight. And
yet here comes Peter and asks, as though Jesus had
been speaking in Greek, "Please explain it to us."

Small wonder that Jesus exclaims, "Haven't you got any sense at all?" It is a mood that we all know. And such a momentary exasperation with dull, heavy, slow-wittedness does not detract from Jesus. It, rather, furnishes a new insight into the greatness of his patience.

For notice, there was no scorn in his question. Jesus on rare occasions expressed scorn. He could make devastating use of it. Some of the Pharisees who had felt its blazing heat could not soon forget it. But he never treated minds of common men with scorn, no matter how slow to understand they might be. He was never betrayed into any form of contempt for average humanity. Scorn is one of the most dangerous emotions anyone can allow himself to feel. It has high uses; but they are rare. No one can make light or frequent use of scorn without having it spoil his whole spirit. Scorn rapidly corrodes the spirit with egotistical superiority, cynicism, and loveless contempt.

The passage furnishes a fine starting-point for a study of Jesus' attitude to the average man, a study which has timely practical values in this day when contempt and derision are current popular poses.

These words of Jesus, "Don't you know anything?" are a common question to-day, in reference to the common mass of people. And the answer is frequently given in a much overworked modern word, "moron." It is quite fashionable to regard common humanity from an infinite height of superiority and call them "boobs," "morons." Moron is a particularly popular word. It has a pseudo-scientific flavor which flatters the self-conceit of the user. The contemptuous attitude of the average mind is helped on by the flood of intelligence tests which have burst loose upon our time. We are told that the "public" has the mind of a twelve-year-old child, and we feel greatly flattered and complacent.

No one ever arrived at a true estimate of men or influence on them by way of contempt. Jesus' attitude furnishes a sharp contrast to this current one of disdain for humanity in the mass. He was aware, painfully aware, of how slow the minds of average men could be, how heavily they got into motion. Yet he had a profound respect for that mind and went patiently to work, over and over again, to share his truth and experience with it. We can learn from him much to warm and hearten us. He never judged men by such superficial standards as knowledge or cleverness. He had a deep penetration into the larger values of common, human stuff. Even though for an instant he wonders whether his disciples were not "totally ignorant," yet always he purposes to bring the kingdom of God in the world through the agency of such average human material. His reverence for the common man, his patience with the common mind, form one great reason why Christianity has survived. It did not depend on experts or geniuses. It never became a self-satisfied little group viewing the common herd with patronage. Whenever any body of Christians have taken on those characteristics—and it has happened often—they have become sterile. Such is always the danger of a progressive group, that it becomes self-conscious and conscious of a superior enlightenment. And the final stage of uselessness is reached when sympathy and patience with average humanity give way to contempt and disdain.

Such a course always spells ruin to any hope of making a better world. It is a measureless distance from the spirit and method of Jesus.

"DISCUSSING SOMETHING"

But they were *discussing something* with one another. —*Matt. 16. 7* (Goodspeed).

AND, of course, they missed the point which Jesus was making. They did not hear him at all. Jesus had just given the disciples a solemn warning against becoming like the Pharisees. It was a truth he wished desperately to get into their minds. But they were discussing something and missed it. They were arguing about the lunch.

How often in all the long centuries since that day have Jesus' disciples been discussing something as trivial as the contents of a lunch basket, and missed the message he had for them!

Only a few hundred years later, before the Christian Church in North Africa there unrolled the opportunity to win a whole continent for Christ. Not often in history, before or since, had conditions seemed to conspire so as to make possible the swift extension of Christianity over so vast an area. But they were "discussing something." All their energies were being spent in acrimonious doctrinal controversies. They were so busy slaughtering each other's arguments, and finally each other, that they had no strength or desire to unite against the paganism. Jesus was saying to them—"Go ye into all of Africa," and "Lo, I am with you alway." But they were too busy with their epithets and arguments.

Again in a later century the high road to China was thrown open in a manner which has never happened since and never can happen again.

H. G. Wells, in his *Outline of History*, tells how the Mongol Emperor, Kublai Khan, who ruled over China and large portions of western and central Asia and Russia, in 1269, despatched envoys to the Pope at Rome to ask that one hundred missionaries be sent to his capital in order that his people might be taught the things of Christ and a better understanding be brought about between the East and the West. This story is told in detail by Marco Polo, from personal knowledge of what transpired, and we quote his words rather than the brief summary by Mr. Wells. Says Marco Polo: "He [the emperor] begged that the Pope would send as many as an hundred persons of our Christian faith, intelligent men, acquainted with the seven arts, well qualified to enter into controversy, and able clearly to prove by force of argument, to idolaters and other kind of folks, that the law of Christ was best, and that all other religions were false and naught, and that if they could prove this, he and all under him would become Christians and the church's liegemen. Finally he charged his envoys to bring back to him some oil of the lamp which burns on the sepulcher of our Lord at Jerusalem."

This remarkable message reached Rome at a time when there was a vacancy in the papacy, because rival factions in the college of cardinals could not agree on the new Pope, and it was two years before Gregory X despatched two Dominican friars to convert the greatest power in Asia to the rule of Christ. The emperor asked for one hundred, and the church answered with two. And those two, appalled by the length and perils of the journey, turned ignominiously back after they had reached Armenia. Most pertinently does Mr. Wells remark, "All Asia was white unto harvest, but there was no effort to reap it."[1]

They were too busy discussing something!

We to-day can wonder, "How can the stupid disciples have been fussing over whether there was any lunch or not, or who was to blame for neglecting it, when Jesus was right there trying to tell them something! Oh, if we had only been there, we would have heard him!"

Perhaps.

Look at our own time. Think of the momentous issues of this post-war world—a broken world, a world with so much disillusion, with old hatreds not put out but only banked, a world still armed to the teeth, with industrial and race conflicts present or impending—yet with a wistful searching for a better way of life. What a time for bringing to all these great human needs Christ's message of life! Yet how many have been in these years "discussing something"—and, like the disciples of old, have missed what Jesus has been saying! Not discussing lunch exactly but things as far removed from the world's needs—competitive ecclesiastical rivalries, denominational peculiarities, fratricidal warfare over details of science, all making such a frenzied clamor that the still small voice of God was drowned.

---

[1] *The Business of Missions*, by C. H. Patton. The Macmillan Company, publishers. Used by permission.

How tragically easy for some comparatively trivial discussion to preoccupy the attention of Christian people and churches—so that they miss Christ's message.

One of the great educational leaders of America has put vividly the same blundering absorption in incidentals to the exclusion of vital needs in the educational world:

Secondary education is asleep. She is dreaming of "I. Q's," of "administration vs. supervision," of dancing and cigarettes, of conformity to the requirements of colleges, of methodologies, of pedagogies, and the isnesses of many inconsequential whys, each in a degree good or bad; but for questions as big as the world and as enduring as eternity she has neither eye nor ear. World courts, leagues of nations, the waxing and waning of dynasties, the crash of nations as they crumble to dust, the struggle of peoples to arise from the horrors of war into the semblance of a decent status, the economic chaos of the world, the moral dilapidation of mankind; hate between nations and races and religions; the disintegration of the fireside; the apparent triumph of material over spirit; starvation among great groups of people; the hectic, post-war tenseness of the world's nervous system; the destruction of ideals and idealism—all of these receive but a passing glance.

Much contained in these words could easily be transferred to the church.

This picture points out the insidious danger to the disciples of Jesus.

We read that, when they were discussing the menu, Jesus "noticed it." "Why did you doubt?" he cried.

Shall we make him continue to ask?

YOU HINDER ME

You *hinder me*, for you do not side with God, but with men!—*Matt. 16. 23* (Goodspeed).

No wonder Peter was surprised at this vigorous outburst of rebuke from Jesus. Hindering was the last thing in Peter's mind. He was merely smoothing out the way, making things easy.

The answer of Jesus makes clear that the most formidable hindrances which can shackle any life are the hindrances of love. They are the forces which crowd a person or an organization of persons into the easiest way; which pull them down from the heights of achievement by well-meaning fears. It was a deeply seeing man who cried, "I can take care of my enemies; save me from my friends." The hindrances of friends are more powerful because more insidious. The direct onslaught of opposition only stiffens the high purpose; the loving remonstrance of friends acts as an opiate.

Friends often hinder each other, till a mistaken love's harping on safety and comfort becomes just what Jesus called it, the very voice of the devil. This easy slide into degeneracy, in the most intimate of relationships, has never been more realistically pictured than by Frances Power Cobbe. She pictures how a wife may play the part of a devastating wrecker to the one she loves:

The higher *moral* good of the husband occupies most wives comparatively little; and often a man who starts with a great many lofty and disinterested aspirations deteriorates, year by year, in a deplorable manner under the influence of a sufficiently well-meaning and personally conscientious wife. If you ask, "How can this be?" the

answer is that, the wife's affections being of a poor and
short-sighted kind, she constantly urges her husband to
think of himself and his own interests rather than of the
persons and objects for which he was ready to sacrifice
himself. "Do not go on that charitable errand to-day:
you have caught a cold. It will answer as well to-
morrow." "Do not invite that dull old friend." "Do
not join that tiresome committee." "Pray take a long
holiday." "By all means, buy yourself a new hunter."
"Do refrain from confessing your unorthodox opinions."
This kind of thing, dropped every day like the lump of
sugar into the breakfast cup of tea, in the end produces a
real constitutional change in the man's mind. He begins
to think himself, first, somewhat of a hero when he goes
against such sweet counsel, and then a Quixote, and then
a fool. And a curious reciprocity is also established. The
husband cannot do less than return the wife's kindness
by begging *her* not to distress and tire herself by per-
forming any duty which costs a little self-sacrifice; and
she again returns the compliment, and so on and so on, till
they nurse each other into complete selfishness.

A memorable phrase that is—"this kind of thing,
dropped every day like a lump of sugar into the
breakfast cup of tea." We read a good deal about
"poisoned liquor." Here is the real thing!

The blind, smothering care of parents sends
children into the world maimed, as far as the possible powers of their spirits are concerned. We
shudder at the story of the slaughter of the innocents in the Gospel of Matthew. But a slaughter
of innocents goes on in our comfort-loving day,
when the main drive of parents is so often to prepare children for conformity and the material
success to which it leads. Every precious individual
difference, giving promise of individuality, every

spontaneous emotion which might lead to original
independent personality is carefully snipped off, as a
Japanese gardener binds back and cuts off branches
in the training of a stunted tree. Thus they are
hindered from ever achieving that self-forgetful
enthusiasm which is the very core of Christianity.
Soul binding is a far deeper hurt than foot binding.

Does it take much of a stretch of imagination to
hear Jesus saying to his disciples and to his church
to-day, "You hinder me"? He still sets his face
toward Jerusalem. "On to Calvary" is still his
watchword. He would lead on to the building of
the kingdom of God, or righteousness, joy, and
peace in this broken world. Yet many of his disciples take their stand with Peter and answer that
call: "Not that, Master. Take the easier way.
Don't be an extremist. We live in a practical
world. Let's stay in Galilee. It is far pleasanter.
There are crosses in Jerusalem." By our easy
accommodations to the world as it is, by our premature satisfaction with unchristian conditions, we
hinder him.

Jesus leads on to a world of peace. Peace means
Calvary. George A. Dorsey, in *Why We Behave
Like Human Beings*, says with a simpering superficiality, "we have discovered how to transmute
imps into angels with miles of smiles."[1] We are
long miles from a transformed humanity, but it is
emphatically *not* "miles of smiles" which intervene.
They are long weary miles up the dark hill of
Calvary. Peace comes as Jesus brought it by costly
sacrifice and self-dedication. Only as we cease

---

[1] Harper & Brothers, publishers. Used by permission.

hindering Jesus, by our clinging to the easier gods of force and aggressive nationalism, will we make a world of secure peace.

We lay hindrances before Jesus' determined onward push to real brotherhood. An air of patronage and condescension to other races is a far more subtle hindrance to fellowship than crude hatred, but it is just as real.

We hinder Jesus' passionate yearning for a church filled with his spirit and utterly at his service by choosing the easier way of a conventional attachment which answers the demands of correct form, without violently revolutionizing our life.

GOD'S OUTLOOK

Your outlook is not God's, but man's.—*Matt. 16. 23* (Moffatt.)

A PICTURESQUE phrase—God's *outlook!* An amazing suggestion, when we think of its implications—that we should have God's outlook. The word suggests rather accurately the one thing we can have in common with God—a point of view, a standpoint from which to look at the world, a common purpose. We cannot have the mind of God—"His thoughts are above our thoughts." But having the mind, the purpose of Christ, we can have God's outlook. It was a more intangible and far-reaching thing than the actual suggestion of Peter which Jesus rebuked; it was the direction in which Peter's mind looked—the limited arc through which his thoughts swung.

Any outlook has four dimensions, depth, height, length, and breadth. And those dimensions may be clues to the inexhaustible meaning of these words—God's outlook.

Jesus revealed a new *depth* to life. He plumbed beneath all outward observances to the heart; beneath all outward acts to the motive. He added a new dimension to righteousness. He uncovered values in the inner life beside which the surface of life shrank in proportion. H. G. Wells, in his novel, *The World of William Clissold*, records a sort of waking-dream experience which symbolizes the new outlook on the world which Jesus brings to men.

I am reminded as I write of this of a queer little thing that happened to me at times, most frequently in my adolescence and when I was a young man. I do not think that it has occurred at all during the last ten or fifteen years. It was this: The visible world, remaining just as bright and clear as ever it had been, would suddenly appear to be minute. People became midgets, the houses and the furniture, dolls' houses and furniture, the trees, mere moss-fronds. I myself did not seem to shrink to scale; it was only the universe about me that shrank.[1]

With the experience of a new depth to life which Jesus brings, material things, while still remaining in the picture, shrink in relative magnitude.

Jesus' revelation of God puts new *height* into man's outlook. Without God we have a worm's-eye view of the world.

The inclusive love of Jesus gives a new *breadth*

[1] Copyright, 1926. George H. Doran Company, publishers. Used by permission.

to our vision and concern. We are so adept at building fences, which shut out other races, nations, classes. On his release from a long prison term, a prisoner looked out across a valley and remarked, "I haven't looked more than two hundred yards in front of me in twenty years." Many men are prisoners in a self-made jail. They have erected walls of exclusion about their minds. Jesus had no use for fences. Paul adduces the fact that Jesus broke down walls of partition as one of the surest evidences of his divinity. Our outlook is not God's when we take in any less circle of humanity in our interest than Jesus did.

Length to our thinking is a mark of God's outlook. "God does not pay every Saturday night." We chop time into convenient blocks, of sevens, thirties, and three sixty-fives. The middle of next week is the usual outpost of our thinking. With God's outlook the present moment partakes of eternity.

DON'T UPSET THE APPLE CART!

He *upset* the tables of the money-changers.—*Matt.* 21. 12 (Moffatt).

A VERY modern outlook to this word "upset." The money-changers had no objection to Jesus until he upset the cash drawer. And in that sensitive spot they represent a powerful section of the business world to-day. The worst crime a prophet can commit is to upset a cash register. Business has nothing but praise for the Christian religion—as

long as it does not really upset anything. But let
it dislocate even so slightly the flow of cash into
the till—and the modern prophet, and the church
which stands by him (if it does) will be in the
midst of the same hubbub which swarmed about
Jesus when he disturbed the profits of the Temple
Merchants' Mutual Protective Association.

One of the great liabilities of the church to-day
is that unintentionally and almost unconsciously it
may allow the injunction not to upset any of the
sacred tables of profit to shape its policies and
throttle its life. A new first commandment might
be written thus:

> A new commandment I give unto thee:
> Thou shalt not upset the apple cart.

These words fairly express the unconscious fears
and timidities of many a congregation. They express
the sense of a never-forgotten obligation to refrain
from collision with current economic traditions and
practices and with financial powers behind those
practices.

Sometimes the elevation of this commandment to
a place of first importance is due merely to an
affinity on the part of many in the church for the
good, the true, the beautiful (and the prosperous!).

Sometimes, however, the bonds which unite the
church to the powers that be in the economic world
are of a firmer nature. The church must go on.
Its overhead runs twenty-four hours a day and
each year seems to see an increase in the amount
of overhead that must be kept running. The under-
lying philosophy is not very different from that

piece of distilled prudence, "Don't bite the hand that feeds you." There is nothing so crude or simple as a deliberate betrayal of the gospel or cowardice in its presentation. The situation is far more complex and subtle and complicated than that.

But like the pressure of the atmosphere of fifteen pounds to the square inch on all of us, there is the ever-present pressure of the ruling ideas of the masters of the economic and business world and the situation of the church itself. That situation is complicated in thousands of instances by the fact that the church has given large hostages to the business world to further a building program. Millions of dollars of mortgages are held over churches. There are unpaid pledges of other millions of dollars. It is for the temporal interest of the church to avoid any disturbance in the placid calm of business prosperity. It is not to be wondered at that the first concern of a large number of trustees and other officials is for carrying through their venture successfully.

Hence there is a very strong feeling to this effect: "There is no use of us or our minister being quixotic. We can very well postpone playing on some notes of the Christian gospel until a more convenient season. Prudence is the better part of valor. *Don't upset the apple cart.*"

With the full organ of the great redemptive message of Christianity to sound in the world to-day, it is tragic if a church harps only on one monotonous string—"Play it safe." The gospel of Jesus is more than a counsel of prudent caution. It is a great message of redemption for the whole of life, redemption from every force that exploits or maims human life.

How can we be real disciples of a Master who upset the world, if we don't upset anything in such a world as ours?

"THAT'S YOUR AFFAIR"

I am innocent of this good man's blood. It is *your affair!*—Matt. 27. 24 (Moffatt).

Four times in the trial of Jesus he was "handed over" to someone else on the plea that he was their affair. The high priests handed him over to Pilate. Pilate handed him over to Herod. Herod handed him back to Pilate. Pilate finally handed him over to the soldiers to be crucified, with a theatrical gesture of innocence and a weak whimper: "It is not my fault. That's *your* affair."

Twice the very words "your affair" are used— once by the high priests and elders to Judas when he brings back the thirty pieces of silver; once by Pilate to the Jews in this passage.

Anything to get Jesus off their hands was the motive. He was a thorny problem. Let someone else handle it. "Here, he is your affair"—each one said as he gave Jesus a push on to someone else. "You do something—anything." This passing of Jesus from one to another is the supreme instance of that circular game of side-stepping responsibility which is so painfully familiar and to which is given the slang name of "passing the buck." There is

no need to describe it; it is part of the daily picture
of life. Nearly every large organization can exhibit
it developed to the point of genius. The matter
at issue is found to belong to "some other department." The other department discovers that it
is really in the province of still another department.
And the game is on. Trying to locate responsibility and getting action becomes a life career.

Every time the words, "That's *your* affair," were
said they were a lie. Jesus was Pilate's affair. He
was the high priest's affair. He was Herod's affair.
Jesus is every man's affair. He cannot be side-
stepped. Men try to hand him over to the church
and evade any personal responsibility by saying,
"He is your affair." He cannot be made an organization matter. He is *your* affair.

The whole trial of Jesus is a looking glass for
humanity. In the play of motives that conspired
to bring Jesus to the cross, in the X-ray light which
the drama throws on human character, we see ourselves and our actions vividly portrayed.

Jesus presented to all these officials a situation
about which they would actually have to do something. And that was bothersome. They preferred
to stand from under any responsibility for so terrifying a thing as a decision. It is easy to judge
these struggling cowards, desperately searching for
an alibi—until we pause to think how often we do
the same thing. When moral responsibility comes
home to us, it is very common and comforting to
shove it on to someone else.

Take the appalling crime record in the United
States. You cannot get into that matter without
hearing on every hand echoes of this claim of

Pilate's, "That's your affair." The blame for
crime is put on the home, on the school, on the
laws, on the police, on the newspapers, on the
movies, on prohibition. Each group or institution
points a finger in some other direction and says:
"That's your affair. It is not my fault." With
the multiplication of accusations and evasions, there
seems less disposition to say: "It's *my* affair. It's
our affair. What can we do to redeem it?"

We do the same with war. We pass on the
responsibility around the circle with a vigorous
shove away from ourselves. That relieves us from
really doing anything about it. Men blame human
nature. They lament it but call for Pilate's wash
bowl and repeat his formula, "That's your affair."
They blame the diplomats; they blame the soldiers; they blame race; they blame trade. Then,
like the high priests, they hand Jesus over to the
government. They allow governments to decide
questions which cannot rightly be delegated to
government officials—the validity of the gospel of
Jesus. And Calvary goes on.

We play this sorry game of "round the circle"
with our personal failings and responsibilities. We
say to heredity: "I'm your affair. I'm not to blame
for my sins, you know. In fact, they are not sins
any more in this day of light. They are psychological tendencies. It's heredity." Or it's environment, an ever-ready scapegoat. Or it's the social
order. Someone has well said that in the face of
an obvious personal call or duty we make the prayer,
"What wilt thou have the social order to do?"
instead of Paul's unevasive response, "What wilt
thou have *me* to do?"

Two warnings among many from this bit of history may be singled out: 1. The whole spectacle is an exhibition of what happens when a man's mind can deal only with routine matters, but shrinks and sidesteps when a genuine moral problem which cannot be avoided comes up. 2. How different it would have been if someone had broken through this vicious circle of evasion and said: "Here, this is *my* affair. I'll stop this murder myself"! Pilate, Herod, Caiaphas, any one of them could have done it. How different our neighborhood, our world would be, if more breaks in the same sort of a vicious circle might happen; if we stopped passing on to others duties and tasks that we might do; if we were as intent on the building of the Kingdom as we are on the building of alibis! For the crucifixion of Jesus shows with a tragic light where this sort of thing leads. It always happens when no one says: "I'll take this upon myself. It's my affair."

A STUDY OF MILITARISM

All the *regiment* round him.—*Matt. 27. 27* (Moffatt).

THE conduct of the Roman military force during the trial and crucifixion furnishes a good basis for a study of many characteristics of militarism in general. This is all the more valuable for an unbiased study, because, throughout the New Testament, soldiers, as a rule, appear in the most favorable light possible. The conduct specified here is not to be taken as characteristic of individual soldiers. The great body of military forces, being just a cross-section of the human race, varies as the race itself varies. It includes multitudes of the noblest men who have ever lived.

But there are characteristics of the strictly militaristic mind, of the system of militarism in government, which are revealed truly and clearly in the historical events of the crucifixion.

1. For one thing the military force never understood what the trial and crucifixion were all about. They did not get to the bottom of the issue at all. They did not bother. Theirs not to reason why, theirs but to jump in and settle it by force. Here was something bothersome to the established order. Suppress it! After it was all over there was a belated recognition on the part of one of the most intelligent of the officers that a tragic blunder had been committed. "Surely," he exclaimed, "this was the Son of God." Now, of course, it is not within the province of the soldier to pass upon the justice of the cause in which he fights. But it *is* a responsibility of militarism in control of the state—or as a predominant influence. And it is a characteristic that it does not bother to get to the bottom of issues. It is not concerned primarily with justice or human values. Above these it sets prestige— nationalistic self-assertion. The crucifixion shows with a white light what happens when justice and human values are forgotten in the determination of action.

2. The treatment of Jesus was marked by unnecessary cruelty and contempt—an abiding accompaniment of war and militarism everywhere.

3. We see the familiar "smoke screen" at work—the falsification of facts, so characteristic of waging war and inciting peoples to war. "We will *screen* you from punishment, if this is reported to the Governor" (Weymouth, Matt. 28. 14), the soldiers are told after the resurrection.

4. Then the military crowd lied about the whole thing—another familiar earmark of the technique of militarism. They noised about a story explaining the resurrection that was a barefaced lie. But that did not bother them so long as it contributed to the security of their caste and order. The "die-hard" militarist will not scorn any weapon that will discredit sincere workers for peace—lies, slander, invective, ridicule.

5. "They took the money" (Matt. 28. 15)—a symbol of the historic relation of the war system and the greed for profits.

It is the persistence of these characteristics in the militaristic mind which makes it such an unrivaled obstacle to loosening the grip of the war system on civilization and the establishment of the kingdom of God.

❧ ❧ ❧

CROWDING CHRIST INTO A UNIFORM

They put on Him a general's short crimson cloak.—
Matt. 27. 28 (Weymouth, 1st Edit.).

THESE words are symbolic of much that has happened in Christian history. In those tragic hours immediately preceding the crucifixion there

were many cruel indignities heaped upon Jesus.
But one of the crowning indignities was dressing
him up in the cloak of a Roman general. What a
piece of irony it was, to dress the Prince of Peace
in the trappings of a war lord! This indignity was
committed by the enemies of Jesus—if those who
had no understanding of him at all could be called
his enemies. But the same indignity has been
often forced upon Jesus by his friends and adherents,
and that wrong is still being done him.

All through the centuries Christ has been crowded
into a *general's uniform*. Each age has made violent wrenchings and distortions of Jesus to make
him fit the war lust of men and the interests of
militarism. In Pilate's day Jesus was put into the
scarlet cloak of a Roman general. Men no longer
use scarlet for war. To-day the color is khaki,
and Christ has been crowded into a khaki uniform
again and again. During the Great War there was
much loud talk about "Christ in khaki," and he
has been made the supporter and inciter of war.
Christ cannot be put into khaki. We may dress
up a mechanical figure and put the sentiments of
angry men into his mouth, but it is not Jesus.
Dean Inge in very vivid words has described how
this process has hidden the real Christ:

Institutional religion does not represent the gospel of
Christ, but the opinions of a mass of nominal Christians.
It cannot be expected to do more than look after its own
interests and reflect the ideas of its supporters. The real
gospel, if it were accepted, would pull up by the roots,
not only militarism, but its analogue in civil life, the
desire to exploit other people for private gain. But it
is not accepted.

But that is not the only uniform which has been fitted upon Christ. He has been dressed up in *ecclesiastical regalia*, smothered with vestments of church officialism. The living Jesus, the Divine Christ, has been lost again and again in the uniform of the ecclesiastical prince, the priest, the monk, the bishop, or any other conventional figure of religion. He has been interpreted as the spokesman for the interests of an intrenched system. By a crowning irony he has been so distorted that he has been made to stand for the very evils of loveless, petrified officialism, against which he contended all his life and which finally did him to death.

We are witnessing in our own day the curious process of dressing up Jesus in a new uniform. Naturally, it is the characteristic uniform of our time—*the business suit*. Jesus has been dressed up in a sack suit and interpreted as the founder of much that the business mind glorifies in our time. He has been pictured as the "go-getter," the "high-powered executive"—a fine man for president of the Chamber of Commerce. This outfitting of Jesus in a new uniform has been done with unconscious perfection by Bruce Barton in his chapters on Jesus, the world's greatest executive and the founder of modern business. But all such interpretations, even though intended as honor, are only another indignity to the real Jesus.

There is no need in the world greater than to strip away from the regal figure of Jesus everything that is foreign and let him stand out unhindered and undisguised!

* * *

THE RESURRECTION AT THE CRUCI-FIXION

Many of the saints who had fallen asleep *rose.—Matt. 27. 52* (Goodspeed).

CONSIDERED as a symbolic picture, the truth of this miracle has been attested through all the centuries. We have here the statement that, at the supreme moment of the sacrifice of Jesus on Calvary, the dead arose. It is profoundly true that whenever the spirit which Jesus manifested on Calvary finds expression in life—it shocks men into life. "Saints who have fallen asleep" arise. There is nothing which has proved so powerful an awakener as Jesus' spirit of sacrificial love incarnate in a personality. It plays havoc with cemeteries, whether in the church or out of it!

When God's springtime has seemed to come again to the church, and new tides of abounding spiritual life are set running, the miracle which has awakened the new life is the old, old miracle of Calvary. When Francis of Assisi took to the road and showed men the love of Christ in its genuineness and simplicity, there was startling awakening of life. It was so with the pioneer souls who began the modern missionary movement, Henry Martyn, William Carey, David Livingstone. "God's trumpet wakes the slumbering world," sings Samuel Longfellow in a stirring modern hymn. God's most effective trumpet is a sacrificial life which brings that love of Calvary freshly into view. Tertullian in the early days of the church expressed the miracle for all time, "The blood of the martyrs is the seed of the church."

How delicately the little verse entitled "Miracle" pictures this awakening of "sleeping saints"!

> "Ten thousand musics never could
>   Stir an image out of wood,
> But let love knock at the church door
> And saints in niches, gray with lore,
> Step from their halos to the floor,
> And laugh, and are alive once more."

There is a world of suggestiveness in the phrase, "saints who had fallen asleep." In depressed moments we feel there are an undue proportion of such sleepy saints in the church. How we long for a General Resurrection—a quickening into life—a new flood of energy!

Resurrection will always follow crucifixion. When anyone takes Jesus seriously, when the sacrificial love of Jesus, instead of being an airy nothing, becomes a local habitation and a name in a human life, that miracle always brings life to the dead. It was simply but effectively expressed in the remark of one student to another, quoted by Bertha Condé, "I've always known what the Bible says about it, but I never saw anyone before who had the nerve to live it. You've given my thinking a jolt."

That is the final hope, and the only hope of the kingdom of God; when that passionate, sacrificial love finds expression in a whole church the resulting miracle will be a quickened world.

❧ ❧ ❧

GOOD MORNING!

"Good morning!"—*Matt. 28. 9* (Goodspeed).

THERE is a touch of genius to Goodspeed's translation of the word "Hail," the first word of the risen Jesus, by the words "Good morning!" The word "hail" has passed out of our common speech as a spoken word. It is now a literary word, relegated to odes and elegies and national anthems. But the words "Good morning" are almost the most familiar words of daily life. To find them used on this highest peak of all history seems to relate Easter a bit closer to common life.

These words are Jesus' victorious greeting to humanity—"Good morning!" It was morning forever, *the* good morning, first among all the days that ever dawned or ever will dawn. Indeed, it was the first full dawn that ever rose on human life. The salutation embodies the truth of Harnack's words—"This grave was the birth place of the indestructible belief that death is vanquished and there is a life eternal."

It was "Good morning" for high and low—the same lifting hope for the furthest extremes of the race in estate and education. Place two instances of the foregoing statement side by side. Sir James Simpson was one of Great Britain's greatest scientists and surgeons. When his heart was broken over the death of his dearly loved little daughter, he had carved on her gravestone the text—"Nevertheless I live." At the other extreme of education the same radiant hope finds striking expression in one of the less known of the Negro spirituals. There is a thrilling and unexpected climax to the verses. The song puts the question: "Who will be a-living when I am dead?" and proceeds to answer it in this fashion:

> "Trees will be a-living and a-waving
> When I am dead.
> Birds will be a-living and a-singing
> When I am dead."

And so it goes on until the listener feels utterly diminished—less than the grass, less than the dust. Then suddenly the song restores his spirit with a triumphant shout:

> "Who will be a-living when I am dead?
> *I will! I will!*"

That jubilant "I will! I will!" is the response to the salute of Jesus to the world—"Good morning!"

The Easter "Good morning" of Jesus is the one great exclamation point of human life on which the height and depth of every joy depend.

> "Joy, shipmate, joy!
> Pleased to my soul at death I cry,
> One life is closed, one life begun,
> The long, long anchorage we leave,
> The ship is clear, at last, she leaps,
> Joy, shipmate, joy!"

Because of that one "Good morning" uttered nineteen hundred years ago every day may partake of its spirit. In Old Russia, on Easter day, after church service the exalted nobleman would without hesitation kiss his coachman three times on the lips, exclaiming, "Christ is risen." This was only a gesture, too soon forgotten, in most cases. But there was a true instinct behind it. The resurrection "Good morning" should be reflected in a new spirit of fellowship which transforms every day and every relationship.

LET'S GO SOMEWHERE ELSE!

"Let us go somewhere else."—Mark 1. 38 (Moffatt).

AT the very outset of the ministry of Jesus, as recorded by Mark, he evades two deadly dangers which have beset his cause ever since: he refuses to become *localized;* he refuses to become *institutionalized.* The future of Christ's church depends to a large degree on the measure to which the paralysis of those same two calamities can be avoided.

It was natural that the townspeople of Capernaum should say, "Stay here!" Jesus' healing had been a blessing to the town. His presence would become a permanent asset. He was among friends. What would be better than just to stay? To Jesus there was one thing better—the road to the world. He came not to be a town doctor but a world's Redeemer.

The play of those two same opposing forces in all life is artistically expressed in the verses of Josephine Preston Peabody,

"The little Road says, 'Go';
The little House says, 'Stay':
And Oh, it's bonny here at home,
But I must go away."[1]

Threatened, for the moment, by loving but mistaken hands which would have imprisoned him in a local provincialism, Jesus said, "Let's go somewhere else." In those words and in that spirit there was the universal destiny of Christianity, its unresting outthrust into all the world. It broke through the bounds of Judaism, broke out of the wider bonds of the Roman Empire, burst the bonds of Europe, across the Pacific. Christianity has lived because as each new frontier came into view, men with a spirit akin to their Master's have cried, "Let's go!" Always that preservation of Christianity as a world force has been won only by overcoming the seductive voices, which demanded, as on that first day at Capernaum, "Let's *stay*." How many snug little homes have had to be left behind! The little house has cried "Stay"—threatening to make of Christianity merely a local tradition. The whole history of the rebirth of the missionary passion in the nineteenth century is the struggle between Go and Stay. The Christianity which degenerates into provincialism and forgets the call of the road speedily becomes a mummy.

Jesus' departure from Capernaum, on the road that led eventually to Jerusalem, Calvary, and all the world, was a refusal to become *institutionalized*. The Prophet, the Teacher, the Redeemer, would

---

[1] From *The House and the Road*. Houghton Mifflin Company, publishers. Used by permission.

have been transformed into a kind of impersonal clinic, a hospital and dispensary. Another institution, a blessed one of course, but still an institution, in the town's life. That subtle danger is never completely escaped and has strangled the spiritual life and power of Christ's church again and again. Whenever Christianity has been expressed in a statement of doctrine, in a form of organization, and men say in satisfaction, "This just fits. Let's keep it this way forever," the institution begins to set like a plaster cast, throttling the spirit within. It is inevitably so. The Christian gospel is *yeast*, not concrete. It should ferment, upheave, grow, not solidify. The hope of the Kingdom depends on the persistence of the Spirit of Jesus, "Let's go somewhere else." When Christianity is identified with any form of organization, the organization is soon substituted for the inner life. Then the church becomes like the man who said to his soul: "Now we're all set. We have goods laid up for many years. We don't need to think, or to plan or to work or to worry." When he reached that stopping-place, of course, he stopped. His soul, his life was gone.

DON'T GET PONDEROUS!

There were some scribes sitting there *pondering.*— Mark 2. 6 (Goodspeed).
Argued in their hearts (Moffatt).

JUST like owls blinking in strong sunlight! Here was something they couldn't quite grasp. Jesus

had just healed a paralytic. That was bad enough
from their standpoint—a breach of ecclesiastical
etiquette. But he had done more—a shocking
thing. He had said, "My son, your sins are for-
given." That set them pondering in a heavy, confused manner. The simile, "like owls," is more
than fanciful. They were exactly that—wise owls—
blinded by the fresh light which Jesus threw on life.
They could find their way around in the dim region
of legal distinctions; in the daylight of clear moral
issues and spiritual values they were lost. They
could only blink and ponder.

Jesus did not fit into any of the familiar pigeon-
holes in the scribes' minds. That was what both-
ered them. They had no ready ticket or label
for him. They did not possess the power or the
inclination to think about him, to grasp his meaning,
to look at him as a human being, to discover him
as a divine revelation. That achievement could
not be done by pigeonholing and all their thinking
was of the pigeonholing character.

It is a pernicious substitute for thinking. The
mental operations in a great many minds are like
the process in a railway mail car in which envelopes
are tossed, with a marvelous mechanical dexterity
due to long practice, into different sacks. New
ideas and personalities are tossed into preconceived notions and prejudices, regardless of whether
or not they fit. That was what the scribes did.
They had a large, roomy pigeon-hole labeled "Blasphemy" and they immediately tossed Jesus into
it. He was speaking a new language. Therefore
it must be blasphemy.

That type of "thinking" unfortunately did not

pass from earth with the scribes of Jesus' day.
It is the favorite and often the only exercise of
lazy and narrow minds. It is responsible for the
persistence of malignant prejudice of all sorts—
race, class, and religious; and for the stagnation
which keeps the world in ruts.

The pondering of the scribes never got beyond
the business of rearranging legalistic precedents and
traditions. When they "argued in their hearts"
they never reached the realm of vital human need
or spiritual realities. They did not live there.
They pondered over quibbles. The deep need of
the body and soul of this poor paralytic, which so
moved the heart of Jesus, never touched them at
all. They were fussing about some impertinent
technicality. They missed the human values. Their
estimate of life is as impertinent as the estimate of
the Lincoln Memorial in Washington, which might be
given by a statistical pedant. He could sum it up
in a catalogue of the materials which went into it, so
many tons of such and such kind of marble, arranged
in such and such architectural patterns. It would all
be true and utterly meaningless as an interpretation
of the building. It would miss two things, both
spiritual realities, the beauty of the structure and the
moral values symbolized. Nor would it convey the
"still small music of humanity" which sounded out
over the world through Lincoln's great soul.

Philip Guedalla in his book, *The Second Empire*,
has a memorable description of a latter-day scribe,
one of the ministers of Napoleon III of France:

. . . He remained, as he had begun, a successful law-
yer with a professional aptitude for detail and a forensic

profusion of second-rate reasoning. Never at a loss for
an argument and untroubled by the doubts which op-
press finer, if less professional, intelligences, his burly
figure dominated the Chamber and in the steady boom of
his uninspired, his inexhaustible eloquence the later empire
had found its accompaniment.[1]

Those words fit closely these scribes in the presence of Jesus—"A professional aptitude for detail
and a forensic profusion of second-rate reasoning!"

Alas, how closely they fit the multitude who
have, like the scribes, "nullified the law of God
through their tradition"! Do they fit us? The
whole scene whispers to us: "Don't get ponderous.
Look what it leads to."

⚜ ⚜ ⚜

JESUS' VALUATION OF OBSTINACY

Hurt by their obstinacy.—Mark 3. 5 (Goodspeed).
In anger and vexation at their *obstinacy* (Moffatt).

THE word "obstinacy" does not occur in the
authorized translation of the Gospels. But it has
played an extensive and tragic part in Christian
history. It did not find a place on the mediæval
list of the seven deadly sins, but it deserves one on
any list.

Goodspeed and Moffatt both substitute the word
"obstinacy" for the words "hardness of heart" in

---

[1] Courtesy of G. P. Putnam's Sons, publishers, New York and
London. Used by permission.

the King James version of this passage. The
meaning, of course, is much the same, but the word
"obstinacy" comes much closer home to us. It
is not so easy for us to escape with the plea, "Not
guilty."

The Century Dictionary makes a good prose-
cuting attorney in the case. Obstinate is "not
yielding to argument, persuasion or entreaty; a
strong and vicious or disobedient refusal to yield;
an unmanageable standing upon one's will." An
obstinate man will try to "carry out his intention
in spite of advice, appeals, remonstrance, or force."

Do you recognize any traces of a portrait of
yourself?

Obstinacy is a deadly sin for three reasons, at
least.

1. *It so easily passes for a virtue.* Who ever admitted he was obstinate? The trait has so many
disguises. It takes on virtuous airs as firmness,
perseverance, strength of will, loyalty, integrity.
The only sin which has so great a repertoire of
plausible disguises is covetousness. Montaigne
paints it in its true colors. "Obstinacy," he says,
"is one of the surest proofs of stupidity. Is there
anything so assured, resolved, disdainful, contem-
plative, solemn and serious as the ass?" Yet this
mental trait, which we share so generously, with
that typical "die hard," the donkey, passes itself
off on us as a virtue worthy at least of the *Croix
de guerre* or the martyr's crown.

2. *Obstinacy is a deadly sin because one rarely
gets over it.* It fastens on the vital centers of personality. It sinks deep. Its grip increases with
expression. Once in a while some rare soul grows

more reasonable, open-minded, and pliant with age, but the spectacle is so rare that we mark it with a double star. The usual process is to get more and more "set in his ways."

3. *It blocks such a wide variety of traffic.* There is not a project for the betterment of life, for an advance on any sector of the kingdom of God, which cannot be obstructed by plain, old-fashioned obstinacy. It has raised barricades on every avenue of human progress.

JESUS CRUSHED BY THE CROWD

So he told his disciples to have a small boat ready; it was to prevent him being *crushed by the crowd.*—*Mark 3. 9* (Moffatt).

How often Jesus has been crushed by the crowd! He has been pushed out of a place of commanding influence, in a life or a community or a nation, by the sheer weight of multitudinous competing interests. He has been flattened out, in the minds of multitudes, till his teaching and purposes have only a shadowy, ghostlike existence.

It is a danger with peculiar intensity in our time, for the simple reason that never before were there so many different things to crowd into the mind like the contents of a ten-story department store. Mass production, both of material things and of ideas, lays upon the mind the necessity of a conscious and stalwart resisting power, if Jesus' interpretation of life and his estimate of values are to be preserved.

1. *The overcrowded mind* is a menace to Jesus'
formative influence on our personality and life.
The diversity of things tends to scatter the attention
and interest until life becomes helter-skelter and
hodge-podge through sheer lack of emphasis. Just
through such a process, often quite unintentional
and sometimes unconscious, has Jesus been crushed
in many lives. Big and little, vital and trivial, get
the same amount of attention. By the overcrowded
mind is not meant a mind richly stored with knowledge. No mind is ever overcrowded in that sense.
The more real knowledge a mind has, the stronger
its powers become. The evil of an overcrowded
mind occurs when there is no selective power to
cast aside the trivial and focus on major issues,
just as a threshing machine tosses chaff to one side
and grain to the other.

2. *Mass thinking* is a cause of Jesus being crushed,
in that his distinctive way of life is lost. The
modern demand for conformity, helped on by a
bewildering increase in the agencies for making
thinking standardized, results in flattening out
individuality. The result of this process in America
is already seen in great multitudes of people whose
minds are about as alike as Ford parts. Standardizing the thinking of the nation usually means
flattening it to a low level. And as a result Jesus
is crushed. Jesus is a mountain. When he is leveled
until nothing is left of his ideals that rise above
the plane of "things as they are," he is lost.

His disciples, on that day when the crowd threatened to crush Jesus, took him away from the throng,
to a place where he could be seen and dominate
the crowd. Only such a care on the part of Jesus'

disciples to-day to preserve and live his peculiar and uncompromising gospel will save it as a redemptive force in an age of mass thinking.

❧ ❧ ❧

THE ART OF SAYING GOOD-BY

After saying good-by to them he went up the hill to pray.—*Mark 6. 46* (Moffatt).

CAN you say "Good-by"? Jesus here illustrates it as one of the highest of the fine arts. When we say good-by it is so often wrung from us by compulsion. We have no other choice. So it is said grudgingly, reluctantly. Jesus said good-by to the crowd, to his public work, to the world, for a period, voluntarily and positively, in the interest of personal replenishment through prayer for larger service.

Unless we can learn to say good-by to things we must inevitably say good-by to the possibilities of largest power and influence. There used to be an old gospel song which had for its refrain, "We'll never say good-by in heaven." The weakness of many lives is that they never say good-by on earth; never get away from the milling of a throng of people or things, never get away to a solitude in which the deep springs that reinvigorate strength and clear the vision are opened up. Without that retirement, the mind becomes like the public waiting room of a railway station—a scene of bustling movement and confusion, not unified in any one object or purpose.

There is a quaint and beautiful custom in Russia for people who are starting on a journey and are leaving the house, to sit down and spend half a minute in silence. Life is just a series of journeys, short, sudden raids into the bustle of events and long marches. If it is to have either poise or carrying momentum, the only effective approach is from what corresponds to "half a minute's silence," when in communion with ourselves and God we can see it steadily and whole.

Our need of this art of saying good-by increases with the complexity and confusion of life. The very noise in which we pass our days disintegrates poise and power. Walter Lippman, in his book, *Public Opinion*, draws a realistic but not exaggerated picture:

Can anything be heard in the hubbub that does not shriek, or be seen in the general glare that does not flash like an electric sign? The life of the city dweller lacks solitude, silence, ease. The nights are noisy and ablaze. The people of a big city are assaulted by incessant sound, now violent and jagged, now falling into unfinished rythms, but endless and remorseless. Under modern industrialism thought goes on in a bath of noise. If its discriminations are often flat and foolish, here at least is some small part of the reason.[1]

The multiplying "shriek and glare" emphasizes as nothing else could the wisdom of Amiel's classic plea for the recreative powers of solitude and prayer:

We are too busy, too encumbered, too much occupied, too active! In an inaction which is meditative and attentive the wrinkles of the soul are smoothed away, and the

---

[1] The Macmillan Company, publishers. Used by permission.

soul itself spreads, unfolds and springs afresh, and, like the trodden grass of the roadside or the bruised leaf of a plant, repairs its injuries, becomes new, spontaneous, true and original.

Reverie, like the rain of night, restores color and force to thoughts which have been blanched and wearied by the heat of the day. With gentle fertilizing power it awakens within us a thousand sleeping forms, and, as though in play, gathers round us materials for the future.

Trader Horn, in that amazing story of a lifetime spent in tramping over savage Africa, called Trader Horn, says in commenting on the savage's utter dependence on his family and kin, "The savage when separated from his kind pines like a dog. The first thing education teaches you is to walk alone. Aye, you can sure stand on your own spear when *you've learned the word good-by and say it clear*."

An imperious "good-by" is the only word which will save the soul alive. On our busy calendars of appointments there must be wedged in an appointment with ourselves, an appointment with God, against the conspiracy of modern civilization against our privacy. There must be a conspiracy with God, as Jesus conspired, ascending the hills of solitude that we may come down into the thronged plain of life with something to give. Without that approach to life, we become like the futile, flustered busybody of Colton's picture, quoted by Glenn Frank:

Like a turnstile, he is in everybody's way, but stops nobody; he talks a great deal, but says little; looks into everything, but sees nothing; and has a hundred irons in the fire, but very few of them are hot, and with these few that are he burns his fingers.

Jesus said good-by to friends, that in the rein-vigorated powers of soul he might be a stronger friend; good-by to work, that he might return to do it better; good-by to the world, that he might overcome it and redeem it.

ARGUING WITH A TRAGEDY

When they reached the disciples they saw a large crowd round them, and some scribes *arguing with them.*— *Mark 9. 14* (Moffatt).

THAT was all the scribes could think of doing in the presence of heartbreaking suffering—argue about it! Coming down from the mount of transfiguration, Jesus finds the epileptic boy in the midst of a dis-tressing seizure. The scribes are waging hot argu-ments with Jesus' disciples. The disciples, help-lessly enough, were at least trying to do something to relieve him. The scribes were merely disputing with them, rushing eagerly from secondly to thirdly and fourthly.

That heartless argument of the scribes represents a permanent liability of humanity confronted by acute need—the danger of approaching it from the angle of a theory, of being lost in arid speculation when the demand is for sympathy and help. Emer-son records a biting picture of a professional mind, more interested in analysis and speculation than in cure. "How is the patient to-day?" he once

asked the village physician of Concord, concerning
the minister, Doctor Ripley, lying at death's door.
"It's the most correct apoplexy I ever saw," replied
the physician. "Face and hands livid; breathing
sonorous, and all the symptoms perfect." And he
rubbed his hands with delight!

Correct apoplexy! Fine comfort for the patient
and his family!

Argument has been a persistent reaction to
tragedy. In the presence of some monstrous social
evil decades of argument and fiery rebuttal have
been engaged in as to whether the State or federal
government should regulate it. What matter that
the tragedy went on unchecked as long as the
argument was engrossing? It has been the same
with war. Men have even gone out to non-Christian
lands and, in the very presence of appalling miseries, have allowed much of their energies to be
dissipated in theological and ecclesiastical pitched
battles.

There is only one Christian response to suffering
—well expressed by Shakespeare's heroine Miranda,
"Oh! I have suffered with those that I saw suffer."
When that Christlike identification with need is
made, there is no heart, mind or breath left for
disputation. The cure for heartless argument has
been perfectly pictured, strangely enough, by the
author of the most terribly pessimistic poems in
the English language, James Thomson, author of
The City of Dreadful Night. Thus he describes a
walk in London:

And I wandered about the city, the vast metropolis,
which was become a vast necropolis. . . . Desolate in-

deed I was, although ever and anon, here and there, in wan, haggard faces, in wrinkled brows, in thin compressed lips, in drooping frames, in tremulous gestures, in glassy, hopeless eyes, I detected tokens of brotherhood, I recognized *my brethren in the great Freemasonry of Sorrow.*

Jesus was the Founder of that greatest of all fraternal orders, the Freemasonry of Sorrow.

Have you ever joined it?

CONSECRATION BY DISCIPLINE

Every one has to be *consecrated by the fire of the discipline.—Mark 9. 49* (Moffatt).

CONSECRATION by *discipline!* It is a great word for an undisciplined age. No doubt it is a slander to call the present age undisciplined. But the description fits a large and very vocal element i-. the life of to-day. The cult of freedom has been exalted as the final wisdom of the ages. "Emancipation" is the watchword of the new salvation. "Discipline" is not a popular word. All the jargon of the truly "advanced thinkers" heaps scorn upon it—"Freedom to experiment," "I must live my own life," "escape from stuffy conventions." To the devotees of the cult of freedom life's only tragedy seems to be the suppression of instincts. Lady Mary Wortley Montagu reported in the eighteenth century a plan on foot for taking the "not" out of the Commandments and putting it in the Creed. That is a flash of feminine satire; but it represents the theory on which whole multitudes lived then and live now.

From another angle, the very idea of discipline is under fire. We live in the age of the short-cut. Mastery of an art, a science, a skill is long, toilsome, dull work. Cut across lots! Our magazines are full of screaming proclamations in the advertising pages that almost anything can be acquired in a few painless doses. "French in six lessons," so that we can astonish our friends by talking to the head waiter, and ordering salad dressing in its native language; fifteen minutes a day spent in the immediate vicinity of a set of leather bound books (bought on easy installments) makes hard study unnecessary; and to many the acquirement of a superficial line of chatter, composed largely of what are known as "wisecracks," is an acceptable substitute for culture.

Short-cuts to wealth are alluring for the same reason, as an escape from the discipline of toil, sacrifice, self-control.

The cult of comfort—the product of labor-saving mechanical genius—works against discipline as an ideal. Pushing electric buttons is so much easier than extending either muscles or minds. "Button, button, who's got the button?" has become our national game. A recent book on camping has the alluring title, Roughing it Smoothly. It promises to eliminate all the hardship and discomforts of life in the open. "Roughing it smoothly" well expresses a current national mood.

For such a day comes this word of Jesus, "Every one has to be consecrated by the fires of the discipline." The real mastery of self and the world can come only by the pathway of discipline. That great conception of life's highest significance, bound up in the word, "consecration," devoting it to a great purpose, depends on discipline for its fulfillment. Kipling has expressed this need in a noble prayer:

> "Teach us to rule ourselves alway
> Controlled and cleanly, night and day,
> That we may bring, if need arise,
> No maimed or worthless sacrifice."[1]

The discipline of Christ, however, is not some compulsion laid on from without, but a growth of mastery from within.

JESUS MAKES A CHURCH SURVEY

And he came . . . into the Temple and *looked it all over.*—*Mark 11. 11* (Goodspeed).

HERE Jesus is engaged in an occupation very familiar to the church life of our day. He is making a church survey. Some twenty years or so ago someone hit upon the world survey as a name for appraisal and evaluation of conditions and the work of a social organization. Since that time it has been one of the hardest worked words in the language in America. Especially since the Great War have churches been beset before and behind

---

[1] "The Children's Song," from *Puck of Pook's Hill*. Copyright, 1905, 1906, by Rudyard Kipling. Doubleday, Page & Co., publishers. Used by permission.

with surveys.   The familiar lines of the hymn,
"Awake, My Soul," might well fit the modern
church,

> "A cloud of witnesses around
> Hold thee in full survey."

Here Jesus walks through the Temple giving that
religious agency an appraisal.   What did he think
of it?   How did he estimate it, as a fulfillment of
its purpose?   How interesting it would have been
to have walked with him.   From what happened
that day we may discern how deep his criticism
went.   He laid the actual conditions alongside of
the original purpose.   That was judgment enough.
The original purpose he stated: "My house shall
be a house of prayer."   The drop from that use was
literally immeasurable—"You have made it a den
of robbers."   When Jesus made a survey of how
God's church was working—it went deep.

The trustees of the church had allowed two
things to be done with it, which have been endlessly repeated in Christian history.   They had
allowed it to be *commercialized;* they had allowed
it to be used as a *convenience*.

It stirs the imagination to picture Jesus making
a survey of the church to-day.   Not the church
in general so much as any local church.   It is so
easy for us to escape general conclusions.   No
theme could be worth more clear honest thinking
about, on the part of a congregation.   How would
Jesus go through our church life and work?   What
would he think about it?   We cannot escape the
probing question, "Would he recognize it as his
own?"

One thing is sure, he would not be the sour, prowling critic who overhauls the church with raking fire every few days. Jesus loved the church. He loved the Temple. The depth of his judgment comes from the depth of his love. The most vital criticism of any institution always comes from a lover of it. It is inevitably so. Only love can see deeply enough and care strongly enough. Only love can know what the institution ought to be.

How would Jesus evaluate our church on the point of retaining his own emphasis? Are the things which were supremely great to him as supremely great to us? Or have we lost his proportions and pushed to the front things which he passed over? It takes honesty and humility to press that question home to ourselves. Our danger was well put by a candid European. "When you Americans get an idea," said he, "at once you make an organization. By the time you have the office organized and the secretaries working you begin to wonder what the original idea was."

Have we lost the "original idea" of Jesus, through the very machinery designed to promote it? An art critic has made a very pointed observation on the over elaboration of detail by Velasquez. He says that it is not easy, in looking at an Infanta by Velasquez, to focus attention on the face, so absorbed is one in the "cascade of crinolined embroidery." Have we ever made it hard for men to "focus" on the face of Jesus Christ by an emphasized "cascade of crinolined embroidery" of ecclesiasticism? The classic story of the artist Whistler points the same searching question. Looking at the work of a pupil drawing a portrait of an old woman holding a candle he said, enigmatically, "How beautifully you have painted the *candle!*"

How would Jesus appraise the church on the score of daring, on the score of breadth of love?

❧ ❧ ❧

THE SOPHISTICATION OF JESUS

He *saw their trick.*—*Mark 12. 15* (Moffatt).

An interesting Rogues' Gallery could be made up of the men who tried to fool Jesus! The inventive genius demonstrated in the intricate snares prepared for him commands high intellectual respect. Yet something always went wrong. He saw their trick! This Galilæan peasant, this simple-minded innocent, as they thought, somehow turns out too sophisticated to be trapped.

One of the eternal fascinations of Jesus is in his uniting characteristics and qualities usually violently opposed or mutually exclusive. Jesus had faith in men, but he was never "taken in." He had a keen eye for the worth of men. He believed in the possibilities of certain men when no one else did. But he had the keenest eye for "tricks" that ever looked into the souls of men.

Many people fail either on one side or the other. They are like the leaning tower of Pisa, out of plumb in some direction. They are either gullible or else cynical. Jesus was neither.

He presents a fine picture, in a day when we badly need such a picture, of a noble *sophistication*. He "knew his way around" both in the obscure recesses of human nature and the tangled lanes

of logic. The word "sophistication" has an enormous vogue in our time. The adjective "sophisticated" is worn as though it were a medal of honor.
The chest is thrown out like that of a pouter pigeon.
But when closely examined, this ideal of "sophistication" is composed of very tawdry stuff. It is
usually made up of an intensive knowledge of a
small slice of life (and a trivial slice at that), an
ignorant contempt for all of life outside of that
slice, and a strange mixture of conceit and an
affectation, at least, of cynicism for humanity in
general.

Such sophistication regards itself as cosmopolitan;
as a matter of fact, as Booth Tarkington has dex-
terously shown, it is always provincial. In his novel,
The Plutocrat, Mr. Tarkington thus lets the air out
of the balloon:

Sophistication is always provincial, because nobody
can know intimately a great deal about the whole world.
The greatest cosmopolitan knows a little about a great
many parts of it and can adapt himself to many kinds of
people; but in his one lifetime he can't become a sophisti-
cate among the Kabyles and among the Esquimaux and
the Patagonians and Samoans and Javanese and Japanese and Russians and Portuguese and Chinese and
Sicilians and Spanish and the French and Germans and
Italians and English and Americans. A lifetime isn't
long enough, my friend. Cosmopolitanism is a little
knowledge about many places and kinds of people;
sophistication is a great deal of knowledge about one
place and one kind of people.[1]

As opposed to this kind of affected sophistication
contrast the wisdom of Jesus. He truly united the

---

[1] Doubleday, Page & Co., publishers. Used by permission.

wisdom of the serpent with the guilelessness of the dove. He was never imposed upon by pretentious frauds or led astray by verbal tricks, as we so often are. Consider some of the commonest "tricks" of specious reasoning which befuddle so many.

1. Take that old, old trick called the "fallacy of the false alternative." What confusion it has led to in Christian history!

Thus we are called upon to choose between two alternatives when both are false and we should take neither, or when both are true and we should take both. We are told by doctrinaires that we must choose either faith or reason, either God or law, either Christianity or evolution, either individual or social gospel. It is not a question of "either or" but of "both . . . and." To imagine that we must choose either one or the other exclusively is to be fooled by a trick.

2. *The delusion of the explanation.* Many in this age of expanding knowledge imagine that when they have explained how a thing works they have explained the thing itself.

3. Many people to-day are helpless before the trick of substituting an epithet or an adjective for an argument. Tell them that religion is "old-fashioned," or "traditional," or a "fairy tale for naïve minds," and they become so paralyzed that their mind resigns. They throw over their faith, for "one must be modern" at all costs!

4. *The fallacy of the majority* acts on the minds of many like chloroform. What "everybody" thinks must be right. At least, it is fashionable, and that is the only meaning the adjective "right" has in many quarters. To have a conviction that

cuts across the grain of current customs and clamors, would make one seem "queer."   And as Dr. Henry Sloane Coffin has said, the one commandment which many people really obey in these days is: *Thou shalt not be queer*.

Should not the imitation of Jesus include his detection of tricks?

⚜ ⚜ ⚜

AN ANSWER TO THE POINT

Then one of the Scribes . . . knew that Jesus had given them *an answer to the point, and a forcible one.*— Mark *12. 28* (Weymouth).

HERE is a new approach to the appeal of Jesus to men—the force of his sheer common sense. Here was a man evidently indifferent to Jesus until he listened to the Sadducees trying to bait him. All the scribes were not pedants and bigots. Here was one with an open mind. Before the clear, forcible reasoning with which Jesus answered the malicious quibbling of the Sadducees every possible bar against Jesus in this man's mind goes down. Pursuing his study of Jesus further, his mind and that of Jesus meet in agreement, and Jesus returns the scribe's tribute with the praise, "Thou art not far from the kingdom of God."

This scribe's response to Jesus' conduct of an argument indicates an effective way of presenting Jesus to a large number of people. The compelling approach to people of this class, thoughtful, open minded, but entirely outside the circle of Jesus' disciples, is not through emotion, sentimentalism, or fear or authority. It is in the demonstration of the truth that *Jesus brings pointed and forcible answers to great questions* which cannot be evaded, such as the existence and nature of God, the meaning and destiny of life and the goal of human effort.

JUMBOISM

"Look, teacher, *what a size* these stones and buildings are!"—*Mark 13. 1* (Moffatt).

THIS exclamation of the disciples, awed by the bigness of the Temple, sounds both very human and remarkably modern. They reflect our awe and reverence for bigness of whatever sort. Perhaps it may not be amiss to call this a peculiarly American text!

Jesus was never overawed by size or bulk. No doubt that is one thing which makes him a baffling personality to many people. Our most delirious enthusiasms are often reserved for the biggest. "Bigger and Better" is assuming the proportions of a gospel. Jesus was unimpressed by the mere size of anything, whether buildings, money, crowds. He had a deeper interest—quality. He weighed the Temple and found it wanting, in spite of its size. Size was no substitute for poor quality of vision or service.

Our obsession with size might be considered either as a national disease or a religion or both. "Jumboism" is a good name for it. One of the most famous animals which ever lived was P. T. Barnum's elephant, Jumbo. His fame rested on one thing. He was the biggest elephant in captivity. He may have had other endearing and noble qualities. If so, they were never widely known. He was the biggest. That was enough.

That is enough for many of us. The city with the biggest population, the man with the biggest fortune, the actor with the biggest salary, the store with the biggest sales, the preacher with the biggest crowd—these are the ones to which popular interest and acclaim run. They are the Jumbos before which the crowd bows.

Booth Tarkington puts this worship into realistic form, in this imagined prayer of a growing industrial city:

"Give me of thyself, O Bigness,
  Power to get more Power;
  Riches to get more riches;
  Give me of thy sweat to get more sweat;
  Give me of thy bigness to get more Bigness for myself.
  O Bigness, for thine is the Power and the Glory
  And there is no end but Bigness for ever and ever.
  Amen."[1]

This awe of size may be well symbolized in a characteristic modern machine—the adding machine. It typifies an attitude toward life which is destructive to the life of the spirit. It is a marvelous invention. The principal trouble with it is that so many people try to make it do things it cannot do. It can add up dollars and things. It can never

---

[1] From *The Turmoil*, by Booth Tarkington. Doubleday, Page & Co., publishers. Used by permission.

add up life or express its meaning, because it deals
only with quantity. The worship of the adding
machine is the enemy of personality when it results
in a person's substitution of quantity for quality.
Such a confusion is a pernicious danger to the church
in the insidious temptation it brings to measure
success in columns of things to be added. For
then the church uses precisely the words of the
disciples of Jesus—"Look, Master, what a size!"

The church is in continual danger of measuring
achievement in terms of size, of crowds, for instance.
Whenever it does so, it always parts company with
Jesus' valuations. Jesus was never impressed with
the cry, "Look, what a size!"

One Sunday in September more than six hundred
thousand people paraded up and down the board-
walks of Coney Island.

What a stupendous crowd! That is a larger
number of people than engaged in all the crusades
of Europe in the Middle Ages. It is a larger number of people than have gone out as missionaries
of the Christian faith since the resurrection morning.

What did such an enormous crowd mean? The
answer can be given pretty largely in one word—
peanuts. It meant nothing! That massive crowd
walked up and down the thoroughfare eating peanuts and popcorn and went home again. It was
not a crowd with any natural unity. It was not
a crowd with any purpose. It was just a crowd.

That crowd of over half a million is well worth
thinking of in an age beset with the fundamental
vulgarity of confusing the size of a thing with its
significance. A crowd, taken just as a crowd, with
not much regard for its purpose, its quality, or its

influence, usually means as little as a Coney Island crowd means.

One of the greatest dangers which the church faces is the continual danger of becoming merely a Coney Island crowd instead of a company of twelve disciples. It is instructive to recall that Jesus feared few things as much as he feared crowds. He knew that the five thousand who got a free dinner made a trivial gathering when compared in influence with the twelve people on whom he so lavishly expended himself.

THE APPALLING HORROR

The appalling Horror standing where he had no right to stand.—*Mark 13. 14* (Moffatt).
The dreadful desecration (Goodspeed).

WHATEVER may have been the exact meaning of the phrase translated in the King James and Revised Versions of the New Testament as "the abomination of desolation," there can be no question of what the supreme abomination is in the world to-day. Goodspeed translates it "the dreadful desecration"; Moffatt calls it "the appalling Horror." Both are vivid and yet restrained descriptions of *war*. War is the appalling horror "standing where it has no right to stand," in the very center of civilization, a devastating explosive force.

Can we think of the four years' nightmare, 1914–1918, and not yield to war this crowning distinction

of being the appalling horror? One vast conflagra-
tion, four and a half years long, spreading over
three continents; one half of the accumulated wealth
of the world destroyed; ten million soldiers killed,
more hate concentrated than in any previous period
in human history.

That is merely a tithe of the cost. War used to
be an affair of armies and navies; now it is a slaughter of whole peoples.

We may give it the worst name we can think of.
(That was literally what this term was—the most
odious and terrible name the prophet's imagination
could devise.) Yet when we are through we must
realize that all previous war has been merely practice, bungling and amateurish, compared to what
can be done in the slaughter of the future. The
chemical warfare service of the United States
government has opened the veil of the future to
cheer us up with this glimpse. It has developed a
liquid approximately three drops of which when
applied to any part of the skin will cause a man's
death. One plane carrying two tons of the liquid
could deposit material enough to kill every man
in a large area by action of the skin.

In one of Joseph Conrad's powerful stories, *The
End of the Tether*, the central figure is an old man
crouching at the wheel of the vessel whose command he will not relinquish although he has gone
blind. It is a true picture of the war system clinging to its grip on the world.

That grip can be broken only by moral and
spiritual force. The old notion that to build ship
against ship and gun against gun and fort against
fort was the way to secure peace has been dis-

credited. The world knows now that men cannot make peace while they have war in their hearts.

To offset this perversion of science men and nations must set their hearts, their minds, and their wills toward lasting peace. Skeptics will meet the believer at every step of his way and tell him that his is a useless mission. But so might any proud Roman, with his cynical culture behind him, have spoken to the twelve humble men in Judæa two thousand years ago. Yet the "pale Galilæan" conquered the material empire. What the friends of peace need to-day is the faith and the spirit of those simple men who made that conquest possible.

DIED OF HEARTBREAK

Jesus uttered *a loud cry* and yielded up his spirit.—
Mark 15. 37 (Weymouth).

DR. ERNEST F. SCOTT thus comments on the actual death of Jesus on the cross:[1]

Jesus died long before the time which was usual in crucifixion, and perhaps his death was not wholly due to the effects of the torture following the terrible strain of the preceding days. The loud cry with which he died seems to betoken a sudden spasm, and the fourth evangelist tells us that when a spear was thrust into his side after death there issued what appeared to be mingled blood and water. It has been conjectured, on medical grounds, that the *immediate cause of his death was a rupture of the heart.*

---

[1] *The First Age of Christianity.* The Macmillan Company, publishers. Used by permission.

The italics are ours. The conjecture is so striking to the imagination that it is well worth the emphasis of italics. We speak, in reference to the deep significance of the death of Jesus, of "the heartbreak on Calvary." It is very suggestive to find the medical conjecture that Jesus died of actual, physical heartbreak. That heartbreak is a vivid physical symbol of the spiritual reality of the atonement.

LIVING ON TIPTOE

She . . . gave thanks to God and spoke about the child to all who were *living in expectation* of the liberation of Jerusalem—*Luke 2. 38* (Goodspeed).

A FINE way to live—in expectation of liberation!

There existed a definite class of people in the Israel of Jesus' day consisting of sentinal souls who lived in the expectation that something was going to happen. And the very expectation that God would do something helped immeasurably to make it happen. For that group of people were the seed plot in which Jesus' message first took root. They received him because they were looking for him.

It is such sentinel souls who make possible the liberation of mankind from the grip of ancient wrong. Nothing really great ever happened without a great many lives being lived "in expectation." Arthur J. Gossip says finely:

They are the kind of folks by whom the world moves forward: who live in a *qui vive* of expectancy, always standing on tiptoe, always sure that something big may

happen at any time. Hush! Is not this it coming now?
With people like that God can do anything. But you
and I keep thwarting him by sheer dullness of spirit.
We are listless, apathetic, blasé, bored; our hopes are
small and thin. There is no audacity in our expectation.[1]

Lorne Pierce traces the same truth back to the
Old Testament:

A. B. Davidson once called the prophets "always terribly one-sided people." That single idea was that "God
is going to do something." "God is surely coming!"
cries Isaiah. "He is here, at our very door!" answers
Zephaniah. And so each and every one by their faith
made it possible, yea, certain, for some great spiritual
surprise to take place. It is upon this that the rest is
builded: "And when the time was fulfilled—Jesus came."
Did it ever happen otherwise? Truth is an emperor that
only comes to visit his subjects along the highway of
great longing. Science advances to its kingdom along
the avenues of expectancy. Religion comes into its own
along the road of loving hearts, that great-hearted clan
of intrepid believers.[2]

But not all of Christ's followers feel this quickened
pulse beat of expectant faith.

Some are *asleep*.

Some are *satisfied*. Their eyes never wistfully scan
the horizon. Their hearts are never hungry.

Some are looking but they are *looking back*.
The golden age for them is in the past. For some
reason yesterday belonged to God but not to-
morrow. They say good-by to sunsets but never
welcome a dawn.

[1] *The Galilean Accent*. Charles Scribner's Sons, publishers. Used
by permission.
[2] From *In Conference with the Best Minds*. Cokesbury Press,
publishers. Used by permission.

There is an even deeper meaning in the words "living in expectation" than appears on the surface. It is this: only as we live in expectation do we truly live at all.

Are our spirits on tiptoe or stretched on a couch? There is one easy way to learn the answer. What is our habitual attitude to the world's "impossibles," to the great dreams of men—the abolition of war, the coming of brotherhood, the curbing of greed, the exploitation of the unprivileged? Do we live, and work, in eager expectation of these things?

A GOOD TIME TO PRAY

It was *in these days* that he went off to the hillside to pray. He spent the whole night in prayer.—*Luke 6. 12* (Moffatt).

WHAT days?

The words immediately preceding these are: "This filled them [the Pharisees and scribes] with fury, and they discussed what they could do to Jesus."

Jesus had just healed a paralyzed man on the Sabbath day and had met the hard, inflexible, closed mind of the scribes and Pharisees. It was a turning point in his ministry. The opposition to him becomes a conspiracy to kill him. It was definitely established that he could not win them by any means. Their hearts were as hard as their heads.

Then it was that he spent the whole night in

prayer. No doubt we should not press too hard the significance of the night in prayer following after this conflict with the Pharisees. Immediately following the night he chooses his twelve disciples. That great step surely had its relation to a night of prayer. Yet the two events in the record, the stubborn and vindictive opposition and the whole night of prayer, have an important relation—and a warning. When this attitude of the Pharisees appeared, Jesus recognized one of the deadliest and most formidable enemies of the Kingdom. Whenever we feel in ourselves or see at work in others anything akin to the attitude and mood and mentality of these scribes and Pharisees, we too ought to recognize it for the malign and terrifying thing it is, one of the chief obstacles to the Kingdom. It was something Jesus could do absolutely nothing with in the Pharisees. He can do absolutely nothing with it in us.

For that mentality of the Pharisees is not a thing very far away from plain, everyday stubbornness that we know so well. Jesus' action was opposed to their tradition. That settled it. Jesus was a new fact in their experience. They had no eyes for new facts. They loved their tradition, their habitual ways of thinking, better than facts. They loved it better than men. Their hearts had not a single twinge of sympathy for the cripple. There was not a trace of common, elementary, human emotion rejoicing over a cured man.

Two characteristics of this mental condition which was Jesus' supreme obstacle stand out glaringly.

1. They had no *flexibility*. Their minds were like

Babylonian tombs, rooms hewn out of rock on which were carved cuneiform inscriptions. Nothing could grow there. Oliver Cromwell once cried out to the Parliamentarians, "For the love of Christ, gentlemen, I beseech you to think that it is possible that you may be mistaken." These Pharisees and their many spiritual descendants could not do any thinking of that type. Edward Carpenter in his autobiography, *My Days and Dreams*, describes a man as "having swallowed a principle like a poker, he would remain absolutely unbending and unyielding." These opponents of Jesus had swallowed their tradition exactly like a poker.

2. There was no warm fire of sympathy, or identification with humanity in their minds. They had catalogued life rather than experienced it— an error unfortunately rather common. Instead of warm, pulsing hearts they had legal storerooms. H. G. Wells has described exactly the mental furnishing of the Pharisees, in writing of a character in *The World of William Clissold*.

His mind was like some great furniture depository, safe from fire, corruption, or admixture; nothing seemed to happen in it, and nothing ever got lost in it, and he could, with every appearance of pleasure, reproduce the most commonplace facts at any time at the fullest length and in the completest detail.[1]

Whenever we feel any symptoms like these—it is a good time to pray.

[1] Copyright, 1926. George H. Doran Company, publishers. Used by permission.

GETTING INTO THE PAST TENSE

Alas for you who are rich, for you *have had* your comfort!—*Luke 6. 24* (Goodspeed).

THE worst accident which can happen to a person is to get into the past-perfect tense. "Have had"—there is a crack of doom about the words. It's all over. There is nothing more.

The most charmed words in human speech are those which frequently irritate us in reading a serial story: *"Continued in our next."* For the glory of life *is* that it is a serial story. When it ceases to be a serial it ceases to be life. When there is no expectancy, when there is no "next" to look forward to and prepare for, when we have majored on the things which end with the consuming, we have wandered into that "never, never land"—and a desert land it is—the Past Tense.

Getting into the past tense—as Jesus uses the tense here—is not to be confused with old age. Jesus was not talking about old age. Age does not lose the future. The tragedy of the past tense goes far deeper than that. It is not anything so superficial as the number of years. It is the tragedy of absorption in things that wind up completely— that have no mysterious remainders. Wealth is one of the most obvious of such dead ends. A person devoted to material accumulation plays a part in life like those characters who get killed in the first act. They fall into the past tense before the real plot unweaves.

One of the reasons for the great hold of the drama of *Faust* on the imagination of men is that it is so true a transcription of human experience.

We have the terrible choice of either grasping things that can be completely encompassed, and so inevitably land us in the past tense, or of pursuing things which move on to ever new horizons.

Robert S. Hillyer has a little poem, terrible in its bleakness, describing an abandoned farm in New England, which accurately pictures the devastation in any life which has gotten into the past tense!

> "Shutters bang in the wind outside;
>   Cobwebs hang from the mildewed walls;
> Stale, damp mould in the lifeless cold;
>   Doors flung wide to the darkened halls.

> "Love and strength of the new keen race
>   Lie full-length where the weeds grow high,
> All things swept to the past, except
>   This ruined place the wind roars by.

> "Blank disaster of empty windows;
>   Broken plaster strewn on the floor;
> Darkness spills from the wild, bleak hills
>   And the winter wind blows under the door."[1]

The glory of life is in its expectancy. Marmont said of Napoleon, "There is so much future in his mind." It has been characteristic of great souls, such as Paul, who have had a far nobler future than Napoleon's in their minds.

It is not merely in materialistic choices that we run the danger of getting into the past tense. There is the same danger in a cosy dogmatism, that leaves no room for the additions of experience; in a finished

---

[1] From *The Hills Give Promise*. B. J. Brimmer Company, publishers. Used by permission.

aim in life; a "fixed" character, or in a religious experience which has petrified.

There is a very common noun which describes getting into the past tense—*death*.

EXPERTS

The . . . *experts* in the Law thwarted God's purpose for themselves.—*Luke 7. 30* (Goodspeed).

AND for everybody else! *Expert* is a favorite modern word. But the expert is not a modern invention. Here he is, face to face with Jesus, a man with voluminous technical information and the slenderest stock of broad human wisdom; able to delve into prodigious researches into the traditions of Jewish ecclesiasticism, unable to grasp elementary spiritual realities, or the significance of a personality like Jesus.

The expert is abroad in the land. And of many of to-day's "experts" the comment of Jesus on some experts of his time is true—"they thwart God's purpose for themselves." We may add— "and for others also."

These words of Jesus are not to be twisted into a disparagement of genuine knowledge or science. Jesus was not disparaging knowledge. The "expert" of his scornful description was the man whose legalistic refinements nullified God's law. There are many experts in our own day who thwart God's purpose for humanity. There is the expert who has mastered the details of one branch of learning and mistaken it for an explanation of the whole universe. He conforms exactly to the classic comment on the English scientist Whewell—"His forte was science; his folly omniscience." There is the expert who builds an imposing theory on insufficient data or wrongly interpreted data. There is the expert who blithely leaves out of view a whole body of facts which do not fit in with the theory he is constructing.

Carlyle gave a picturesque description of one of this class of experts. "He is a slightly impertinent man with several dictionaries about him but with small knowledge of God's universe."

There is the *psychological* expert (not to be confused with all psychologists, by any means) who expounds a materialistic "behaviorism." He bows the soul out of the universe and by counting and describing nerve cells, molecules, atoms, and electrons imagines—or pretends—that he has explained the mind and soul of man.

Albert E. Wiggam's conclusion is fairly representative of the tribe: "The universe stands revealed at last in all its gaunt nakedness, as a mere machine without sympathy or purpose."[1] Anyone who by prestige or the pressure of intellectual fashion imposes that conception of the world on others is "thwarting God's purpose" as revealed in Jesus.

Take a few examples at random:

Dr. Irwin Edman, of Columbia, teaches that "man is a mere accident." George Santayana, the author, makes man "a little luminous meteor in an infinite abyss of

---

[1] From *The New Decalogue of Science*. Copyright, 1922–1923. Used by special permission of the publishers, The Bobbs-Merrill Company.

nothingness; a rocket fired on a dark night." Everett Dean Martin maintains that "religion is primarily a defensive mechanism," while Professor John Watson, of Johns Hopkins, asserts that the soul, consciousness, God, and immortality are merely mistakes of the older psychology. Bertrand Russell, the high priest of mechanism, wails "that man is the product of causes which had no prevision of the end they were achieving; that his origin, his growth, his hopes and fears, his love and his belief, are but the outcome of accidental collocation of atoms; that only on the firm foundation of unyielding despair can the soul's habitation be safely built."[1]

Then there is a vastly different type of expert—of the same variety that Jesus was speaking of—the ecclesiastical expert. He is the leader so intent and fussy over ecclesiastical procedure, manipulations of church machinery, animated over superficial issues, and with what Carlyle calls "explosions of all the upholsteries," that the great matters of the law such as mercy and justice in human relations receive but scant attention. He too grievously thwarts God's purpose.

Their name is legion—the *anthropological* "expert," whose labored arguments for the inherent superiority of the so-called Nordic races over all others of God's creatures thwarts God's purpose of human brotherhood; the *military* expert, whose technical impossibles block the movement of the human race toward peace.

A little learning is a dangerous thing.

[1] From *The New Decalogue of Science*, Copyright, 1922-23. Used by special permission of the publishers, Bobbs-Merrill Company.

A TRINITY OF SUFFOCATION

The message is stifled by the *anxieties, wealth, and gayeties* of time.—*Luke 8. 14* (Weymouth).

HERE is the only Trinity of which many people have any real experience: a trinity of suffocation; anxieties; wealth and gayeties. These are three very different things—anxieties and gayeties seem at the very opposite poles of human emotion and experience. But they are strangely alike in their effect—they suffocate the spirit. In that respect their effect is much like the frequent effect of the application of ice or fire to the skin—they both feel the same. They give the same shock to the nerves in spite of a difference of one hundred degrees of temperature. So these three enemies of the spirit —as different as human experiences can be—"stifle the message," as these words of Jesus declare. They suffocate the soul.

Anxieties do it for more of us than either of the other two. Most of us do not have wealth. With most of us, our "gayeties" are a rather slight and pathetic array. But anxieties are the very atmosphere we breathe. In a very real respect they are an essential to sensitive life. They need not asphyxiate the spirit. They do so only when we have not acquired the art of selective attention, when we allow a flood of concerns to assume the same magnitude. The person suffocated by anxiety cannot take out of the central place in his mind any fears, irritations, worries. He is like a radio set without any selective power in which six or eight jazz bands destroy any melody, any harmony that might be won through concentration. Jesus brought the great secret of preventing suffocation through concentration—"Seek ye *first* the kingdom of God."

Wealth, or the vain pursuit of it, can stifle the message of life. It need not necessarily do it, but the process by which it does is one of the commonest spectacles of our time. That process is pictured strikingly in Frank Norris' novel, *The Pit*, in which a grain speculator is trapped in a wheat elevator and buried in an avalance of wheat. Here was the means of supporting life, the wheat, becoming the agency of destroying it. The high purpose of life is obscured with the clutter of its material accessories. Emerson put it in a single sentence, "The worst thing about money is that it so often costs so much." So life loses its deep significance; its spiritual flame is snuffed out.

When gayety becomes a conscious pursuit it becomes chloroform.

There is only one preventive against this trinity. Jesus described it in this very passage. "But as for that in good ground, it means those who, having listened to the message with open minds and in a right spirit, hold it fast and patiently yield a return" (Weymouth).

"GET OUT!"

Then all the people of the neighborhood of Gerasa *asked him to go away from them*, for they were terribly frightened.—*Luke 8. 37* (Goodspeed).

IT would be very instructive to make a list of the

people who said to Jesus, "Get out!" It would provide not merely a study in New Testament history but likewise a picture of many forces in present-
day life. For the burden of the world's attitude
to Jesus in many areas of life to-day is exactly the
same as in many towns of Galilee and Judæa. It
can be expressed in two words—"Get out!"

1. The people of Capernaum threw Jesus out of
town (Luke 4. 29). He had healed a man and challenged their traditions.

2. The people of Gerasa cried feverishly, "Get
out!" They were afraid for their property and the
placid order of their town. His coming had been
the occasion of the loss of property. They preferred pigs to a miracle-worker.

3. Herod told Jesus to "get out." His ideas did
not suit the purposes of the government, Herod
being the government.

4. A Samaritan village kept him out. They had
a violent, ineradicable prejudice against his race.

Here were four instances of people who threw
Jesus out of their town, and as far as possible out
of their life and affairs.

The same four antagonisms to Jesus operate
powerfully to-day. Jesus is told to get out because
his teachings run counter to sacred traditions and
practices; because they would reduce business
profits, if applied; because they challenge some
purposes of governments; because they condemn
cherished race and class and nationalistic prejudices.

❧ ❧ ❧

THE BLUNDERING CHURCH

How long must I . . . *bear with you?—Luke 9. 41*
(Moffatt).

How long must I . . . *put up with you?* (Goodspeed.)

THE ninth chapter of Luke is a wonderful portrait panorama of the problems which Jesus had with his disciples, the blunders, the dullness and the failings with which they continually confronted him. It is also a panoramic picture of church history and of present-day church life. For the problems which the disciples presented to Jesus are the same ones which the church at one time and another and in one way or another presents. If Jesus was driven to the point of asking them, "How long must I put up with you?" must he not ask the same question over us?

In the short space of this one chapter there are nine separate occasions where the disciples exhibited an attitude or engaged in an action which illustrated a failure to share his spirit or his purpose. Each of these nine situations is paralleled in the common everyday life of the church to-day.

1. *"Send the crowd away."* This was the only solution which the disciples had for the need of a hungry crowd. Get rid of them somehow. Why should we worry? It isn't our affair. It is exactly the spirit of many of Jesus' disciples to big human need to-day—"Send them away."

2. *"Who am I?"* Jesus asks them. And some of his disciples make replies indicating a failure to grasp the real significance of Jesus in the world. To-day, in deeds, if not in the words, we often deny the lordship of Jesus over life.

3. *"Let's stay on this mountain."* The conception of Christianity as a selfish emotionalism unrelated to human need.

4. *Failing to heal the paralytic at the foot of the mountain.* An instance of failing to supply the resources of God for the world's evils.

5. *Failing to understand the approaching suffering and death of Jesus.* How common it is for Jesus' disciples to overlook the demand for sacrificial living! The twelve shrank from the hard way. So do we.

6. *The dispute about who should be greatest.* What a glorious history Christianity would have had if this had been the last as well as the first dispute among Jesus' disciples on this subject! What a future it would have if there should never be another!

7. *Wishing to stop another disciple* of Jesus who did not belong to their circle. Comment is unnecessary!

8. *Calling down fire* on an inhospitable village. Here is the familiar experiment of attempting to use the weapons of hell in the service of the kingdom of heaven.

9. *Delayed discipleship,* in the case of the man who wished to follow Jesus, but only after something more pressing had been attended to.

What a mirror for us to look into!

Yet, lest this picture be one of unrelieved pessimism, there is the sublime truth to be recorded that it was from this same strangely mixed human stuff that Jesus formed the force that launched his gospel and his church in the world!

❧ ❧ ❧

THE BEST DISH AT THE BANQUET

"Mary has *chosen the best dish*, and she is not to be dragged away from it."—*Luke 10. 41* (Moffatt).

LIFE is not a *table d'hôte* affair. It is an *à la carte* menu. You can't have everything, though many are trying, with an impossible eclecticism, to take everything in the world in an indiscriminate gorge. Life's business is a terrible choice.

Moffatt translates Mary's action in listening to Jesus' conversation as the choice of "the best dish" at the banquet. He says in one of his rare footnotes: "I translate 'merida' by 'dish,' to bring out the point and play of the saying." The best dish at life's banquet is fellowship with God—the nourishment of the teaching of Jesus.

It is a timely figure of speech for our day, when so many forces of social compulsion are reducing life to a severely standardized *table d'hôte*, where people take what is laid down for them and go through life without any real exercise of sovereign choice. The lives of many people are characterized not so much by wrong choices as by the failure to make any deliberate choice of the "best dish" on life's bewildering menu.

And choice there must be, if life is to have any coherent meaning. What shall it be—the upholstery of a house or the spirit of a home; fashion or the fine and mellow graciousness of spirit which can ennoble the routine of everyday living however simple; a shifting vaudeville or the concentrated purpose of the New Testament?

Henry James, in a letter to a friend, advises a choice of the best dish, in a word of counsel, that might very well have come from this tenth chapter of Luke—"Let your soul live; it is the only life that isn't, on the whole, a sell."

Have you placed your order on life? Is it just a conventional demand for everything with no graduation of values—or is it the dish that satisfies life's deepest hunger?

There is a quaint story from the life of the English poet Coventry Patmore which throws a bright light on the business of living.

He always refused to marry any one (he was three times wed) until he had lent the lady a clean copy of his favorite book. He would then ask her to mark the passages that seemed to her important. If they were what he considered the right bits, the matter went forward.

The Book of Life is opened up before each of us with the injunction—"Mark the best."

"DON'T PESTER ME!"

"Do not pester me."—*Luke 11. 7* (Weymouth).

THIS word "pester" is almost audible. We can hear the irritated snarl of this man wakened up out of the first moments of sleep; hear his loud protest over the vast injustice of his being called on to move and get some food for belated guests. He could not possibly do anything, he cried. He had balanced his books for the day. There couldn't be any new entries. "Everything is set. I'm all fixed for the night. I can't make any changes now."

That phrase, "Do not pester me," is the perfect expression of a mind that is completely set, that cannot readjust itself to any new set of facts or a new situation. Such a mind is a static thing, like a trunk neatly arranged, tightly packed, all locked and strapped. It's too much trouble to open it, and nothing will go in anyhow.

It represents vividly a risk that life has for all of us—of becoming so set and finished in our ideas and views of life that anything new, which demands an opening of the mind or a revision of opinion or an unexpected action, is a mere "pestering." We come to look at a new idea, not on its merits but simply as a disturbance of our snug nap.

It is the voice of reaction against any change or new demand—"Don't pester me." Stephen A. Douglas once cried out in a speech during the political conflict over slavery, "Why can't they let our country remain as our fathers left it?" That is the chief response of many persons to the experiences of life. They are "pestered" by anything that requires movement. It is partly due to an inborn inertia in human nature which resists change. Bergson stresses the tendency of animal life to relapse into the vegetable kingdom. "Torpor and unconsciousness," he says in *Creative Evolution*, "are always lying in wait for animal activity." Torpor and unconsciousness are always lying in wait for mental life and frequently "get" it. Habituated to some use or tradition, men prefer to leave well enough alone. They prefer to stay in bed to risking an adventure into the unknown. Richard Roberts has described the process:

Every class and caste, every community and country, has built for itself a house of life, has elaborated for itself a code of orthodoxies and habits, of familiar ideas and customs, within the pale of which the individual is at home. But let any new idea enter into this circle; immediately the community scents danger, feels its security imperiled, closes its ranks and is up in arms against the intruder. It will have nothing to do with it; it hurls hard and ugly names at it; it charges it with criminal intention and as often as not it kills the individual who imported it.[1]

This was precisely the attitude of the static minds of the religious authorities of Judaism to Jesus. "Don't pester us!" they shrieked. Early Christianity met the same irritated crowd. In Jerusalem Christianity was treated as an outrage upon religion; at Philippi as an outrage upon patriotism (Acts 16. 21).

It was the attitude of the Established Church toward Luther, toward Wesley. Later—by a strange repetition of history—that same Methodism, which had a century earlier been accused of "pestering" religion with wild, new demands, said to William Booth: "Don't pester me about your poor and outcasts. I'm all set and can't change my ways."

The early pioneers and prophets of the modern missionary movement met the same closed door, in the early days, and the accusation of being a pestering nuisance. It took half a century for the churches to begin to get up and provide the bread of life for the hungry.

And how often it has been the attitude of business

---

[1] From *The New Man and the Divine Society*. The Macmillan Company, publishers. Used by permission.

and industrial interests to any new insight of Christian social ethics. "Don't bother me," is the reaction. "Business is business. We're all fixed for good."

There are many large meanings to this story of Jesus. One which comes close home, with its challenge to self-examination, is this: "Don't get all set. Don't snuggle down into such a deep sleep that the call of human need for action and change strikes you merely as a nuisance."

"CONGRATULATE ME!"

Congratulate me.—Luke 15. 6 (Weymouth-Goodspeed).

How often we use these words! And frequently in what trivial connections!—over a new dress, an automobile, a choice bit of flattery, a new decoration of some kind, an increase in salary; graduation from school. At other times the words, or the unspoken emotion, at least, mark a real red-letter day in life—the coming of life's great gifts and trusts, marriage, the birth of a child, or some significant toil and achievement.

The words here as Jesus uses them picture life's deepest and most lasting cause for congratulation —*that somehow we have become part of the redemptive forces of the world*. Beside that, congratulations on other scores are like the chatter of a child's tea party. Here is a real graduation—life's true Commencement Exercise!

Twice in Weymouth's and Goodspeed's translation of the fifteenth chapter of Luke these words occur—over the finding of the lost sheep and the lost coin. They are both works of redemption; a force out of use and circulation is restored; a life wandering in aimless and baffled circles has been saved from waste.

There is pictured here a double cause for rejoicing. For one thing, life was organized into a *search*. Anyone has reached the place for supreme congratulation when his life has in the furtherance of a great purpose, an exploration, focused on a high quest. For another thing—any life is blessed, no matter what toil or pain it struggles through, which has become a restorative, reclaiming, building force in other lives. In this fellowship of redemption are the great spirits of humanity, names like Pasteur in medicine; Froebel, Pestalozzi, and Horace Mann in education; servants of men like John Howard and Florence Nightingale; and such indefatigable "finders" as William Booth, and that innumerable company who have shared their spirit and purpose.

What is true for an individual is, of course, true for a nation. "Congratulate me" may be the selfish, boastful, complacent expression of national wealth and egotism. The only final and valid basis for national congratulation is the basis of Jesus, that it has graduated from childish assertion into a redemptive force. National greatness is not to be measured by efficiency in *production* but by wisdom in *use*.

Many people, if their inward heart should speak, would frame their national anthem after this fashion:

"O beautiful for dividends
   Of twenty-five per cent
On oil and steel and real estate,
   On money freely lent.
America! America!
   May riches be our fate;

"Increase our wealth
And guard our health,
   America, the great!"

Katharine Lee Bates wrote the original anthem
with a deeper insight into the only cause for real
congratulation:

"O beautiful for pilgrim feet,
   Whose stern, impassioned stress
A thoroughfare for freedom beat
   Across the wilderness!
America! America!
   God mend thine every flaw,
Confirm thy soul in self-control,
   Thy liberty in law."[1]

SLAVING

"All these years," replied the son, "I have been slaving for you."—*Luke 15. 29* (Weymouth).

THE perfect word for the spirit and attitude of
the Elder Brother—*slaving*. That was just what
was the matter with him—he slaved. The word

---

[1] From "America the Beautiful." Used by permission of author.

"serve" has such high uses in common speech that it cannot convey accurately the quality of the Elder Brother's relation to the father and to his work. That relationship never reached the height of a joyful partnership; it was conscript toil. It was labor without love; without the energizing force of a great affection either for the father or for his brother. The father calls him, "My dear son" (Luke 15. 31). The son never says, "Father." He gives an unconscious picture of himself in his persistent refusal to use the word "brother." He substitutes the contemptuous expression, "This son of yours."

There were no wings to his service. It was dull, heavy, unloving, plodding. And that kind of slaving ends up with a snarl. The return of his brother brought no explosion of emotion to him.

This last act of the drama of the Prodigal Son— the drama of the Two Lost Sons as it should be called—is an eternal warning, always needed, of the tragedy and futility of trying to do God's service without the spirit of sonship and love. There are multitudes of Christians in the position of the elder brother, not to the extent that they share his harsh, bitter feeling, but in that they are plodding along at the tasks of the church and Kingdom, without the lifting, propelling force of a real experience of fellowship with the father. Their lives are not replenished and sustained by the joy of communion. They know no ecstasy.

There is none of that liberating force in the soul which Emerson calls "latent joy." His words are a valid description of the fruit of sustained Christian experience:

Latent joy performs a great office in nature, so does latent joy in life. You may have your stock of well-being condensed into ecstasies, trances of good fortune and delight preceded and followed by blank or painful weeks and months; or you may have your joy spread over all the days in a blank, vague, uniform sense of power and hope.

One of General Foch's military maxims is this: "Every soldier must see his General—must feel himself in communication with him, and never be allowed to consider himself merely a poor pawn maneuvered by an unknown power." The conditions of modern warfare have rendered that maxim well-nigh impracticable. But it is a maxim of Christian warfare that can never be outdated. "Every soldier must see his Leader." Without that vision and communion service becomes slavery.

The propelling force of the Christian enterprise is emotion, it is love. It must get forward in the world as an automobile gets forward by *a series of explosions*.

The danger is that a fussy preoccupation over the technicalities of services of one sort or another may displace the replaceable power of an energizing outburst of love. Emerson has drawn the classic picture of the tragedy of substituting meticulous care over incidental details for the great experience of fellowship of soul.

I pray you, O excellent wife, not to cumber yourself and me to get a rich dinner for this man or this woman who has alighted at our gate, nor a bedchamber made ready at too great a cost. These things, if they are curious in, they can get for a dollar at any village. But let this stranger, if he will, in your looks, in your accent and behavior, read your heart and earnestness, your thought and will, which he cannot buy at any price in any village or city, and which he may well travel fifty miles and dine sparely and sleep hard in order to behold.

We merely slave when there is no renewed experience of joy in God. Samuel Rutherford, from his Scottish prison, wrote, "Jesus Christ came into my room last night and every stone flashed like a ruby." That is exalted language, but millions of Christians could testify from their own experience that it is not the language of madness but the word of truth and soberness.

We slave when there is no spontaneous exuberance of our own personality or no active sharing of the father's love for our own brothers.

THE SNEER

The Pharisees, who were fond of money, . . . *sneered.* *Luke 16. 14* (Moffatt).

JESUS had just proclaimed, "You cannot serve God and mammon." And in doing so, of course, he had described one of the cornerstones of the philosophy of some of the Pharisees. No wonder they sneered. They were "lovers of money." They were adepts at fitting in the lust of acquisitiveness with their religion. This bald simplicity of Jesus' alternative, "either God or mammon, but not both," aroused their scornful contempt. They had been choosing both all their lives.

Doctor Moffatt has done well to give this word "sneer" a place in the New Testament, for it has had a large place in Christian history from the very opening of Jesus' ministry. It is one of the most unlovely words in the language; and that is fitting, for it is one of the most unlovely things in the world. It has been one of the most destructive and malicious enemies of Christianity. It is not an open fighter's weapon but the favorite dagger of the coward and the snob.

Always used at every stage of Christian history, it has never been more popular or widely used than to-day. That is one reason why this word of Moffatt's brings such a timely insight. It links across nineteen centuries the earliest opposition of Jesus to the latest. The art of the sneer has reached an amazing perfection in our day. The hiss of the sneer is one of the most familiar sounds in our modern medley of noises. A whole literary cult has thrived on the perfection of the technique of the sneer. Some acclaimed as major prophets are simply past masters of the sneer.

A whole school of biography has been founded on the art. These sculptors of life do not work in marble or granite; they work in mud. They count that day lost which does not see "debunked" some figure which has commanded reverence and admiration. This school might well be called the "Three Sneers for Anybody" school of biography. These sophisticated minds do not live by such ridiculous things as admiration, hope, and love; wit, mockery, and slander are so much more clever and modern. One of our own American poets has thus described these apostles of the sneer:

"They trample on their youth, and faith and love.
   They cast their hope of human kind away.
With heaven's clear messages they madly strove
   And conquered—and their spirits turned to clay."

There are many reasons for the vogue of the sneer.

It is *inarticulate*. It does not deal in reasons, but in epithets. Paley well asks, "Who can refute a sneer?" It is vague, like a fog, and just as deadly. It creates an atmosphere of reproach.

To sneer is *easy*. It is not a mental operation. It requires no mastery of knowledge or skill in reasoning. A sneer begs every question. It is more like a physical operation, which any mind, no matter how shallow, can readily manage, like sticking out the tongue in derision.

The sneer ministers to *conceit* in the one who uses it. It gives that feeling, rated so highly among life's tickling sensations by many, "How much smarter I am than these poor simpletons!"

Accordingly, it gives a reputation for wit, that chief end of man according to the shorter catechism of to-day.

Three times this word "sneer" is used in Luke and Acts. Each occasion interprets a current trend of our own time.

1. There was the sneer at *ethical loyalties*. That clear division between allegiance to the righteousness of God and the serving of mammon was sneered at by lovers of money. In A. D. 1928 as in A. D. 30 it may be called "The Golden Sneer." Confronted with a choice between God and mammon an easy ethical inclusiveness says, "Take them

both." Three of the vital issues before the church to-day—God against materialism, Christian industry against an old regime, and a warless world against one filled with war—call forth the same contempt. When taking Jesus seriously interferes with the profit side of the ledger the answer is frequently the easy sneer. "Sentimentalists," "idealists"—these words become, by a vicious perversion of values, terms of reproach.

2. There was the sneer at *love and sacrifice*. In Luke 23. 35 we read, in a description of the crowd at the foot of the cross, "The people stood and looked on and even the rulers *sneered* at him." The love of Christ as a motive of life often meets the same response.

3. There was the sneer at the *spiritual foundations* of life. In the presence of the great experience of Pentecost, when the transforming energies of the Spirit of God entered the souls of men and marked a new epoch in the evolution of humanity, "some others *sneered*" (Acts 2. 13)—the same ignorant disdain, unwilling to examine, preferring to flee to the refuge of ignorant contempt. The realities of the spiritual nature of man meet the same reaction in many quarters to-day, both on the score of the content of faith and its expression in practical life. To meet that sneer there is need that the air of apology for our faith be dropped. Jesus Christ is one of the facts of the universe as truly as the elements of chemistry; the experience of religion is as genuine and authentic as the experience of heat and cold. As Dr. Harry Emerson Fosdick well puts it:

Christ must be recognized as a fact just as much as the readily accepted facts of chemistry and mechanics. The universe is not composed of newts only; it has its Newtons. Crystals do not make up all of the facts of existence; there is Christ. We must recognize that there are two worlds existing now, the temporal and the eternal.

But the sneer is futile. It has always proved so and the sneers which are the fads of the hour will prove equally so. To Paley's question, Who can refute a sneer? there is one devastating answer. *Time* can refute a sneer. The trail of the years is scattered with the remains of the forgotten sneers of yesterday.

THE FINE ART OF PESTERING

I will give her justice to prevent her from *constantly coming to pester me.—Luke 18. 5* (Weymouth).

JESUS told this story as an encouragement to prayer. But its insight into human motives and human nature make it an encouragement to persistent pestering for justice as well.

A great many steps in human progress have been reluctantly taken by people who did not particularly revere God or respect man but who did respect "pestering." The judge in Jesus' story well stands for officials of every sort, from kings and emperors down to the corner policeman. They have one important trait in common—an aversion to being pestered. They have to get on with the job in some fashion, and their love of justice is frequently far less conspicuous than their love of quiet. A "pest" is a nuisance, an embarrassment, and may precipitate a crisis. Consequently, wrongs have been frequently remedied, not at the command of a troubled conscience, but on account of a troubled ease.

William Lloyd Garrison is one of the notable examples of a man with a genius for constantly pestering. Even the theoretical opponents of slavery as well as its defenders, as a rule, regarded him as a "pest." He was a fanatic, and contemporary records do not paint him as an altogether pleasant man to live with. But he did not worry about being pleasant any more than this "unreasonable" widow did. Both got things done. In the whole field of social progress the degree of Doctor of Philosophy is frequently of less use than that of Master of Arts of Pestering.

THE APPETITE FOR SALUTES

They are *fond of getting saluted.—Luke 20. 46* (Moffatt).

THESE words are translated in the King James Version of the Gospel of Luke as "They love greetings in the markets." Obviously, that might be taken as a wholly innocent and commendable fondness for the friendly talk of the market place. Moffatt's translation makes clear the kind of greetings the scribes hankered for. It was not the hail of fellowship but the salute to a superior in rank.

How fond of that exhilaration one can become!

Good morning, Doctor!
How do you do, Colonel!
You're looking well, Bishop!
I'm proud to know you, Senator!
Salutes! They are among the most corrupting
words in the world. The love of salutes has wrecked
more careers and more good causes than almost
any other obstacle or opposition. "Give us this
day our daily salute," becomes the prayer of multitudes. The salute is more necessary than bread.

The lust for pre-eminence, for flattering recognition, is deadly because it is a habit-forming drug.
Alfred Austin counsels,

> "Friend, be not fretful if the voice of fame
>   Along the narrow way of hurrying men,
> Where echo unto echo shouts again,
>   Be all day long not noisy with your name."[1]

And he describes just what happens in a distress-
ingly large number of cases—the one whose ear
does not catch the echo of his name "frets." And
a fretter is a poor fighter in any cause. He is too
preoccupied with "fretting" to make any effective
moves against the enemy. Again and again throughout Jesus' training of his disciples it appears that
one of his chief cares is to prevent their preoccupation with other things, things which would prevent
concentration on the kingdom of God. Three
possible preoccupations are stressed—worry, the love
of money, and the desire for pre-eminence. Those
three pitfalls occupy a surprisingly large portion of
his teaching. The reason is plain—he needed in

[1] From "The Door of Humility." The Macmillan Company,
publishers. Used by permission.

his disciples one great preoccupation and one only
—Seek ye first the Kingdom.

The lust of salutes, titles, precedence, destroys
the effectiveness of a disciple's work for the cause
of Christ, as does any other kind of lust. It becomes an end in itself; it becomes a substitute for
real achievement. Moreover, the craving for salutes,
the manipulating to get them, has demoralized the
working force of the Kingdom, and with ruinous
results.

He that findeth his life must lose his dependence
on flattering recognition. Emily Dickinson, in a
characteristically humorous verse, laughs at this
itch for honors:

> "I'm nobody! Who are you?
> Are you nobody too?
> Then there's a pair of us—don't tell!
> They'd banish us, you know.
> How dreary to be somebody!
> How public, like a frog,
> To tell your name the livelong day
> To an admiring bog!"

Jesus offers two sure cures for this enervating
disease: the grip of his great enterprise itself upon
the mind and heart and the enlistment of the disciples to win a far higher order of merit, the most
glittering decoration and title ever worn by any
one—"I have called you friends." That, in the
most literal sense of the words, is a Distinguished
Service Cross.

SOPORIFICS

From hour to hour keep awake.—Luke 21. 36 (Moffatt).

ONE of the finest and most difficult arts of life
—that of keeping awake. There are so many
opiates and soporifics, "knock-out drops," which
deaden and cloud the spirit and lull it to sleep.
Keeping the soul awake is a continuous vigil. It
cannot be done by a sudden or even frantic arouse-
ment every thirty days or every seven days. It is
only to be done "hour by hour." Doctor Moffatt's
expansion of the word "always," a word we tend
to pass over lightly, into the detailed and picturesque, "hour by hour," gives a real insight into one
of life's persistent problems.

There are in literature two striking pictures of
the liability of the soul to be deadened by opiates
and the senses to be narcotized. They are both
cases where this is done by a false sense of attain-
ment and arrival, perhaps the most subtle opiate of all
life's experiences. One is Bunyan's chapter on "The
Enchanted Ground" in *The Pilgrim's Progress*,
where the onward push of the pilgrims is lulled into
a drowse. The other is Tennyson's "Lotus Eaters."

The success of a transatlantic air flight depends
not only on wind and weather, or on the engine's
going for forty hours without missing a beat. It
depends supremely on whether the pilot can keep
awake. The net result of the longer flight of life
depends on the same variable factor.

Most anything has possibilities of becoming a
soporific to the spirit and making it oblivious both
of dangers and high possibilities. We must be
adept workers of magic and exorcism. We need to

exorcise the yawn, for the yawn is one of the most evil demons we will ever meet.

Habit is the most common narcotic to the alertness of the spirit and senses. It comes as an old familiar friend. More than that, it *is* a friend. Almost every advance in psychology is a new chapter in the amazing story of how habit makes life, in the human sense, possible. Without the help of habit we would never emerge from helpless infancy. Life would be consumed in buttoning and unbuttoning buttons. But habit will take over everything in life instead of merely the physical basis of life, if we let it. It can smother the higher centers of the brain like coal gas. That is what has happened again and again. Many people "think" with their spinal column, not with their brain. Their responses have become instinctive. The enterprise of their life is conducted like a business of which the head is absent, ordered to a sanitarium perhaps. Nothing is referred to the head of the firm; everything is handled by a lower department. "There is plenty of room at the top" —of the spinal column. Hour by hour—use it!

The fallacy of arrival drugs the aspiration of the soul like a field of poppies. The premature satisfaction, the mistaking the means for the end, the beginning for the conclusion, the blue print for the finished building—these things have snuffed out the achievement of many a promising life, when the life had barely started. This is the picture drawn, as has been indicated, both by Bunyan and Tennyson. There is only one safe tense to the verb "arrive"—the future. Browning uses it in the only way it should be used:

> "I go to prove my soul. . . .
> . . . I *shall arrive*."

When we use it in life in either the present or past, life withers.

Popularity is a habit-forming drug which, like many other poisons, paralyzes the higher centers of the brain. It beclouds the mind like alcohol. Trying to get a clear vision of the world while intoxicated with adulation is like trying to look out on a landscape through a mirror. The subtle danger of this kind of opiate to the man who deals with crowds is well pictured in an incident told in the life of Silvester Horne.

Once when Mr. Horne was a boy he had gone to see Doctor Dale, in the vestry of a church where he was preaching, bearing a letter from his father hinting at Silvester Horne's inclination toward the ministry.

"My lad," said Dale, looking kindly down at me, "remember our temptation is not, as a rule, money." Then he pointed through the open door to the church, where the crowds of people were still slowly straggling down the aisles: "*That* is our temptation." Boy as I was, I felt instinctively what he meant; and a curious surprise came over me that he should feel the snares of popularity so keenly.[1]

The *easy chair* lulls to sleep, spiritually as well as physically. Try reading a solid book, that requires close thinking, in a soft, friendly reclining chair. Your wits sink back with an easy sprawl as well as your body. Ambition must be made of sterner stuff. Wealth, the pursuit of comfort, absorption

---

[1] From *The Life of Charles Silvester Horne*, by W. R. Selbie George H. Doran Company, publishers. Used by permission.

in the pillows and upholstery of life show down the eager movements of the spirit.

The *eye turned inward*, afflicting our vision of the world, like a cataract on the eye, dulls the divine powers of sympathy.

"From hour to hour keep awake *praying*"—there opens the avenue of escape. It is life's crowning miracle, and yet a daily miracle that the mind can so open itself to the quickening of the spirit—that it moves alive and awake. Carlyle, in words of rare and beautiful tenderness, has recorded the wonder of the miracle:

Daily I am taught again the unfathomable mystery of what we call a soul radiant with Heaven even while capable of being overclouded and, as it were, swallowed up by the bottomless mud it has to live in in this world.

THE COMMUTER'S SERMON

His habit at this time *was* to *teach in the Temple by day*, but *to go out and spend the night on the Mount* called the Oliveyard.—*Luke 21. 37* (Weymouth).

For the last week of his life Jesus was a commuter. Every morning he went into the city to do his work. Every evening he went back to the little quiet place in the country to spend the night. It may seem an act of violence to use such a distinctively modern word as "commuting" to describe the daily journeys of Jesus. Yet in this physical aspect of his life he followed exactly the habits of

that great, thronging modern tribe of suburbanites
who flock into the city to work in the morning and
at five or six in the evening go out again to the
little village on the outskirts of the city.

Here is an aspect of Jesus' last week which comes
home very closely to a great army of hurrying,
thronging people. The trains, the street cars,
busses and ferries bring into the cities every day
millions of people whose regular movements on the
shuttle of traffic are exactly those of Jesus as he
journeyed back and forth from the hillside of Olivet
to the crowded streets of Jerusalem.

If we look closely at the life of Jesus during these
days and nights, we find more than a physical
resemblance to the motions of the modern suburbanite. His life has, in those last five days, a
peculiar message to those who go back and forth.
He avoided the peculiar temptations of the commuter.

To look at just one aspect of the moral risks of
living in the suburbs we may truly say that the
great danger of the commuter is that he may avoid
responsibilities at both ends of his trip. The railway train may be used—unconsciously at times—as
a way of escape from burdens and responsibilities,
both in the city and at home. Jesus bore the burdens and responsibilities at both places.

The suburbanite easily finds an excuse for slipping
out of responsibilities in the city to which he goes
to work. He does not live there. He merely pays
a daily visit. His church is not there. His family
and friends, for the large part, are not there. The
social problems of the city, its needs, its appeals,
come to have the character of things afar off. He

does not know how "the other half lives." It is easy not to care. He is in a hurry to catch the five-fifteen.

At the other end of the line the process of side-stepping is just as easy and insidious. Listen to snatches of conversation painfully familiar to every pastor in a suburban town: "I'm so tired when I get back from the city that I really can't take up any work here"; "I moved out here to rest"; "I was active in the church in the city for fifteen years but I really can't start in again out here." And so it goes through the whole catalogue.

The tasks of the Kingdom remain undone for the lack of energy that is lost somewhere on the road between the two points. Many a suburbanite is truly "a lost soul" as far as any genuine partici-pation in the causes of human welfare are con-cerned, outside of his own business affairs.

The road between Jerusalem and the Mount of Olives was not a road of evasion for Jesus. He gave himself supremely in both places.

After the great earthquake of a few years ago in Tokyo no one was admitted into the city unless he came bearing rice and a candle; in other words, food and light. There was no room for merely another person to be carried. That same passport ought to be ours whether we come into the bustling city or the quiet countryside—food and light—strength and sympathy, skill, brought and shared.

჻ ჻ ჻

DELIGHTED TO SEE JESUS!

Herod was *greatly delighted* to see Jesus.—*Luke 23. 8* (Moffatt).

THE word "delighted" expresses exactly the superficiality of Herod. The word is ordinarily used of such trivial affairs, and it is fitting here, for every event in Herod's life is a trivial affair. He could not have any other kind. He is the perfect example of the genial, superficial curiosity seeker.

Of course he was delighted to see Jesus. It was a sort of picnic for him. You can just see him rushing about rubbing his hands in anticipation. "Isn't Jerusalem the most interesting place. Here one meets all the interesting types. Perhaps he'll do a miracle for us. Wouldn't that be exciting!" And he chatters, chatters on, empty-headed fool that he is. There is not to be found in literature anywhere a more powerfully dramatic scene than this loquacious empty-pated chatterbox confronted with the regal silence of Jesus. The silence of Jesus is the perfect tribute to utter insignificance.

John Masefield, in his noble and reverent play, "The Trial of Jesus," takes exactly this conception of Herod as a superficial chatterer, curious over the latest sensation. Herod is quite irritated that Jesus refuses to work a miracle for him.

As we read the story, far away and incredible it all seems, that a man should try to use Jesus as an entertainer, that a man could look him fairly in the face and never get any conception of the greatness of the man. Pilate, at least, had the mentality and judgment to escape that ignominy.

And yet, is it so far away? Are there not people

like Herod, many of them, some in the ranks of Jesus' professed followers, light-minded chatterers who never remotely understand the stupendous meaning of Jesus? Just as Jesus was the latest curiosity and Herod was delighted to see him, so He has become a fashion. There are multitudes on whom the crucifixion of Jesus and the whole sacrificial conception of life have made no real impression at all. Jesus' uncompromising claims are treated with an unconscious indifference. Like Herod, they are delighted to see Jesus; like Herod, they never see him at all.

It is so easy to say "they" in the preceding sentence. Had we not better say "we"?

PILATE'S COMPROMISE

I shall release him with a *whipping.*—*Luke 23. 16* (Moffatt).

I will *teach him a lesson* (Goodspeed).

I will . . . give him a *light punishment* (Weymouth).

THE alternatives before Pilate in the trial of Jesus were simple and plain—either condemnation or release. Pilate tried to straddle them. His real desire, of course, was to release Jesus. But he didn't have the moral character for that. He reasoned, rather: *"I can't* condemn him. *I won't* champion him. I'll just insult him and thus make a compromise between the two. I'll release him with a whipping. That will be a sop both to my conscience and to the Jews!"

What a cheap attitude it was!

Yet what a common attitude to Jesus!

It is exactly the attitude of many whose actions, if not their conscious reassuring, proclaim: "I can't condemn Jesus. I won't acclaim him. I'll just strike a cross between the two. I'll give him the moral equivalent of a light whipping. I'll give him some fair words and throw him out."

"Fair words and throw him out"—this modern equivalent of Pilate's action is so common that it has almost become standardized. There has been worked out for it, in our day, a well-recognized technique. The very form of words with which it is done have almost become a ritual.

The modern form of this shuffling compromise in regard to Jesus which will neither condemn nor loyally follow takes several forms.

One of the most common is that impertinent patronage of Jesus which pays formal tribute to his teachings and then disdainfully dismisses them as impractical, visionary, "idealistic." Why idealistic should be an adjective of contempt is a mystery, but it is so. The company who take this position welcome Jesus to the front door with protestations of hospitality, and once in the house, roughly throw him out the back door as an encumbrance, a fanatic touched in the head, a troublemaker, and a bore. The apology for this is the well-worn sophistry, "We live in a practical world."

A frequent modern parallel to Pilate's compromise is: "I'll allow Jesus a small place in my life—in the show window. But I'll keep him cooped up there and never let him get loose in the whole house." So men give him one day and fence off the other six secure from his trespassing. They admit him to rule over minor etiquettes but give him no vote in the decisions on the major issues of life.

An orthodox form of Pilate's heresy is the attitude, happily growing less common, which says: "I'll grant Jesus jurisdiction over individual conduct, but let him keep away from society. When he tries to enter where he does not belong he needs to be scourged."

Rome has passed into history. Pilate, with his cowardly compromise on the case of Jesus Christ, remains.

❧ ❧ ❧

"NONSENSE!"

But this story of the women seemed in their opinion to be *nonsense.—Luke 24. 11* (Moffatt-Goodspeed).

THIS was the first verdict on the resurrection of Jesus—Nonsense! Yet with the words scarcely out of his mouth Peter gets up and starts on a break-neck run to the tomb to look into this nonsense! The wild hope proved too much for the first snap judgment of "Nonsense!"

That experience of Peter's is a symbol of the experience of the race. "What? Resurrection—Immortality—Life after Death?" has been the incredulous question. "Nonsense!" comes the ready answer.

And then humanity, like Peter, has rushed to meet the wild hope. The urging within the breast

of man has been an explosive, propulsive force send-
ing him with a leap to the great faith.

Bliss Perry in a noble sentence has described the
movement of mind and heart in Peter and in the
heart of humanity. "Easter," he says, "like all
deep things, begins in mystery and it ends, like all
high things, in a great courage."

The mystery is so deep that the first verdict is
nonsense. And without the background and foundation of the God and Father of our Lord Jesus Christ,
even the final verdict may well be "nonsense."
But with that foundation, life takes on the high
courage of a great faith.

What changed the mystery of the resurrection
for Peter from nonsense into reality? One thing
only—experience. It is the experience of God in
Christ which throws out the first verdict. There
is no other altogether sufficient evidence. We can
listen to all the banging tambourines in the dark-
rooms of mediums and still render the verdict—
"Nonsense!" We can listen to the well-worn analogy
of the butterfly emerging from the cocoon and
remain unmoved. The resurrection is to be proved
from Jesus Christ and not Christ from the resurrection. It is from the experience of what God is that
we hold the faith in our immortal destiny. "Even
if Christ had shown himself to no one after his
death," declares Dean Inge, "we might still be sure
that he has risen. *Being what he is*, he could not
be beholden to death. And the same applies to
our immortality. Because we are spiritual beings
we cannot wholly perish."

The question of our immortality is not so much
a matter of God by a special exertion rescuing us

from extinction and oblivion, but whether, quite aside from the body, we are possessed of life such that, by its very nature, it is inextinguishable, inherently eternal; whether our spirits have become so possessed with the spirit of God that we cannot be canceled out, so long as God lasts.

When we think deeply, it is the "faith of unbelief" which is nearer "nonsense" than the faith in God as revealed in Christ. To believe in a blank meaningless universe requires a far more staggering act of faith than to believe in a universe through which runs an increasing purpose of God.

Dr. T. H. Martin, of Liverpool, has put this burden of the faith of denial in a paragraph so strong that it cries for quotation:

Man in his primitive state, gross and sensual, nevertheless laying hold of great ideals, believing in an eternal right, an eternal truth, an eternal justice, an everlasting goodness and love, making great ventures for it, and sublime sacrifices because of it, and at the end, thinking over it all, trying to understand it all, talking about "God." So unpromising a beginning, so glorious an end! How came this to be? Where did he get the idea from? Can science tell us? Is it blind force or chance? Is it the result of a fortuitous assemblage of atoms? And Jesus, the top and crown of things, in whom we see the very face of God—can he be explained so? Only an idiot could think or believe that. Our old earth is more than matter, or force, or atoms. Something calls, constrains, pulls, draws, holds, lifts, saves, satisfies, cares. Someone is out there in the distant, here in the near, who speaks, subdues, silences me. God! Is it really so? And the answer comes gentle and low: "E'en so: it is so!"[1]

---

[1] Quoted in *The Christian Century*.

So on the foundation of the God of Jesus—as revealed in Jesus, the mystery ends in the high courage expressed in the words of Walt Whitman:

"I know I am deathless.
I know this orbit of mine cannot be swept with a carpenter's compass,
I know I shall not pass like a child's curlicue cut with a burnt stick at night."

THE FIRST CHRISTIAN EXPERIENCE MEETING

Then they related their own *experience.—Luke 24. 35* (Moffatt).

HERE, on the evening of the day of resurrection, the first institution of Christianity came into existence. It was not baptism, not the Lord's Supper, not the mass, not even formal Christian worship. It was an experience meeting. "Then they related their own experience" of meeting Christ. It was a little prayer meeting—and its sole content was the relation by those present of how Christ had appeared to them. It was not argument; it was not eloquence, save for that supreme "eloquence" of Christian experience.

It was not merely the first Christian institution. It was more. It was and is the only permanently effective Christian institution—the recital of actual experience of Christ. It was the first demonstration of the methods by which the Christian faith and life were to spread and did spread. It was also the first demonstration of the method by which it must always win its way, if it is to be more than a thin veneer on the surface of life, more than a pitifully transparent coat of paint over a foundation of paganism.

"They related their own experience." That is the unfailing Christian apologetic, and the gates of hell cannot prevail against it. It is the one sure basis of Christian conquest.

From the very birthday of the Christian Church there comes across the centuries a tremendously timely and urgent message for our own time.

This Easter evening experience meeting points the way to the answer to the great bewilderment and search of multitudes of our day—the need for an unshakable authority and certainty in religion. Many of the conventional foundations of authority are no longer adequate for men of the modern world.

An infallible church, an authoritative creed, a literally inspired Book—all of these sources of authority are still offered the world by Catholic and Protestant dogmatists. Yet these cannot meet the needs of earnest multitudes. As Dr. Raymond Calkins says, "The gravest religious problem of our modern world is the discovery of the grounds of religious certainty, apart from Roman Catholicism, on the one hand, or of unscientific dogmatism, on the other."[1]

Here it is—Christianity's endowment on its birthday. In the first chapter of *The Eloquence of Christian Experience* Dr. Raymond Calkins gives an impressive and moving study of the religious certainty of the early Christian fellowship in the New Testament, showing that it was just what came

[1] The Macmillan Company, publishers. Used by permission.

into being at this first Easter prayer meeting—the disciples' experience of Christ.

That amazing certainty and assurance which glows in the book of Acts and the Epistles had this unfailing basis. The certainty and authority was not in the *church*. There was no church. It was not founded on an authoritative *creed*. There was no creed. It was not founded on an inspired and infallible *book*. The New Testament did not exist.

The ground of their assurance was their experience of God in and through the historical Jesus. This the New Testament affirms is the unshakable and immovable reality. Here we seem to have touched bottom. These New Testament writers have found solid ground for religious certainty.

The Christian experience of God is the one thing needful. It is the one thing that we can positively least afford to lose. The practical wisdom of men of affairs, the philosophy of our universities, the culture of our schools—these are all a necessary and important part of our equipment as ministers of Jesus Christ. . . . Underneath every other discipline of mind and body there must be a deep, warm, passionate experience of God in Jesus Christ. Paul well calls this a sacred deposit, a holy treasure, a priceless possession. The Christian experience of God alone answers the quest of the human soul for certainty. It alone is the unshakable ground of Christian faith and of Christian knowledge.[1]

This little company of a few souls, met in the gathering dusk of eventide on the first Easter, found the sure foundation not only of New Testament preaching, but of Christian achievement always and everywhere.

---

[1] From *The Eloquence of Christian Experience*, by Raymond Calkins. The Macmillan Company, publishers. Used by permission.

BUBBLES

Bethesda, . . . where a crowd of invalids used to lie,
. . . *waiting for the water to bubble.*—*John 5. 3* (Moffatt).

THE healing of the impotent man at the Pool of
Bethesda has many values for thought and action.
But among them one thing stands out clearly—
here were a group of invalids depending for their
cure on some external commotion. They put all
their trust in "bubbles." They sat there waiting
to seize the periodic disturbance and bubbling of
the pool to plunge in and be saved.

It is not pressing an allegory too far to catch in
this company of folk, eagerly scanning the surface
of the pool for bubbles, a suggestion or picture of
a church, or those within it, hoping to find, in the
coming of some new craze or agitation, the means
of supplying a deficiency in its own inner life. The
weakness portrayed is a dependence on externalism,
a superficial opportunism which looks to the stirrings of popular interest, the rise of a new fashion
of the hour, with the hope of exploiting it. It is a
faith in bubbles on the surface of life.

Society is very much like a boiling spring. It
has its periodic fashions and crazes. A new word,
a new interest, leaps into prominence; the surface
of the pool of life is disturbed; it bubbles. And a
church, in a mood of invalidism, sees the new upheaval, and says, "Lo, here! This is the thing
which will put me on my feet. I can jump into
the center of these bubbles and grow strong again!"

Now, of course, it is not to be denied that there
have been great periodic movements in the minds
of men which have been tides which, taken at the

flood, lead on to fortune. There were such deep stirrings of the world's mind in the first Christian century, in the Reformation and the evangelical revival of the eighteenth century. But these have not been bubbles on the surface. They were not external, not mere fashions, but veritable gales of the Spirit of God which bloweth where it listeth and we see the effects.

Faith in bubbles is quite another thing.

One recent pathetic instance of trust in external commotion to bring results which can be secured only by inward renewal of life and power was the Great War. Only by going back to the contemporary records, the newspapers, magazines, pamphlets, and books of 1914 and 1915 can we realize the hopes and expectations which multitudes of people had of what the war was going to do for religion. The war was the most agitated bubbling which has ever disturbed the pool of the world's life. Superficial thinkers, interpreting certain manifestations in the light of their own hopes, said: "Here it is. Here is an agitation that will turn people to God. The war will save religion and the church. The bubbles will be our cure."

It is too early to measure the effect of the war on Christianity. A balance sheet of assets and liabilities cannot be struck. Forces good and bad have been set in motion which will run for years. But it is not too early to realize that the expectation that the upheaval of the war would result in an increase of spiritual life and power, in salvation for the church, was a tragic illusion. The tumult and the shouting die and the war left what it always leaves—blight, devastation, death. The disturbance passes, and, like the poor man at the pool, we are not saved by it.

Each new intellectual fashion which agitates the minds of men is seen by some as a way of salvation. There is a great overestimation of what such new interests and developments can do. The new trends in religious education have been greeted, not for what they are, legitimate aids to religious life, but as wonder-working panaceas which would effect an automatic salvation. "Jump into this pool and all our troubles will be over." Take the word "community," for example. It has had an immense vogue. Some have vainly imagined that by baptizing their church with a new name and calling it a "community church" they would be rid of all the ills a church is heir to.

So with the stunts and tricks constituting that modern form of unfaith which is so besetting a sin to preachers who must proclaim the gospel to a motion-picture age. "We will plunge into this pool and be saved," a great many bewildered preachers and churches have said, as they have grasped at the showman's tricks. It is a form of exchange of faith in the living God for faith in bubbles.

The man at the pool was saved not by the coming of an external disturbance but by the advent of a Person. It is the advent of Jesus Christ into the midst of our life which is the one hope of salvation. By faith are we saved—faith in the meaning of that fine definition of it given by Doctor DuBose —"the setting of our entire selves Godward."

The kingdom of heaven cometh not with observation of bubbles.

THE TRAFFIC JAM

The man who had been cured did not know who it was;
for *Jesus had passed out unnoticed*, there being a crowd in
the place.—*John 5. 13* (Weymouth).

WHAT a theme for a crowded age—the unnoticed
Jesus—"there being a crowd in the place!" How
perilously closely it fits large aspects of our world
—the Son of man lost in a traffic jam! So dense a
crowd, such a weaving to and fro that even the one
who was the most in debt to Jesus lost sight of him.

This word of Weymouth's translation expresses
the most formidable and characteristic obstacle to
the Christian faith in our day. The opposition to
Jesus most often met is not of the kind typified by
the crucifixion or the relentless antagonism of the
Pharisees. These still exist. But it is, rather, here,
tucked away in an incident of the day's work of
Jesus, that we find the supreme hindrance to the
cause of Christ. He was simply lost from view
in the crowd.

In it is a shaft of light which illuminates great
stretches of history, both personal, political, and
ecclesiastical. Jesus' work done, he is allowed to
be elbowed out to obscurity. Indeed, both in individual and social life Jesus often suffers the fate
of that very familiar figure of the modern newspaper world—the person whose name and story
fills the front page for a few days and then drops
back to smaller type on page six.

This is especially true in these years of the twentieth century in the most fabulously prosperous
land under the sun—the United States.

There is such a staggering crowd of things in

the world's show windows that it is easy for men not to notice Jesus.

The enormous hodgepodge of things has served also to crowd Jesus out of many minds and lives. He is not so much thrown out by set purpose as dropped out. He cannot be kept amid the clutter of interests.

On a much higher level of life the same crowding out process goes on simply through the mere accumulation of knowledge and facts and data of all kinds. Some have even feared that the mass of facts has become too great for the mind to carry. Richard Roberts has said:

The mind is breaking down under the weight of its own achievements. With the growth of the world's population, the facts, external and internal, that have to be dealt with are too numerous for any single brain. Salvation by knowledge is becoming a desperate undertaking. The paths of education are blocked by mountains of books. There will have to be greater specialization and a return to the elemental facts of existence.

The scientific approach to life—so dominant an influence to-day—has the effect of crowding God off the main avenue of life into a corner. Many people have come to feel that in knowing and obeying scientific laws they have no further needs. They leave no place, because they really feel no need of personal relationship to God. The idea of a life sustained and renewed through fellowship is foreign to them.

Shall this be the verdict on our time and our society—"And Jesus passed out unnoticed, there being a crowd in the place"?

Shall it be the verdict on our lives?

Whether written of a nation or a person, it is a verdict of doom—an epitaph.

❧ ❧ ❧

CONTEMPT FOR THE MOB

As for this mob . . . —*John 7. 49* (Moffatt).
This rabble . . . (Weymouth).

THERE spoke the snob.   The words voice the contemptuous scorn of the aristocrats of the Sanhedrin for the common people of the nation.   You can almost see the curl of the lips as the words are spoken: "This mob—this rabble, these ignorant louts unversed in the niceties of the law—they are accursed."

That same snobbery for the great mass of humanity has always been manifest, but it is active in new and vicious form to-day.   It has become so much a fashion that it constitutes a real moral, intellectual and spiritual pitfall for our time.   A recent novelist has thus described the expression of one of his characters, "His eyes seemed fashioned for small contempts."   That description would stand for a large number of self-constituted Sanhedrins to-day.

There are many causes for this rising tide of snobbery in these present days.   One is unquestionably the apparent justification for it furnished by statistics.   We have taken to tests and statistics with all the eagerness of a child for a new toy. And the far-reaching generalizations made on the basis of arbitrary tests are frequently those of a child with a toy that he does not know exactly how to work. On the basis of the army tests made on soldiers in training during the World War, we have learned that the intellectual attainments of the so-called average man make a showing that came with a shock of surprise. We have learned such facts as these:

The average man leaves school at the eighth grade. He has a smattering of local geography, and knows a little bit about history and a few elementary facts of physiology. In spite of the fact that he is to be accepted as a citizen, he has no general knowledge of civics, science, politics, or literature. He is able to speak one language only. On a standardized intelligence test he makes about the same score as does an average boy of fourteen. He never develops the intelligence required for satisfactory high-school work.

These facts regarding the scholastic attainments of the average man have been made, in a wholly unjustifiable manner, the basis for a whole school of contempt for the rank and file of the nation. A Eugenic Conference held in New York a few years ago exhibited a chart which indicated that thirty billion persons had been reared to maturity in civilized countries since the dawn of history eight or ten thousand years ago, and adds that the thing of unique interest which the chart pointed out was that only about five thousand persons out of the whole thirty billion ever "amounted to much."

A. E. Wiggam, one of the high priests of this cult of contempt for the mob, thus sums up the truth as he sees it: "The strength of mind and body, of soul and spirit, of these few precious people is worth more than all the rest of humanity put together."[1]

Three things should be remembered about this modern expression of the old contempt of the Sanhedrin for the "rabble."

1. It is the refuge of every autocratic force in society, of every reactionary, of every exploiter.

2. It has been historically and is to-day the "defense mechanism" of empty conceit and privilege frantically grasping its advantages.

3. It is a vicious denial of the spirit of Jesus and the Christian gospel.

The pretensions of this modern cult of aristocracy demand a new understanding and proclamation of the attitude of Jesus to this same "mob" and "rabble" on which the Sanhedrin poured its cynical contempt and loathing. His sympathy for people knew no limits and his faith in the possibilities of mankind was unwavering. His central teaching of the sacredness of personality and the worth of man is the charter of democracy and human freedom.

That great faith of Jesus is quaintly and beautifully but with profound truth expressed in the words of that Negro spiritual, "All God's Chillun Got Wings."

This is not the affirmation of a sentimental blindness to the facts of human evil. It is not a superficial estimate of humanity seen through rose-colored glasses. It is a simple and noble expression

---

[1] From *The New Decalogue of Science.* Copyright, 1922–23. Used by permission of the publishers, The Bobbs-Merrill Company.

of the spiritual capacity of man. It is a melodious declaration of the truth that "To as many as received him, to them gave he power to become the sons of God." John Wesley records somewhere in his *Journal* that he preached on the text just quoted and he adds the note, "They seemed greatly encouraged." Small wonder! The only bit of encouragement that can come to the human soul strong enough to outlast every vicissitude is the assurance that he is the child of God with divine possibilities.

Days such as ours need the assertion of the faith that is embedded in the gospel in the possibilities of man through the action of the Spirit of God. The faith expressed in the words, "All God's chillun got wings" is also timely in that it asserts the sacredness and value of human personality at a time when a rampant materialism puts property values before the values of the soul.

A SPECTACLE OR A PERSON?

Those to whom he had been a *familiar sight* as a beggar.—*John 9. 8* (Moffatt).

A familiar *object* (Weymouth).

THESE townsmen had seen this beggar for years as an "object," a "sight," a familiar spectacle of the village life. Jesus was the first one, apparently, ever to see him as a *person*. In other words, they had never really seen him at all. He was merely part of the landscape.

The way of these villagers in regarding a man as

a sort of depersonalized object or spectacle points out a continual danger to which our power of selective attention lays us open. We develop very readily an ability to blot out from our conscious vision things to which we are not giving our immediate and intense attention. We cross a crowded street and the blazing electric sign in front of our eyes does not really exist for us. Neither does the crowd of hurrying individuals a hundred yards away. If we could not do this, we would soon be killed, no doubt. While letting our eyes roam indiscriminately an automobile or street car would pick us off.

But while this power of partial or voluntary blindness makes for physical safety, it carries grave moral and spiritual dangers. It is the danger of failing to put ourselves in the place of another and really see him as a person. To the neighbors of this man he was only a sight; to the disciples of Jesus he was an interesting theme for theological discussion. Only to Jesus was he a brother in need.

It is so easy to get that way. Bishop Francis J. McConnell shows this very strikingly in telling of the terrible pull on one's sympathies which the coughing of the tubercular coolies who pull jinrickshas in Chinese cities makes on one. He says that for the first few nights he could hardly sleep at all. At the end of thirty days the coughing becomes so familiar one hardly hears it.

The same process goes on in regard to the major portion of life with many people. Persons with peculiar characteristics and needs have become just "spectacles" or "types." Let us beware of the word "type." It is one of the most vicious words in the English language. It is the perfect astringent on sympathy. When we get to regarding people as "types" of this or that, the sensitive soul has died. An American visitor to London wrote home to a friend: "You must visit the Victoria embankment and see the people sleeping on benches. There are the most interesting 'types.'" That heart-breaking panorama of aching, homeless woe was just a child's peep box of "types" to her. An extreme instance of the same callousness of this Palestinian village is that of a great architect, on the deck of a ferry boat in the Hudson River, when a stoker fell from the stern of a tug and was smashed by its screw to pulp that left on the waters a lacquer of bloody oil. He merely cried, "What *color!*"

PUTTING JESUS INTO A PIGEON HOLE

We do not know *where this fellow comes from.—John 9. 30* (Weymouth).

THE fundamental objection to Jesus on the part of many was that he would not fit into a pigeonhole. The Pharisees had a cut-and-dried universe. Things went into arbitrary and traditional classifications. They could get around in that kind of a world. Here they are trying to fit Jesus into two of their most standardized classifications—the geographical pigeonhole and the hereditary one. They are nettled because they cannot "place him." All their holes were round. Jesus would not fit into

them. He was a square peg. He could not be
disposed of as just another stock sample of a familiar
class. To understand him they had to think. They
didn't like to think. They didn't know how. They
wouldn't learn. Pilate is trying the same thing
when he demands of Jesus, "Where do you come
from?" He was trying to evaluate Jesus on the
basis of a geographical pigeonhole.

It is a very common state of mind. It led eventually to the crucifixion and leads to much of the
evil and tragedy of the world.

We cannot pigeonhole Jesus. We cannot force
him into any conventional classification. He is
unique. We cannot tie him up with any number
of individuals as just "another sample of the same
thing." There are no other samples of the same
thing. Jesus, to use Edwin Arlington Robinson's
fine phrase in "Merlin," is

> "The man who had made other men
> As ordinary as arithmetic."

When Jesus becomes to us merely one of any
group he becomes nothing.

LIFE TO THE FULL

I have come that they may have *life* . . . *to the full.*—
John 10. 10 (Moffatt).

ONE of the many vivid pictures in the writings
of William James is his comparison of the position
of man in the universe to that of a dog in a draw-

ing room. He says that just as there is a world
of powers, ideas, and values quite beyond the dog's
sight, so there is a world of experience and values
beyond the world that is obvious to our eyes.

The mark of the abundant life, the "life *to the
full*," to the limit of our possibilities, which Jesus
desired to bring to men, is awareness and grasp of
that world of values and ideas and powers beyond
the elementary senses. That world is called "life"
in the Gospel of John. It covers much that is
called the "kingdom of heaven" and "the kingdom
of God" in the synoptic Gospels.

The problem of life, then, is to get out of the
realm of fractions; to cease to live on a mere fraction of our inheritance and powers, and to live *to
the full*.

The truth that ordinarily man does not live
more than a fraction of his possible life is made
clearer with every advance in the study of the
mind. Many lives are like a ship, creeping along
slowly on one small auxiliary engine, with the main
engines out of commission, giving none of the powerful drive of which they are capable.

Modern psychology brings real light to this
problem of living to the full of our possible powers.
It supports the theory that the chief cause of
fatigue is not exhaustion. When our energies fail
it is not because our definite, limited supply of
energy is used up. That was the old physical
theory of energy, now pretty largely abandoned.
The present new theory is that there are "resources
of power whose existence we do not ordinarily recognize, but which can be made available for the
purposes of our daily life."

Dr. J. A. Hadfield gives some remarkable instances of persons making available untapped resources of power:

A corporal, whose courage won the V. C., was for several days cut off from our troops, was exposed the whole time to bombardment (subsisting meanwhile on the barest rations), and yet, in spite of the awful strain, he came out feeling cheerful, elated, and without fatigue. Several men with him had the endurance to pass through the same experience, but at the end were exhausted and broke down. The corporal had evidently discovered sources of power which were not exhausted by the terrible strain he underwent, but provided an ample resupply.

Four years ago, at midnight, I witnessed an explosion at a great munition factory, and afterward heard that a woman, after her day's work, had risen from bed and, in anxiety for the safety of her husband and son, had run practically the whole distance of seven miles to the scene of the explosion in an incredibly short time.

We tend to live on a mere fraction of our possibilities not only in regard to energy and power but in regard to *joy*. Jesus expressly emphasized that normal result of the life he could impart—"I have spoken to you, . . . and that your joy may become perfect." It requires no labored assemblage of evidence to convince us that in our civilization, overflowing with opulence, the supply of joy is tragically depleted. Our rightful inheritance seems to be tied up in chancery. We can't get at it. The stupendous and brilliant feats of our civilization bring us no deep joy or content. Our buildings are higher but our joy is not more profound. As one has said, "We have machinery to manufacture everything except the peace which passeth understanding."

In a letter to the New York World a writer has described in picturesque detail people living on a fraction of life's energy and content vainly reaching out for impossible material panaceas:

All over the country there are muddled people seeking a sad Carlylian entrance to light. Everywhere you turn there are fuzzy-minded incompetents, unhappy idealists, and pathetically ambitious idiots who are looking for panaceas which will enable them to face life—the Darwinian unfit, seeking frantically for miracles with which to save themselves. These go in for beauty clays, gland treatments, miracle foods, mental sciences, and psychoanalysis indiscriminately. They don't go in for Roentgenanalysis or operations. They want something dazzling and infallible.

Our age has given great study to the task of adding years to our life and has succeeded marvelously. In the last fifty years the span of the average life has been increased by fifteen years. But the deepest problem is not to add years to our life but *life to our years*. That is the gift Jesus came to impart—*"life* to the full."

It cannot be acquired by a frantic plunge after acquisition of either things or sensations. That is a popular modern method. A character in one of William J. Locke's novels expresses this conception perfectly—"I would like to take life by the throat and *choke* something out of it." Life to the full never comes by choking; it must grow.

It is in contact with the Spirit of God that the gates are opened by which a liberating divine energy and joy come into life. The New Testament experience of the Spirit of God brought and brings the power of living life to the full. We cannot go through the New Testament without being struck again and again by the truth that the normal Christian experience brought a new increase of power. "I have strength through him who gives me power."

Love of God brings a unifying power to life. It harmonizes the emotions of the soul, bringing chaos into one inspiring purpose, and abolishing conflict. But it must be a love that shakes the whole life. That pale kind of emotion suggested by Matthew Arnold's unconsciously satiric definition of religion as "Morality tinged with emotion" will never do it. A "tinge" will not bring life to the full or turn the world upside down.

Sacrificial love to man brings strange recreative power. As the author of *The Lady of the Decoration* says in words worthy of a place in the New Testament: "The most miserable, pitifully smashed up life could blossom again if it would only blossom for others."

❧ ❧ ❧

SAVE OUR HOLY PLACE!

The Romans will come and *suppress our holy Place.*— John *11. 48* (Moffatt).

No wonder the Pharisee wanted to hustle Jesus off the scene. In these words the *real* reasons for their antagonism to Jesus crop out as opposed to the many *good* reasons, piously put forward by many to justify their conspiracy against him. In these words it is as though an unexpected gust of wind blows aside the curtain from the inside room of their mind and discloses the interested, material reasons for their fear and hatred of Jesus.

"We do not want our Holy Place disturbed." No doubt it was partly a religious fear. But it was also a disinclination to be jolted loose from a special privilege and order which paid them well.

They didn't want the established order upset.

That is an eternal objection to Jesus. We can hear the same angry and fearful cries flying through the air to-day from all parties, orders, Sanhedrins, whose settled advantages would be disturbed by the real dominion of Jesus over life.

"Our Holy Place," runs the real argument, no matter how plausibly it may be dressed up for show purposes—"our sacred twenty-per-cent interest, our traditional power over the lives of men, our war system, our race supremacy—will be suppressed!"

"Away with such a fellow!"

GET IT FINISHED SOMEHOW

Pilate *came outside* to them.—*John 18. 29* (Moffatt).

A CLOSE study of Pilate's movements during the trial of Jesus gives an overwhelming impression of *fidgets*. Pilate bobs in and out through the curtain like a nervous wreck. Now you see him and now you don't. He rushes out to the porch to bargain

with the crowd. Then he rushes back into the
house to work out a new scheme to get Jesus off
his hands. For that was the one idea behind all
this dashing back and forth—get rid of him somehow!

Six times he goes in and out between the crowd
and Jesus in the court room: (1) John 18. 29; (2)
John 18. 33; (3) John 18. 38; (4) John 19. 4; (5) John
19. 8; (6) John 19. 13. In that last passage he
reaches the end of his tortuous path of shuffling
evasions. He gets rid of the bothersome nuisance
at last. "Then Pilate handed him over to them to
be crucified. So they took Jesus" (John 19. 16, 17,
Moffatt).

So they took him away, did they? That was
what Pilate wanted, just to put Jesus down somewhere and be rid of him.

Took him away, did they? In that last scene in
this sordid drama of six acts the soldiers tied Pilate
so tightly to Jesus that all the centuries of a million
years will not dissolve the bonds. "Crucified by
Pontius Pilate." Who ever achieved an immortality like that?

This nervous, irritated effort of Pilate's to get
Jesus' case disposed of somehow is not merely one
man's tragedy. It is a picture of a way of meeting
responsibilities that is deeply embedded in human
life, which goes on endlessly. The white light
which beats about Calvary reveals where it leads to.

Get rid of it somehow! That becomes the ruling
motive or mood of many in dealing with problems
and responsibilities. Like Pilate, they have a
genuine desire to deal with them justly. But if
the problems hang on long enough, that first motive

is lost in a feeling of irritation and the chief desire becomes to shake loose from the problem some way —any way—as long as the thing is settled, and we escape the responsibility!

When a responsibility, a burden, a problem, gets on our *nerves* rather than on our mind or our heart or conscience, we are lost, as Pilate was. Watch your "nerves"! They are the most impertinent members of your whole being. They will usurp the seat of judgment. Pilate allowed Jesus to get "on his nerves." His "nerves" usurped the place of his mind, his heart, his conscience. Our own "nerves" will do the same if we allow them the run of the house instead of holding them to their legitimate place of service.

A major problem in the growth of character and the ordering of life is to refuse to allow the judgment to be stampeded by irritations, or the impatient insistence to get rid of the bother some way. For it was just that which led to Calvary. It always leads to some kind of a cowardly evasion.

EACH GIVING A BLOW

And they marched up to him, . . . each *one giving him a blow.—John 19. 3* (Goodspeed).

Doctor Goodspeed individualizes the scourging and torture of Jesus by stressing the particular blow given by each one. It not only adds to the grimness and horror of the scourging; it is also a vivid reminder of individual responsibility. Jesus did not suffer any general indignity. There is no such thing. He suffered a succession of particular insults and assaults—each one as definite and responsible as if it stood alone.

Try to imagine this grim parade of roistering soldiers marching up to Jesus—one by one—and each one weighing the question—"Where shall I strike him—on the head or over the heart? Shall I give him a blow with the bare hand or a club?"

It is not mere imagination. These questions did flash through the minds of these men.

It is not a pleasant thing to run through one's mind, for it has another question trailing after it —what kind of a particular blow do *we* give Jesus? What is our special peculiar way of striking Jesus and his cause?

Several considerations come to mind as we think of ourselves as possible members of this company.

Some undoubtedly must have struck Jesus merely because they were in a parade where it was the fashion. That is the subtle danger of fashion parades.

It is inconceivable that each one of these men had a definite reasoned animosity to Jesus. It is very probable that none of them had. Brutality had merely become a thoughtless tradition, a barrack-room sport. The crucifixion was a sport event —of a sort—to the guard. The parade formed, marched past Jesus—the blows started, and each one, following along the almost automatic march, delivered his own personal blow.

The parade still goes on. We follow modes of life, indulge in ways of thinking, which are cruel blows to Jesus, to all that he stands for in the world's hope, to all that he died to accomplish. We do not choose deliberately to do it. We are in a fashion parade. We take our cue from the crowd.

These men struck Jesus publicly. Alas that so many of our blows are given in secret! We do not repudiate him publicly. But in the secret places of the heart—in the depths of life where motives are formed and the costs of sacrifices are weighed—we strike.

We cannot forget that the disloyalties of Jesus' disciples hurt more than the rough, crude assaults of enemies. The blow that hurt Jesus most was one that never touched him physically. It was not a blow on the head. It was a thrust through the heart. Can we imagine that any cruel stinging blow on the mouth given by a soldier hurt Jesus as did the denial of Peter?

"I never saw the man," cried Peter.

"Yes, I'm a Christian, but I don't really take it seriously," is the modern echo of Peter's words.

We do not say the words. We merely act them. "Each one." . . .

FINDING A WAY AND MAKING ONE

This made Pilate try *to find a way* to let him go, but . . . —*John 19. 12* (Goodspeed).

WHAT was needed was to *make* a way to let Jesus go. Pilate merely tried to *find* one. Pilate lived by finding things. He dodged all over the place looking for a way out of the responsibility of dealing with Jesus. He was pathetically eager to find a way. He did not lift a finger to make one.

When he couldn't find an easy, ready-made way of duty, instead of making one, he set out to *find* something else, a ready-made excuse, an alibi.

Josephine Daskam Bacon, in a sharp little portrait called "Pilate's Wife," has drawn this search of Pilate, first for the easy way of disposing of Jesus justly, and failing that, for the excuse consoling to his conscience. Pilate's wife is speaking of the crucifixion of Jesus:

"I have been worried, ever since his death,
  About my husband.
  I warned him many times of that young Jew—
  'Don't let those ignorant natives kill him,' I begged,
  'You will be bitterly blamed for it,
  Sometime, somewhere!'
  He was too fair, too logical, my husband.
  'But think,' he said, 'what I am bound to do,
  In these outlandish districts!
  Rome rules by tact, by suppleness, by smoothness.
  It seems they want to kill him—we must let them.
  Bloodthirsty rabble!'
   He washed his hands in water before them, later.
  They were so crude, one spoke to them in pictures—"[1]

This text throws into bright light two types of character—two ways of living.

There is the haphazard, impersonal, lucky way of *finding* something.

There is the personal, costly, creative way of *making* something.

---

[1] From *Truth o' Women*. D. Appleton & Company, New York, publishers. Used by permission.

Unconsciously or consciously we choose one or the other method of life.

We find plenty of things in life. Even Pilate finally found a way of getting rid of Jesus. But the ways we find are like the way Pilate found; they lead to nothing or they lead downward.

We never find a way to real achievement. We speak of Columbus finding a way to America. He didn't find a way. He made it. Goodyear didn't find a way to manufacture rubber. He made it, through a weary road of endless obstacles.

We do not find a way to character or great service. True, life has its great surprises and we find chances and opportunities, as Jesus portrayed in the parable of the man finding the treasure in the field. To get it, however, he had to sell all and fashion life into the deliberate business of winning it by a great concentration.

Mankind will never find a way out of great social evils. We must make it, through toil and tribulation. One of the greatest obstacles to social betterment has been the lazy, blind optimism that in some way the world will accidentally stumble on to an easy, painless way out of the wrong. One of the striking things in Beard's *Rise of American Civilization* is the recital of the manner in which politicians both of the North and South, for a whole generation before the Civil War, refused honestly to face the slavery issue, and clung to the vague, baseless hope that some way of settling the issue would appear out of the clouds.

Many now take the same attitude to war. Every one would be glad to find a way to get rid of it. No way will ever be found; it must be made. One

of the great soldiers of our time, Foch, in one of
his principles of war, has indicated a first principle
of peace-making: "We must always seek to create
events, not merely to suffer them."

❧ ❧ ❧

THE LEGACY OF A LIFE

The upper room where they were *in the habit* of meeting.—*Acts 1. 13* (Moffatt).

A MODERN realist attempting to assess what
Christianity actually was in the world in these first
days of its existence would have presented a rather
sorry invoice. To the materialistic eye it was not
much more than is contained in this verse—a
rather loosely formed habit among a few obscure
and insignificant people from among the lower
strata of Jerusalem society. The whole crowd,
including the fringe, was a hundred and twenty
altogether. There was no "program" or organization. The paraphernalia of a modern "movement" were absent.

It was a very tenuous and slender legacy which
Jesus left in the world—just a few people with
personal devotion and a few reminiscences.

No great character ever left so *little*.

No one ever left so *much*.

It was enough to transform the world.

One striking thing about this legacy of Jesus is
that it is just what most of us leave when we pass
out of this world—a few devoted friends and some
reminiscences—a pathetically meager legacy. And

yet it all depends on the quality of the reminiscences. If the quality is fine and strong, this same legacy which Jesus left and which we leave may be a real transforming and abiding force.

Some men leave more and other than this. Some have left a large estate, to bless or curse. A very few men have left a compact body of thought as their gift to the world. Some have left a name or an institution. Jesus, from one point of view, left what we all do—friends, on whom the quality of our lives has made some impress and the abiding memory of our spirit.

The force of a sunbeam, modern science tells us, gives the world as real a push as dropping a stone upon it. The force of a particular beam is infinitesimal but real and perceptible.

Is there light enough in us to give the world any kind of a push?

THE PIONEER OF LIFE

You killed the *pioneer of Life*.—*Acts 3. 15* (Moffatt).

THIS description of Jesus, "the pioneer of life," is one of the great poetic insights of Doctor Moffatt. It is a great service to launch into the stream of thought such a truly illuminating and inspiring phrase. It is one of those great phrases described by Professor Simon N. Patten as being worth more than books because "they work harder and live longer."

A pioneer is one who enlarges the possible area of life, one who pushes back horizons and blazes the trail into new habitations for humanity. The word catches many of the essential and unique meanings of Jesus for the world. He, above all others, was the great enlarger of life; the one who pushed back the horizons of men's minds, sympathies and lives; the trail breaker to new heights.

The greatest thrills of history lie in the glory of the world's pioneers, from Abraham on his westward hazard of faith, pushing out into unknown domains, down to the lonely flyer making the first trail through the air across the seas. The great human epic is the long daring trek of humanity pushing steadily westward. Tennyson puts into the mouth of Ulysses the very spirit of those great pioneer souls who have led the parade:

"For my purpose holds to sail beyond the sunset
And the baths of all the western stars
Until I die."

Steadily through the centuries have pushed the pioneers across the Atlantic, over the mountain ridges into the great central plain of America; then on over the prairies and deserts to the path of the western stars in the Pacific. The Santa Maria and the Mayflower, Magellan and Drake, Daniel Boone, Lewis and Clark, and Livingstone—pioneers!

There is a deeper thrill in "the pioneer of *life*"— Jesus. He was not merely a horizontal pioneer, pushing back the horizons of continents. He was a vertical pioneer, opening up a way into the high heavens and the depths of the human heart.

Jesus pioneered a new and living way into the
heart of the Father. He threw open a new home
to the race—in the very heart of God himself.
Because he was the way, we may follow. "Where
I am, there ye may be also." "From God, *who is
our home*," says Wordsworth.

Jesus opened up a new quality of life; he led
men into new regions of power. That new habitation which he pioneered Paul well described. "The
life I now live ... I live by the faith in the Son
of God."

Jesus crossed old frontiers. The ancient barriers of race and clan and color and class, with all
their fearful taboos, with their high walls of exclusion, had no meaning for him. The whole course
of social betterment has been but following the
footsteps of Jesus through the wilderness of human
suffering and need. Still, he is far ahead in the
unconquered wastes of life.

This conception of Jesus as the pioneer of life
saves Christianity from being merely a refuge.
Christianity has been too much regarded as a
harbor from storms, a refuge—a retreat from the
conflicts of life. To escape from penalties and
dangers and risks of life has been regarded as the
chief end of a Christian. Many have learned only
one hymn:

> "Hide me, O my Saviour, hide,
>   Till the storm of life be past,
>   Safe into the haven guide,
>   O receive my soul at last!"

Glorious as that is, deep and genuine as the need
which it expresses is, it is inadequate. Chris-

tianity is an achievement, a venture, a discovery.
Its motto cannot be "Safety first." It must pioneer
to open up new achievements in living together.

> "The men of the East may watch the stars
>   And signs and seasons mark,
> But the men signed with the cross of Christ
>   Go gaily in the dark."

To-day this conception of Jesus comes as a
needed impetus to the spirit of daring and risk, so
sadly waning in many quarters. Dr. Francis Green-
wood Peabody has described a prevailing mood
among us, even among Christ's disciples:

Most of us devote a great part of our time to insuring
ourselves against the risks of life. We accumulate money;
we fortify health; we guard ourselves against uncertainty;
we lay our plans for leisure, comfort, and old age. Abraham going out, not knowing whither he was going, Pilgrims launching forth into a stormy sea, soldiers risking
all in the great adventure, Jesus Christ finding peace and
joy at the end of his short career—all these seem remote
from a prudent and judicious way of life. An assured
income, a good digestion, an undisturbed conformity to a
venerable creed—what can make one safer than these?

This is emphatically not the mood or spirit of a
pioneer. And it is emphatically not the mood or
spirit of Jesus.

The great aspiration needed to lift life to Jesus'
level of courage and the risk represented by the
cross is put into a remarkable modern prayer first
printed in the London *Spectator*. It worships Jesus,
the pioneer of life.

"Jesus, whose lot with us was cast,
Who saw it out, from first to last:
Patient and fearless, tender, true,
Carpenter, vagabond, felon, Jew:
Whose humorous eye took in each phase
Of full rich life this world displays,
Yet ever more kept fast in view
The far-off goal it leads us to:
Who, as your hour neared, did not fail,
The world's fate trembling in the scale,
With your half-hearted band to dine
And chat across the bread and wine,
Then went out firm to face the end
Alone without a single friend:
Who felt, as your last words confessed,
Wrung from a proud unflinching breast
By hours of dull ignoble pain,
Your whole life's fight was fought in vain;
Would I could win and keep and feel
That heart of love, that spirit of steel."

ANNOYED OR AMAZED?

The priests, the commander of the Temple, and the
Sadducees, *who were annoyed* at them teaching the people
and proclaiming Jesus.—*Acts 4. 2* (Moffatt).
Greatly disturbed (Goodspeed).

THERE are two kinds of people in the world,
judged by their characteristic reactions to life.

One kind is annoyed by incidental things. Their
prestige is not enhanced, their comfort is disturbed,
their routine is broken up, their exaggerated sense

of order is outraged. They are annoyed, because they live mainly for these things.

Another kind is too gripped with amazement over life's wonders, its surprising graces, its positive good, to waste nervous energy in fussy explosions over inconveniences or incidentals.

The crowd in the Temple praised God for the astounding miracle of abundant life, in the healing of the cripple and the preaching of Jesus the life-giver.

The Temple bureaucrats were annoyed. They had not seen anything but "disorder" and a blow to their self-esteem.

What is your most characteristic mood—annoyance or amazement? They are the opposite poles of life.

❧ ❧ ❧

OUTSIDERS

"By what authority, in whose name, have *men like you* done this?"—*Acts 4. 7* (Moffatt).

THE translation "men like you" is a bit of very dramatic interpretation found in a note of Doctor Moffatt's on this verse. He says, "With a touch of superciliousness ('men like you!'), which is perhaps better expressed in reading aloud than by any verbal periphrasis."

It is a feeling of snobbish contempt for an outsider, without ordination, without the authority of the religious caste. It is better expressed by a gesture than by a word. Indeed, the word "superciliousness" is a gesture originally. It comes from the Latin word *supercilium*, meaning "eyebrow." It is a lifting of the eyebrow in haughtiness and disdain.

The eyebrow is a fine test of mental quality and moral character. It can be lifted in disdain or lowered in thinking. These Temple aristocrats never lowered their eyebrows in real thinking over a new force or event. They were supercilious— eyebrow lifters. Snobbish contempt was so much easier than open-minded study.

Here was the haughty pride in being an insider, in being ordained, in being regular—ecclesiastical caste. You can see the arrogance in the expression accompanying the expression, "men like you!" "How could the grace of God possibly come to the world outside of the regular official channel?"

You can hear the sneer of the official insider all down the centuries. There is something very ironical in this conversation. Here was Peter, on whom the whole structure of apostolic succession depends, being challenged because he didn't have it!

"Men like you" has the sneer of official priestly complacency, flung at every prophet with the living word of God in his heart and on his lips, men who have come in from the outside with no diploma of official sanction—men like Martin Luther, George Fox, John Wesley, Roger Williams, William Booth, the woman Anne Hutchinson, and the whole company of God's Irregular Volunteers.

This sneer at "outsiders," directed against men who were furthest on the inside of the *mind* of Christ of any men who ever lived, ought to check our easy habit of testing the value of a prophet's message by its source rather than by its contents.

This chapter of New Testament history should teach us to beware how we call anybody an outsider. A person may be on the outside of every ecclesiastical caste and tradition and be on the inside of God's purpose and revelation. It should warn us effectively—a warning continually needed —of taking regularity of order or opinion or procedure too seriously. God has never appeared to notice it at all. God's revelations frequently come outside of the regularly appointed channels. This has happened often because the channels were closed, through arrogant complacency and contempt akin to that of these rulers, elders, and scribes.

That was one of the deep truths manifested in the birth of Jesus in a barn—a truth so easily forgotten.

WHAT WILL HAPPEN NEXT?

Wondering *what would happen next.*—Acts 5. 24 (Weymouth).

As long as the church had the world on the *qui vive* it had measureless power. These Roman soldiers and officials after Peter's escape from jail were in a state of baffled expectancy. They couldn't figure where some strange unknown power would break loose next. But they paid the little church the magnificent tribute of expecting something to happen. It was a company in which things happened.

That attribute of throwing the world into amazed expectancy was one of the secrets of its vital power. It is always an indispensable secret of power. The church has reached the bankruptcy court when the world expects nothing to happen, when its life flows on in placid routine from which no great upheaval is looked for.

This wonderment which the church of the apostolic age caused affords a good test with which to measure the church of our own time and our own lives. Is there such an abounding vigor and resourcefulness of Christian faith in us that the world is constantly wondering what the next manifestation of power will be? Alas, to ask the question is frequently to answer it that the world doesn't expect anything to happen. We are not in the business of producing amazement. We grow tame. We slide into routine about which the prediction of an unheroic sameness is only too easy.

Dr. H. R. L. Sheppard, the beloved rector who served Saint Martin's-in-the-Fields, London, for many years, and who in his own person and message possessed just this power of apostolic amazement, has said recently in a characteristic utterance:

Many onlookers "find our brave assertions and poor achievements irreconcilable. . . . We appear to them like Alpine climbers who, after boasting of the height they were about to scale, take their ice-axe, rope, and other equipment, and are discovered later proceeding cautiously up Ludgate Hill."

This power of creating amazed expectancy cannot be acquired by a spurious sensationalism. It is not outward sensationalism in the apostolic church but a startling wealth of inner power and conviction that made the world wonder. The church cannot rally the world by blowing on a penny whistle, as is the superficial practice of many.

The real reason why the world does not expect more to happen *through* us is that so little has happened *in* us. Dr. James Denny put a finger on the creeping paralysis when he observed, "The number of people who suppose that they are Christians while it is all the same to them if Christ had never lived is appalling."

Christendom in the Middle Ages united in crusades to recover a lost tomb. Is there not a finer quest for our day—to recover a lost question mark? Not a question mark concerning the gospel's power or the church's mission, but the search for that abundant spiritual life and daring, that the world may continually ask the old question, "What will these astounding Christians do next?"

AND AT HOME

Not for a single day did they cease to teach and preach . . . in the Temple *and at home.—Acts 5. 42* (Moffatt).

WE have not ceased to preach at the temple. But we have, rather largely, ceased to do it *at home*. And therein lies one of the major differences between the church of the book of Acts and the church of our own day.

Preaching at the temple is not enough. Indeed,

it is rather apt to be sort of futile unless there is the teaching "*at home*."

It is an urgent and timely word which comes from this exhilarated, creative day and company of the first Christian church at Jerusalem. Here was a secret, a largely forgotten secret of our time. Its recovery transcends many other much more imposing "programs" set before the church of our time.

Nothing can be a substitute for the shaping of Christian character at home. George Santayana, the poet and philosopher, a master of exquisite English, though born in Spain, writes with great insight concerning his use of the language. "The roots of the language," he says, "do not quite reach to my center. I never drank in in childhood the homely cadences and ditties which in pure spontaneous poetry set the essential key."[1] How beautifully and truly these words fit the spiritual experiences of millions of Christian homes! "The pure spontaneous poetry" of the Christian gospel has set the essential key of life—and the note has never been lost. The homely cadences of a faith learned and experienced in childhood can never be matched.

That apostolic age was much like ours in the deadliness of things which swarm in to crowd out religion from the life. It is a sobering thing to ask, "What will a generation be like which has grown up with no Christian teaching and molding at home?" Henry Seidel Canby asks the alarming question:

---

[1] Charles Scribner's Sons, publishers. Used by permission.

In the last war there were regiments of poor, stunted devils, syphilitic, tubercular, crooked in body, incapable of anything but menial work and the kind of fighting where hopeless endurance counts. They were the grand-children of the factory slaves. What will the grand-children of the tabloid readers be like? Healthy of body perhaps, for this exploitation is by flattery; not poor, not oppressed, for it is their economic power which makes them exploitable; but in emotions, ideals, intelligence, either wrought into fantastic shapes or burnt out alto-gether. Soiled minds, rotten before they are ripe.

In the face of such liabilities, shall we lightly let slip out the *"and at home"* part of that grand strategy of the apostolic age?

The question is far more serious than that—we are *already* doing it. The only question is, Shall we go on doing it?

❧ ❧ ❧

THE EARTHQUAKE PRAYER

Enable thy servants to proclaim thy message with *fearless courage.*—*Acts 4. 29* (Weymouth).

HERE was a prayer that shook the place like an earthquake. It was a prayer for just one thing—fearless courage. When a church prays for that, it always precipitates some kind of an earthquake.

This prayer is the key to an understanding of the abounding vigor and power of the apostolic church. It is a remarkable evidence of an indom-itable spirit. After their leader's escape from jail and death, while they all stood in slippery places of peril, they prayed for just one thing—reckless, bold courage. Not a syllable about protection. Not even, in the excitement, a word of thanksgiving—just courage to carry on.

No wonder the house shook. You can lean your ear and heart down close to the fourth chapter of the book of Acts and hear the vibration to this day. It is like the ground swell of a new springtime. And that was exactly what it was—bursting life.

This is one of the first recorded prayers of the Christian Church. Suppose it had been a model of all Christian prayers—forgetful of safety and gain; intent only on the fearless courage of proclaiming Christ.

So many prayers of individuals and churches have the deep bass accompaniment, whatever the air, of "me, me, me"; "Save us from danger; increase us, magnify our organization"—these are rather constant notes in our prayers, not necessarily unchristian, save as they predominate. But this little company were desperately reckless—"Never mind what becomes of us, O Lord, only give us fearless courage!"

What house would not shake with that prayer to-day? Some houses of God do shake with it. Some towers of evil shake before it. Suppose it could be recovered as the normal burden of Christian prayer. What could not be accomplished? The solidified rocks of intrenched evil would experience an earthquake.

The newspapers a few months ago recorded a story of a clergyman in Vermont who recovered his voice and spoke aloud after whispering for seventeen years. Many a disciple of Jesus has need of the same miracle. Many have been "whispering" the message of Jesus for more than seventeen years—such a suave, velvety whisper that it startled or restrained nobody.

Milton's "Areopagitica" contains a strong, inspiring sentence concerning the heroic stand which he took against great odds: "God intended to prove me, whether I durst take up alone a rightful cause against a world of disesteem, and found I durst." This is the great poet's explanation of the heroic stand which he took against the social, political and religious opposition of his day.

"And found I *durst*." What an instinctive response the quaint and noble old English word awakens! It is matched by that simple, modest word of Lindbergh in his story of his flight across the Atlantic. "I decided," he wrote, "that I must not think any more about going back." That was the moment of triumph.

It was the moment of triumph of the little company of disciples and will be the only lasting triumph of any company.

We need to make that the chief burden of prayer, for we are so open to the mounting hesitations of what Wordsworth calls "the uncourageous elder years." Whether we are so elderly or not, we soon meet the uncourageous years. Instead of the assault on the world's evil, so full of risk and toil, we begin to play what is known in sport as "a defensive game."

We need a fearless courage to proclaim a spiritual universe amid a growing fashion of materialism; to proclaim a gospel of moral austerity in a day of tolerated license; to proclaim a gospel of justice and brotherhood in the face of powerful forces of exploitation.

❧ ❧ ❧

THE "HEATHEN"

The Jewish believers . . . were amazed because the gift of the Holy Spirit had been showered *upon the heathen too.—Acts 10. 45* (Goodspeed).

AFTER nineteen Christian centuries this is still hard to believe and act upon. For these men of privilege, these Jews, with a strong consciousness of race and national superiority, it was a staggering amazement to be asked to believe that the Holy Spirit had been showered on "the heathen" as well as upon themselves.

Goodspeed's translation of the word usually rendered "Gentiles" as "heathen" undoubtedly better preserves the original values of the word. It gives us more of the emotional content which the word "Gentile" had for the Jew. To our ears there is nothing objectionable in the word "Gentile." It is even a designation that carries a tinge of superiority. But to the Jew it had just the feeling of condescension and implicit arrogance which the word "heathen" has.

This problem raised at the very birth hour of distinctively foreign missions in Christianity is a very timely and momentous one for the present stage of missions.

Can we readily and wholly and gladly admit the

Christian churches of what have been called "heathen" lands to a full equality with us of another race and older privilege?

This is the major question in missions in China and India to-day—as it was a major question in Cæsarea. On the way it is answered depends much of the future of Christianity in the Orient.

The development of a self-directing, self-governing church on mission fields has been proclaimed as an objective of the missionary activity of churches in Western lands. Are we willing to face all the implications of that announced purpose, and do it not grudgingly—with a tight grasp on property that will relax only by force—but eagerly?

Are we, the church at home and missionaries on the field, willing to give over the direction of the church to nationals, to take a subordinate place, to yield authority we have always held, to turn our property, to serve under native direction—in other words, to admit that "the heathen" have been showered with divine grace in as copious a manner as the white race?

The question takes another form: Have we ourselves been showered with enough grace to do it? It will mean renouncing the patronizing attitude to the "heathen" which has been a part of our racial and national inheritance. Kipling's phrase, "half devil and half child," as a description of "new-caught savage peoples," well expresses that patronizing attitude. Indeed the whole poem, "The White Man's Burden," might well serve as a Bible for the cult of Nordic supremacy.

To-day—as in Peter's day—the future of missions hangs in the balance.

BLOCKING THE ROAD TO CHRIST

We ought not to put *fresh difficulties* in the way of those who are turning to God from among the Gentiles. —*Acts 15. 19* (Moffatt).

We ought not to put *obstacles* (Goodspeed).

Against inflicting *unexpected annoyances* (Weymouth).

HERE was a great principle of Christian faith— a Magna Charta of the church—unhappily so often forgotten. If it had been kept in the high central place to which the apostle James, with a great reach of faith, elevated it in this Christian assembly in Jerusalem, the history of Christianity would have been a far more glorious story. "We have no right," he declares, "to put fresh difficulties, obstacles, unexpected annoyances in the way of those coming to Christ from heathenism."

Circumcision, which was the matter under discussion, was a Jewish rite. It had no place whatever as a requirement for Christian faith and discipleship. It was exactly described in the words, "fresh difficulties" and "unexpected annoyances." It blocked the way like a stone fence erected at the entrance of the house of God. "Believe on the Lord Jesus Christ, and thou shalt be saved" was the sufficient Christian evangel. Rites and tests which were not an essential part of this one great message were an insufferable annoyance. They not only blocked the path to Christ; they obscured him.

Yet down through the centuries to this day men have done the thing here condemned. They have imposed legal and intellectual difficulties and annoyances which are not vital parts of Christian faith. Frequently the essential simplicity of being a

Christian has been lost in the mazes of metaphysical and philosophical speculations to which the convert has been required to subscribe. Frequently wandering around amid these conjectures embodied in creeds and confessions, expressed in the thought forms of other long-past centuries, the simple-minded man has been tempted to cry, "They have taken away the Lord . . . and we know not where they have laid him."

This priceless inheritance from the first days of the church is a charter of liberty, freeing the Christian from burdens and tests which Christ himself did not lay down. We have no right to make it harder to become a member of the church than Jesus made it to become one of his disciples. We have no right to impose burdens which Jesus himself did not impose. The requirements for inclusion in Christ's church have often contained, and in many instances still do contain, elements alien from and additional to essential Christian faith according to Jesus. What an absurdity it has been to make membership in the church depend on things which the apostle Paul himself would not understand and never even heard of. Yet it has often been done.

And how the churches have exported these extra, illegal burdens to non-Christian lands! The relics of old conflicts, of the theological battles of the Middle Ages, of the later physical battles of the Civil War in America, incidentals of the history of Western nations which are saddled on to the Christian faith—though no real part of it—have been carried across the seas and set up as requirements of faith in Christ.

Would anything mean more to the cause of Christ

than that we might recover for our time this faith
and vision of James, able to distinguish the essential
from the incidental in our gospel, and to present
Christ, unencumbered by any "unexpected annoyance"?

❦ ❦ ❦

THE MOB MIND IN THE BOOK OF ACTS

They got hold of some idle rascals *to form a mob.*—
Acts 17. 5 (Moffatt).

THE book of Acts furnishes a fine field for study
of the mob mind in action.   In the unthinking
mobs which assaulted Paul again and again there
is the play of one of the most malignant and destructive forces in the world.   About society to-day the
old entail of the herd mind still clings and becomes
the mob mind, which is one of the most ugly and
horrible manifestations of all human nature.   It is
in truth no mind at all, but a wild, contagious
impulse which puts the mind out of action.   The
mob mind is humanity on a wild, blind buffalo
stampede.

Any real progress which the world may make
in the future depends on the liberation of mankind
from the herd mind.   This involves substituting
thought for blind instinct, stirred by fear, hatred,
and prejudice.   In a word, it depends on education.
It is a help in this process to recognize the blind,
irrational action of the mob in the events recorded
by the book of Acts, how it is skillfully played upon
by all the arguments and incitements so familiar in

our day until it rushes and roars and kills with the
rage and cruelty and blindness of an angry bull.
We see that Christianity here runs the familiar
gauntlet of charges well calculated to stir up the
herd instinct of the mob, that it endangers social
security, is an enemy of the state, is not patriotic,
hurts business, is impious.

The familiar incitement that business will suffer
is made and the inevitable result follows, "The city
was filled with confusion . . . they rushed like one
man."

How many efforts at social betterment to-day
suffer the same frenzied mob cry!

In Acts 16. 20 we find the familiar mob frenzy
stirred up by an appeal to patriotism. The crowd
is urged to stamp out Christianity and mob its
adherents because it is not patriotic! "These fel-
lows are Jews [there was the eternal appeal to race
prejudice] who are making an agitation in our
town. They are proclaiming customs which as
Romans we are not allowed to accept or observe."
They are subverting the empire. It sounds like a
modern blacklist put out by one of our fussy societies
of professional patriots, charging some of the out-
standing Christian personalities of the country with
being Bolshevists because they do not take all their
ideas ready made from military bureaucrats.

In John 19. 12 we find this sort of threat was
used very successfully on Pilate during the trial
of Jesus. "If you let him go, you are no friend
of the emperor's!" urged the Jewish politicians.

In Acts 14. 2 "Refractory Jews stirred up and
exasperated the feeling of the Gentiles against the
brothers."

Acts 21. 28 shows the same raucous cry of appeal
to race and nationalistic prejudices, making an emotional atmosphere in which straight and fair thinking is impossible. "To the rescue, men of Israel!"

Acts 22. 23. The modern art of camouflage
appears. During a heated discussion the enemies
of the apostles and of Christianity threw dust in
the air to prevent reasoning and to obscure the
issues. Compare that blind appeal to chaotic passion with the clear mind, the self-control, the deep
wisdom of the town clerk of Ephesus, a man who
deserves far more fame than he has ever received.
For he represents the hope of the world, that the
individual judgment, unclouded by fear or hate,
may have growing dominion over that heritage
from our subhuman past, the herd mind and the
mob mind.

WHAT IRRITATES YOU?

His soul was *irritated* at the sight of the idols.—*Acts
17. 16* (Moffatt).

ARE you irritable?

Modern science has shown that, in a real sense,
to ask this question is equivalent to asking, Are
you *alive?*

Irritability, as the word is generally used, is
regarded as a defect of character. It is the mark
of a runaway nervous system which has gotten
out of control. And we are all anxious to avoid
a collision with that kind of a runaway. We give

the "irritable" person a wide berth—when we can.

But that nervous tendency to explode on the smallest provocation is merely a perverted sensitiveness. It is a degenerate irritability, focused on the wrong objects. Science tells us that irritability is the real glory of life, the essential power which distinguishes life from inert matter. "A living body is an organism," says G. T. W. Patrick, "and the peculiar feature of a living organism is the possession of a group of unique properties, of which the two most conspicuous are *irritability* and reproduction."[1]

Dr. George A. Dorsey thus describes the essential place of *irritability* as the basis of life:

All life is irritable. This irritability inheres in every living cell of every living body. Because of that quality the amœba is excited to explore its world and man his. That quality leads to the ego in the individual and to culture in the human race.

The enemies of Socrates were so excited that they put him to death. Hunger can so excite an amœba that it commits cannibalism. Moisture and heat so excite a grain of wheat that it sprouts; if it does not respond to sprouting stimuli it is dead. An amœba beyond the stage of excitability is dead.

Irritability is in the nature of living things, regardless of size and shape, whether plant or animal, one-celled or many-celled, and of every cell in every living body. Because of this irritability, life responds. Without excitability there could be no response to physical or chemical change in environment.[2]

---

[1] *The World and Its Meaning*, p. 77.   Houghton Mifflin Company, publishers.   Used by permission.

[2] *Why We Behave Like Human Beings*.   Harper & Brothers, publishers.   Used by permission.

An amœba without "excitability," "irritability," is dead. So is a human soul.

Paul was alive. His soul was so sensitive that he could be irritated ("exasperated," Goodspeed translates it) by the sight of idols and all that they represented.

One of the chief differences between human beings lies in the kind of things which arouse their irritation. Of course there is perhaps another group whose chief characteristic is torpor, sluggishness of mind and spirit, who don't get irritated or stirred by anything. Their family line seems to draw heavily on the vegetable kingdom. They emulate, amid life's alarms, the fine placidity of the cabbage.

But most people are richly dowered with sensitiveness, capacity to respond, an excitability in the physical sense. Hence the vital question for each of us to face, How does this divine gift of irritability manifest itself? Is it a noble thing like Paul's, which stirred the soul over wrong or injustice or human degradation? Or is it an ignoble thing, a fussy energy which explodes when our coffee is cold, when we miss the morning paper or our self-esteem is wounded?

Paul went through enough hard experiences "to exasperate a saint." The noteworthy thing about that common expression is that the things which are "enough to exasperate a saint" never do exasperate saints. Shipwreck, stoning, imprisonment— none of these things irritated him. The sight of idols did. The vision of the ruin and degradation brought to the sons of God by a pagan ideal of life stirred his whole being.

Here are two men, both endowed with the same

high power of irritability. One is that unlovely creature, the overgrown baby. He is intensely "irritable." His prestige, his comfort, his crotchets and opinions, his "rights"—any invasion of these things touches off Vesuvius. But great human injustices, suffering of others, aching needs do not jar him at all. Another man, like Paul, has so risen in the scale of life that his irritability is connected with higher centers of the mind—his sympathies are stirred and his energies are moved to action.

Where do we stand in the scale of life? Have we retained a capacity for moral indignation which Paul here displayed?

Two of the gravest dangers which threaten to atrophy this high endowment of the soul are cynicism and cloistered selfishness. That latter danger is well put in a satirical quatrain which recently won a prize offered by the London Spectator:

> "St. Francis of Assisi
> Was incapable of taking things easy;
> That is one of the advances
> We have made upon St. Francis."

Is our irritability of the Christlike character of Paul's?

ARDOR AND ACCURACY

He preached and taught about Jesus with *ardor and accuracy.*—Acts *18. 25* (Moffatt).

A DIVINE combination of qualities, twin jewels of

the mind and heart—ardor and accuracy—fire and precision—poetry and geometry!

What a superb ideal for Christian teaching and preaching!

If we wish to realize what an essential combination for the proclamation of the gospel it is, we have only to glance at the ills which follow where one of these qualities appears without the other.

There has been plenty of preaching with ardor, but, alas, with little discernible accuracy. Such a flame is like a fire which has gotten out of control. Such ardor has often come from the hot flames of animosity, of polemical controversy, of unrestrained emotion, or a debauch of exaggerated passion. It has often shown a lack of discernment, condemned, like the Prince in Tennyson's "Princess," to mistake the shadow for the substance.

On the other hand, accuracy alone is often sterile. It may be a soul without a body. The most correct and precise logic on earth can never say to an impotent soul, "In the name of Jesus of Nazareth, rise up and walk." Macaulay has described the best parliamentary oratory as "reason penetrated and made red-hot with passion."

It is the same high fusion of mental qualities which Apollos possessed. Emerson's tribute to ardor is all the more effective from one of his temperament: "The eloquent man is no beautiful speaker but one who is inwardly and desperately drunk with a certain belief."

This description of the preaching of Apollos presents the only ideal which can meet the need of our time—the need of an intelligent faith, quickened and emerged with life-giving emotion.

There is the danger of what has been well called an arid liberalism—so intent on stating the position that the gospel seems to be an academic exercise of intellectual formulation, with no consuming passion or redeeming power. On the other hand, there is the danger of an "inaccurate" gospel, in which the great simplicities of Christ are lost in a confusion of accessories, or smothered in a din of outworn shibboleths.

❧ ❧ ❧

COMMISSIONED TO ATTEST

The commission I received from the Lord Jesus *to attest the gospel* of the grace of God.—*Acts 20. 24* (Moffatt).

To attest is to "certify as true." Paul's commission was to certify the gospel of the grace of God as true, to prove it.

Every disciple's commission is a commission to prove the truth of the gospel, to furnish the evidence from experience by which it can be recognized as true.

This is a much larger commission than to talk about it, to sing about it, or to praise it. Proving it is a more considerable undertaking.

"Come let us *live* the poetry we sing," cries Edwin Markham. That is every man's commission.

It is proof the world waits for. As it is stirringly expressed in the statement of aims of the British Conference on Christian Politics, Economics and Citizenship:

If the Christian ideal vividly expressed and plainly translated into terms of action could be proclaimed, we believe that the new age now opening might be fashioned according to the pattern of Jesus Christ. We Christians can only fail if we are either not intelligent enough to understand our gospel or not honest enough to apply it.

"It is not enough to sit together in heavenly places; we must stand together in unheavenly places."

The only possible method of proof is to furnish in actual experience in individual and collective living, that the unblurred features of Jesus, his mind and spirit, in the words of the text, the very "gospel of the grace of God" shine through.

We frequently succeed, in our efforts to portray Jesus, in giving more of a portrait of ourselves than of him. Philip Guedalla, in *The Second Empire*, says of the Life of Cæsar written by Napoleon III, "The portrait of the artist was excellent but it was less easy to reconcile it with the hard features of Julius Cæsar."[1] A common failure of portraiture, constructing a mirror for the artist instead of a portrait of the subject.

William Lyon Phelps thus notes the same common blunder in portrait painting and another equally fatal one:

A portrait painter may show more of the personality of the artist who copies than of the subject copied. Like stained glass is more conspicuous for its own bright color than for the amount of sunlight it transmits.

He may take more of the accessories than of the person. It is easier to copy incidentals and furnishings.

---

[1] G. P. Putnam's Sons, publishers. Used by permission.

Either of these will cause us to fail in our commission to attest, to prove true, the gospel of God's grace in Christ.

❧ ❧ ❧

WHEN DO YOU STOP LISTENING?

Until they heard this last statement the people listened to Paul.—*Acts 22. 22* (Weymouth).

EAGERLY, sympathetically, approvingly these Jews listened to Paul until he mentioned his being sent as "an apostle to nations far away"—to the Gentiles, the heathen.

Then it was all over.

Bang went the door of their minds!

Snap went the shutter!

Boom went the explosion!

For in that statement he touched sensitive nerves—their pet prejudice of aversion to the Gentiles, their sense of race superiority and special privilege. Nations far away? Disgusting! So the cordiality of the hearing ended instantaneously with the cries: "Away with such a fellow from the earth. He ought not to be permitted to live."

Thus end most challenges to dearly loved pet prejudices and set opinions.

How modern it all sounds! How like yesterday's meeting, to-day's conversation, the upheaval over last Sunday's sermon!

In our hearing of the gospel many of us are exactly like the Jews in their hearing of it when it was first proclaimed so many centuries ago. We

listen up to the point where the gospel as preached
or taught clashes with our favorite aversion, our
cherished animosity, our prejudices, our profit and
privilege. Then, inwardly at least, we cry, "Away
with such a fellow!"

Max Beerbohm has drawn our picture as well as
his own in his humorous confession: "I am a Tory
Anarchist. I should like every one to go about
doing just as he pleased, short of altering any of
the things to which I have grown accustomed."
So many are glad to have Jesus Christ go about
the world doing exactly as he pleases—short, of
course, of *altering any of the things to which they
have grown accustomed!*

What is the point at which we stop listening to
the teaching of Jesus, and shut the door of our
mind with a bang? It is a very humbling but rewarding question to ask ourselves. The very act of
asking it and searching honestly and frankly for
an answer will be a means of growth in grace.

Sometimes it is this very point at which the
Jews flared up in explosion. Some Christians, any
more than these first-century Jews, cannot heartily
join in carrying the gospel to nations far away.

"I don't believe in foreign missions," and snap
goes the shutter of the mind. "We have enough
to do at home"—true, far too much for one who
talks like that ever to accomplish. Such people
do not live on God's globe. They live on a man-
made hemisphere, or, worse yet, in a bailiwick, a
county, a township. God's love is the equator of
the spiritual universe; it circles the whole earth.

Sometimes the prejudice that marks the end of
our hearing the gospel is political. When it seems

to come to a difference between Cæsar and Christ, the issue to many people is simple and clear. Cæsar always wins.

Sometimes the boiling point is economic. A man can "stand" the gospel as long as it keeps away from business. The sacred customs of the present order in the business world are an ark of the covenant which must not be touched. As long as the preacher sticks to individual morals or theoretical theology he will listen. But let him follow where Jesus leads —into the moral basis of society, social justice—the response is all too frequent. Reinhold Niebuhr has well pictured the difficulty of preaching the gospel in America to-day to an opulent, successful age:

In the history of the world it has probably never been more difficult to preach the gospel than in America in the twentieth century. . . . Your average American is really a pessimist because he is superficially an optimist; he is so thoroughly satisfied with his mechanical achievements that he cannot imagine a world very much better than the one in which he lives. He therefore defends the *status quo* with frantic enthusiasm against every attempt to change it. To such a generation it is not easy to preach repentance. Its people are willing to repent of comparatively insignificant sins, but they are proud of the very limitations of their civilization and tolerance of every effort to make their good seem evil.

In such a world it is very difficult to preach a gospel which demands that we prove our greatness through service and which measures the worth of a man by the contributions which he may be able to make to the spiritual development of his fellow men. There are many pious men in our churches who are perfectly ready to pray with the poorest beggar in the street, but they are not willing to embark upon the adventure of trusting their workingmen and of so organizing their industry that the life of the work and his personality will achieve significance. Many of these men could be won for a Christian adventure in business and industry by careful and courageous Christian pedagogy. But most of them are so proud of the very limitations of our modern life and so oblivious to its sins that they will make short shrift of any teacher of religion who tries to teach them the way of God more perfectly.[1]

When we stop the truth of Christ as soon as it threatens to reach us, we are still living back in B. C. with these Jews and not in A. D., the Year of Our Lord.

* * *

FINDING TIME AND MAKING IT

"When I can find a moment, I will send for you."— *Acts 24. 25* (Moffatt).

"I will *find time* later" (Goodspeed).

FELIX gives utterance here, in postponing the decision due on Paul's appeal, to one of the oldest and most persistent fallacies of the human mind —that one can ever *find* time. There is a strange delusion which hangs before the mind like a mirage —that we will accidentally stumble against a great big chunk of time that will be available for a hard or disagreeable task which we are trying to escape.

There is this unique characteristic about time which we overlook: we can *lose* time, but we can never *find* it. We have to *make* it.

---

[1] From The Christian Advocate, March 4, 1926.

This translation introduces a new idea to the familiar version—"When I have a convenient season." It contains that idea and more. It is not merely a convenient moment but *any* moment which cannot be found accidentally, without deliberate and costly effort.

Felix illustrated this perfectly. He found lots of moments for what he wanted to do—to satisfy his curiosity about Paul and open the way for a bribe. We read that he sent for him "pretty frequently" (Acts 24. 26), but he found no moments to face the big issue squarely and render a judgment. Such moments are never found. They must be made.

It is a truth to be especially remembered in an age when such a marvelous new variety of time-filling and time-stealing employments are let loose upon us. "The world is so full of a number of things" that the river of time rushes on like the rapids above Niagara Falls. We are swept irresistibly on unless we anchor ourselves by deliberate choice, as an island is anchored by an unshakable foundation. We live in a time surpassing all others in the multiplication of time-saving devices and inventions. Yet by a strange irony—like one of time's "revenges"—we have less time for many of life's major enterprises, such as self-discovery and the growth of personality, than any previous age. So the very multiplication of mechanical wonders has proved a boomerang in that it defeats often the *use* of time saved.

We have a common bit of advice that runs far deeper into life than usually appears. It is this: "Take your time!" That is, take it *yourself*. Seize it. For if you don't take it yourself and use it, be sure someone else or something else will take it for you.

Felix's vain and vague hope of accidentally finding time is a picture of the measureless amount of the spending of time lavishly by people who make no selective choice in what they buy with it. Life is like going into a department store with a severely and definitely limited amount of money. If you buy this, you *can't* buy that. And the expedition of life—unless planned with a painful and inflexible consecration—turns into a shopping expedition which spends its capital at the first counter. It may happen to be cheap, gaudy beads, but if they catch the eye, that settles it.

Christopher Morley has speculated suggestively about this appalling waste of time—figured statistically by the thoughtful dog hero of *Where the Blue Begins*, Mr. Gissing:

One of the things that struck him about the city was its heedlessness of Time. On every side he saw people spending it without adequate return. Perhaps he was young and doctrinaire: but he devised this theory for himself—all time is wasted that does not give you some awareness of beauty or wonder. In other words, "The days that make us happy make us wise," he said to himself, quoting Masefield's line. On that principle, he asked, how much time is wasted in this city? Well, here are some six million people. To simplify the problem (which is permitted to every philosopher) let us (he said) assume that 2,350,000 of those people have spent a day that could be called, on the whole, happy: a day in which they have had glimpses of reality; a day in which they feel satisfaction. (That was, he felt, a generous allowance.) Very well, then, that leaves 3,650,000 people whose day has been unfruitful: spent in uncongenial work, or in sorrow, suffering, and talking nonsense. This city, then, in one day, has wasted 10,000 years, or 100 centuries. One hundred centuries squandered in a day! It made him feel quite ill, and he tore up the scrap of paper on which he had been figuring.[1]

A feature of our modern life which keeps us from deliberately making time for the highest uses, and betrays us into the old fallacy of Felix, is the note of *strident immediacy* so characteristic of the mood of to-day. So many things must be done right away to keep up with the "swim" that those long processes of growth which are life's finest fruit find no sufficient time to mature. Many have substituted a kind of telegraphic impressionism for long-process fruitage.

William H. Davies has voiced in simple, powerful lines a protest against this ruthless tyranny of external things—a true declaration of independence of the spirit:

> "What *is* this life if, full of care,
> We have no time to stand and stare?
>
> "No time to stand beneath the boughs
> And stare as long as sheep or cows.
>
> "No time to see, in broad daylight,
> Streams full of stars, like skies at night.
>
> "No time to turn at beauty's glance,
> And watch her feet, how they can dance.
>
> "A poor life this if, full of care,
> We have no time to stand and stare."[2]

---

[1] Doubleday, Page & Co., publishers. Used by permission.
[2] *Leisure.* Jonathan Cape, Limited, London, publishers. Used by permission.

Are you a vagrant? A vagrant lives by finding things. Life has no high choices, no seizing of time for creative purposes. A vagrant, in his relation to time, ambles through life a helpless Micawber, hoping time will "turn up." Felix was a vagrant, even though he sat on a throne.

✤ ✤ ✤

THE METHOD OF INQUIRY INTO RELIGION

"I felt *at a loss about the method of inquiry* into such topics."—*Acts 25. 20* (Moffatt).
I was *at a loss as to how to investigate* (Goodspeed).

THE baffling topic to Festus was "a certain Jesus."
Festus is not the only one who has felt at a loss about the method of inquiry into that topic.
There is only one sure method of inquiry, Festus, and you did not find it. Paul told you but you did not listen to him. You asked Agrippa, and he knew nothing about it. The one and only method of inquiry is *experience*. You wish to know whether there is anything in this way—this Jesus? *Try it.* That's the only really scientific method of investigation.
There are many methods of inquiry that have been tried. Men have tried logic. They have discussed Christianity as an academic problem—a thing to be proved or disproved by a clever entanglement of major premise and minor premise and conclusion. But a living thing can never be investigated in a vacuum of formal logic.

Men have "investigated" Christianity by the method of analyzing the physical universe—with physics, chemistry, astronomy, biology they have scrutinized the earth, sea, and sky. They have reported: "The earth is resolvable into so many elements. But our test tubes do not report God or the soul."

So this school of materialistic science has exiled from the universe all unresolvable mystery and wonder. Its revised form of Jane Taylor's "Star" would begin like this:

> "Twinkle, twinkle, giant star,
> I know exactly what you are,
> An incandescent ball of gas
> Condensing to a solid mass.

> "Twinke, twinkle, giant star,
> I need not wonder what you are,
> For seen by spectroscopic ken,
> You're helium and hydrogen."

So by that inquiry God is resolved into a myth. Jesus becomes a bedtime story fit for the race's childhood, and man is told, "You, my dear sir, are nothing but a chemical formula."

There is only one valid method of inquiry—for the Festus of yesterday or to-day. Try it. Try living on the hypothesis that Jesus' revelation of God the Father is true and that his way of life leads into the largest values. That experience will yield *facts* on which to build life.

❧ ❧ ❧

VITAL RELIGION

With a sense of what is vital in religion.—*Rom. 2. 18* (Moffatt).

THIS is Doctor Moffatt's translation of the words rendered in the King James version, "approvest the things that are more excellent." The phrase is put forward in Romans as one of the chief glories of the Jew in his religious heritage.

What a chief glory it is in Christian faith and experience, "a sense of what is vital in religion"! It is surely one of the highest endowments of mind and personality—an instinct for the essential, a discernment between the incidental and the living heart. Indeed, most of the evils, the blunders, the failures of the church through all history have come from a tragic absence of just this sense of the vital. The days when the church has specialized in irrelevancies have been the Dark Ages, no matter at what date they have appeared on the calendar.

What a gift for our confused day this would be —a wide acquirement of this high power of discerning the vital in religion! It is true that the longer the course of Christian history the greater the need for this sense, for the obvious reason that there are more accumulations to discriminate between; in the long years of its history Christianity, like a river, has made vast accumulations from the territory and years through which it has passed. Some of these accretions are true wealth; some are impediments. They are of many kinds, forms, organizations, formulations of beliefs, made at different periods. Without a keen sense of the **vital,** we are hopelessly encumbered with accumulations and are unfitted for the battle of faith to win the world.

We need, especially in America perhaps, to be on our guard against an external and superficial understanding of this over-worked word "vital." Vitality is frequently confused with vehement action. People who externalize their restlessness or energy are regarded as "vital." As a matter of fact, they may be merely noisy or fidgety. A man may have plenty of vitality and yet keep still. By the same token, he may be exuberantly noisy and have little real vitality. American "vitality" often expresses itself in terms of speeding automobiles, of crowds, speeches, drives, slogans.

The vital in religion is not the elaborate or the spectacular or the noisy. It is the essential source of life. It resides in the elements without which religion dies or becomes paralyzed.

Jesus' revelation of God is a vital center of the Christian religion. The truth that God is Christlike is, as Bishop Francis J. McConnell insists in *The Christlike God*, the vital center of the Christian faith. Everything in the Christian tradition must be brought to that test.

Likewise the central thing in our religion is the person of Jesus, not any theory about him. Theology has often missed this point. Jesus sometimes has been made a figure without life or beauty. As Dr. Herbert Gray has said, "He is used as a support for difficult and involved terms, such as 'the Incarnate Deity,' 'Very God of Very God,' 'the Logos,' 'the Second Person in the Trinity.' He is made the central figure in a transaction called the 'atonement,' to which many differing theories attach themselves. The central thing is the person of Jesus, and what matters more than anything else is to see him and know him, and then to love him."

Jesus' way of life, his ethics as incarnated in his person and life, are vital in Christianity. Almost everything conceivable has been substituted for this. Wearied with the substitution of superfine spirituality for the elementary business of Christian living, John Wesley cried out in his Journal:

My soul is sick of this sublime divinity. Let me think and speak as a little child! Let my religion be plain, artless, simple! Meekness, temperance, patience, faith, and love be my highest gifts; and let the highest words wherein I teach them be those I learn from the Book of God!

Sharing Jesus' compassionate sacrificial sympathy with the whole human brotherhood and all human need is a vital part of Christianity. Professor Blakie had it:

"On me nor Priest nor Presbyter nor Pope,
    Bishop nor Dean may stamp a party name;
But Jesus, with his largely human scope,
    The service of my human life may claim.
Let prideful priests do battle about creeds,
The church is mine that does most Christlike deeds."

ENDURANCE PRODUCES CHARACTER

Endurance produces character.—*Rom. 5. 4* (Moffatt).

Both these translations bring to light a larger principle of life than the more familiar words "tribulation worketh patience." "Patience" covers a much smaller area of the moral life than "character"; and "endurance," likewise, has a much larger significance as a way of life than the more detailed and specific word "tribulations."

As here translated, there is a truth as indisputable as the law of gravitation or the law of harvest, and as large as life itself. It is the law of harvest in the moral and spiritual realm. Character is the accumulated result of a long-period investment. It is not a mysterious "gift," as lawless and irrational as the gift of a fairy godmother in Grimm's Fairy Tales. It is not a mushroom which springs up after a summer rain. It is not produced by a clever trick, like the manipulation of a sleight-of-hand performer. Character comes from endurance, from fortitude. As Booker T. Washington said finely, "Character is the sum of all we struggle against."

Insistence on this great law of moral growth is always necessary, but never perhaps has it had a greater timeliness and urgency than to-day. For "endurance," to say the least, is not one of the favorite ideals of a large section of our generation. To escape the discipline of endurance has become the chief end of man. To substitute the short-cut, the clever evasion, for the hard and grueling discipline of obedience is the vogue of the moment. On the other hand, character to-day seems to many a prize of doubtful value, hardly worth the painful and costly striving of the years. To multitudes in the full flush of the gospel of self-expression, character is no longer life's pearl of great price, but a tarnished jewel left over from quaint Victorian days. So both the ripe fruit of character and its rigorous method of production have been discounted.

A popular mood of the hour is the exaltation of cleverness. Let a thing be bright enough, modish enough, and in the dazzle its moral quality is overlooked as inconsequential. As has been said of a certain section of British society on the Riviera, "They have no God and Michael Arlen is their prophet." This sort of cleverness as an ideal of life is the very opposite of what Paul here terms endurance or fortitude.

It is no wonder that this cult of the flashing, the stimulating, the superficial smartness has resulted in a lack of *staying power*. Without fortitude, endurance, staying power, life consists of many dashing starts and futile abandonments. Arnold Bennett says of novel-writing, "*Anybody* can write a good *first* chapter." Then comes the really difficult time for the conscientious writer. Then it is that if there is to be any character it must come through endurance. To carry life through to the working out of any significant plot, to the growth of any ripe fruit, the same quality of endurance must find play.

Lines of least resistance are lines leading away from character. The substitution of pleasure for discipline as the end of all our seeking, inevitably makes thin souls. There are not enough rigid vertebræ in the backbone to support a full soul. The shriveled fruit of pleasure and the emptiness of its rewards is well described in Robert B. Hamilton's famous lines:

"I walked a mile with Pleasure;
    She chattered all the way.
But I am none the wiser
    For all she had to say.

"I walked a mile with Sorrow,
    And ne'er a word said she.
But, oh, the things I learned from her,
    When Sorrow walked with me!"

The painful superficiality of many lives to-day comes from the unlearned lessons that fortitude, in the face of hard and rough conditions, depends on tribulation, endurance for the sake of a great ideal. It is disturbing to think of the appalling extent to which the rugged school of character described with such warm sincerity, born of personal experience, by Richard Hovey, has dropped out of millions of lives:

"Thank God for poverty
    That makes and keeps us free.
And lets us go our unobtrusive way,
Glad of the sun and rain,
Upright, serene, humane,
Contented with the fortune of a day."[1]

We cannot artificially create the material environment of other days which so often ministered to the growth of character by endurance, a ministration not produced by our present environment. But we can do much so to kindle the aspiration for Christian character that endurance and fortitude

[1] Copyright by Dodd, Mead & Company, Inc., publishers. Used by permission.

against all the withering influences of modern life
will seem overwhelmingly worth while.

✿ ✿ ✿

GOD WORKS WITH THOSE WHO LOVE HIM

We know also that those who love God, those who
have been called in terms of his purpose, *have his aid and
interest in everything.—Rom. 8. 28* (Moffatt).

We know that in everything *God works with those who
love him* (Goodspeed).

It is doubtful whether any fresh rendering of a
New Testament text brings more light and prac-
tical help than these translations of Moffatt and
Goodspeed of this great verse of Romans.

One of the hardest texts in the New Testament
for many to understand and believe has undoubtedly
been Romans 8. 28, "We know that all things work
together for good to them that love God." No
doubt the difficulties of the text have been largely
due to faulty exegesis. But the difficulties have
been there. Few texts have been more often
preached upon, and it is a rather rare experience
to hear a satisfactory sermon on the text.

The usual tendency is to claim too much. And
the result very often has been to read into
Paul's statement a superficial optimism which does
not face the hard and tragic facts of sorrow and
sin. The text has been interpreted to mean that
everything in the world is for the best—a doctrine
scarcely, if at all, above the line of an unchristian,
pagan fatalism. Both Moffatt and Goodspeed

express the meaning of this great word of Paul's in terms that avoid an easy misreading of superficial optimism and fatalism.

"Those who love God have his aid and interest in everything."

"In everything God works with those who love him." Here is a comforting faith to the highest degree, which looks full in the face the whole of life, with all its tragedy and evil, which does not palsy the nerve of effort, but energizes for great endeavor.

This great word—so rendered—meets a characteristic unfaith of our time, the feeling, sometimes unconscious and unexpressed, that God has forgotten the universe and the race that he created, that he stands impassably outside of its whirling, its struggles, its agony, a sort of absentee designer. This mood has been expressed with terrible vividness by Thomas Hardy in his poem, "God Forgotten."

"I towered far, and lo! I stood within
　　The presence of the Lord Most High,
Sent thither by the sons of Earth, to win
　　Some answer to their cry.

"'The Earth, sayest thou? The Human race?
　　By me created? Sad its lot?
Nay: I have no remembrance of such a place:
　　Such world I fashioned not.'

"'O Lord, forgive me when I say
　　Thou spakest the word and made it all.'
'The Earth of men—let me bethink me. . . . Yea!
　　I dimly do recall

"'Some tiny sphere I built long back
  (Mid millions of such shapes of mine)
So named. . . . It perished, surely—not a wrack
  Remaining, or a sign?

"'It lost my interest from the first,
  My aims therefore succeeding ill;
Haply it died of doing as it durst.'
  'Lord, it existeth still.'"[1]

Against the freezing conception of a God who "dimly recalls" his strange creation stands, as the only foundation which makes life sane or tolerable, this warm living faith of Paul's—"We have his aid and interest in everything."

PUTTING AFFECTION INTO YOUR LOVE

Put affection into your love.—Rom. 12. 10 (Moffatt).

In other words, learn to *like* people as well as to love them in a formal sense.

The best commentary on the meaning of these words, which here look a trifle redundant but are not so, is the marvelous 16th chapter of Romans which is at once Saint Paul's catalogue of heroes and friendship. For in that chapter his heart reaches out to a score of people in divine love and warm human affection. Read it in the Authorized and Revised versions, in Moffatt, Goodspeed and Weymouth. Then you will know better what Paul means by "putting affection into your love" than you could learn in any other manner.

---

[1] The Macmillan Company, publishers. Used by permission.

There we feel intensely that Paul did not merely love such people as "Rufus, that choice Christian, and his mother who has been a mother to me," because they were of the same faith and church as himself. He *liked* them; he had an outrushing human affection for them. It was not love as a theological virtue but love as a human joy and necessity.

The shade of meaning which "affection" puts into the word "love" is necessary to the full meaning of love as used in the New Testament.

It is very possible and common to have love for other people chiefly as a kind of abstract theological virtue. That kind of a correct formal attitude may have a genuine desire to help others and to serve them with sacrificial cost and yet preserve at the same time a feeling of aloofness touched even with a certain condescension and contempt. That is the ever-present danger of missionary work at home and abroad. We may love our fellow men without any affectionate liking. But in doing so we miss two things—we miss half the fun of life and we miss the true Christian attitude and relationship to men.

Of this frigid relationship Emerson writes with keenness,

When I have attempted to give myself to others by services it proved an intellectual trick—no more. They eat your service like apples and leave you out. But love them and they feel you, and delight in you all the time.

Whitman puts the positive ideal of human affection filling up the formal attitude of love—

"Behold, I do not give lectures or a little charity.
When I give I give myself."

Even more so did Paul. And Jesus.

The bonds of the church often set loosely and ineffectually because there is not that human grasp of heart to heart pictured here and in Romans 16. Members of the same church are often merely cordial strangers, sometimes even that description is a hope rather than an exact description. And a fellowship of cordial, tolerant strangers will never become that miracle, a church of Jesus Christ. Only where the Christian virtue of love flowers into human affection ardent enough to overcome all repellent rough edges can there be generated the vehement flame which will fuse humanity into a brotherhood.

MAINTAIN THE SPIRITUAL GLOW

Maintain the spiritual glow.—Rom. 12. 11 (Moffatt).

THESE four words are a great poem. There are color and fire and music in them. They should never be analyzed and killed by neat, precise, homiletical partitions. The one, two, three, homiletical tradition is too often like picking the petals from a flower—murder for the sake of dissection.

Baker Brownell makes one of the best illuminations of this text in words written without any thought of the text at all. "Life is not the wick or the candle. It is the *burning*."

Stephen Graham, in his *With the Russian Pilgrims Jerusalem*, describes the receiving of the Sacred Fire, which for many of the pilgrims is the crown of their pilgrimage.

Once they have received it, they seek to carry the pure flame back with them to their homes, and to "treasure as they would the water of life or the philosopher's stone." That is, of course, no easy matter. "It is often a difficult matter keeping the lamp a-burning all the way, through rain and tempest, and through stress of circumstances on the road. Some Russian writer will perhaps collect one day stories of the Adventures of the Sacred Fire; it would be a piece of national literature."[1]

The keeping of the sacred fire has already become an international literature. For this great injunction is not merely an ideal but a world-wide experience. Paul lived, as well as pictured, the possibility of having the spirit of Christ which makes the whole life glow; not merely past history but present experience.

The difficulties of the Russian peasants in carrying the lighted candle back home, "through rain and tempest," have a close parallel in the spiritual life. It is the highest of all fine arts to keep the spiritual glow from dimming—to keep the candle from being snuffed out, by gusts that blow from all directions, chilling winds of indifference or hot blasts of passion. It is not merely the task of sheltering the flame, but kindling new fire to maintain the glow.

It cannot be done by a false or overstrained emotionalism or sentimentalism. The spiritual glow

---

[1] The Macmillan Company, publishers. Used by permission.

can be maintained only by contact of the soul with the life of God which first brought light, warmth, and power into the life.

The alternative to maintaining the spiritual glow must inevitably be a dying fire, a hearthstone of the heart and mind filled with embers. In *Penguin Island*, Anatole France describes a freezing globe, such as was foretold by the now discarded nebular hypothesis of our planet's origin. In that picture we see in imagination the last forlorn man shivering over a pile of dying embers and the disappearance with him of all life and hope. It is a true picture of a freezing world on which the glow of faith has been allowed to die. It is also a true picture of an individual life when the candle of the Spirit of God has flickered out.

It is the sustained glow of a living religious experience which preserves life from the destructiveness of that plague so malignant to life's happiness and highest uses—boredom. When the glow which a living faith brings to life is gone a baffled sense of futility creeps into the heart in its place. That empty place which might be filled with a real religious experience is the explanation of much of the restlessness and disillusionment characteristic of our day.

This boredom is well summed up by a London physician quoted by G. A. Studdert-Kennedy. Through the dull roar of London traffic, as it floated in through the open window, the surgeon said quietly:

After all, the greatest of human miseries, the most deadly of diseases is one we cannot touch with the knife or save men from by drugs.

"What do you mean?" I said, "cancer?"

"Oh, no," he replied; "we'll get that little devil yet. I mean—boredom. There is more real wretchedness, more torment driving men to folly, or to what you parsons call sin, due to boredom than there is to anything else. Men and women will do almost anything to escape it; they drink, drug themselves, prostitute their bodies, and sell their souls; they will take up mad causes, organize absurd crusades, fling themselves into lost hopes and crazy ventures; they will torment themselves and torture other people to escape the misery of being bored. Any-one who discovered a cure for that would put an end to more tragedy and misery than all of us doctors and physicians put together."

Jesus Christ has discovered the cure. In the enlistment of the heart in a great affection for God and man, he keeps life's powers occupied and alive in the warm kindling glow of the presence of God.

❧ ❧ ❧

RALLY ROUND ME!

Rally round me by praying to God.—*Rom. 15. 30* (Moffatt).

Every day is Rally Day on the Christian's calendar.

This plea of Paul's voices one of the deepest needs of life—that of re-enforcement through other wills and hearts. It pictures one of the largest services we can render in life—that of being the supporting battalion, without which the best powers of some other life would never find expression or be brought to fruition.

Paul's own life is perhaps the finest demonstration of this truth which could be found. His battles were won not only by his own daring, intrepid spirit and forceful thrust, but by the auxiliary troops who "rallied round him" and made his best achievements possible. No one ever recorded more joyously or gratefully his dependence on a glorious and sometimes nameless company of people who could rally royally: "Onesiphorus, who often refreshed me"; "Andronicus and Juinas, fellow prisoners"; "Fortunatus and Achaicus—they refresh my spirit as they do your own, you should appreciate men like that"; "the brothers beside me."

So the tale runs on. He was ten times himself from the multiplication of personal power through rallying friendship.

It is not merely in prayer, with which this particular request is linked, but in the whole bearing and attitude that we really turn the tide of battle in another's life. Many a man and woman whose modesty and humility would prevent them from using the boast of Galahad,

> "My strength is as the strength of ten
> Because my heart is pure,"

would nevertheless gladly and gratefully cry "My strength is as the strength of ten, because it is literally the strength of ten who rallied around me."

The hours for rallying to another's need are varied S O S hours, even though no shrill call is ever sent out! There are the hour of adversity and

the often more fateful hour of prosperity; the hour
of the loneliness of grief and the equally needy hour
marked by the thronging of crowded popularity;
the dark day when one has failed to live up to his
best; when one has slunk to the rear or run up the
white flag; or when one has courageously taken a
Christian position far in advance of the majority and
the hue and cry of condemnation arises; or when
one sails by the siren voices of prudence which bid
him haul down the belligerent flag of a fighting
faith—all the hundred shifting fluctuations of the
battle of life.

Have we ever mastered the technique of rallying, that fine dexterity of love which, without pre-
sumption or magisterial dogmatism, can re-enforce
the heart and mind of another?

Have we ever mastered that particular brand of
the art of rallying mentioned by Paul—rallying
round in prayer—that rare art of Secret Service?

PARTY CRIES

I beg of you all to drop these *party-cries.*—*1 Cor. 1. 10*
(Moffatt).

THIS expression, "party cries," gives a very different impression from that of the translation in
the Authorized Version—"I beseech you . . . that ye
all speak the same thing." Those words, "that
you all speak the same thing," have been used as
though Paul were enjoining a deadening uniformity;
as though he were urging the Corinthians all to

chant the same form of words, thus saddling a hopelessly literalistic and mechanical conception of Christianity on the church. The whole spirit of Paul's First Epistle to the Corinthians is opposed to this conception and Moffatt's substitution of the words "party cries" makes such a misleading interpretation of Paul's thought impossible. The meaning is amplified by the rest of the verse: "There must be no cliques among you; you must retain your *common temper and attitude*."

Paul was not pleading for the unvarying repetition of any shibboleth; he was not setting up any superficial or mechanical test of orthodoxy. He was warning against the fatal results of a divisive, fighting partisanship.

No one needs to labor the point that this plea, "Drop these party cries," has been needed and has been forgotten all through Christian history, or how it is needed and is so often forgotten today.

It is the eternal danger of the substitution of the lesser loyalty for the greater; of the burning of a hotter devotion to a segment of a thing than to the whole thing, or to the shadow of a thing rather than to the thing itself.

It is one of the crowning ironies of history that every great truth of Christianity and every institution which it brought to the world to be a great welding, uniting bond for humanity has been perverted at some time or other into a divisive party cry—a jagged, barbed-wire fence.

The incarnation, the atonement, even the doctrine of the Fatherhood of God, the sacrament of the Lord's Supper, baptism—all these divine harmon-

izing, unifying ideas—have been made the hoarse,
polemical shouts of fratricidal warfare.

It is a vicious thing to attach the primitive,
unreflective emotions of partisanship to Christian
truth.　It substitutes the lust of battle for the
love of truth and the love of God.　It substitutes
the joy of breaking heads for the joy of winning
hearts.

In the business of shouting party cries the distinctively Christian virtues are lost.　Humility,
meekness, long-suffering, peace-making, forgiveness
—what place have these essential Christian traits
in a partisan clamor and fight?　What could be
possibly gained for Christ if these, the indispensable
marks of Christ, are lost?

All party cries drown the still small voice of God.

Over the centuries comes the clear voice:
"Brothers, for the sake of our Lord Jesus Christ,
I beg you all to drop these party cries?"

THWARTING THE SHREWD

"I will thwart the *shrewdness of the shrewd!*"—*1 Cor.*
1. 19 (Goodspeed).

THIS is an "American" translation which is very
disrespectful to a popular American ideal and idol.
"Shrewdness" is not an exclusively American trait.
The prophet quoted here was speaking to Hebrews
and they have acquired at least the beginnings of
a reputation for "shrewdness."　But the shrewd
man, the fellow who "beats the game," who out-

wits the other with a clever ruse, the sharp trader, the money-maker, is the hero of a large and reverent multitude among us to-day. It is a trait which rates high in a commercial civilization. Many of the largest fortunes are made, not by any production of new goods or additions to the world's welfare, but simply by shrewdness in manipulating the labor of others and goods produced by others.

But shrewdness does not seem to rank so high with God.

Here he is pictured as saying that the big winnings of life do not go to the wise manipulators, to the shrewd.

"I will thwart the shrewdness of the shrewd."

To explore the truth of this word we do not need to think of God as confounding the best laid schemes of the nimble witted. It is rather the truth that the shrewd schemers for self-advantage are thwarted by the spiritual laws of God's universe which cannot be altered and cannot be beaten.

The very maxims in which this ideal of selfish calculation are expressed are specious lies.

"He travels fastest who travels alone"—a shrewd observation on life, surely! Yes? But what of it? He never gets anywhere except to a lonely desert. The lone speeder in life misses its chief point, which is the fellowship of love and labor along the road. This was the motto of the priest and the Levite who passed hurriedly by on the other side of the road in the story of the good Samaritan. They made good speed and missed life. God thwarted the shrewdness of the shrewd.

"He who fights and runs away lives to fight another day." Innumerable inglorious retreats have been

conducted under this bright shining banner. It seems the quintessence of prudence. It is. It is also the motto of all the cowards in the world. It is also a lie. For "he who fights and runs away" may live a good many days but he doesn't live to fight. The habit of running away becomes ingrained and he spends his life in a dreary succession of shuffling evasions. He never knows the fun of a good fight. He is thwarted by his own shrewdness.

Life's deepest insight does not come from cleverness but from love.

THE HUNDRED PER-CENTER

The spiritual man is *alive to all true values.*—*1 Cor. 2. 15* (Goodspeed).

HERE is the real One Hundred Per-Center—the man alive to *all* true values.

The phrase, "one hundred per-center," has had many trivial and cheap associations and uses in our day. It has been used in the interests of racial and national prejudice and intolerance.

Contrasted to such use is Paul's picture of life at One Hundred Per Cent—a personality sensitive to every sort of true worth, with every human power developed for use.

The sentence holds a fine definition of the spiritual man. It corrects a very common conception of a "spiritual man" as an essentially weak man. There has grown up a very frequent idea of "spirituality" as a deliberate retreat from large areas of life, coupled with a sort of disdainful attitude to common human interest and enjoyments, concentrating on a rather abstract and obscure virtue known as "spirituality." There has been much in the monastic practices of Christianity which furnishes a foundation for this idea.

The spiritual man is not the one alive to only partial values, not one who wears blinders shutting off a large portion of the human scene. He is one fully alive.

As opposed to this full-sided life of the man alive to the spiritual world as well as to the material, the fractional life is paralyzed. The sensory nerves of a man living a fractional life are alive on one side, or part of one side only, like those of a person injured on one side of the brain.

Such "paralyzed" souls are common. How many Peter Bells there are, for instance, who can see yellow primroses and catalogue them efficiently, if necessary, but are dead to any magic a primrose might work on the imagination!

Others are paralyzed so far as being alive to the values of the common fellowship of life is concerned.

Others are *dead to intangible, unponderable ideals.* They are blunt to the moral "feel" of things. Mr. A. G. Gardiner, in his sketch of Lord Birkenhead, gives a picture of a man dead to many intangible values:

The note of Lord Birkenhead's political life is the note of an easy flippancy. As the graces of youth vanish his bankruptcy of the deeper wisdom of affairs and of the disinterested attachment to a considered philosophy of government becomes more apparent. Perhaps he had too early and too intoxicating a success. His brains, as Lady Oxford wittily remarked, went to his head.[1]

How true that may be of Lord Birkenhead we cannot and do not need to judge. It is a fair picture of a large number of people.

Others are not *alive to God*. In Emily Dickinson's fine phrase they have "lost the Face that made existence home."

The word "half-wit" is much used in these days, in a flippant contemptuous manner. There is a real "half-wit," however. Our wits include the faculty for coming into the knowledge and experience of God. When we allow that faculty to become atrophied we are living on only a part of our wits. We are not alive to the highest of life's values.

GOD'S FARM

You are *God's farm.*—*1 Cor. 3. 9* (Goodspeed).

"GOD's farm" has exactly the same meaning as the words, "God's husbandry," of the Authorized Version. But "farm" is much more of a colloquial word. It is a part of the daily speech and life of all—the very theater of life for millions of people, and, by so much, the word brings Paul's great figure of speech more immediately and arrestingly to our minds.

---

[1] *Portraits and Portents*. Harper & Brothers, publishers. Used by permission.

It is a perfect metaphor—the soil of our personality made fruitful by the influences of heaven rained upon them. Commerce with the sky is the secret of the productive life.

The words bring to mind also the wide varieties of "farms" God has to work upon. Some are as fertile and luxuriant as an opulent river bottom. Some are like the slanting field of a New England mountainside, full of bowlders, with a thick crust almost impervious to rain and sunshine, which grudgingly yields only a scrubby, scraggly growth. On some of God's farms the soil is exhausted; life is never replenished. On others the weeds have strangled any useful growth.

You are God's farm. What kind of a farm does He have?

NOT ENGROSSED

Let those who mix in the world live as if they were not *engrossed* in it.—*1 Cor. 7. 31* (Moffatt).

Not *absorbed* in it (Goodspeed).

THE Authorized Version renders this text, "use this world, as not *abusing* it." Goodspeed and Moffatt bring out quite a different shade of meaning.

The word "abusing" suggests the waster, perhaps the profligate, who makes perverted use of life's powers and possessions. He "abuses" the world; does not use it reverently; makes it minister to wrong purposes.

The words, "Let those who mix in the world live

as if they were not engrossed in it," bring to mind an entirely different problem and bring a message to an entirely different need and class of people.

Most of us are far more in danger of being engrossed and absorbed in the world than we are of abusing it. The person who runs the risk of being engrossed in the material world is not only the waster; he is the eminently solid substantial respectable citizen. He is all of us, who in the multitude of interests, none of them perverse in themselves, allow the life of the spirit and the task of the kingdom of God to be pushed out of sight into a corner.

A GIFT FOR BABEL

To another the power of *discriminating between prophetic utterances.*—*1 Cor. 12. 10* (Weymouth).

THIS promised gift of the power of discriminating between prophetic utterances is a boon for a civilization of Babel. To "try" the prophets is hard at the best, when conflicting philosophies, cults, and gospels clash in the market place. The difficulty is magnified a thousandfold in the clamor of prophets to-day. The most characteristic feature of the present city architecture is the tower. The Woolworth and Singer Towers dominate the skyline of New York; the Tribune and Wrigley Towers of Chicago; other towers rise up to mark and symbolize other cities. They are all only too reminiscent of their great forerunner, the Tower of Babel. Like the original Babel, they signify confusion; not merely the superficial confusion of the clash of a score of languages but the deeper, more fundamental confusion of the uproar of competitive prophets and prophecies bidding for popular following.

For prophecy, in the large sense of the interpretation of life, is a national industry. If all the practitioners of the art, busily engaged in proclaiming, "This is the way, walk ye in it," should take out a union card in The Amalgamated Prophets' Union, the craft would become one of the considerable factors in the American Federation of Labor.

We have the Prophets of Doom, a flourishing order. The Dark Ages are upon us. Inexorable laws are steadily working out our destruction. Different sects of this great order specialize on different varieties of coming catastrophes. The Spengler School takes up the rôle of Gibbon and describes the Decline and Fall of Western Civilization. Wiggam specializes on heredity and portrays the race going to seed. The Nordic school of prophecy fills the air with laments over the color scheme. The resulting "Literature of Despair" is enormous.

On the other hand, we have the order of Saint Pollyanna, with its anthem of praise to the best of all possible worlds, in which we live. We do not pay much attention to Saint Polycarp in these days; but Saint Pollyanna is very much with us. Captains of Industry are her special devotees. Everything is for the best so long as dividends flow steadily for God's chosen children.

To enumerate even a portion of the contending

prophets would call for an appraisal of the whole thought world of our time. We have the prophets inveighing against democracy, a cult which makes such surpassingly strange bedfellows as Dean Inge, Mussolini, and H. L. Mencken. We have the prophets of self-expression, as the chief end of life (whether there is any self worth expressing or not); the prophets of contempt; the prophets of materialism, eternally reading the funeral service over religion.

What a gift, then, is this promised power of discrimination!

How may we discriminate? Is there any surer basis than fear, wishing, prejudice, or popular majority?

Paul's basis was to bring all interpretations to the test of the purpose of God as revealed in Jesus Christ. He approached the world and life with that as the key to their meaning and mystery. With that key he was, to use his own phrase, employed in another connection, "unafraid with any amazement."

That same test of the clamorous prophets in the world to-day is our possession. We can ask of every "prophetic utterance" the question—"Does its interpretation of life accord with God's purpose revealed in Christ?" With that starting point we can learn from all the literature of despair whatever it may have of instruction and warning, without being engulfed in a pagan fatalism and without being led off into blind alleys.

❧ ❧ ❧

THE CHEMISTRY OF CHRISTIANITY

We have all been *saturated* with one Spirit.—*1 Cor. 12. 13* (Goodspeed).

THIS translation which Doctor Goodspeed makes of the words rendered, "We are all baptized into one body," in the Authorized Version, gives a much more vital insight into the nature of the Christian experience.

Baptized is in the realm of physics. *Saturated* is in the realm of *chemistry*. The transformation of personality by saturation with the Spirit of Christ is far more like a chemical change that it is like a physical, mechanical operation. Baptism may be an outward, mechanical, rather superficial affair. Saturation, the infusing of the whole mind and heart with the attitude and outlook and purpose of Christ, is inward, complete.

The word "saturation" also preserves another fine insight. It makes clear that the Christian life cannot be divided into compartments. Faith in Christ is not something added to life, like an extra room built onto a house. It is something which penetrates all of life, as the sea is saturated with salt.

ORGANIZATION—SERVANT OR MASTER?

By God's appointment there are in the church . . . powers of organization.—*1 Cor. 12. 28* (Weymouth).

IT is worth more than a passing notice that in this classic list of God's gifts to the church, which Paul draws up, the power of organization comes *seventh.* Of course the significance of this ranking must not be pressed too far. Very probably the apostle Paul was not drawing up such a list with any idea of ranking the different gifts in the order of their importance in his mind. It should always be remembered that Paul did not write theological treatises; he wrote letters. The list cannot be rightly taken as expressing his exact comparative valuation of the gifts of the Spirit.

Nevertheless, here is mention of eight gifts to the church which flash to his mind, while he is emphasizing the diversity of service. And of these eight gifts six come to mind before "powers of organization." Only one, the "gift of tongues," comes after it.

Surely, this is worth reading in an age sorely tempted to exalt organization to the place of first importance. Put this fact in glaring and frankly exaggerated form: We often rank organization first. Paul ranked it *seventh.*

Committees, bureaus, boards, secretaries, budgets, drives, publicity—these are the background and foreground of so much ecclesiastical activity. As someone has said overlooking the scene, "The cry of the churches to-day is not so much 'Save the world' as 'Raise the budget.'" An age of machinery demands a new metaphor. We could sing most properly, not, "Like a mighty army," but

> "Like a mighty *engine*
> Moves the Church of God."

The pistons plunge back and forth, the wheels interlock, the whistle screams, the organization moves.

The danger of all this, of course, is that it may blind us to the fact that the Christian life is a *biological function*, not a *mechanical* one. "Ye must be *born* again." "In him was *life*." The things which come first in Paul's list of gifts are those having to do essentially with the communication of life—apostles, prophets, teachers. These are supreme. When they are present other things, such as miraculous powers, organization, supplement helpfully. But they are not indispensable. To fall into the delusion that they are of first importance is, in the literal sense of the word, insanity. It turns the whole genius of Christianity upside down.

To-day bodies of Christians are depending on organization for things it can never produce any more than an automobile engine can give birth to an orchard.

To realize this is not to disparage the value of organization or administration. Paul counts it a distinct spiritual gift. But he keeps it in its place —seventh!

The irony of great mechanical achievement is that the machine becomes the master of its creator instead of its slave. This has been the history of the industrial development of the nineteenth and twentieth centuries. The machine comes as a labor-saving benefactor and then a new slavery develops, in which men are forced to tend the machine in a deadening monotony of standardized motion.

That same calamity threatens the church, that as the machine grows greater and more complex the task of keeping it going grows more and more

insistent and engrossing, until the machine itself
demands the greater part of the church's energies
and the purpose it was designed to serve is obscured
or forgotten.

The real source of a church's life and power is
not in the engine or boiler room in the basement;
it is in the prayer room and sanctuary. It is in
lives that have the life of the Master. As it is
strongly put by A. E. Zimmern:

> The long history of European Christianity, if it ever
> comes to be written, will be the history of a submerged
> and hidden movement—the tracing of the course of a
> pure but tenuous stream of living water which has re-
> freshed the souls of innumerable men and women who
> have penetrated to its secret recesses, but has but seldom
> emerged into the open, to flow through the broad and
> dusty cities where the world's main activities are carried
> on.

THE BIG PARADE

Love makes no parade.—*1 Cor. 13. 5* (Moffatt).

To make any change in the wording of the thirteenth chapter of First Corinthians seems like a
sacrilege. The cadences and the music of this
great masterpiece of divine poetry have a place
in the world's heart that is unique. It will ever
remain undisturbed.

At first thought, then, it would seem that here is
a portion of the New Testament where no new translation can render any service. Yet the fact is that

it is right here that the renderings of Moffatt, Weymouth, and Goodspeed are particularly rich in suggestive insights. They are not intended to be used as substitute versions but as interpretative comments. So used, they present details and expressions which lead us into new appreciation of the chapter, like the play of fresh sunbeams on a tower of jewels.

This particular translation of Doctor Moffatt, "Love makes no parade," has a veritable touch of genius in the use of the word "parade." It is hard to imagine any word which would so clearly and picturesquely express the very opposite of the true spirit of love. It expresses vividly the subtle egotism which is so often alloyed with love or even substituted entirely for it and yet passes for the real thing. Making a parade is a gratification of the insidious and deeply planted desire for self-display; the concern for getting personal credit in every action and relationship. When the parade instinct is let loose the parade itself becomes the chief thing, and the distinctively Christian virtue of spontaneous, self-forgetful love is lost amid the fuss and feathers and display.

True love makes no parade. The person who parades his affection and benevolence always has at least one eye on the mirror, generally two. He is like the little bird with a white patch in his tail in Robert Frost's poem, in "North of Boston," which keeps flying from branch to branch in front of you and takes everything said as personal to himself.

The subtle danger is that when a parade of affection, whether in words, motions, or deeds, is staged, the parade exhausts the emotion. It satis-

fies with a premature substitute the real energy
of love which should expend itself in deeds and
not in formations and gestures.

That is true of a parade of personal affection.
It is almost always true that the more of an outward splurge there is, the less of deep sacrificial
love to the uttermost there is. It is true of benevolence. How easy it is to make a parade of service!
We can make it impressively in preambles and
resolutions and ringing declarations of sympathy.
These are innocent enough if they are only preambles. But they have a pernicious way of becoming the whole thing. When the parade is over,
all is over.

EAGER TO BELIEVE THE BEST

Love is . . . always *eager to believe the best.*—*1 Cor.
13. 7* (Moffatt).

VERY directly this word goes to the heart of one
of the commonest human failings. "Failing" is too
mild a word. It is a distinct and destructive vice.
A kind of appetite for bad news, a zest for calamities, a reluctance to put the best construction on
an incident or personality, crops out with appalling
frequency in human nature. Sometimes this degenerates into a ready ear for scandal, a delight in
evil report, a malignant enjoyment in talebearing
—a vice which receives the severest condemnation
in both the Old and New Testaments. But frequently it is not a simple matter of recognized evil.
It is a much more subtle tendency to persistent

pessimism in human relations, or a tendency to cynicism, a grudging unwillingness to kindle into generous faith in another's best powers and possibilities. It was an avowed cynic who reported, "There is something not entirely unpleasant to us in the misfortunes of our best friends." That is a slander upon human nature; and yet the crabbed and acid remark does preserve a rather accurate observation of queer twists of human minds. That disposition is the result of competitive feeling in regard to others and of an undisciplined egoism.

Doctor Moffatt's rendering, "eager to believe the best," adds an important meaning to the rendering of the original Greek text as "Love believeth all things." The rendering in the Authorized Version has often been mistakenly understood as praise of credulity; of an unsophisticated readiness to believe anything, a type of mind easily imposed upon, and therefore weak. That unfortunate trait is not what the apostle is praising as an attribute of real love. It is, rather, the "set" of the mind to believe the best possible, as soon as it is possible and as long as it is possible.

The priceless value of that quality of mind and soul is that such eager faith to believe the best is one of the greatest creative forces in life. Such love actually *creates* the best in others which it is eager to believe in. Such eagerness to believe the best is like the chemical solution which brings out the lights and shadows of a photographic plate or film. It was exactly in such a way that the eagerness of Jesus to believe the best of men brought out from the recesses of their personality powers which neither they nor others had ever suspected.

It is the steadfast persistence of this eagerness to believe the best of others which has made some of the most glorious history of the world possible. This history has been largely unwritten, buried deep in the secret recesses of the heart where character is developed. But it is the world's most important history nevertheless. For such persistent faith has acted on souls like the breath of spring-time sweeping over a garden, bringing out the buried power and beauty which could never emerge in a killing December climate of distrust.

In race and national relations there is no attitude of mind more supremely necessary than this eager love and faith to believe the best. It is the beginning of all wisdom in international and interracial relationships. It is so easy to give up this attitude of steadfast eagerness to believe the best and to slouch back into prejudices and contempts and fears and hysterics which demand no effort.

But that way lies madness. That way lies conflict and war. One of the worst things about war is that it generates a spirit in which any tendency to believe the best of other nations or races, with which tension points arise, is killed. It becomes a patriotic duty to believe the worst. Nothing seems to be too bad to believe of any "enemy" nation or an alien race, when fears or antipathies are played upon. This trait of eager faith, so absolutely essential to the kingdom of God, is obliterated.

❧ ❧ ❧

BLAZING AND BROODING

Nor irritable, nor mindful of wrongs.—*1 Cor. 13. 5*
(Weymouth).

HERE are two of the most destructive perversions
of emotion and imagination—the blazing of hot,
uncontrolled anger and the sullen nursing of injuries and wrongs. These are at the opposite ends
of the mental thermometer; they are the extremes
of the emotional register—anger is at the boiling
point, brooding down near the freezing point.
But they are about equally destructive, both to
the spirit which engages in them and those who
have to endure them.

Where love controls both blazing and brooding
no longer ravage.

Blazing anger, when aroused over some personal
slight or injury, is a sign of weakness frequently
mistaken for strength. It is not strength, but
power running loose. It is a disastrous explosion
touched off by the fuse of selfish sensitiveness. It
is a survival from undisciplined babyhood into an
undisciplined manhood. An adult in a sputtering
fit of anger is an exact physical picture of a baby
in a spasm of rage. And the interior of the head
is just as faithful a picture as the contortions and
color of the exterior. While the language of an
adult in an uncontrolled flame of anger is quite
different from the screams of the baby, the ultimate meaning is very often the same—"Somebody
took my rattle!"

A sullen, smoldering brooding over wrongs, either
real or imaginary, is like a fire which does not
blaze but runs underground. Or, to change the

figure of speech, it is like a poison, secreted in the heart and cherished there, which pervades one's whole being. Such a habit is far more of a calamity than any wrong in itself can possibly be. It gets to be a blighting preoccupation—unfitting one for a constructive part in the onward movement of life. It rapidly grows into an obsession, and the habit has probably unhinged more minds than any other cause.

Love, because it is the strongest thing in the world, cannot manifest itself in either of these weak and defeated reactions to life.

Love saves us both from blazing and brooding by focusing both of those capacities of human nature on new and nobler aspects. Both are perversions of high endowments of personality. To blaze in indignation, when it is a noble indignation like that of Moses over the oppression of his people, or Amos over the wrongs of the exploited poor, or Jesus over the violation of the Temple—to do that is to give exercise to one of the finest and most unselfish capacities of human nature. So it is with brooding, when the object of our meditation is not our own injuries or advantages, but some of the great themes and questions of life.

Love does not suppress these powers; it does not obliterate them. It directs them into a fresh channel. It redeems them. It transforms them from being a destructive fire or a slow poison by directing them to the accomplishment of high purposes.

❧ ❧ ❧

THE GIFT OF SILENCE

Love . . . knows *how to be silent.*—*1 Cor. 13. 7* (Weymouth).

THIS is Weymouth's translation of the words rendered in the Authorized and Revised Versions, "Love . . . beareth all things." It emphasizes the self-restraint of real love, which does not go about in a noisy harangue about its wrongs, does not shout its troubles through a megaphone. It is not filling the air with charges and incriminations against others. (Moffatt's translation is, "Love is . . . always *slow to expose.*") There are some people who play the part of a district attorney in life. They are full of charges and indictments. Against this resort to noise under trials and burdens, Paul etches this picture of a love which beareth all things in strong, serene, trustful silence.

That is the primary meaning of this picturesque rendering of Weymouth, "Love . . . knows how to be silent." Until one has learned that fine art he has not entered into the noble heritage of fully Christian self-command.

But the words are suggestive of other aspects of love—aspects which are not directly emphasized in the original translated by these words, but which are worthy of emphasis because they are profoundly true pictures of the insight of a sensitive, sympathetic love. The words, "Love . . . knows how to be silent," suggest the great variety of occasions when the supreme gift which love can bring is the sympathy and understanding which expresses itself in silence. There is vast true meaning in the phrase, "a healing silence." It frequently comes with a positive blessing like the stopping of a riveting machine.

It is one of the rarest refinements of sympathy which is able to discern occasions which call not for speech, however tender or eloquent, but for that deeper ministry and communication of heart possible only through silence. To recognize this is not to minimize the healing and creative gift of words. Anna Hempstead Branch has beautifully expressed this wonder of words:

> "God wove a web of loveliness,
>   Of clouds and stars and birds,
> But made not anything at all
>   So beautiful as words.
>
> "They shine around our simple earth
>   With golden shadowings,
> And every common thing they touch
>   Is exquisite with wings.
>
> "There's nothing poor and nothing small
>   But is made fair with them.
> They are the hands of living faith
>   That touch the garment's hem."[1]

Yet beyond and completing this divine art of words is the divine art of silence. A love that knows how to speak but does not know how to be silent has not entered the deepest places of human intercourse.

There are so many calls in life—mute, unspoken calls—for the love that knows how to be silent. They are as various as the many mysterious silences

---

[1] Houghton Mifflin Company, publishers. Used by permission.

of the natural world. These particular silences, each with a quality of its own, have been suggestively enumerated by Edgar Lee Masters in his poem, "Silence," in which he speaks of the "silence of the stars and sea, of the sick, of a great love, of a great hatred, of a spiritual crisis, of defeat" and of many other high hours of life.

This silence of love is not indifference; it is not merely poverty of something to say. It is a positive form of self-communication. Just as silence is needed to hear a watch ticking, so silence is the medium through which heart beats are heard.

There is the silence of love when someone makes a mistake, when a shallow soul would let loose a stream of comment and advice; the silence of grief, when any conventional stereotyped words are a noisy sacrilege; the silence of worship, of whose healing we have far too little in a vocal, chattering age; the silence of a parent when a child is making a decision and whose love restrains him from making the child's decision for him, and allows the child the great but glorious risk of growth; the silence of loving trust, which asks no hesitant questions even when baffled.

These are but a few moments of love at its best.

THE PAGEANTRY OF LIFE

He makes my life *a constant pageant* of triumph.—
2 Cor. 2. 14 (Moffatt).
He always leads me in *his triumphal train* (Goodspeed).

THESE translations make clear that Paul is using the imagery of the public triumph of a victorious Roman general in the streets of Rome. To his own life he applies the figure of such a glittering pageant. That word "pageant" does a large service, not only in making evident at first glance Paul's comparison, but also of emphasizing an element which so easily drops out of the Christian life— its pageantry, its richness, its triumphant power and victory.

It is a strange description of a life like Paul's— a pageant! This man who entered the very scene of these great triumphs of conquering war lords in chains? He limped along the road to Rome a prisoner where the conquerors had swung in resplendent chariots.

A pageant? A strange kind of a pageant, from his own description,

I have been often at the point of death; five times have I got forty lashes (all but one) from the Jews, three times I have been beaten by the Romans, once pelted with stones, three times shipwrecked, adrift at sea for a whole night and day; I have been often on my travels; I have been in danger from rivers and robbers, in danger from Jews and Gentiles; through dangers of town and of desert, through dangers on the sea, through dangers among false brothers—through labor and hardship, through many a sleepless night, through hunger and thirst, starving many a time, cold and ill-clad, and all the rest of it.

A queer pageant! No wonder Paul was told, on occasion, that he was beside himself. Yet who, considering realities, rather than upholstery and

spangles, would deny that he was using the words
of truth and soberness?

Call the roll of the conquerors who enacted the
pageants of Rome—Pompey and Cæsar, Anthony
and Augustus, Titus and Hadrian—call them all!
Which one of them, compared to the drama of
Paul, ever achieved anything more considerable than
the tinsel performance of a doll's theater?

Paul's pageant of life surpassed the triumphs of
the Forum just as the drama of "Hamlet" sur-
passes an exhibition of fireworks or a chariot race
in a circus. It moves in the realities of life rather
than its material accidents and incidents.

Paul's life was a real pageant of life because in
it was the play of divine, creative forces. "Christ
liveth in me"—that was life's pageant for Paul—
an energy that flowed from inexhaustible springs
in God, an opulence of fellowship divine and human.
That made every dingy prison into which he was
cast literally a throne room. There was also the
element of glorious action, the creation of a fellowship of people who have "tasted the powers of the
age to come." So in imagination he does not cross
the Roman Forum alone but there follow in his
train a company in whom Christ has been formed
—prophets, saints, apostles, martyrs—who are to
create a new world.

How many of us would describe our lives as "a
constant pageant of triumph"? Yet is that not
what they ought to be, literally and truly? We have
the same divine creative forces available for us as
found play in Paul's life. Our great loss is that
so often we allow this possible pageantry of life
to drop out of our minds and hearts.

It is a tragic anti-climax to life when, instead of a confident, erect triumph, progressing to new discoveries of the power and love of God, it becomes a pedestrian trudge "over the hills to the poorhouse." No matter how richly colored the trimmings of life may be, life is a parade to the poorhouse if its spiritual resources dwindle, if the realities of God's grace become frozen assets which are not available for daily use; if we face the oncoming bankruptcy of ideals and purposes and joy.

GOSPEL HUCKSTERS

We are not *fraudulent hucksters* of God's Message.— *2 Cor. 2. 17* (Weymouth).

I am no *peddler* of God's message (Goodspeed).

HUCKSTER—Peddler! The words echo with the street cries which float into our windows. Yet they give us the warm, present-day, colloquial equivalent of Paul's impassioned denial of the charges of insincerity made against his ministry. He was no traveling merchant of adulterated goods, trafficking with the name of Jesus for what he could get out of it. He was no peddler of second-hand stuff which he had picked up at a cheap price and passed on at a bargain. He was an apostle by the call and will of God, declaring at the cost of his whole life the full, uncorrupted gospel of Christ which he had first experienced in his own soul.

That word "huckster," which Paul throws so scornfully from his lips, is an uncomfortable one to

look at for every minister of God and every one
who speaks in his name or bears the name of Christ.
It is a challenging and rewarding word to study.
It gives us a glimpse, as of a sudden unsuspected
abyss, of the process by which a prophet and apostle may degenerate into a huckster and peddler.

There is a shade of meaning in the word "huckster" as used here which must be kept in mind, lest
we miss its chief point and do wrong to many who
are engaged in an honest and highly useful business
of retailing goods from house to house and town to
town.   Weymouth is careful to attach the adjective "fraudulent" to the noun "huckster."   It is the
peddler of corrupted and adulterated goods which
Paul had in mind.   The peddler did not have a
high reputation for honesty in the Roman Empire.
He was in a game of wits, and palming off inferior
stuff was usually part of the game.   That has been
one of the moral risks of the itinerant huckstering
business in all history.   The legend of the Yankee
peddler and his wooden nutmegs testifies that frequently his reputation for shrewdness far outranked
his reputation for trustworthiness.

In one sense Paul was a peddler of God's message.   He went from place to place, from house
to house, beseeching men, as Christ's envoy, that
they be reconciled to God.   What he rejected was
the idea of adulteration which was almost insepar-
ably associated with the peddler's trades.

How do we become "fraudulent hucksters" of
God's message?   Not often by deliberate choice.
It is far more subtle and insidious than that.

We become "gospel hucksters" *when we substitute anything else or anything less than the message*

of God in Christ. Paul never trimmed his message down to meet the antagonisms or prejudices or aversions of his audience. The message which brought him a stoning at Derbe was the very same message which he delivered later at Philippi and Ephesus, with prison and mob violence staring him in the face. Wherever and whenever he spoke he declared the real thing and the whole thing which he had received from Christ. Yet it should be emphatically noted that he never indulged the luxuriant feeling of the martyr complex.

Paul never became a court chaplain, serving up small portions of a diluted gospel adroitly denatured so as to be palatable. He knew where to draw the line between dignified courtesy and flattery. He never emphasized a part of the gospel, leaving the impression that it was the whole message.

All of these things are the chief stock-in-trade of gospel hucksters until the gospel of the Kingdom has so lost its life and bloom that it resembles the withered vegetables of an unscrupulous peddler.

Paul never offered substitutes for the gospel. A common form of huckstering to-day is the reliance on stunt and trick services of one sort and another; a giving up of relying on faith to move mountains of indifference and substituting a pathetic belief in little shovels. We have a large cult worshiping at the shrine of Saint Phineas—Phineas T. Barnum, the greatest showman on earth, apparently expecting a showman's tricks to accomplish what the sincere preaching of the gospel of the Son of God is unable to do. In a recent discussion of fiction Mrs. Edith Wharton has made an observation which applies with peculiar force to preaching.

"Too many writers," she says, "are forgetting that true originality consists not in a new manner but in a new vision."

A huckster is a trafficker in second-hand goods. He gets his stock from the producer and passes it on. It is not his own production—he is merely the jobber. We become mere peddlers of God's message when there is no prophetic passion; when we are merely following a trade or fulfilling an office, or when we glibly discourse on themes that have never become part of our inner life and experience.

It is easily possible for a minister or other Christian to become like a clerk in a travel bureau, who spends his days directing people how to go to the ends of the earth, but who himself has never traveled beyond his native county. It is all a matter of hearsay and time-tables to him. But it is never possible to impart the life of Christ unless that life is first our own.

A NEW TESTAMENT LIBERAL

For if I have a *liberal* share of Christ's sufferings' through Christ I have a liberal share of comfort too.— *2 Cor. 1. 5* (Goodspeed).

STEVENSON says that man does not live by bread alone but mostly by catchwords. One of the hardest working catchwords of our time is the word "liberal." It is a great and noble word, standing for an attitude and spirit indispensable to the progress of the kingdom of God. But it has also been seized upon as a catchword by many whose interest in religion is largely intellectual, who have lost the keen edge of the redemptive passion of Christ. It is that condition which has given rise to the phrase "an arid liberalism." Any liberalism can be perfectly arid if it exhausts itself in stating its position and working over its ideas.

Here in Second Corinthians is a glimpse of an indispensable kind of "liberalism," often forgotten in a war of words and labels—"a *liberal* share of Christ's sufferings."

Liberal ideas will never save the world. Only a liberal share in Christ's sufferings is adequate to form the redemptive agency needed for that task. This is a description of a true New Testament liberal, and unless twentieth-century liberalism preserves that quality it will be arid and sterile.

THE ART OF TACKLING

My mind is made up to *tackle* certain people.—*2 Cor. 10. 2* (Moffatt).

PAUL'S vigorous word, rendered here as *"tackle"* by Moffatt, gives a glimpse of one of the fine arts of Christian warfare, the art of tackling. It is no armchair enterprise.

Some people never tackle anybody. They are only guards. They are willing to "defend the faith," at least by argument. But they never get into an "offensive" movement which requires tackling.

Some tackle other people and things only when their own advantage is the thing at stake. Then they throw timidity to the winds and plunge into the mêlée, hoping to bring out some kind of a prize.

Others tackle only the weak and unimportant. They choose their opponents carefully and cautiously. It is possible to make a great bluster and parade of audacity when we are assaulting something that can't hit back, or something which will arouse no one's ire or defense. Mr. E. W. Howe, the Kansas journalist and author, says that he has learned in forty years of newspaper experience that the only safe thing to attack is the man-eating shark! That expresses the platform of some doughty warriors exactly—"Down with the man-eating shark!" They pick out some "safe" demon to attack, from which there can be no "comeback" from the allies of the poor demon, because it has no allies.

When Paul "made up his mind to tackle certain people" he did not study first to make sure that he could do it with impunity. They were "certain people of importance" whom he went after, because they were blocking the onward movement of the gospel. He was not afraid of getting his clothes ruffled. They had been torn from him frequently. He was not afraid of getting into "hot water." He lived and moved and had his being in hot water all of his career as an apostle.

There is no particular in which the church has always needed a baptism of Paul's spirit more than in this art of "tackling." In nothing has the church lost more than in being afraid of the positive thrust of action, of joining the issue with powerful

and well-intrenched forces of evil, particularly of
respectable evil. The only way effectively to defend
the faith of Christ is to project it into all life. Otherwise it becomes a limp, negative, impotent thing.

The church needs this spirit and art of Paul
also to keep it from centering its attack on minor
vices or individual vices, and neglecting great social
and corporate wickednesses. The spectacle, which
Christian people have sometimes furnished, of
crusading against boys playing baseball on Sunday
and yet being as dumb as an oyster on such iniquities as child labor, economic exploitation, or war,
is not a very inspiring spectacle, considered as
warfare for the kingdom of God. For a church
which never tackles the master iniquities of its age
will never dominate the heart and mind of the
people of its age.

THE MASQUERADE BALL

"They are *masquerading* as apostles of Christ."—
2 Cor. 11. 13 (Moffatt).

THE things which have masqueraded as apostles
of Christ would make a long and weird parade.
In fact, across the centuries they do make a varied
parade, a sort of masquerade ball, in which every
base motive of human conduct, every scheme of
personal or national advantage, has appeared in
the trappings of the Christian gospel.

In some ways this masquerade is the most sincere tribute which has ever been paid to Christianity. No praise could surpass the testimony to

the greatness of the Christian gospel given in the
trouble taken by its enemies to appear in imita-
tions of its clothes.

Here Paul throws the searchlight of his indignation on one of the most persistent masqueraders
—*partisanship disguised as piety.* Through his
letters to the Corinthian church we can catch
echoes of the oily sanctimoniousness with which
these trouble makers at Corinth spread schism and
animosity. The technique has been the same to
the present day with the holy robes of a professed devotion to godliness covering the claws of
hatred, jealousy, bigotry, and self-seeking.

The back files of history show every monstrous
evil dancing at the masquerade ball in the veritable
garments of light. In *The Rise of American Civilization* there is quoted a defense of slavery as a fundamental Christian institution, made by a Virginia
member of Congress on the floor of the national
House of Representatives. With impassioned eloquence he declared:

I believe that the institution of slavery is a noble one;
that it is necessary to the good, the well-being of the
Negro race. Looking into history, I will go further and
say . . . that I believe it is God's institution. Yes, sir;
if there is anything in the conduct of his chosen people;
if there is anything in the conduct of Christ himself who
came upon this earth and yielded his life as a sacrifice
that all through his death might live; if there is anything
in the conduct of his apostles who inculcated obedience
on the part of slaves toward their masters as a Christian
duty, then we must believe that the institution is from
God.[1]

[1] By C. A. and Mary R. Beard. The Macmillan Company, publishers. Used by permission.

What could be more noble and complete?

The war system has hardly ever failed to fit itself out with the garments of religion. Few wars of the Christian era have ever neglected to get themselves baptized as "holy wars," no matter how outrageous or imperialistic their real purposes were. In the spring of 1927 a monk in Italy died, and after his death it was discovered that for years he had worn under his monk's robe the uniform of a soldier. That concealed uniform is a very fair symbol of militarism masquerading as religion.

We do not need to go back at all to find the ugly spirit of race hatred and prejudice, and religious animosity, and bigotry dressed up as apostles of the gospel of Christ, deceiving multitudes whose understanding of that gospel was sadly distorted.

And how often is a mere satisfaction with class privilege and material advantages therefrom disguised as being the very essence of the gospel!

Paul's advice was in his own time, and is to-day, "Unmask every pretense."

DEAD WEIGHT

I myself never hung as a *dead weight.*—*2 Cor. 12. 13* (Weymouth).

THIS phrase, "Hung as a dead weight," is a perfect picture of the inertia which is the most formidable handicap of thousands of churches.

Paul is making his defense against the charges

of his slanderers that he has been a burden to the churches, that he had profited from their support. "I make my own living," he cries, "working with my hands. I never hung as a dead weight."

The very phrase makes our muscles ache. Try to lift a perfectly limp and inert human body. It seems to weigh a ton. It is almost impossible for us to raise it to a position where it can be carried.

Yet that is the arduous task of multitudes of churches—trying to make headway for the gospel in the world, staggering under people who hang as dead weights.

Such people do not move the load; they *are* the load.

They would be the first concern of a spiritual engineer who might be called in to study the causes of lost motion and energy in the church.

Perfectly delightful people, most of them. They would scorn the suggestion that they could ever be classed as liabilities of the church. They never bring any open disgrace upon it. The simple trouble lies in their whole conception of the church as a sight-seeing bus rather than an engine pulling a load up a mountain. They insist on riding in a Pullman. They never get out of the realm of statics into that of dynamics. They never make the most glorious pilgrimage of life—that from the dark Egyptian captivity of the passive voice into the Holy Land of the active voice. They come and go with the same sense of responsibility that a passer-by has who stops at a street corner to listen to a speaker long enough to get a dim idea of what he is talking about, at least enough to decide whether he is advocating socialism, conducting a gospel meeting, or selling a new patent collar button, and then hurries on. Nearly every church has members whose appearances are like those of a magician giving a mystifying performance—"Now you see him, now you don't."

"I myself never hung as a dead weight."

And you——?

TURNING THE GOOD NEWS AROUND

Some people who . . . want to turn the good news of the Christ around.—*Gal. 1. 7* (Goodspeed).

THEY frequently succeed.

Some people turn the good news around that it looks *backward* instead of *forward*.

Some turn it upside down so that it looks *downward* instead of *upward* to God's sky.

Others turn it so that it looks *inward* entirely, instead of *outward* to a world of need.

TWENTIETH CENTURY SLAVERY

We were slaves to *material ways of looking at things.*—*Gal. 4. 3* (Goodspeed).

BETTER words could hardly be chosen to describe one of the dominating obsessions of a large part of the twentieth century, slavery to "material ways of looking at things." To say this is not to indict

our time as materialistic beyond all other ages.
It is but to recognize the facts of life about us.
There is a kind and degree of pressure upon the
generation living to-day to conceive of the world
and life in material terms which is different and
perhaps greater than that put upon any other age.

For one thing, the present day has given us a
view of the universe whose immensity is staggering.
There is revealed a bulk of matter and space in the
universe of which no previous age ever remotely
dreamed. The figures with which astronomers try
to give us a conception of the size of the universe
are beyond the power of the imagination to conceive. The rows of ciphers run beyond any names
we have. Professor Shapley, director of the Harvard University, does some careful figuring and
reports thus about the galaxy of stars of which our
sun is a minor member.

Our sun, which is one of the dwarfs, is in its
decline. The great galaxy, however, of which it is a
remote and a minute part will continue for billions of
years to show its white ring around the sky to any
beings who may be here or elsewhere to see it and
call it perhaps something else than the Milky Way.
It will continue to draw into itself the great star
clusters and distribute them, though Mr. Shapley
does not know whether it will ever affect the faint
star cloud called N. G. C. 6822, which is about 4,500,-
000,000,000,000,000 (four quintillions five hundred
quadrillions) miles distant from us. He does, after
all, indulge in a few figures. He remarks that the
probable diameter of our galaxy is 1,800,000,000,000,-
000,000 miles.

A universe, the diameter of a small part of which

is expressed by eighteen followed by seventeen ciphers, is a large place to live in. It has been an inevitable result from this discovery of our universe that the material bulks so large that the spiritual element of life has been diminished in the thought of many people. The psalmist's question, "What is man, that thou art mindful of him?" has received a tragic emphasis in this age of science. And the answer is frequently only a question mark.

The prestige of science, due to its dazzling progress and achievements, has led many into a complete captivity to material ways of looking at things. If God is not always "bowed out of the universe," the spiritual aspect of the world is frequently "laid on the table," like a parliamentary motion quietly forgotten.

From quite another angle, another form of material outlook on life is imposed upon our minds with a pressure like that of the surrounding atmosphere on our bodies. That is the astounding development of an industrial and commercial civilization, with the resulting tendency to measure everything in the heavens above, the earth beneath, and the waters under the earth with a material and financial foot rule. Machines and industrial progress come with the gift of freedom from burdens, but soon develop a new and galling slavery of their own.

The physical slavery has its tragic counterpart in the bondage brought to the mind and soul in the mental outlook and habit described in Goodspeed's rendering of Paul's words—"material ways of looking at things."

The climax of the process is when the same tendency to measure life by material things insinuates its way into the church itself. If the agency set in the world to extend and preserve a distinctively spiritual measurement of life's significance falls into the same slavery to material valuations, the hope of redemption from that bondage grows pale. Yet that happens in a disquietingly large number of cases, where size, numbers, wealth, prestige, the ready measurements of the world of trade, are made its language and aims.

The words of this text occur in Paul's story of a redemption. "We *were* slaves to material ways of looking at things," *but*—thank God for the "but"! —but something happened! "God sent his Son . . . to ransom!"

The world needs ransom. About twenty years ago Henry van Dyke wrote his book, *The Gospel for an Age of Doubt*. A timely volume might be written to-day—*The Gospel for an Age of Things*. That gospel is the imperishable gospel of a spiritual order behind and above things. It will meet in two great respects the needs of an age when material-ism is in the very atmosphere. It will redeem man from the tyranny of a vast material universe in its revelation of the God and Father of our Lord Jesus Christ whose personal relationship to each child transcends all the bulk of the universe. It will reveal man as the measure of all things—the human values as the chief end of life.

The tremendous preaching of such a gospel is the only hope of leading mankind out of a new form of old bondage.

❧ ❧ ❧

THE STEWARDSHIP OF TRUTH

It is the *stewardship of the truth* which from all the
Ages lay concealed in the mind of God . . . —*Eph. 3. 9*
(Weymouth).

A PHRASE to grip the imagination this—*"the
stewardship of the truth."* It brings out clearly
what is not so easily visible in the older versions,
that preaching was to Paul not only an undeserved
privilege of God's grace but an intensely solemn
responsibility, a trusteeship. In his hands was
placed the truth of the incarnation of God in Christ.
He was a steward of that truth. From him would
be demanded an accounting of his handling of
that truth.

This rendering of Weymouth's brings a welcome
enlargement of the idea of stewardship. The great
New Testament conception of stewardship has suffered from exploitation for the purpose of immediate results. In recent years, at any rate, in many
quarters, the church has suffered from an emergency view of stewardship, emphasizing the payment of the tithe of material income.

The primary stewardship of a Christian is the
stewardship of truth, a far more germinal and vital
thing than money. The question each must face
is this—what kind of an investment have we made
of the truths of the gospel of Jesus, of which we
were made trustees?

Jesus' great parable of stewardship, that of the
talents, rushes inevitably to mind. Think of the
five, two, and one talents distributed to the servants
for employment, not as money, but as truth. Have
we taken the truths of Jesus' teaching and person-

ality and buried them in some dead, sterile vault, or have we put them to work in life, that they grow in meaning and power?

Take his great truth of human brotherhood. What kind of an individual stewardship of that truth can we render? Does that truth get into living expression through us? Do our attitudes and actions make it gleam with reality as we move among men? Could such a truth be logically deduced from the evidence of our habitual spirit, or does it grow dead, blunt, and impossibly utopian through our handling?

How about our collective, national trusteeship of that luminous truth of human brotherhood? What kind of a steward of that truth can a nation be if it is imperialistic, contemptuous, quick to employ force, ready to exploit weaker peoples, nations, or races?

Or take that primary truth of Jesus—that life is more than meat and the spirit more than things. Are we faithful stewards of that truth, so that it is not lost or dulled in an age so given to the feverish lust for things as ours is?

Arthur Train wrote a few years ago a fantastic story called *The Lost Gospel*. The action centered around the supposed finding, in an Egyptian monastery, of an ancient manuscript containing a collection of words of Jesus, never before brought to light. These words dealt largely with social questions such as Jesus' teaching against war and economic oppression. The finder of this document was an officer in the army of one of the European powers, and the manuscript was destroyed by order of the emperor, for fear of the volcanic disturbance such a gospel would bring to the established order of life if it were ever published.

That is only fiction. It is fact, however, and tragic fact, that there is a "Lost Gospel" of Jesus. It has not been lost in an ancient monastery. It has been published as no other writing in the world has been published. But it has been lost through a careless stewardship of truth. The social implications of Jesus' words have been allowed to become fogged, skipped over, forgotten. One insight of Mr. Train's story is sure—the realization with sunlit clearness that the knowledge of what Jesus actually taught about war, about oppression, about the lust of acquisition would upset the imperialistic and militaristic regime on which so much of the world is ordered.

The recovery of that "Lost Gospel" of Jesus is a major responsibility of our stewardship.

THE TRAGEDY OF PETER PAN

Till we should all attain the unity of the faith and knowledge of God's Son, *reaching maturity*.—*Eph. 4. 13* (Moffatt).

THE expression frequently found in the Authorized Version, "The perfect man," or "unto a perfect man," as here, is rendered by Moffatt *"reaching maturity."* The rendering brings the ideal much more within the range of possibility by eliminating the word "perfect." It is not mathematical perfection which Paul has in mind so much as full-grown maturity, adult manhood and womanhood. It is the alluring ideal of growing up into the maturity of our powers as full-grown children of God, as Moffatt continues the verse, "reaching the full measure of development which belongs to the fullness of Christ."

The expression shows vividly the great tragedy of life—failing to grow up. It is the common tragedy of Peter Pan. As Barrie wrote that wonderful drama of the spirit of youth—the immortal story of the little boy who never grew up—it is a joyous fantasy, a comedy. But in real life it is so often a tragedy—the dreary history of a person who never reaches maturity. Such a Peter Pan never comes into the heritage of mature fellowship with God; he never takes a man-sized burden of the world's load on his shoulders. He pleadingly insists that he is under twelve years of age and must be let off with a half portion or be pushed in a perambulator. He never learns to bear a cross, and the years which should be melodious with the notes of love and service resound with the petulant whine of an insistent selfishness.

❧ ❧ ❧

THE MASTER SPIRITS OF THE AGE

We have to struggle . . . with . . . *the master-spirits of this dark world.*—*Eph. 6. 12* (Goodspeed).

HERE is the battle line of Christianity stretched out against the ruling ideas of the age which oppose and deny the whole Christian interpretation of life. With this major engagement ahead, a veritable life-and-death struggle for the dominance of the world, it is an unspeakable blunder that so much of the energy and man power of the church has gone and is going into rear-end engagements, skirmishes with snipers of minor importance, while the master iniquities of the age have gone unchallenged.

Saint Paul was a strategist of the first order. He had an instinct for the pivotal points in the struggle with paganism. He had also the audacity to storm the main strongholds. He was never led off into a fretting guerrilla warfare with subsidiary and minor enemies. He struggled with the *master* spirits of darkness.

Two of General Foch's "Ten Commandments of War" have immediate bearing on all Christian effort: "Never fire at an empty trench," he says, "and never fire an empty gun." We have done a good deal of both. Effective warfare, whether in the struggle between warring conceptions of life or warring armies, does neither. "Empty trenches" —how many times have they been fired on and charged in Christian history—things that don't matter much one way or another, irrelevant to the vital purposes of the Christian enterprise. Empty guns—how loudly they have resounded and with little execution! "Pretty sermons" loaded with nothing but rhetoric, with no profound explosive message in them; often "duds," shells that never explode, so innocuous that the real enemies of Christ never even notice them.

What are the master spirits of this dark age with which we must struggle—the anti-Christian ideas, the major problems we must solve? Two very suggestive lists will give a view of the battle line of to-day and to-morrow. The first is from Dr. Henry Sloane Coffin, from an address given in the summer of 1927. Doctor Coffin says that there are five potent factors in the thought and background of the present situation which make it difficult for religion to get a chance:

1. Emphasis is put upon the superior powers of man without any recognition whatever that God may have contributed anything.

2. The second factor is the scientific attitude toward the world which is developing to a high degree to-day. This imperial process of cutting up and dividing life into neat and careful parcels will never help us find God nor discover the real man.

3. The industrial organization of mankind is the third factor that is making it hard for us to find a place for religion. Accompanying virtues such as thrift, push, and industry are good, but they are not the best. If ranked with those of the Sermon on the Mount, they fall far short.

4. Another factor is democracy. Democracy levels down as well as levels up. Real religion never entered the world via the mass movement.

5. The fifth factor is psychology. In its emphasis upon the materialistic view of life and its depersonalization of God, religion faces a real difficulty.

The second is the list of what Dr. E. Griffith Jones, of England, calls the six great problems of the next few centuries. He says that these six problems must in some way or other find a settlement in the next few hundred years. These are the six:

1. "Moralizing" man's power over nature.
2. The just distribution of wealth.
3. International and racial relations.
4. Birth control and problems of population.
5. The conflicts of religion.
6. The religion of the future.

Christ's foes are legion.   His injunction to his disciples in this confused age is surely to keep on the front battle line.

1. *A materialistic view of the world* which bows God and even the soul itself out of the universe is one of the master spirits of the age.   A. E. Wiggam gives this picture of what he calls "naturalism."

The universe stands revealed at last in all its gaunt nakedness as a mere machine without sympathy or purpose.   Man is found to be a brother not only to the brute but to the clod and crystal.   He sweeps for a brief moment round his little orbit and passes into the trackless void with the same mechanical precision as the stars.[1]

Faith in a Christlike God is the supreme object of struggle.   If that is lost from the world, it makes little difference what remains.

2. A dark spirit to be met is that of *vulgarity* which is rushing over many areas of life like a spring flood.

3. *The spirit of acquisition* is surely a master spirit, molding the very soul as well as the form of our present-day industrial civilization.   Mr. Sigfried, in his book, *America Comes of Age*, says that modern civilization is a debate between Henry

---

[1] From *The New Decalogue of Science.*   Copyright, 1922–1923. Used by special permission of the publishers, The Bobbs-Merrill Company.

Ford and Gandhi, between the production of things and an interest in the moral and spiritual content of life. Deeper than that it is a debate between the profiteer and Jesus Christ.

4. *Christ or Mars.* That battle is nowhere pictured with more shocking clarity than in the Invalides in Paris, where over the tomb of Napoleon is a large figure of Christ on the cross. Civilization can serve one or the other. It cannot serve both.

A COLONY OF HEAVEN

We are a *colony of heaven.—Phil. 3. 20* (Moffatt).

THIS is one of the high peaks of Doctor Moffatt's New Testament translation. It is perhaps as well known and much used as any of his renderings. And with good reason. There is in it a touch of genius which presents Paul's meaning far more clearly than the translation in the Authorized Version, "Our conversation is in heaven." And it comes with a wealth of inspiring suggestion.

Paul grew up in a Roman colony. He knew what the acknowledgment of allegiance to a distant authority meant—its high gift of citizenship. It is the analogy between a Roman colony and the Christian community owing its allegiance to heaven which Paul has in mind. The figure of speech carries endless suggestions for the Christian life and task in the modern world.

It suggests the *high adventure* of the Christian enterprise, both in individual personality and col-

lective effort—the thrust out into new and un-
claimed and unconquered territory. Some of the
most romantic and stirring events of all human
history have been in the founding and development of colonies. Colonization is not an armchair
job, not a "white-collar job," not a job for weaklings.
Only stout spirits thrive, or even endure, on a
frontier. To think continuously of our task as that
of colonizers will put iron into our blood.

To most Christians to-day the business of founding and extending a colony of heaven is not the
physical adventure of bringing new territories into
Christian allegiance but *the entrance into unre-
deemed areas of life* and claiming them for Christ's
dominion—into wild, unconquered areas of industry, into the jungles of race conflict and international relations. A "colony of heaven" is a fine
conception of the kingdom of God on earth. A
colony is not a crowd on a journey through hostile
country. It is not an expedition passing through
a place, like a Pilgrim's Progress to some celestial
city. It is a settlement. It establishes a permanent
dominion for the laws and authority of another
power. Our business on earth is to be colonizers of
heaven, to redeem the world and set up in it an
order of life which will incarnate the spirit and
principles of Jesus. As Walter Rauschenbusch
put it:

This high task of making human life and human society
the realization of the Father's loving will for his children
—this is the substance of the spiritual life, of which the
services and the devotion of the church are but outward
forms.[1]

---

[1] The Macmillan Company, publishers. Used by permission.

The figure of a "colony of heaven" keeps to the forefront the *higher allegiance* of the Christian and the church. The church is not to be conformed to the world but is to transform the world itself into the likeness of its Master. Just as a thousand mystic ties run back from a colony to the homeland, the colonist of heaven finds a thousand daily reminders of his allegiance—"There is another king, one Jesus."

One of the most impressive places in the United States is Pilgrim Hall in Plymouth, Massachusetts. No familiarity with the history of Plymouth Colony can take away the poignant eloquence of those relics preserved there. Every one of the things which came over in the Mayflower and which were used in those high days of the planting of the colony— every bit of furniture, the cradle, the kitchen implements, the dishes, the clothing, the Bible—all speak of the loved and noble heritage of England. These men and women did not come to the wilderness to live like savages, to drop their ways of life and "go native." They carried on the dear and loved tradition of their English home, its laws, its high sanctities. They carried England with them.

They were a colony of England.

We are a "colony of heaven."

THE ZEST FOR PRAYER

Maintain your zest for prayer by thanksgiving.—*Col. 4. 2* (Moffatt).

THIS exhortation of Paul's touches one of the commonest problems of the personal life to-day—how to maintain a zest for prayer. That word "zest" is far too keen and lively and strong to express exactly the attitude which multitudes of sincere and earnest Christians have to prayer. The trouble isn't that there is any reasoned disbelief in prayer; it is not that there has been any disillusioning experience of its futility. But the zest, the insistent eagerness of a keen appetite that will not be denied—that is a rather rare thing to find.

The recovery of a lost zest is a difficult quest.

Paul suggests a remedy. He does not argue for it. He does better than that. He says, "Try it." Maintain your zest for prayer by *thanksgiving*. And he had never heard of the fourth Thursday of November. He did not have in mind an annual day, chiefly notable in these latter times for dinner and football. He meant a constant habit of mind, as fixed as breathing.

The mood of thanks—the quick, wakeful heart to discern and receive a mercy—that in itself is a possession richer than all the other gifts Heaven can bestow. That habit of mind and heart maintains a zest for prayer. Then prayer can no more be repressed than a spring can be kept from bubbling up out of the earth. You can't help praying, for you will have something to talk to God about.

The art of keeping the zest of life by thanksgiving is much akin to the faculty of a true poet for alert and loving observation of the beauty of the earth. The love of life in a poet, the passionate quest for detailed loveliness, like that of a detective on the trail for unnoticed beauty, maintains zest

in the poet's heart and words. A critic has well
described this process in Edna St. Vincent Millay:

She loves life for its beauty, *which she finds in very
definite objects*, *not in abstractions*. She loves the special
countenance of every season, fragrant names, the salt
smell of the sea along her native Maine coast, the sound
of sheep-bells and dripping eaves and the unheard sound
of city streets, the homely facts of houses in which men
and women live, tales of quick deeds and eager heroisms,
the cool, kind love of young girls for one another, the
color of words, the beat of rhythm.[1]

The person who has learned to look on the world
with such a sense of its beauty and its gifts brings
to life the high art of a poet, and has opened an
unfailing spring of zest. Mr. Chesterton has pictured the gift of youth which a wakeful and thank-
ful heart preserves:

> "Men grow too old for love, my love,
>   Men grow too old for wine,
>   But I shall not grow too old to see
>   Unearthly daylight shine,
>   Changing my chamber's dust to snow
>   Till I doubt if it be mine.
>   Behold, the crowning mercies melt,
>   The first surprises stay;
>   And in my dross is dropped a gift
>   For which I dare not pray:
>   That a man grow used to grief and joy
>   But not to night and day."[2]

Paul wrote poetry rather than geometry. But
much of his writing, including this injunction and

[1] *American and British Literature Since 1890*, by Carl and Mark
Van Doren. Century Co., publishers. Used by permission.
[2] From *The Ballad of Saint Barbara*. Dodd, Mead & Company,
publishers. Used by permission.

promise, has one thing in common with a proposition in geometry. It is this: *You can prove it.*

❧ ❧ ❧

DIED OF DIGNITY

We might have *stood on our dignity.—1 Thess. 2. 6* (Goodspeed-Weymouth).

As apostles of Christ we *have the power of claiming to be men of weight* (Moffatt).

PAUL always found something better to stand on than his dignity. That is one of the reasons he has stood so long in the world's history. The people who are always standing on their dignity have little else to stand on, and as dignity is a rapidly crumbling sandstone, when alone, it makes a poor pedestal.

Paul rightly declares, in Moffatt's rendering, that he had *"the power of claiming to be"* a man *"of weight."* Is there any more subtle pleasure to a small-minded man than the consciousness of appearing as a man "of weight"? But Paul was not a small-minded man, nor was he out for pleasure. He was an apostle of Christ. He had too urgent business on hand to strike a pose, an attitude. He had something better than dignity to work with. He had the love of God. So instead of the cheap satisfaction of strutting as a man of weight, he showed himself as "gentle as a mother is when she tenderly nurses her own children."

If the followers of Paul and of his Master down through the centuries had always managed to escape the snare of dignity, the course of Christian history would have been vastly different. For dignity is very often only another name for paralysis. More institutions have died of dignity than from any other cause. Or, if they have not actually died, they have been so crumpled up with rheumatism that they could not get up from an invalid's chair. The church has had tragic seizures of the paralysis of dignity, when she has been unable to rise, gird herself, take a towel, like her Master, and follow him in lowly service.

Think of that phrase—a contradiction in terms so glaring as to be blasphemous—"Princes of the Church." Paul didn't invent that phrase. He continually used one slightly different, "slave of Jesus Christ." The difference between those two phrases is the difference between dignity and love, between death and life, between a forgotten statue rusting in the rain and a living incarnation of Christ.

Watch self-regarding "dignity" strut futilely through the world:

> With lofty pride she entered the room.
> "I," said her carriage,
> "I," said her eyes,
> "I," said her careless, yet well-thought-out nod.
>
>
> She sat down in a high-back chair,
> Unbending.
> Her glasses glittered in the cold bright glare
> Of many pointed prism-lights.
> "I," said her glasses, trying to shine the brightest.

She spoke,
Breaking the silence that her presence made.
With sounds like pebbles dropping on cracked ice.
"I," said her well-posed gestures,
Then:
"I," said her voice.

So as individuals and as a church we make our choice between the childish satisfaction of self-conferred pompousness and importance and the self-forgetful plunge into life's scramble and struggle.

The open secret of it all is, of course, that only by forgetting dignity do we ever achieve the real thing. Has the world ever gazed on a truer dignity than that of Abraham Lincoln? Can anyone imagine him trying to look "dignified"? Dignity, like happiness, is always a by-product. The surest way to lose it is to seek it. The surest way to find it is to lose it; to forget it as Paul did, in a preoccupation with love and service. Then it comes, as it came to him, as the inevitable coronation of a sacrificial life.

A PROFOUND RELIGION

Who does not admit *how profound is the divine truth of our religion?*—*1 Tim. 3. 16* (Moffatt).

Great is the mystery of our religion (Weymouth).

MUCH more clearly does this word "religion" express the meaning of Paul's emphasis here than the more familiar words, "great is the mystery of 'godliness.'" "Godliness" emphasizes, in our use of the word, an ideal of personal devotion, of ethical

conduct. Paul is concluding his exhortation in the
third chapter of Timothy with something different
than that—something much deeper—an exhortation to remember the profound religious truth of
the gospel, the deep realities of spiritual truth
which are the basis of it all.

And his reminder that in Christianity we have a
"*profound* . . . religion" is a word of tremendous
urgency and timeliness in a time when superficial
and sloppy thinking about the Christian religion
has a wide and popular vogue.

For many, Christianity has dwindled down from
a profound religion into *a didactic collection of wise
maxims*. It is a Western counterpart to Confucian-
ism, which is not properly a religion at all but a
system of ethics, a glorified Book of Etiquette, a
social code of conduct. There is a comfortable
suggestion of liberality and progress about the attitude of many who are saying, "We will keep the
morality of Christianity, but throw over its religious
teaching." In other words, we will pass it up as
a profound religion and keep it as guide, philosopher,
and friend in the field of conduct. It is a very
pleasant program. The only trouble with it is that
it can't be done. The teaching of Jesus is a seam-
less texture, a robe which cannot be divided. The
ethics of Jesus can no more be separated from his
religious teaching than a tree can live with its roots
lifted out of the earth.

Professor Ernest F. Scott, in his *Ethical Teaching
of Jesus*, emphasizes this truth clearly:

Whether we like it or not, the moral teaching of Jesus
is rooted in his religion and cannot be detached from it.

Even his demand for social justice and human brotherhood is based on a religious postulate and is left hanging
in the air when this is withdrawn. *There is no way of
saving Jesus' ethics at the expense of his religion;* but it
can no way be sufficiently emphasized that he builds
always on the central things in religion. . . . From the
faith in the sovereign God who is at the same time Father
of mankind, the morality of Jesus cannot, at any point,
be separated.[1]

*The substitution of a "pretty" religion for a pro-
found religion* is common. By a "pretty" religion
we do not mean that emphasis on æsthetics, which
is concerned with the beauty of the Christian religion. It is not so dignified as that. It is not so
much a beautiful religion as it is merely "pretty."
It is concocted of superficial optimisms. It gives
a world view done in pale-pink pastels. As an
equipment with which to face the realities and
tragedies of life it has about the lasting value of a
child's book of fairy tales. Such a pretty religion,
blind to the harsh bewilderments and agonies of
life, can do no more for us than we can do for ourselves. It is open to the comment made by A. G.
Gardiner on an American political leader—"He
moralizes but he does not spiritualize."

*Christianity as a profound religion is frequently
lost by its distortion into a subservient religion.* No
message can be profound, going to the very roots
of both the universe and the human heart, and at
the same time be subservient to any ruling dynasty
—whether that dynasty be a thirteenth-century
feudal nobility or a twentieth-century Chamber of
Commerce.

---

[1] The Macmillan Company, publishers. Used by permission.

CREATIVE LIVING

Model yourself on the sound instruction you have had from me in the faith and love of Christ Jesus.—*2 Tim. 1. 13* (Moffatt).

As your example in wholesome instruction, keep before you what you learned from me (Goodspeed).

THESE translations give a dynamic interpretation to a text which has been repeatedly used to fasten upon the Christian a static and liberalistic conception of his faith.

"Hold fast the form of sound words," says the King James Version.

"Model yourself on the sound instruction," says Moffatt. There is a world of difference between the two. The expression, "the form of sound words," has been used with a misleading emphasis on the word "form," which does not render Paul's primary meaning at all.

The phrase, "form of sound words," has been pressed into the service of insisting on the repetition of verbal shibboleths, as the essence of Christian faith. It is a static, lifeless conception of faith and may be made as mechanical as the grinding out of worn phonograph records.

Paul's plea is in the active voice, not the passive. What he is urging as the enterprise of faith is not the parrot-like repetition of a formula but the creative task of taking great truth and actively modeling life upon it. He is concerned with the creation of personality, not the mere repetition of words.

❧ ❧ ❧

FAITH

"Now faith is."—*Heb. 11. 1* (Weymouth).

IT would be hard to find a passage in the New Testament where the three translations of Moffatt, Weymouth and Goodspeed perform a larger service in clarifying a definition of great importance than the first verse of the eleventh chapter of Hebrews.

That verse is one of the highest peaks of a great mountain range of New Testament truth.   But it has suffered the fate of many mountain peaks in that it has been frequently clouded with mist and fog.   Its language is familiar; it has a well remembered scriptural ring about it, yet its meaning is vague to multitudes of readers.   Its phrases lack clear definition, like a photograph slightly out of focus.

These new translations throw a shaft of morning sunlight on to the nature of faith as set forth by the author of Hebrews.

Compare the four translations:

1. King James Version:

Now faith is the substance of things hoped for, the evidence of things not seen.

2. Moffatt:

Now faith means we are confident of what we hope for, convinced of what we do not see.

3. Weymouth:

Now faith is a well-grounded assurance of that for which we hope, and a conviction of the reality of things which we do not see.

4. Goodspeed:

Faith means the assurance of what we hope for; it is our conviction about things that we cannot see.

THE GOSPEL FOR AN AGE OF DISILLU-SION

Born anew to a life of hope.—*1 Pet. 1. 3* (Moffatt-Goodspeed).

MANY would ask—How can anyone be born anew to a life of hope *to-day?*

A mood of disillusionment has settled down over the minds and hearts of multitudes to-day, a mood which is a long, long distance from "a life of hope."

Is there virility and life enough in the gospel to achieve such a miracle as a new birth to "a life of hope" would be?

That is a major and insistent question which the Christian forces of the world must answer. If it cannot be answered convincingly in the affirmative, the church will still have a career of years before it, but its function in the world will not be much more than that of a high-class concert company—a purveyor of music and æsthetics.

H. G. Wells has a powerful story of a man who is left in a room in a house reputed to be haunted. The terror of the story is furnished by the effect on the man's mind of a row of candles slowly going out one by one. That story is a picture of what has happened and is happening to-day to a large number of people. One by one lights in which they have trusted have gone out. And the room is dark.

Multitudes of thinking people have suffered mental and spiritual shell-shock. A mood of pessimism and cynicism has replaced that of faith and hope. Some of this disillusion is an *asset* for the spiritual life of the world. For in the failure of many things in which men put their trust is a

force that will fling them back to deeper foundations.   There has been a very wholesome bankruptcy of superficial and complacent optimism that
made the nineteenth century and the first decade
of the twentieth century blind to malignant forces
working under their very eyes.   Many a Humpty
Dumpty has come down never to be put together
and set up again.

But much disillusion is of another sort—the loss
of a noble and inspiring faith.   When a man reels
back from a great faith he usually drops into one
of three attitudes—or all of them together: into
despair, into superstition, or into a "grouch."   We
have much of all three.

The causes and forms of disillusionment are
many.   Only a few that first spring to mind are
here listed:

1. Overdevotion to scientific method inevitably
ends in a kind of intellectual disillusion.

2. Absorption in material tasks, the scramble for
material things, has blotted out for many the
spiritual aspect of life.

3. A bankruptcy of moral standards is a natural
outcome of lost landmarks.

4. Prophets of pessimism are abroad in the land.
Bertrand Russell unfolds eloquently the doom, piti-
less but sure, that will overtake the human race,
"When the whole temple of man's achievement
must inevitably be buried beneath the debris of
a universe in ruins."

5. The terrible disillusionment of the Great War
is not a thing which will lightly pass in a few years.
Dr. Raymond Calkins says that many are asking,
"Is God in his heaven, since hell's in the world?"

Pleasant chatter, brocaded rhetoric, stunts and tricks, a policy of escape—none of these can ever speak healingly to such an age or such a mood.

It must be "an imperishable gospel."

To bring a new birth to a deep and lasting hope calls for a gospel which can look all the facts of life in the face without evasion.

It must be a demonstration of the adequacy of Christ to interpret the world and save it from all destructive forces.

It must be a gospel of experience—both in the life of the individual and of society.

BRACE UP!

Brace up your minds.—1 Pet. 1. 13 (Moffatt).

THESE words are a reveille, a memorable sermon in themselves. Especially when minds so easily tend to slouch, to grow soft, invertebrate, and to collapse in fatigue.

KEEP COOL

Keep cool.—1 Pet. 1. 13 (Moffatt).

THESE words may be the expression of an ignoble selfishness, a loveless indifference, or of a calm unterrified faith.

"Keep cool"—that was undoubtedly the motto of the priest and Levite who passed by on the other side of the man lying wounded on the Jericho road. It is the motto of many whose self-control in the presence of the wrongs and sufferings of others is nothing short of marvelous. One of the most subtle and soul-deadening voices to which we are exposed is that counsel which continually tells us to keep cool, not to get worked up about things, to do nothing rash; after all, other people's troubles are not ours. Some of the most appalling miseries of human history, some of the cruelest wrongs, have gone on because people who watched them decided to "keep cool."

Needless to say, that is not the exhortation here. It is the poise and calm of faith, "unafraid with any amazement," which is urged. Instead of the flustered fever of unbelief, the bewildered panic of fear in the face of danger and risk, keep the head cool by having the heart fixed in an unshaken faith.

It is a word with a great message for a day of intellectual and moral confusion. But in this day, when an attitude of complacent indifference has almost been elevated to a national ideal, guard should be taken lest the injunction of this New Testament word be distorted. There is an apostolic virtue of keeping cool, but it is never self-possessed coolness in the face of injustice and wrong. Then is the time to get "red-hot."

Cowtown--

Metropolis

By

ROBERT H.
Professor of
Texas Christi

—Foreword—

Austin L.

LEO POTISHMAN FOUNDATION
TEXAS CHRISTIAN UNIVERSITY
Fort Worth, Texas

Cowtown--

Metropolis

Case Study of A City's
Growth and Structure

By

ROBERT H. TALBERT
Professor of Sociology
Texas Christian University

Foreword—

Austin L. Porterfield

LEO POTISHMAN FOUNDATION
TEXAS CHRISTIAN UNIVERSITY
Fort Worth, Texas

1956

Printed in the
United States of America
by the *MANNEY COMPANY*
Fort Worth, Texas

To

Christy—native of the metropolis—

who has never ridden a cowpony

iii

No longer do cattle trains move through the streets of Fort Worth, to pause momentarily on the drive to the northern railroad junctions; now they come by truck and railroad to be processed in the local packing plants. The cowpony is seen on the streets only on ceremonial occasions, but the cowboy, both the real and the imitation, is seen at all times.

While the cattle industry no longer dominates the economy of the city, its influence is still important, and local citizens and visitors are probably most aware of this in January at the time of the Southwestern Exposition and Fat Stock Show. Less glamorous but more significant is the steady operation of the packing plants, and the people the industry brings to town for business, shopping and pleasure.

Today the cowboots, broad-brimmed hats and suburban "ranches" are reminders of the past as the city faces an industrial and metropolitan future. "Cowtown" is a trade-mark of distinction. *Cowtown—Metropolis* is a picture of a cowtown turning metropolis.

PREFACE

This is the story of the growth of one American city—of the processes involved and the factors of causation. In addition, it shows broad outlines of the current structure of the community. The historical facts of Fort Worth's development are not particularly different from those relating to the growth of other American cities. What may be different herein is the interpretation of the facts, and particularly the emphasis on local leadership and its influence on the growth of the community. From frontier settlement to cowtown and on to metropolis—in approximately one hundred years—is something of a transformation, even for Texas. It is particularly so since there was little logic for the community's existence, and even less for it to become a railroad center and the gateway to West Texas, or recently to become an industrial giant on the Texas horizon.

Certainly the city has achieved its present status partly because of the growth of Texas and the Southwest, and because of the related processes of industrialization and urbanization apparent throughout the country; but, in addition, there has been the factor of local leadership. That is, at various times in the past opportunities presented themselves requiring local action and leadership. To borrow from Toynbee, the community was confronted with "challenges." The "responses" were such that development was furthered. It must be added, however, that in many instances the "challenges" were ignored.

Today, Fort Worth is faced with additional challenges. Metropolitan status leads to problems which cannot be ignored without dangerous consequences. Increasing demands for expanded educational facilities and the resolving of other educational problems, more effective prevention of housing blight and dilapidation, an arresting of the decay of the central area of the city, an improved system of vehicle traffic, rapid expansion of hospital and health facilities, and continuing awareness of increasing welfare needs, are only a few of the current problems facing the metropolis. Certainly of paramount importance for the future is the adjustment which the city will make to the recent decisions of the United States Supreme Court in the area of race relations.

Only recently, expansion of the school system was assured with the approval of a bond issue for this purpose. Also of recent development is the Gruen Plan for the rehabilitation of the downtown business area. These and similar efforts show an awareness of current problems and a recognition of the need for local leadership in planning for the future.

A second emphasis herein, and particularly related to the current structure of the community, is found in the presentation of a variety of factual data in tables and charts. Such material may make the book less readable, but should make it more useable.

Anyone familiar with the modern metropolis is aware that it is a complex organization of individuals, groups and activities. In a broad sense it has common interests, values and goals; but more specifically, the large city is composed of somewhat heterogeneous elements, of functionally different social worlds. For the individual citizen, busy with his daily activities, a comprehensive understanding of the over-all functioning of the city is next to impossible. Yet the interested citizens would like to "know" their city, and many are willing to look at it realistically; but understanding and evaluation require factual information.

Definite limitations need to be indicated. The decision to present an over-all picture and to select only the facts which reveal the processes of community development has resulted in the omission of many historical details. Further, this type of study cannot present adequately the "human" facets in the growth and functioning of the city. The saints and sinners must appear only by inference. The human conflicts as well as the many more instances of cooperation are suggested only in terms of descriptive and statistical measures of the end product. Also, it must be stressed that this book is designed primarily for the layman. It is hoped, however, that professional sociologists and social scientists will find, as one instance, the emphasis placed on the role of leadership worthy of consideration. Finally, because of insufficient factual information, reference to certain important phases of the total community life has been omitted. Thus, the significance of the family is beyond question even though no separate chapter or section dealing with this basic institution is included. Similarly, religion has been and still is a vital influence in the life of the people.

For convenience, and because of the evidence, the community's general development will be treated in terms of stages or levels which represent successive phases of relative equilibrium. This general approach is presented in Chapters I and II. Chapter III provides an analysis of the composition of the population, because such information is considered essential for intelligent understanding and planning. For similar reasons Chapter IV, which shows intra-city similarities and contrasts, is included. The chapters thereafter consider particular phases of the total socio-cultural situation which are thought to be important. For these latter chapters the general procedure has been to present for each phase, (1) selected facts which reveal the process of development, (2) information about the present structure, and, (3) comparisons with other large Texas cities and with cities of similar population throughout the United States. The final chapter seeks to establish "bench marks" for the qualitative analysis of urban life. Under the title, "What Makes a City Good?" an attempt is made to evaluate the conditions which are considered essential to achieve stable and effective urban community life.

ACKNOWLEDGEMENTS

The research on which this book is based was made possible by a grant from the Texas Christian University Research Committee, operating with funds provided jointly by the Carnegie Foundation and the University, and by later grants from funds provided solely by Texas Christian University. *Cowtown—Metropolis* is one of several publications made possible by these research grants.

Many people in Fort Worth, as well as elsewhere, have been most generous in providing desired aid and information. In addition, the chapters on the economy, social welfare, health, and education were read by local specialists in these fields. At appropriate places in the pages which follow particular reference will be made to such assistance and criticism.

Publication was assured by the Leo Potishman Foundation, by Mr. Neville Penrose of Fort Worth, and by almost two hundred individuals, business firms, and organizations in Fort Worth who agreed prior to publication to purchase one or more copies.

The entire manuscript was read by Professors Austin L. Porterfield, Estus C. Polk, and Herbert L. Mundhenke, and by Kathryn Talbert. For their generosity in giving freely of their time and skill the writer is deeply indebted. To Austin L. Porterfield, Chairman of the Department of Sociology in Texas Christian University, goes my deepest gratitude. Throughout, he has given unlimited encouragement, assistance and valued suggestions, not the least of which was the title, *Cowtown—Metropolis*.

"Insofar as sociologists are concerned," Robert Bierstedt once observed, "community studies have probably reached the law of diminishing returns. We do not need," he said, "another Middletown or Plainville, or Yankee City, nor indeed studies of Ypsilanti, Escanaba, Kokomo, and points west, unless we have an intense practical interest in these communities."[1]

Professor Robert H. Talbert, as the author of *Cowtown—Metropolis*, manifests both a practical and a theoretical interest in his field. Practically he presents us with a fact-book without committing himself to the fallacy that science is but a compendium of facts. At the same time, he relates fact to theory in such a way as to escape another criticism of sociological community studies advanced by Bierstedt. The latter believes that "there is subtantial ground for the assertion that the sociologist . . . has no present business in the field, unless he is testing an hypothesis or trying to corroborate one."[2]

Running through *Cowtown—Metropolis* implicitly and, at times, most explicitly is an emphasis upon the idea that conscious leadership has interacted with factors inherent in the social process in the development of a frontier cowtown into a modern metropolis. The data seem to bear the author out. Yet Talbert claims nowhere that "detailed examination of a single case or community" provides him with all "the corroboration he needs."[3]

While relating facts indicative of the part played by conscious leadership in the making the city, the author remains at all points thoroughly aware of the onsweep of the social process in the making of all cities. He knows, to begin with, that no city is owned exclusively by the people who live in it. It be-

---

[1]Robert Bierstedt, "A Critique of Empiricism in Sociology," *American Sociological Review*, 14 (1949), 584-592, p. 590.
[2]*Loc. cit.*
[3]*Loc. cit.*

longs to the larger society which has made it possible. Business corporations carrying on strictly local operations—city transportation or bus lines for example—may be largely in the hands of absentee owners. Office buildings which house local professional men or large stores may be owned by non-dwellers. The Jesse Jones interests have huge investments in not a little of the Fort Worth skyline. Utilities form a vast international web of which local systems in most all cities are only nuclei. Railways utilize cities as major loading zones; and they have to pull out when there is no longer anything to load and unload. Defense plants and military bases sit down in whatever metropolitan areas military logistics may demand, *if they are welcome.*

Still Professor Talbert is essentially correct in suggesting the importance of local initiative in the building of cities: not only in the part it plays in calling attention to the strategic values of locating city-building industries and operations at given urban spots, but in determining the city's social and ecological structure, as well as the nature of its local institutions.

To have a railroad or not to have a railroad may depend upon local support or opposition, as the author in a stirring story clearly shows. To read a history of railroads is to see other instances of the part played by local leaders in obtaining rail lines through their cities.[4] On the other hand, the reader of railroad history can hardly escape seeing how the obvious indifference—if not active opposition—of leaders in some cities results in the rails being laid elsewhere to the city's later sorrow.

Likewise, local leadership in cities has proved to be an important factor in determining the nature and quality of other institutions which influence their development. The city of McAlester in the neighboring state of Oklahoma could have had either a college or a penitentiary. It chose the penitentiary! Durant, to the South, took the college. In such cases, conscious and personal rather than impersonal factors are clearly determinants.

---

[4]Cf. S. G. Reed, *A History of Texas Railroads* (Houston: St. Clair Publishing Company, 1941).

The author of *Cowtown—Metropolis* recognizes well enough that geographical and cultural factors conspired quite impersonally in the development of the oil industry which has meant much to Fort Worth. One pioneer, the name of whose family became attached to more than one building overlooking downtown streets used, before the coming of cultural demands for petroleum products in the larger society, the oil that oozed up in the back yard of his ranch house to kill the fleas on his hogs! It was really good for nothing else. Impersonal aspects of the social process made his riches possible and led to his part in the development of Fort Worth. Likewise, Amon G. Carter owed much to "the world out there." Yet he and others clearly demonstrate the importance of the factor of foresight in making a city what it becomes. Each recognized that he must want something for his city before he could get anything he wanted for himself. Thus the city grew.[5]

There is, however, another aspect of conscious attention to city growth involved in *Cowtown—Metropolis*. It is the factor of organized leadership seeking insight into the best way to get from today to tomorrow in city building, with tomorrow finding the city "better" than it is today economically and socially. It is the function of planning in the light of research which makes insightful leadership possible. It is a process which implements the ideas of Lester F. Ward without completely refuting William Graham Sumner. Ward believed that effective social planning is possible. Sumner did not.[6] The

---

[5]In relation to the force of impersonal factors, it is interesting to observe how many of the cities of Texas are located on the famous old trails which followed a Northeast-Southwest course as a result of the nation's drive toward the Rio Grande. On *Trammel's Trace and the El Camino Real* sat Texarkana, Jefferson, Marshall, Nacogdoches, Crockett, Caldwell, Bastrop, New Braunfels, San Antonio, and Carrizo Springs. On the *Chisholm Trail* and *Preston Road* were cities like Denton, Fort Worth, Cleburne, Temple, Belton, Austin, Dallas, Waxahachie, Hillsboro, and Waco. On the *Atacosita and La Bahia Roads* were Madisonville, Anderson, Brenham, La Grange, Cuero, Victoria, Re Fugio, Beaumont, and Victoria. Pecos, El Paso, Alpine, Fort Stockton, and Presidio were points on the *Butterfield Route and the Chihuahua Trail*. San Antonio was a center of convergence for trails connecting cities such as Boerne, Fredericksburg, Mason, Menard, Laredo, Goliad, and Del Rio. These old trails fed into all the Northeast-Southwest routes. At Houston and Galveston, "sails meet rails." Events in these cities situated on famous old trails, however, indicate differences in the extent to which their people "cashed in" on these early advantages.

[6]Cf. Austin L. Porterfield, *Wait the Withering Rain?* (Fort Worth: Leo Potishman Foundation, 1953), Chapters II-V, for evaluation of Sumner and the science of planning.

Gruen plan, for example, which seeks to reverse the business exodus from downtown areas in Fort Worth can be defeated by the tendency of firms presently located in the heart of the city to follow the ecological drift to outlying areas, simply because, as individual businesses, they think it is to the advantage of themselves and their customers.

Ward knew, however, that planning insights themselves must take full account of all factors at work in the social process in order to be realistic and, thereby, effective. It is the merit of Talbert's treatise that he suggests research techniques which are simple, but make it possible to obtain the information needed to grapple realistically and intelligently with trends in both the internal and external relations of the city.

Much that *Cowtown—Metropolis* contains will be largely of local interest. Even so, it shows how students who "have an intense practical interest" in other communities may proceed to satisfy that interest. Thus it becomes a case study in the gathering and ordering of data for organized planning, as well as in the growth and structure of a modern city. Every city chamber of commerce and all city managers need a copy of it. Sociologists who are interested in action-related research will find it highly useful. In *Cowtown—Metropolis* helpful facts abound for the local planner, along with intimations of significant theory and procedures for students of cities in colleges and universities.

AUSTIN L. PORTERFIELD

CONTENTS

CHAPTER I

THE GROWTH OF FORT WORTH: GENERAL
DEVELOPMENT*

General Pattern of Development.[1] Fort Worth had its origin when a troop of United States cavalry established a fort on the banks of the Trinity River to give protection to the settlers who were pushing westward from the north and east. A few years later, because either the area was found to be undesirable as a military camp, or the "frontier" had moved farther west, the troop was transferred. The fort buildings constructed by the soldiers were immediately occupied by nearby settlers. Others soon came, including storekeepers, a doctor, and a school teacher, so that by 1860 possibly 200 people were living in the immediate vicinity of the present city. Part of the growth which had been achieved by 1860 was apparently due to the fact that the settlement had been able to establish itself as the county seat of its newly organized county.[2] However, from its inception as a military fort until its incorporation in 1873, Fort Worth remained essentially a frontier settlement with a few hundred inhabitants during most of the time.

Stage-coach connections, started in 1856, gave some contact

---

* In this and the following chapter, attention will be turned to the growth and development of Fort Worth. In this chapter certain general trends will be briefly mentioned, and some of the factors which were instrumental in the growth of the city will be indicated. The next chapter will seek to trace in more detail the major changes which occurred in the transformation of a frontier settlement into a metropolitan city. The emphasis is upon the major factors and forces in the community's growth rather than upon attempting a history of Fort Worth. In succeeding chapters similar treatment will be provided for particular phases of the local culture.

[1] The historical facts used in this section are derived mainly from three basic sources: Oliver Knight, *Fort Worth: Outpost on the Trinity* (Norman: University of Oklahoma Press, 1953); Fort Worth *Star-Telegram*, "Fort Worth's First 100 Years," October 30, 1949; and *Research Data: Fort Worth and Tarrant County*, Texas Writers' Project (available in Fort Worth Public Library).

[2] The population of the county grew from 664 in 1850 to 6,022 in 1860.

with the outside world and, beginning after the Civil War, one of
the cattle trails over which cattle were driven to railroad ter-
minals in Kansas passed through Fort Worth, and the town became a resting and relaxing place for the men driving the cattle.
Even so, at the time the railroad came into the town in 1876
there were, according to available reports, fewer than 60 business establishments. Most of these had been opened only
shortly before, in anticipation of the coming of the railroad.

Beginning in 1858 leading local citizens became imbued with
the idea that their community could become a terminus for one of
the railroads being built westward. Even though their dream
was interrupted by the crisis of the Civil War and the Panic of
1873, such actions did serve the purpose of unifying the local
citizenry, and indicated the development of some community
spirit. Following the Civil War a renewed effort was made to
secure a railroad. Local money and land were provided, and the
state of Texas was induced to set aside land for the railroad.
By 1873, track had been laid to within 24 miles of the town, and
settlers had arrived in anticipation of future business opportunities; but the financial panic of that year, which occurred
nationally with the crash of the Jay Cooke empire, brought
local reverberations. The company building the railroad lost
its financial backing and stopped work, and the population of
Fort Worth dropped from around three or four thousand to
600 people within the year. However, Fort Worth did get its
railroad three years later, when the Texas and Pacific tracks
were extended from the east to the city's limits, partially
through the efforts of local citizens.

Besides the courthouse, early interest in the cattle industry,
and the railroad, four other additions stand out as being vital in
the growth of the community. In 1903 the meat packing plants
of Swift and Armour began the processing of products of the
nearby cattle ranges. In 1917 oil was discovered at Ranger,
approximately 80 miles to the west, and Fort Worth became a
center for the expanding oil exploration in West Texas, as well
as an important center for oil processing. At about the same
time, during World War I, the city secured one army canton-

ment (Camp Bowie) and several air fields. Although as military installations these were short-lived, they were of permanent importance in the city's development. The most recent major economic event in the city's development was the opening of the Consolidated-Vultee aircraft plant in 1942. At peak periods this one plant alone has had as high as 30,000 employees.

In the main, a city develops because of the existence of primary economic activities—activities which can be traded for wants produced elsewhere. This fact is shown in the growth of Fort Worth. As an isolated frontier county seat community it could support only a small population. Its use as a stop-over place for cattle trains being driven northward was of some significance, but not until its development as a railroad center did the city acquire the means for adequate economic functioning.

The location of the meat-packing industry meant not only additional jobs but also a significant addition of incoming money for the local economy. In the same way, the establishment of military facilities during World War I, the development of Fort Worth as a center for the expanding oil industry, and most recently, the introduction of airplane manufacture, have all been vital influences in providing not only jobs but also "outside" money for the local economy.

Other less spectacular primary economic activities have been added, often directly or partly related to the major developments. In this connection, Fort Worth's position as a retail and wholesale trade center, as an educational center, as a medical center, and as an office and residential center for both governmental and non-governmental work and workers, has been significant in its development.

The Growth of Tarrant County. In general, Fort Worth and Tarrant County have developed together. Just as Fort Worth is being transformed from a trading center to an industrial and trading center, so Tarrant County is being changed from an agricultural area to an industrial and agricultural area. During the 20th century many county municipalities have been established; but both by Census Bureau definition and because of actual interdependence, they are a part of the metropolitan area of Fort Worth. The growth of population of the city and county is presented in Table 1 and Figure 1.

Table 1. Population of Fort Worth and Tarrant County, by Decades 1850-1950*

Year	Fort Worth		Tarrant County	
	Number	Percent Increase	Number	Percent Increase
1950	278,778	56.9	361,253	60.2
1940	177,662	8.7	225,521	14.2
1930	163,447	53.5	197,553	29.3
1920	106,482	45.2	152,800	40.7
1910	73,312	174.7	108,572	107.3
1900	26,688	15.7	52,376	27.3
1890	23,076	246.3	41,142	66.3
1880	6,663		24,671	326.3
1870	————		5,788	-3.9
1860	————		6,022	806.9
1850	————		664	

*Source: United States Bureau of the Census, decennial reports for corresponding years.

Since 1890 over half of the population of the county has resided in Fort Worth, and since 1930 three fourths have lived within the Fort Worth city limits. While part of this trend is due to the expansion of the Fort Worth city limits, it is also due to the growing dominance of Fort Worth in the county. Prior to the advent of rapid means of communication and transportation, each of the county towns was something of a separate entity, with its own social and economic life. Today, the county towns, and particularly those closely adjacent to Fort Worth, are a part of an interdependent social and economic situation. As additional industries come into the area it is likely that many will locate outside Fort Worth, while utilizing its metropolitan advantages.

Growth of Business and Industry. Fort Worth began as a trading center for the immediate farming area. With the coming of the railroad it became also a center of trade for a larger area. The addition of industries gradually changed the economic and social picture, but until recently Fort Worth was essentially one of the important retail and wholesale trade centers of the Southwest. Only since 1940 has manufacturing achieved a dom-

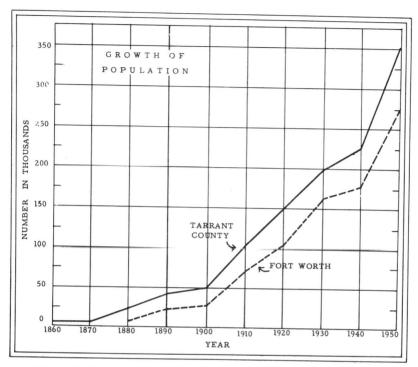

Figure 1. Growth of Population of Fort Worth and Tarrant County by Decades, 1860-1950. (Original data from U. S. Bureau of the Census, decennial reports for corresponding years.)

inant place in. the culture of the city. The impetus for manufacturing expansion after 1940 was the location of the Convair aircraft plant of the Consolidated-Vultee Corporation, but because of war needs many established local industries expanded their output, and new manufacturing activity was added to the local economy.

The economic growth of the city is particularly apparent in the expansion of manufacturing. This can be illustrated through reference to the trends in "value added by manufacture,"[3] and wages, as shown in Figure 2 for the period from

---

[3]"Value added by manufacture is calculated by subtracting the cost of materials, supplies and containers, fuel, purchased electric power, and contract work from the total value of shipments ... Value added provides the most satisfactory measure of the relative economic importance of given industries." U. S. Bureau of the Census, *Census of Manufactures: 1947*, Volume III, p. 20.

1909 to 1947. In this figure the data have been transferred to index scores, with the 1909 figures representing index values of 100. For Fort Worth for the period from 1909 to 1947 the

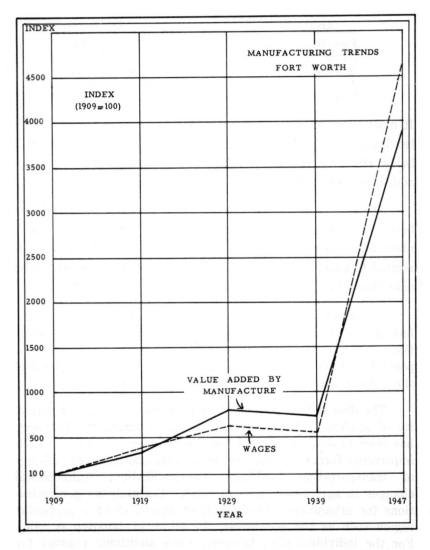

Figure 2. Indices of Growth of Manufacturing in Fort Worth, 1909-1947. 1909 = 100. (Original data from U. S. Bureau of the Census, Census of Manufactures for corresponding years.)

"value added by manufacture" increased 3,949 percent. Percentage increases for other areas for the same period showed smaller gains as indicated in the following:

Area	Percent increase
Fort Worth	3,949
Dallas	2,093
Houston	2,956
Texas	1,824
United States	912

It must be emphasized, however, that even though Fort Worth led Dallas and Houston in percentage gain, in 1947 it was still below the other two Texas cities in actual volume of "value added by manufacture."

The growth of manufacturing in Fort Worth since 1947 has been even more pronounced, with considerable expansion in airplane and related industries. In addition, many industries unrelated to airplane construction have been established within or near the city.

Besides the growth of business and industry, the community has experienced phenomenal changes in its practices of education, government, recreation, health, and social welfare; important changes have occurred in the functioning of religion and the ways in which the citizens are housed.

The Role of Leadership in City Growth. In the great majority of studies of urban community development the tendency has been to describe growth and functioning in terms of such impersonal forces as nearness to natural resources, availability of transportation facilities, industrialization, technological changes in agriculture, and so forth. Certainly as generalizations for urbanization in the United States, or of a particular region such as the Southwest, the above explanation is valid. For the individual city, however, some additional reasons for growth—or lack of it—may be necessary. That is, why is it that one town in an area grows into an urban center while others nearby remain small or disappear?[4]

In the growth of Fort Worth, at least, it appears that a basic factor has been the part played by local citizens in giving their time and money to secure new industries and other primary economic activities, and to achieve within the community improvement of facilities for education, religion, and so forth. In the pages that follow it will be seen that some local resident or residents apparently played the strategic role which made the difference between securing such additions as the courthouse, a railroad line, or the location of a government plant in the city. Even in the beginning when Fort Worth was just another frontier settlement, at the time cattle were being driven from South and West Texas to railroad facilities in Kansas, local citizens took an active interest in making Fort Worth a resting place in the drive by arranging to secure plenty of "entertainment" for the drivers. "Hell's Half Acre" in the early settlement did not represent community planning in the present-day sense, but also it did not develop without some local assistance. Later, local citizens raised cash bonuses to get railroads and other industries. Between 1873 and 1899 a total of $377,000 was raised for railroads and depots.[5] In 1902, alone, $100,000 was raised to bring two packing plants to the city.

As used herein, leadership refers to the position. Effective leadership refers to a condition in which the leader makes choices which are favorable in terms of the needs of the society in general. This course involves working toward established goals or cultural values which are commonly held to be valid and important. Such goals may be mainly those of increase in population size and economic opportunities, but they may include also improvements in education, health and sanitation, housing, recreation and many other areas of community life.

---

[4]There is no intention here to imply that growth or industrialization of a community is good or bad. Certainly for many people, growth, and particularly rapid growth, is not the ideal for which they strive. The addition of industries to an agricultural center brings drastic changes in community organization which are undesirable to many local citizens. Others, however, benefit materially from growth. Hence, the purpose here is merely to catalog growth—not evaluate it. In our last chapter some evaluation will be attempted.

[5]"Transportation," Fort Worth *Star-Telegram*, loc. cit., p. 2.

Certainly there are limits to effective leadership. These would include individual ability, resources of the community, and general level of culture. Also, there is no implication intended here that leadership can accomplish miracles, that "wishing will make it so." Finally, it must be emphasized that effective leadership can function on various levels. Some men may take the lead in bringing about the movement of large industry into the community, while others serve mainly in establishing such needs as a successful boy scout troop.

The thesis here is that in the development and functioning of communities today one of the variables of importance is local leadership.[6] That is, in addition to the commonly given factors affecting community life, there is the influence of individual citizens or organized groups of citizens who take an active interest in promoting the addition of primary economic units, and in the development internally of institutional structures and organizational patterns. This we will call the leadership factor.

Simply stated, the leadership factor involves those conditions where one or a few men have sufficient power, interest, and ability to utilize their resources in a manner which influences the direction of socio-economic change. Such men are able to rise above the impersonal competitive struggle and use their greater resources to implement desired change.

Such conditions can be referred to as power blocks—composed of men who through their wealth and or position have considerable influence on the structure and functioning of the urban community.[7] At many points, but not all, such groups control vital decisions affecting a particular community. In a negative way power groups can prevent certain developments; or positively they can provide a cultural climate which is receptive to certain developments. In addition, those power blocks

---

[6]Other variables would be natural resources, population composition, transportation and communication facilities, technical skills, geographic location, general cultural values and ideological preconceptions, or the general level of culture.

[7]For a study with this emphasis, see Floyd Hunter, *Community Power Structure* (Chapel Hill: University of North Carolina Press, 1953).

can at certain points have an influence on the larger culture as it affects the local community.[8]

It is of course true that in some communities the leadership may use its power to secure additional primary economic units, but at the same time fight attempts to expand community services to meet the needs of an increased population. Or it may manifest considerable foresight in one area of internal development, and almost complete blindness in other areas.

At this point it seems appropriate to raise some questions about certain prevailing theories of urban area development. One question concerns the emphasis of urban sociologists, and particularly those who write textbooks in urban sociology. That is, have they failed to recognize an important influence in the development and functioning of cities and metropolitan areas? More particularly, why have they generally ignored the influence of local leadership and local power blocks? One obvious answer would be that they think such of little or no importance. But possibly another reason may be related to the history of urban sociology in the United States.

With some important exceptions, most of the academic research in the field since around 1920 stems rather directly from the University of Chicago. Professor Robert E. Park laid the foundations for the emphasis in a paper published in 1915 and entitled: "The City: Suggestions for the Investigation of Human Behavior in the City Environment."[9] This emphasis was continued almost without change in the publication of *The City* in 1925, with chapters by Park, Ernest W. Burgess, and Roderick D. McKenzie.[10] Although there is some evidence that Park

---

[8]In a sense the community is somewhat like a young lady of marriageable age. In the case of the lady, she may (1) shun suitors by neglecting her appearance, (2) discourage them by intentional rudeness, (3) attract them by being—within the limits of her capacity—the kind of female she thinks will attract men; or (4) she can wage a positive campaign designed to interest men in general, and oftentimes a highly effective campaign to corral one particular male.

[9]*American Journal of Sociology*, XX (March, 1915), 577-612.

[10]Robert E. Park, Ernest W. Burgess, and Roderick D. McKenzie, *The City* (Chicago: The University of Chicago Press, 1925).

and Burgess were mainly interested in setting down "bench marks" for their graduate students, it seems apparent that they succeeded in establishing what can be called a school of urban social theory. We need not become involved regarding the validity of the ecological approach of Professors Park and Burgess and those who worked with them, or whether they were mainly interested in providing "leads" for their graduate students. Whatever the intent, Park and Burgess have had considerable influence on the point of view and content of urban sociology. In the main, they seem to have viewed the forces determining the urban structure as impersonal.

Walter Firey, in summarizing the theory of Burgess' *concentric zonal theory*, gives a statement which, while intended as a criticism of only the zonal theory, seems applicable to the general emphasis of Park and Burgess:

> The total configuration is envisioned as a self-regulating mechanism whereby 'a process of distribution takes place which sifts and sorts and relocates individuals and groups by residence and occupation.' Each increment of population gravitates naturally to its predestined zone, so that the city's growth consists of an outward extension of each zone into the one lying just beyond it.[11]

In commenting on the zonal theory of Burgess, Firey concludes,

> Nowhere in the theory is there a definite statement of the *modus operandi* by which people and groups are propelled to their appointed niches in space. Yet the whole emphasis upon the inevitability of the pattern implies a disavowal that they have any active part in the locational process.[12]

Essentially the same type of analysis and criticism is found elsewhere.[13]

---

[11]Walter Firey, *Land Use in Central Boston* (Cambridge: Harvard University Press, 1947), p. 7.

[12]*Ibid.*

[13]Emma C. Llewellyn and A. E. Hawthorn, "Human Ecology," in George Gurvitch and Wilbert E. Moore, *Twentieth Century Sociology*, (New York: Philosophical Library, 1945), esp. pp. 492-498. See also, William L. Kolb, "The Social Structure and Functions of Cities," *Economic Development and Cultural Change*, 3 (October, 1954), pp. 30-46. Kolb contends that Park and Burgess and the "human ecologists" who followed their lead ignored in the main the influence of human values on the particular pattern of a city. While Kolb is concerned mainly with the importance of values as they influence a particular urban pattern, it seems logical to assume that his thesis would include emphasis on the various forms of leadership as a value which for some urban communities is considered important.

The significance of the Park-Burgess influence lies in the large number of sociologists who have been trained in Chicago, and the number who, although not trained at Chicago, have followed the Park-Burgess emphasis on impersonal forces creating the urban environment. Again, it must be emphasized that there is no intention here to evaluate critically the total urban theory of Professors Park and Burgess. Reference to them is made merely to raise the question as to whether urban sociologists in general have failed to consider local leadership in the development of the urban environment. Moreover, exceptions to the conclusion concerning the interests of urban sociologists must be given. One is found in the two urban sociology textbooks for which Stuart Queen was the senior author.[14]

With regard to the growth of Los Angeles, Queen and Carpenter write:

> All these trends, which might have gone forward of themselves, were accelerated, if not forced, by the advertising of the Chamber of Commerce and the All Year Club, heralding to the world the health, beauty, and romance to be found in Southern California and especially in Los Angeles. Here, then, is the tale of a city built by man's ingenuity in engineering feats and his persistence in propaganda—the two quite overcoming the natural disadvantages which might have prevented the spot from producing any important urban development.[15]

Other exceptions need to be mentioned. Floyd Hunter in a study of community power structure emphasizes the influence of power groups on the internal structure of an urban community;[16] and E. W. Burgess suggests the necessity of research

---

[14]Stuart A. Queen and Lewis F. Thomas, *The City* (New York: McGraw-Hill 1939), pp. 73-75; and Stuart A. Queen and David B. Carpenter, *The American City* (New York: McGraw-Hill, 1953), pp. 69-71. In this connection, it appears appropriate to refer to a practice of the National Municipal League and *Look Magazine.* For the past four years the League and *Look* have designated certain communities as "All-American Cities." Those chosen have achieved the award because in each instance local problems, such as slum housing, corruption in government, and the like, have been eradicated or the situation has been materially improved, through local efforts and local leadership. See *Look Magazine*, January 10, 1956, p. 32. Leadership as a factor in group behavior in general has, of course, been emphasized in a number of the earlier sociological writings, and its importance denied in others. Representative of the former is the emphasis of E. S. Bogardus in his *Leaders and Leadership (New York:* D. Appleton-Century Co., 1934) and more recently in his *Sociology* (New York· The MacMillan Co., 1954), pp. 498-514.

[15]*Ibid.*, p. 71.

[16]Hunter, *op. cit.*

on the influence of power groups:

> We have almost no studies of power groups in urban areas. Yet such groups are among the most effective in influencing community behavior. Studies need to be made of associations of commerce, civic associations, property owners, professonal associations of various types, and political organizations.[17]

It would appear from this statement that Professor Burgess has modified his interpretations of the significant factors in urban community behavior, or his earlier position has been misinterpreted. But in the same report edited by Bogue, W. F. Ogburn appears to discredit the influence of promotion. Under the title, "Urbanism and Aggression," he suggests,

> There are certain regions of the United States that have had very great growth. During the periods of growth the people have appeared to exhibit an attitude of great and buoyant optimism. Chicago at the time of the World's Fair, Seattle in the 1920's and Texas at the present time are examples of this correlation between growth and optimism.

> Closer examination will show that optimism is followed by confidence. Men and societies tend to take full credit for whatever prosperity comes, even though it may really be an unearned increment. Thus, social and economic growth are credited to their own virtues, giving rise to confidence.[18]

Emphasis must be given also to the work of Robert C. Angell on the moral integration of cities. While Angell is mainly concerned with the contrasts in internal functioning of cities, and concludes that leadership is an important factor making for significant differences between cities, at least by inference it would seem that he believes that leadership can be influential in urban growth.[19]

It is, of course, next to impossible to measure the precise influence of the leadership factor. We can only attempt to make logical deductions from the available evidence which is presented herein. Yet, in the main, this is precisely the manner in which the more commonly accepted reasons for city development were derived. In considering the influence of leadership, two related

---

[17]Donald J. Bogue, *Needed Urban and Metropolitan Research* (Oxford, Ohio: Scripps Foundation, Miami University, 1953), p. 83.

[18]*Ibid.*, p. 88.

[19]Robert Cooley Angell, "The Moral Integration of American Cities," *American Journal of Sociology*, LVII (July, 1951), Part 2 (140 pages). The emphasis of Angell will be presented in greater detail in our final chapter.

questions seem appropriate. First, if it can be demonstrated from the evidence that some cities have been significantly influenced by effective local leadership, is the condition sufficiently widespread to permit generalizations? Second, if generalizations are possible, must they be limited to particular time periods and regions? While evidence concerning these two questions is not the primary purpose of this work, they do appear to be worthy of further consideration.

Types of Leadership. Two general types of community leadership can be differentiated. These are (1) leadership which is predominantly interested in growth of population and economic growth, and (2) leadership concerned mainly with internal affairs and the solution of local problems. Concerning leadership primarily interested in city growth and the assumed-to-be-necessary promotional activities, there are at least two types which can be described. These can be labeled the "shotgun" approach and the "directed" approach. The former includes the mailing of brochures, booklets, maps, and so forth, in a more or less broadside manner. Here also should be included the various techniques and stunts used to secure favorable publicity. The danger here is that a city may draw many new residents without the necessary economic activity to support the newcomers.

The directed approach involves working to secure income-producing economic units—factories, transportation lines, government offices, and other institutional structures. This includes detailed brochures directed at a particular industry, or to a particular company, and the work of community leaders, who through their contacts and power can arouse interest and make promises which will be fulfilled by the interested community. An integral part of the directed approach is the willingness to provide attractive concessions. In the past such concessions often included an outright grant of money. Today in the larger cities the promises may include favorable site locations, tax concessions, promises of a congenial labor supply, and other related services. In. addition, the willingness of local capital to invest, and to expect only a small return, has been important in some instances.

It also must not be overlooked that community prestige can be an important influence motivating community leaders to action. Certainly a good case could be made for this in the rivalry between Fort Worth and Dallas. In fact, there is considerable evidence that the leaders in Fort Worth have worked hard in part to try to keep up with or to surpass Dallas.[20]

One illustration of the influence of individual leadership in community development is the story of the activities of Amon G. Carter, who until his death on June 23, 1955, was publisher of the Fort Worth *Star-Telegram.* For almost a half century he worked diligently to expand the city. Coming to Fort Worth in 1905, he helped to start one of the early 20th century newspapers, the Fort Worth *Star.* Later, he and his associates bought out a rival, the *Telegram,* and eventually established the *Star-Telegram,* with morning, evening and Sunday editions, a policy which has continued to the present. In addition to his newspaper interests, Carter acquired extensive holdings in real estate, and during the oil boom period became a successful independent operator.

Carter was much more than merely a successful business man. He adopted the role of super-salesman for the city of Fort Worth, for West Texas, and for Texas. The evidence leads to the conclusion that he was successful in his adopted role. Through his interest and desire to publicize the city he led "the business community in one expansion after another, frequently involving the location in Fort Worth of factories, stores, branch

[20]One of the early local newspaper editors, B. B. Paddock, was possibly the first to develop a spirit of rivalry. In his newspaper columns he regularly chided his fellow citizens, apparently with one eye on the accomplishments of Dallas, and, when Fort Worth achieved something special, hastened to laugh in Dallas' face. What Fort Worth needs has often been determined by what Dallas has. Typical of this was the situation in 1936, when Dallas was selected as the site for the Texas Centennial Celebration, after Dallas business men agreed to underwrite the affair. Fort Worth citizens rushed to create a rival attraction, and advertised, "Go to Dallas for culture; Come to Fort Worth for entertainment." For an "outsider's" account of this rivalry, see George Sessions Perry, *Cities of America* (New York: Whittlesey House, 1947), pp. 57-70. See also, The Dallas *Morning News,* February 5, 1956, part 7, for a report of the 100th birthday of Dallas. This provides a brief account of the development of Dallas during the 100 years since it became an incorporated city. (Fort Worth was incorporated in 1873).

plants, and warehouses of important national corporations."[21] His activities in trying to secure government installations for Fort Worth led John Nance Garner, who at the time was Vice-President of the United States, to remark, "That man wants the whole government of United States to be run for the exclusive benefit of Fort Worth and, if possible, to the detriment of Dallas."[22]

An important method used by Carter was that of personal friendships. He was a friend of Will Rogers and gained fame as his flying companion on one of Rogers' round-the-world flights. His contacts are attested to by the fact that few important visitors passed even close to Fort Worth without a visit with him and to his Shady Oaks Farm. Early he established the practice of collecting hats. Every visitor at his farm would be requested to leave his old hat and take away a "Shady Oaks" hat, the "trade-mark" which Carter adopted. The name labels in the hats which remained at Shady Oaks Farm are indicative of the level of Carter's friendships. Included are hats belonging to Franklin D. Roosevelt, Harry S. Truman, Charles S. Lindbergh, John Nance Garner, Otto Kahn, Robert Lovett, W. S. Knudsen, Generals Eisenhower, Arnold, Doolittle, Spaatz, Wainwright, and Admirals Stark, Halsey, and Nimitz.[23] There are hundreds of others, including leading business men, foreign diplomats, and a number of foreign chiefs of state. Significant in the list of names above is the fact that all but one (Kahn) at one time held high positions in the Federal Government, and particularly in the military services.

It is, of course, difficult to evaluate the role of friendship and personal contacts in government and business actions, but the history of American government action and of business programs provides many instances where personal friendships did play a decisive part in certain new developments. Suggestive of the probable role of friendship, is the fact Fort Worth "acquired"

21Knight, *op. cit.*, p. 222.

22Dallas *Morning News*, June 24, 1955.

23Knight, *op. cit.*, p. 225.

the U. S. Public Health Service Hospital, the Carswell Airforce Base, U. S. Quartermaster Depot, Convair, a considerable number of federal regional offices, and federal money for the development of the Fort Worth International Airport (Amon G. Carter Field) and Benbrook Dam. Certainly other Texas and southern cities secured federal projects, and it must be recognized that there is a danger in attributing achievement to any one man, or for any one reason, but even with such cautions in mind, it seems apparent that Carter was instrumental in the successful acquisition of the developments mentioned, as well as many others.

Carter was interested not only in securing things for Fort Worth; he also took an active part in developing the city internally. For a time he was president of the Chamber of Commerce, and was chairman or honoray chairman of just about every important movement to improve the city. His interest, however, was not alone for Fort Worth. West Texas was also important to him. He was instrumental in the location of Texas Technological College at Lubbock and served as the first chairman of the board of that state college.

Of particular interest to Carter was the development of aviation. He was successful in getting many early barnstormers to include Fort Worth in their itinerary, in securing money from Congress for the International Airport, and was long a director of American Airlines. For his interest in aviation, he was awarded the Frank M. Hawks memorial award in 1950 for "his many contributions to the development of aviation in America."

Some measure of Carter's influence can be secured from the story of his death in the Dallas *Morning News*. The front-page story began, "Amon Giles Carter, perhaps the most internationally famous Texan of the 20th century, died Thursday night."[24] Many people, of course, have achieved international fame. The importance of the statement quoted is that Carter apparently at all times sought to translate his friendships into benefits for Fort Worth and Texas. In a very real sense he was a roving ambassador for the city and the state. And as any good

----

[24]Dallas *Morning News*, June 24, 1955.

ambassador would do, he worked diligently to further the inter-ests of his homeland.[25]

Expansion of City Limits. Another reason for the growth of Fort Worth has been the expansion of the city limits. In one sense, however, the expansion of the city limits is merely the logical incorporation of interrelated areas. Even so there are separate legal municipalities immediately adjacent to the city which are an integral part of the social and economic fabric of the city. The legal expansion of the city, with the incorporation dates of the adjacent municipalities, is shown in Figure 3.

In the main, the growth of Fort Worth from the time of its incorporation in 1873 to the present has been of a horizontal rather than of a vertical nature. That is, as the town became a city the growth was outward to the periphery rather than up-ward. This fact is shown in Table 2. Thus, it can be seen that in relation to population per square mile, the city was more densely populated in 1910 than it was in 1950.[26]

Table 2. Total Population, Total Square Mile Area, and Population Per Square Mile, Fort Worth: 1890-1950.*

Year	Population	Square Miles	Population Per Square Mile
1890	23,076	7.20	3,205
1900	26,688	—	—
1910	73,312	16.83	4,356
1920	106,482	—	—
1930	163,447	61.57	2,655
1940	177,662	65.65	2,706
1950	278,778	103.20	2,702

*Source: City of Fort Worth, Department of Public Works. For 1950 comparisons with other cities, see Table 47, herein.

Additional evidence of the predominantly horizontal growth of Fort Worth can be secured from the 1950 Bureau of Census reports. This evidence indicates that Fort Worth's pattern of growth has been more horizontal than is true for comparable

[25]The above account is intended only to present some of the ways Carter functioned as an effective leader. Understandably, a man in his position made enemies, and many disagreed with his value orientations.

[26]The low density per square mile is related to the large amount of land in parks and lakes. When such areas are excluded, the square-mile area of Fort Worth in 1950 was approximately 83 square miles (83.849). On this basis, the population per square mile in 1950 was 3.325.

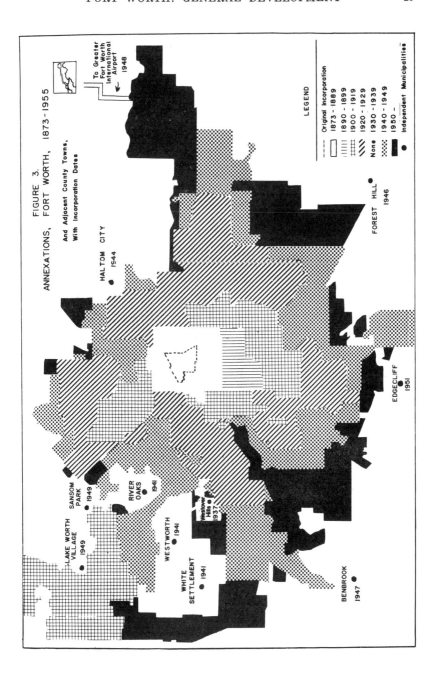

FIGURE 3.
ANNEXATIONS, FORT WORTH, 1873-1955
And Adjacent County Towns,
With Incorporation Dates

LEGEND

Original Incorporation
1873 - 1889
1890 - 1899
1900 - 1919
1920 - 1929
1930 - 1939
None
1940 - 1949
1950 -
Independent Municipalities

To Greater
Fort Worth
International
Airport
1948

HALTOM CITY
1944

FOREST HILL
1946

EDGECLIFF
1951

SANSOM PARK
1949

LAKE WORTH VILLAGE
1949

RIVER OAKS
1941

WESTWORTH
1941

Westover Hills
1937

WHITE SETTLEMENT
1941

BENBROOK
1947

cities in other parts of the country. Thus, for renter-occupied
dwelling units, the percent of Fort Worth units which were
single-detached structures was greater than was true in representative Eastern cities. Also, Fort Worth had a lower percent
of its units in structures of 10 or more dwelling units. For selected representative cities the following tabulation provides revealing contrasts.[27]

| City | Renter-Occupied Dwelling Units | |
	One Unit Detached Structures	Ten or More Units in One Structure
	Percent	
Fort Worth	39.7	4.5
Dallas	29.8	8.0
Akron, Ohio	22.7	6.5
Dayton	19.7	13.4
Rochester, N. Y.	11.8	16.4
Buffalo	9.0	6.9
Providence, R. I.	4.9	7.9
Chicago	3.7	36.4
Baltimore	2.2	7.5

Of importance in peripheral growth are the factors of transportation facilities, the desire for more living space, and the
activities of residential developers. The role of the developer is
particularly important because he tends to operate where he can
secure large acreage at low cost, which is usually on or near a
city's outer edge.

Interestingly, expansion of city limits meets with varied
response from the residents of the acquired areas. One of the
first sections added to the original city limits in Fort Worth was
on the southside and occurred because the people wanted city
services. Apparently the annexation of Arlington Heights on
the west and Polytechnic on the east occurred for the same
reasons. In contrast, Niles City on the northside which grew up
around the stockyards was added only after a court fight.[28]
The fear of annexation is probably one of the reasons for the
number of recent incorporations on the periphery of Fort Worth.

[27]Source: U. S. Bureau of the Census. *U. S. Census of Housing: 1950.* Vol.
II, *Nonfarm Housing Characteristics,* (Standard Metropolitan Area reports, Table
B-3).

[28]"Community Life," Fort Worth *Star Telegram, loc. cit.,* p. 2.

The desire to have more living space is an important factor in the functioning of the urban community. It has had a profound influence on land and housing values in the inner sections of the city. In addition, this trend has added to the cost of city government. On the one hand, the tendency has been for the city to expand its limits to newly developed areas, thus necessitating new sewer and street construction, as well as expanded fire, police, and school services. Often this means that already established facilities and services of the inner areas of the city are not used to their maximum capacity. In other instances, the suburban area establishes a separate municipality. This often creates problems of duplication of services, conflicts of legal authority, and raises the issue of whether the residents of the independent suburbs are paying for services they use in the central city.

Summary. In the section dealing with leadership, certain questions have been raised concerning the nature of urban development. Most pertinent are those concerning the validity of the evidence presented for Fort Worth, and the question as to whether the conditions which seem to have been influential in Fort Worth are unique or of a more general nature. Will further evidence reveal that promotion is significant in implementing urban growth? In the case of Fort Worth it seems apparent that at certain periods in the city's history a leveling process occurred. A new stage of growth was entered when important new economic units were introduced into the community's economy. Generalizations, however, will have to be based on similar investigations in other urban areas.

Also, it may be suggested that the questions raised here apply not only to the nature of urban expansion. If urban sociologists have in general ignored an important factor in city growth, can it not be argued that they have ignored a factor which should be considered in the functioning of the urban area in general?

CHAPTER II

THE GROWTH OF FORT WORTH: STAGES OF DEVELOPMENT

In this chapter the history of the community is considered in terms of seven stages or levels. In each instance, it is believed, a new period began after the introduction of some new element of major socio-economic significance. Although the new elements which are considered important are essentially economic in nature, there is no intention to give only an economic interpretation of the town's development. While it must not be overlooked that changes in education, religion, government, and other institutional practices were vitally important, yet the economic innovations seem to have been of major importance, and particularly in the general growth of the community from a frontier settlement to a metropolis. In these changes local leadership had a part, sometimes a major part, in the introduction of the new element. It might be argued, as an illustration, that the introduction of public education was of more lasting importance than any of the factors which are listed below. Certainly public education is important, but many villages have introduced free schooling without becoming metropolitan centers.

In later chapters the importance of other developments will be discussed in some detail. The stages which will be outlined in the following pages are:

1. Military outpost

2. County seat of Tarrant County

3. Oasis on the cattle trail

4. The coming of the railroad

5. Development as a livestock-processing center

6. Development of West Texas oil fields, and role of the

city as a center for military installations during World
War I.

7. Aircraft manufacture and diversified industry[1]

As a convenient, if oversimplified, method of presenting
historical sequences in the development of the city, it is assumed
the periods between these innovations represented levels of
relative equilibrium. The city reached a new level when
the old equilibrium was disturbed by the addition of some distinctive and significant cultural element. Thus, at a particular
time the then existent economic base could support a community
and a population of rather well defined limits. The addition of
a new economic unit of importance meant the movement into a
new stage and significant expansion of the community and
growth of population. In line with the theory of leadership
presented in the previous chapter, the information suggests that
each new stage or level was achieved in part at least because
local leadership was effective in bringing into the community
important new economic activities.[2]

---

[1]The particular factors in the growth of Fort Worth were first suggested to
the writer by Mr. C. J. Watson, who at the time was manager of the Research Department, Fort Worth Chamber of Commerce. For a classification similar to the
one used herein, see, Oliver Knight, Fort Worth; *Outpost on the Trinity* (Norman:
University of Oklahoma Press, 1953), pp. 216-17.

[2]While the particular stages or levels listed above are in the main unique
to Fort Worth, the procedure has been widely used. The use of constructed typolo-
gies as theoretical constructs to show community processes in time has been a common device in sociological literature as well as elsewhere. Representative of this is
a study by Albion W. Small and George E. Vincent which was published in 1894.
In this report the authors trace community development from village to town and
from town to city. There is a close parallel between the development of the community described by Small and Vincent and that of Fort Worth. See, T. Lynn Smith
and C. A. McMahan, *The Sociology of Urban Life* (New York: The Dryden Press,
1951), pp. 141-151 (quoted from, *The Study of Society*, published by the American
Book Company, 1894). For a list of other early studies of community development,
as well as another example of constructed typology, see, Robert H. Talbert, "The
Emergence of Ruraltown" (unpublished Ph.D. thesis, Duke University, 1943). For
a discussion of the emergence of urban centers in the South, see, Smith and Mc-
Mahan, *op. cit.* pp. 159-171.

Stages In Fort Worth's Growth

Military Outpost. As seen earlier, Fort Worth had its origin
in 1849, four years after the annexation of Texas to the Union,
when a troop of United States cavalry established a camp and,

later, a fort on the banks of the Trinity River to protect the band of settlers pushing westward.[3] The fort was one of nine planned for the Texas frontier on a line extending from Oklahoma south and slightly west to the Rio Grande River.[4] At the time, Dallas to the east was already an established community. In what is now Tarrant County, settlements were located at Bird's Fort (Birdville), seven miles east of the Fort location, and at Johnson Station, a few miles southeast of present-day Fort Worth. The fort (Fort Worth), located on the bluff overlooking the Trinity River, near the present site of the Tarrant County courthouse, consisted of a few green timber log and mud cabins built by the soldiers. The military force at the time consisted of one officer and 25 privates, which was hardly sufficient for scouting activity.[5] Later additional strength was added.

The fort apparently lent some stability to the area. More settlers arrived, and a few businesses were established around the fort. The state legislature provided further stability by having established Tarrant County in 1849; organization occurred in 1850.[6] In 1853 the fort was abandoned, and the military forces were moved to Fort Belknap, 100 miles to the west and north. But the civilians remained, and others joined them, including a few professional men. In 1856, however, according to Peak, the population of Fort Worth was 67.

In this first stage of Fort Worth's development there was little to lead to a permanent community. It had the potentials— settlers, a water supply, a farming area, and a few business and

---

[3]Camp Worth was named in honor of Major General William Jenkins Worth, who at the time was Commandant of the Eighth and Ninth United States military departments which included Texas and New Mexico. See, Howard W. Peak, *The Story of Old Fort Worth* (no date, publisher, or pagination; available in the Fort Worth Public Library). Peak was the first white male child born in the settlement.

[4]For a map showing this line, see Knight, *op. cit.*, p. 10.

[5]*Ibid.*, pp. 15-16.

[6]The county was named for General E. H. Tarrant. At the time the area was a part of Navarro County. General Tarrant was a member of the state legislature, representing Navarro and Limestone Counties. He was an old Indian fighter and onetime member of the Texas Congress. See Knight, *op. cit.*, pp. 19-20.

professional men, including a school teacher[7]—but many other
frontier settlements had similar opportunities for development.
There was nothing in this original stage which destined it inevitably to survive, let alone achieve its present metropolitan
status.

County Seat of Tarrant County. An event of major importance for the future of the settlement occurred in 1856. In that
year the residents of the Fort Worth area succeeded in having
their town designated as the county seat of Tarrant County.[8]
When the county was established by an act of the state legislature in 1849, Birdville was named as the county seat, apparently because it was the largest settlement in the new county. But
in 1856 Fort Worth residents convinced the state legislature that
a local election should be held to determine the county seat. In
the election, held in November, 1856, Fort Worth won by seven
votes, but apparently only because of the "ingenuity" of Fort
Worth citizens and friends. This ingenuity consisted primarily
in having available a goodly supply of free whiskey, the successful stealing of the Birdville whiskey cached away for the occasion, and the assistance of a former resident, who brought 14
friends from an adjoining county to the voting booth.[9] The
court equipment was immediately moved to Fort Worth, but the
issue was not permanently settled until 1860, when a second
county election gave Fort Worth 548 votes out of a total of 853
votes cast. Probably the deciding factor in the 1860 election was
an agreement made by 38 men to pay for the cost of a permanent
courthouse building in Fort Worth.[10]

---

[7]John Peter Smith opened the first school in 1854 with 12 pupils. See Peak,
op. cit. Smith's contributions to the early life of the community have been recognized with a public school named after him, and recently the changing of the
name of City-County Hospital to John Peter Smith Hospital.

[8]For the early history of Tarrant County, see Verna Elizabeth Berrong, "History of Tarrant County from its beginning until 1875 (unpublished M. A. thesis,
Texas Christian University, 1938).

[9]See Peak, *op. cit.*

[10]For a list of men, see B. B. Paddock, *Fort Worth and the Texas Northwest* (Chicago: Lewis Publishing Company, 1922), Vol. II, p. 837.

The importance of this victory lay mainly in the fact that it gave to the settlement a basis for permanence. In addition, Fort Worth became the logical place of settlement for lawyers, doctors, businessmen, and other settlers moving into the area.

Oasis on the Cattle Trail. The decade from 1860 to 1870 was one of serious setbacks for the struggling frontier village of Fort Worth. During the war years the county population dropped from 6,000 to approximately 1,000. Little money was in circulation, and the few merchants who remained found it almost impossible to get goods to sell. The difficulties of the time are described vividly by Peak:

> During the four years of the Civil War Fort Worth was in the throes of despair. It was stagnant. No business. No trading. Marooned as we were with the frontier on the west with its Indian enemy, and no railroad within 200 miles, our condition was desperate. But thanks be, the Indians were at peace at the time and had it been otherwise, with our able-bodied men away fighting for their Southland, God knows what would have become of us.[11]

Knight reports one case in 1865 of a local resident's using a $20 gold piece to pay a medical bill, and then later in the day receiving the same piece as payment for a debt owed to him. In checking back, the man discovered the gold piece had been used to pay over $200 in debts in a single day. Following the War, some settlers returned and new ones arrived, but even with the returnees and new arrivals the population of the county in 1870 was less than it was in 1860, and Fort Worth was described as, "a sluggish settlement of no more than three hundred souls, 'a dirty, dreary, cold, mean little place.' "[12]

However, a third factor in the development of Fort Worth began to operate even before 1870. With the end of the Civil War the people of the North were hungry for the meat that was plentiful on the West Texas range land. The problem was to get the cattle to market. This was partially solved by driving the cattle north to westward-moving railroad lines. When the Kansas and Pacific Railroad reached Abilene, Kansas, in 1867,

---

[11]Peak, *op. cit.*

[12]Knight, *op. cit.*, p. 59.

large herds of cattle began to move from the Texas plains to the Kansas town. According to one report,

> ... it is estimated that around 250,000 cattle were trailed North from 1866 to 1870. The year 1871 is considered the peak year when a total of more than 600,000 went up the trail. Then the decline in trail movements set in and by 1885 the trail herds had practically faded from the cattle picture. However, there were some trail herds moved around 1890.[13]

Fort Worth played an important part in the movement of cattle eastward, first as a stopping place in the trail drives, and later as a place from which the cattle could be shipped. On the trail drives Fort Worth was "about the last place where the trail hands could reprovision and take a last fling before striking out for the Indian country to the north."[14] Later, when the railroad came to Fort Worth, it became a focal point for the economic activity of the cattle industry. In addition, the village soon gained the reputation as a place where the men of the industry could have a good time. Whiskey and women were apparently easily available. And after the coming of the railroad in 1876, "Fort Worth erupted into the wildest town in western Texas."[15]

The Coming of the Railroad.[16] As suggested in chapter I, by 1858 leading local citizens became convinced that their community could become a terminus for one of the railroads being built westward. Even though their dream was interrupted by the crisis of the Civil War and the Panic of 1873, such actions did serve the purpose of unifying the local citizenry, and indicated the development of some community spirit. Following the

---

13"Ranch and Farm," Fort Worth *Star-Telegram, loc. cit.,* p. 2. The first trail herd of cattle moved through Fort Worth in 1866. See *Research Data: Fort Worth and Tarrant County,* Texas Writers' Project, Vol. I, p. 250 (available in Fort Worth Public Library).

14Knight, *op. cit.,* p. 61. See also, Peak, *op. cit.*

15Knight, *op. cit.,* p. 87. See also his Chapter VI, "Blood, Lust and Gold."

16For an account of the local interest and of the difficulties which developed as well as the final success in securing the first railroad, and those which came later, see Paddock, *op. cit.,* pp. 611-614, and Peak, *op. cit.*

Civil War a renewed effort was made to secure a railroad. Local money and land were provided, and the state of Texas was induced to set aside land for railroad use.[17]

The first attempt came in 1873, when, through the leadership of a Fort Worth citizen, the Fort Worth and Denver City Railway Company was granted a charter by the state legislature.[18] While this line did not become a reality as far as Fort Worth was concerned until 1890 (construction was started from both ends of the line),[19] it did serve to arouse local interest and enthusiasm. One energetic citizen had prepared a huge canvas map which showed nine railroads passing through Fort Worth. This map was displayed prominently in the courthouse square. Although no line was at the time within 30 miles of the city, the map served as a challenge. "And lest the citizenry forget their destiny with the iron horse, Captain B. B. Paddock (editor of the Fort Worth *Democrat*) succeeded in reproducing the map in his paper and persisted in publishing it for weeks on end."[20]

By 1873, tracks of the Texas and Pacific Railroad had been laid to within 24 miles of Fort Worth, and settlers had arrived

---

[17]"The state's first railroad, designed to link Harrisburg (now a part of Houston) and the Brazos River, put its first twenty miles into operation in September, 1853. That was the beginning of a network that gradually worked northwestward from the Gulf Coast to reach a total of more than seven hundred miles by 1870. The next three years saw construction that was especially pertinent to the plans of Fort Worth. In Midsummer, 1872, the Houston and Texas Central (now Southern Pacific) reached Dallas from the south, thus opening a continuous line from Galveston and Houston. Later that year the Missouri, Kansas and Texas brought its main line from Kansas City across the Red River to Denison, at which point the Houston and Texas Central joined it in March, 1873. At almost the same moment, the Texas and Pacific began construction of its Shreveport-Dallas line, even then projected to continue to Fort Worth and El Paso," Richard C. Overton, *Gulf to Rockies* (Austin: University of Texas Press, 1953), p. 27. By 1876, when the first train moved into Fort Worth, there were 1,910 miles of track. By 1952 the number of miles of main track had increased to 15,511. See the Dallas *Morning News, Texas Almanac,* 1954-55, p. 262. Figures compiled by the Railroad Commission of Texas.

[18]Overton, *op. cit.,* p. 31.

[19]*Ibid.,* p. 95.

[20]*Ibid.,* p. 34.

in anticipation of future business opportunities. The town's population increased from around 300 in 1872 to 3,000 in 1873.[21] However, the financial panic of that year, which occurred nationally, led to local difficulties.

The company building the railroad lost its financial backing and stopped work, and the population of Fort Worth dropped to about 600 people within the year. The crisis is described by one writer in the following manner:

> There was little or no business left to Fort Worth, except the spring cattle drive. That brought business to a few. The town was dead as far as business and development went. The grass literally grew in the street. This was not a metaphor to indicate stagnation, but a doleful fact. There were more empty stores and vacant dwellings than those that were occupied.[22]

But in spite of this crisis the railroad line was brought into the town in 1876, at least partly through the energy and work of local citizens. A newspaper account shows the local interest:

> Fort Worth's men and women went to work on the problem. It wasn't hopeless. The Legislature had voted the T & P a land grant of 16 sections per mile, provided the tracks reached Fort Worth by Jan. 1, 1873. As each succeeding Legislature met, it extended the deadline for a year. The Fort Worth donors did likewise. The extensions continued until the Constitutional Convention of 1875 made the time limit 'the date of adjournment of the first legislature held under the new state constitution.'
>
> Fort Worth acted rapidly. In 1875, citizens organized the Tarrant County Railway Construction Company and told the T & P they would build roadbeds, culverts and bridges from Eagle Ford to Fort Worth. The T & P agreed to lay ties and tracks. Stock was bought by residents who promised to pay in money, labor, material, supplies or anything else of market value. A contract was given to Riche Brothers & Tierney.
>
> The 'deadline Legislature' convened on the second Tuesday of January 1876. Again the T & P asked for a time extension. Opposition to the request was strong. Fort Worth, too, demanded action. By July 7, the tracks began to creep forward and the work train whistle 'roused the natives of Johnson Station.' Tracks were laid at the rate of a mile a day. The company purchased 20 locomotives and 400 cars. 'As soon as the track is laid the cars will begin delivering timber and lumber for the most extensive cattle yards in the state,' the Fort Worth Democrat reported.
>
> Meanwhile, in Austin, the Legislature finished work and strained to go home. The Senate sent an adjournment resolution to the House for approval. Adjournment meant the T & P would

---

[21]"Transportation," Fort Worth Star-Telegram, loc. cit., p. 2.
[22]Paddock, op. cit., Vol. II, pp. 606-607.

lose the land grant and Fort Worth the railroad. Vote after vote was taken. The go-home block needed but one vote to win. Tarrant County's representative, Nicholas Henry Darnell was ill. For 15 days, until the railroad reached Fort Worth, he was carried into the House on a cot to vote 'nay' on adjournment.

Graders sweated, track layers kept at their heels, mule-skinners swore and the railroad forged ahead. The tracks crossed Farmer E. J. Tandy's fields, four miles east of town on July 15. At Sycamore Creek, the feverish contractors decided it would take too long to build a trestle. The bridge over the creek was strengthened. Ties and rails were laid on the dirt county road which paralleled the railroad right-of-way. The ties were weighted at each end with stones. 'It was as crooked as the proverbial ram's horn but it bore the rails,' Editor B. B. Paddock wrote in the Democrat the next day.

On July 15, the laborers began to work nights, too. They took an hour off for supper, worked until midnight, rested until dawn, then started out again. To help things along, City Council met and extended the city limits a quarter of a mile east. Fort Worth women organized sandwich squads, bringing hampers of food morning, afternoon, and night. The rough workmen cheered and called them 'angels.' As the tracks neared the depot site at E. Lancaster and Main, a duck pond impeded work. Draining and filling would take time, so the tracks were curved around the pond.

On July 18, the city began filling up with visitors from miles around. The railroad was due the next day! And it arrived on schedule. Chugging and puffing, crawling forward slowly to keep from jumping the shaky track, Engine No. 20, the T & P work train, came in at 11:23 the next morning. She weaved and rocked, but advanced steadily through the lines of frenzied settlers, cow-boys, business men, housewives and children. Thousands dressed in Sunday finery strained to get to look at the 'contraption.' The 12-piece Fort Worth Cornet Band tootled manfully.

The celebration lasted all night. Contractors paid off the laborers. Most of them thronged to the saloons to celebrate. 'Our police officers should exercise discretion and leniency to the hands paid off,' Editor Paddock counseled. 'D. D.'s (drunk and disorderly) must be treated with leniency for a few days.' In Austin, the Legislature voted to adjourn but Fort Worth didn't care.[23]

Some of the results of the coming of the railroad are reported by Peak in the following manner:

With the advent of the first train on July 19, 1876, the young city took on a new energy and immediately stepped into high gear. New and better hotels were built, lumber yards and cement plants were added, gas works and flour mills were established; an ice plant and factories were built . . . the hitherto muddy streets were paved, first with wood and stone, followed with asphalt and cement[24]

---

[23]"Transportation," Fort Worth *Star Telegram, loc. cit.,* p. 2.

[24]Peak, *op. cit.*

Apparently, however, Fort Worth did not become a modern city immediately. Knight reports that until 1878 hogs were a major nuisance on the streets, where they curdled mudholes into sties; in 1878 public opinion against the hogs was shown in a referendum which favored an anti-hog law by the narrow vote of 377 to 324.[25] In 1905 mud was still a major problem, according to the Mayor's report of that year.[26]

The decade beginning in 1870 was a vital one in the transformation of a frontier settlement into an established community. The town was incorporated and the first city government formed in 1873. In addition to the railroad, the town secured during the decade telegraphic connections with the outside world; the first newspaper was started, the first bank was organized, mule-drawn street cars were introduced, and artificial gas was made available. In 1870 there were 59 business concerns in the town. In 1878 the first artesian well was completed. Prior to this time water had been secured from a spring on the Birdville road and delivered by wagon for domestic purposes. Before the artesian well, water to fight fires had been collected, when it rained, in cisterns.[27] By 1880 the town could boast of a population of 6,663, as reported by the United States Census Bureau, and approximately 460 retail and wholesale business establishments.[28]

The coming of the railroad gave Fort Worth contact with the east but it also helped establish more firmly socio-economic relations with West Texas. It "assumed a greater stature as the cattleman's town, supplying ranches and serving as a transit point for livestock shipped north."[29] Recalling this period, B. B.

---

[25]Knight, *op. cit.*, p. 116.

[26]*Research Data, loc. cit., Vol. I*, p. 247.

[27]B. B. Paddock, *Early Days in Fort Worth: Much of Which I Saw and Part of Which I Was* (no date or publisher; available in Fort Worth Public Library), p. 17.

[28]"Transportation," Fort Worth *Star-Telegram, loc. cit.*, p. 2.

[29]Knight, *op. cit.*, p. 105.

Paddock who arrived in Fort Worth in 1872 and stayed to become a newspaper editor and one of the town's leading promo-
tors, wrote in 1922:

> Progress and development have been so swift in obliterating
> the primitive order of things and introducing all the accomplish-
> ments of modern life that even old-time citizens have forgoten
> the 'wild and woolly' aspects of existence in Fort Worth during
> the later '70s. The railroad brought its evils as well as its bene-
> fits. For several years Fort Worth was the clearing house between
> the legally constituted society of the East and the free and un-
> trammeled life of the West. Here the currents of humanity met,
> and in the swirling vortex that ensued could be found every class
> of mankind.[30]

Soon after the Texas and Pacific arrived, stage lines were established to the surrounding area.[31] In 1878 Fort Worth became the
eastern terminus of what was called, "the world's longest stage
line—1,500 miles from Fort Worth to Fort Yuma, Arizona."[32]

As a one-railroad town, however, Fort Worth's future was
definitely limited. Being the western terminus of a line was of
considerable importance, but with extension further westward
there was danger of the town's becoming just another stopping
place along the main line. Apparently local citizens realized this
danger, because after 1876 they began working to bring other
lines into the town. At least partly through such efforts, which
included bonuses and grants of town land for depots and yards,
other lines did come. A northern outlet developed first when the
Missouri, Kansas and Texas came into Fort Worth in 1880, via
the Texas and Pacific tracks. In 1881 a southern outlet was provided with the arrival of the Santa Fe. The Cotton Belt lines
came in 1887, and as mentioned previously, the Fort Worth and
Denver City connections were completed in 1890, although tracks
were laid to within 5 miles and connections established with

---

[30]Paddock, *Fort Worth and the Texas Northwest, op. cit.,* p. 614.

[31]Beginning somewhat earlier, but coming into prominence with the advent
of the railroad, was the development of the wagon yard. This type of business establishment provided supplies and service for both local residents and settlers
moving west. Commonly, the wagon yard was built in a large enclosure, and provided hay, water, horseshoeing, wagon repair. supplies, and some had cabins for
the weary travelers. In a very real sense the wagon yard was a forerunner of the
present-day filling station and tourist court.

[32]Knight, *op. cit.,* p. 102.

Denver by 1888. The last of the railroads was the Rock Island, which arrived in 1893.[33]

In retrospect, it may be argued that the railroad lines would have come through Fort Worth without local assistance, since they were spreading in all directions through Texas. This may have been true for the later roads, but in the beginning other towns might have been chosen just as well. In the early days in the West, railroads helped to develop population centers, and to a considerable extent influenced their exact locations. Only later did they connect already established centers; and in Central and West Texas, with few natural barriers to roadbed construction, the railroad companies could vary their rights-of-way to meet local conditions—meaning in the main, cash bonuses and gifts of land within a town's limits.

Development as a Livestock Processing Center. As indicated previously, almost from the beginning, Fort Worth has been closely connected with the live-stock industry in Texas. And as conditions in the industry have changed, Fort Worth's role as a "cow-town" has changed, but since 1860 it has been a major role. During the trail-driving period, Fort Worth was a "favorite spot for herds and hands to lay over for a while, and stores and salons catered to that trade. Many northern buyers made the town their headquarters."[34] Later when the railroads took over much of the shipment of cattle to Eastern and Northern markets, Fort Worth continued its importance as a "break in transportation."—cattle being trail-driven from West Texas and then being shipped by rail.

However, the rail shipment of cattle did not solve all the problems and bring the perfect arrangement. First, the freight rates were too high to suit the cattlemen. Second, there was difficulty in shipment because the long horns of early Texas cattle

[33]See Paddock, *Fort Worth and the Texas Northwest, op. cit.,* pp. 611-614; see also, Paddock, *Early Days in Fort Worth; op. cit.,* p. 5, ff.

[34]"Ranch and Farm," Fort Worth *Star-Telegram, loc. cit.,* p. 16.

limited the number of head to the carload. Then there was the problem of the cattle tick. Northern buyers tended to discriminate against Texas cattle because of ticks. For these and possibly other reasons cattlemen and Fort Worth citizens saw the need for processing the meat in Texas before shipment.

Soon after the invention of the refrigerated car, local entrepeneurs in 1877 shipped meat by refrigeration eastward, but apparently this was not successful.[35] In 1883 a local meat-packing company was organized, but lasted only a year or so. Another attempt was made in 1890, with the organization of the Fort Worth Dressed Meat and Packing Company. In the same year a permanent stockyards was constructed. The stage was set for Fort Worth to become the meat packing center of the Southwest, but not on the basis established at that time. The local packing company soon found it difficult to compete successfully with the larger companies centering around Chicago. Thus, when the Swift and Armour Companies began to look for Texas sites for branch plants, Fort Worth was quite willing to welcome them with open arms. However, as was true of the railroads, there were many towns in Texas which were suitable locations. Fort Worth may have been logical, but the packers demanded money from the successful town; so it was that Fort Worth citizens again turned to the task of raising funds to add something new to the local economy. After several months the bonus of $100,-000 for the two packing companies was pledged. The day after the bonus was raised the local newspaper reported the success:

> Fort Worth made history for herself and Texas last night. Fort Worth today will be on the lips of every man, woman and child who reads. Fort Worth, the packing house center of all the South and Southwest. Fort Worth the metropolis of Texas—the metropolis of the South and West. Fort Worth started on her road to greatness last night.[36]

Fort Worth did not quite become *the* metropolis of Texas or the South and Southwest—in Texas, Houston, Dallas, and San

[35]For the early trials and failures in attempting to make Fort Worth a meat-packing town, see Paddock, *Fort Worth and the Texas Northwest, op. cit.*, pp. 657-59.

[36]Fort Worth *Register*, Oct. 8, 1901, p. 1, quoted in Knight, *op. cit.*, p. 174.

Antonio were and still are larger in terms of population—but it did become the leading livestock center as predicted.[37]

Today livestock and meat packing are only two of many economic activities of Fort Worth, but cattle are still vitally important, and certainly cattle have helped to propel Fort Worth from just another cowtown to *the* Texas cowtown and on to an important Southwest metropolis.

Development of West Texas Oil Fields and Influence of Military Installations During World War I.[38] Between 1910 and 1920 the population of Fort Worth increased from 73,312 to 106,-482. Part of this increase was due to the addition of many small primary economic activities. But certainly an important influence in the population growth during this decade, and even more so in later decades, was the role Fort Worth played in the development of the oil industry in Texas.

As early as 1911 Fort Worth had achieved some importance in the industry. In 1911 and 1912 the Gulf Refining Company and the Pierce Oil Company established refining plants in the city. According to one source, these establishments and related activities made Fort Worth, at the time, the state's leading inland refining and pipe line city.[39] However, the influence of oil on the economic life of the city did not become important until after 1917. In that year discoveries were made at Ranger, and in the following year at Desdemona. Both of these fields are located in Eastland County, some 90 miles west of Fort Worth. Also of importance were the fields developed, beginning in 1918, around Burkburnett to the northwest in Wichita County. In a

---

[37]Along with Swift and Armour, the Libby, McNeil and Libby Company established a packing plant in the area, but this was later closed. See *Research Data, loc. cit.*, Vol. I, p. 250. This same source reports that as a result of the packing houses, many wealthy cattle barons were attracted to the city.

[38]For a more inclusive treatment of the development of the oil industry, see Knight, *op. cit.*, pp. 195-99, and "Oil and Gas," Fort Worth *Star-Telegram, loc. cit.* As used here, the oil industry includes the distribution of oil drilling and related equipment, the process of actual well-drilling, the processing of oil, and necessary business structure to finance the operations.

[39]"Oil and Gas," Fort Worth *Star-Telegram, loc. cit.*, p. 2.

very real sense these three fields laid the foundation for Fort
Worth's continuing interest and importance in the West Texas
oil industry.[40]

The part played by Fort Worth in the development of the
West Texas oil fields has varied somewhat in time. In the beginning, because of its established facilities, it became the center
for the oil operators, and in Fort Worth many of the financial
transactions necessary for oil development were carried out.
Knight describes this period in the following manner:

> By being a concentration point for oil operators, Fort Worth was
> a hotbed of oil transactions. Men crowded the streets, clamoring
> for a chance to invest money that would bring quick, manifold re-
> turns. The center of activity was the Westbrook Hotel, where the
> management was forced to remove all furniture from the lobby
> to clear space for the oil mart. But even that seemed hardly to
> lessen the congestion, for the daily crowds overflowed through
> the big double doors to the sidewalks and into the street.[41]

Apparently not all of the operators were interested in honest
transactions. Knight also records this part of the early picture:

> The excitement bordering on hysteria was a perfect incubator for
> shady operators who specialized in bogus stock. Scores of such men
> hurried into Fort Worth, where the rush and bustle of legitimate
> oil undertakings gave them both cover and concealment. The shady
> operator had a batch of fictitious stock printed and peddled on
> street corners. Men were only too anxious to place their money in
> an oil well, sight unseen, operator unknown. In front of the bogus
> operator standing on the street corner, long queues of men formed.
> They waited patiently in line to hand over good money for worth-
> less paper. Not infrequently an impatient speculator far down the
> line could be heard to shout, 'Save some for me.'[42]

The available railroad connections of the time made Fort
Worth the logical central point for the early West Texas developments. The main line of the Texas and Pacific Railroad
connected Fort Worth with the Ranger fields; after the discoveries at Desdemona branch lines were extended to that area.
Connections for the Burkburnett fields were provided by the

---

[40]With regard to these developments, Knight writes, "These were the three
great oil developments: Ranger, Burkburnett, and Desdemona. They were going
full blast at the same time, carrying over from World War I into the twenties. And
Fort Worth was the town that derived lasting benefits from the booms." Knight,
op. cit., p. 197.

[41]*Ibid.*, p. 197.

[42]*Ibid.*, p. 198.

Fort Worth and Denver Railroad to Wichita Falls and then via the Missouri, Kansas and Texas to Burkburnett.

In addition to the influence of oil, Fort Worth was for a short time During World War I a military center. Camp Bowie was located on the edge of the city in what is now the Arlington Heights section, and three airfields were located nearby. The importance of the military installations will be considered in Chapter V. Here it can be suggested that they were helpful in bringing people to the city, and in showing local people what could be accomplished through cooperation.

The more lasting benefits for Fort Worth of the oil discoveries became apparent in the 1920's, although the general developments during the decade cannot be attributed entirely to oil expansion. At the beginning of the decade the Fort Worth metropolitan area (Tarrant County) was the leading manufacturing area in the state in terms of "value added by manufacture,"[43] and the city, with its railroad connections was the main gateway to the growing West Texas area. Thus, while oil apparently provided a new element to influence the city's economy, the already existing trade and manufacturing were also important factors in growth.

For Fort Worth the 1920's were particularly prosperous. In 1922 the city annexed several of the suburban sections, including the tax-rich area of the stockyards and packing plants, to double its land area. Between 1915 and 1925 the assessed valuation for tax purposes increased from $67,046,941 to $152,000,000.[44] In 1921 the Chamber of Commerce could report that the city's Farmers and Mechanics National Bank building was the tallest in the Southwest (24 stories).[45] The same

---

[43]*Fourteenth Census of the United States*, Vol. IX, *Manufactures*, pp. 1449-1459. Dallas County had the largest number of establishments and Harris County (Houston) the highest number of wage earners.

[44]"Fort Worth," annual report of the Chamber of Commerce, 1926. Part of this increase, of course, was due to increased prices and values of the post-war period.

[45]The Farmers and Mechanics National Bank later became a part of Fort Worth National Bank. The Fort Worth National Bank was organized in 1884.

account reported 50 concerns manufacturing oil field supplies, and 342 oil company offices.[46]

By 1925 Fort Worth was claiming to be the leading pipe-line (oil) center in the United States, with six and eight-inch pipe lines bringing oil to the city's refineries from the fields at or near Electra, Ranger, Wichita Falls, Burkburnett, and Healdton.[47] In 1922 there were 9 refineries operating in the city area. By 1925 the Chamber of Commerce was reporting petroleum products as second in importance in manufacturing, below packing-house products and ahead of flour and feed products.[48] In 1921 the Chevrolet Motor Car Company and the Texas Motor Car Association were assembling 120 vehicles daily.[49] Between 1915 and 1924 yearly grain inspections had increased from 11,792 cars to 34,475.[50]

The year 1925 saw the establishment of the present council-manager form of city government and the passage of a bond issue of $7,659,000 for street widening, paving, sewer and water extension, swimming pools, additional park sites, and an annex to the City-County Hospital. This was reported as the largest bond issue a Texas city had ever voted.[51] Significant in terms of new community attitudes, was the fact that $500,000 of the issue was earmarked for park development. This was not the first local interest in parks, but it showed a new awareness of the varying needs of a metropolis.

---

[46]"Fort Worth and the Billion Dollar Circle," Fort Worth Chamber of Commerce, March, 1921.

[47]Annual Report of the Fort Worth Chamber of Commerce, 1925.

[48]Annual Report, 1926. For 1925 the annual value of manufactured products were reported as: packing house products—$120,000,000; petroleum products—$50,000,000; and flour and feed products—$20,000,000.

[49]"Fort Worth and the Billion Dollar Circle," loc cit. Both plants were later closed.

[50]"Fort Worth," Annual Report of the Chamber of Commerce, 1926.

[51]"A Story of the Progress of Fort Worth, 1925-1926," Annual Report of the Fort Worth Chamber of Commerce, 1926.

Other additions during the early part of the decade included the present Hotel Texas, the first radio stations (WBAP and KFJZ), the Pennsylvania Hospital, the city's first municipal airport, the Fort Worth Club Building, Bell Telephone central office building, and the Worth Hotel Building.

Between 1928 and 1932 the expansion of facilities was particularly significant,[52] and apparently was partially responsible for the delayed local effect of the national depression. During the five-year period the major additions included the following, all of which are currently in use: Texas and Pacific railroad yards and shops; Texas and Pacific Passenger Station Depot and Terminal Building; additions to grain storage and oil refinery facilities; Texas Christian University Stadium; Fair Building; Blackstone Hotel (now the Hilton); Trinity Life Building; Sanger Building; Sinclair Building; Electric Building; Montgomery-Ward wholesale and retail facilities; First Methodist Church; Methodist and Cook Hospitals; Masonic Temple; Elks Club; Forest Park Apartments; Central Fire Station; city water filteration plant; central Post Office building; and the Lake Worth Casino; and the completion of major projects in street paving, widening and the construction of overpasses.

More recently, many of the oil operations have centered in towns closer to the oil fields, but Fort Worth still has an interest in oil and many of the larger independent operators have their headquarters in Fort Worth and live in the area. Thus, Knight reports:

Fort Worth became the gateway to the West Texas oil fields. Companies in need of a major supply base, yet not wanting the inconvenience of a boom town, made Fort Worth their headquarters. Oil-rich ranchmen and farmers moved to Fort Worth, where they lived in luxury. With oil, the skyscraper era arrived. Oil earnings were responsible for the Life of America, Sinclair, and W. T. Waggoner buildings. Oil meant refineries—nine were operating in 1922 as an important addition to the city's industries.[53]

---

[52]"Five Years of Progress: A Final Report on the Five Year Work Program of the Fort Worth Chamber of Commerce," 1932.

[53]Knight, *op. cit.*, p. 199.

Certainly the evidence which is available indicates that the oil discoveries have had a significant and lasting influence on the economy and social life of Fort Worth. However, relatively little of this type of growth can be attributed to the planned efforts of local community leaders. In contrast to other developments, Fort Worth greatly benefited mainly because it was the logical center for certain types of activity. It is true that Fort Worth was receptive to the possibilities of making the city a center for the oil industry, but unlike the united effort which leading citizens of Fort Worth made to get railroads and other primary economic activities, the rewards from oil have accrued more or less in the nature of an unearned increment. In another sense, however, the city was capable of benefiting from the discoveries in part because earlier leaders had worked to establish a permanent community with the necessary facilities. Moreover, there is some evidence that local leaders were instrumental in securing or holding on to some of the oil refineries.

Important also is the fact, as indicated above, that after the oil money began to pour into the city, private interests and the public were willing to expand the facilities of the community and invest in the future.

Aircraft Production and Diversified Industry. The seventh period in the development of Fort Worth began after 1940,[54]

---

[54]Apparently the depression years of the 1930's caught Fort Worth unprepared. As in the rest of the country, the prosperous years of the 1920's had led people to assume that nothing could happen to change the course of events. This was particularly true in Fort Worth, since the previous decade had been one of significant growth and expansion. Although the economic difficulties did not become all-important in Fort Worth as early as was the case in some urban centers, partly because of the city's extensive building program and partly because manufacturing was not predominant, Fort Worth did suffer along with the rest of the country. And like the rest of the country, Fort Worth took an active part in the recovery program of that decade. The City Council asked for its first federal project in 1933, and, as a result of this request and others, received many permanent improvements which are in use today, including the present City Hall, Library, the Will Rogers Memorial Auditorium and Coliseum, and much in the way of street, sewer and overpass construction.

The decade which began in 1920 was for Fort Worth one of internal expansion and sharing in the prosperity of the country. The following decade was one of crisis rather than disaster. The city suffered along with the rest of the country, but with few exceptions its basic economy remained intact. As war began in Europe, the local economy began to awaken and, with the entrance of the United States, the city took an active part in the war effort.

when the city became a major production center for military aircraft needed during World War II. Except for temporary cutbacks after 1945, the city has continued to turn out military planes, through the Korean conflict and the preparedness program of the present. In addition, since 1951 the area has been a production center for helicopter planes.

The present period of Fort Worth's industrialization began to take shape in 1942, when the Consolidated-Vultee Corporation opened its Convair plant and began to make military planes during World War II. At about the same time what is now Carswell Airforce Base was opened. The essence of this achievement is suggested by an event which occurred in 1949 when a B-50 bomber of the United States Air Force made the first military non-stop around the world—Fort Worth to Fort Worth.

The city is not the leading aircraft production center of the country, but certainly aircraft production is the leading industry of Fort Worth. As the production center for the giant B-36 bombers, and more recently with contracts for their substantial modification, Convair has made Fort Worth air-minded. The drone of planes being tested by Convair, those from Carswell Airforce Base, those using Fort Worth's new $15,000,000 International Airport, and those from the recently added Bell Helicopter plants, as well as a large number of private planes, most of which are based at the municipally owned Meacham Field, are potent reminders of Fort Worth's interest in the air age.

The selection of Fort Worth as the site for the Convair plant was certainly related to strategic considerations—to the advantages of long periods of flying weather, to transportation facilities, an available labor supply, and so forth—but since the decision as to location was made by federal agencies, it seems evident that successful local pressure was used to secure the plant. Certainly other cities in Texas or in the South had most or all of the desired advantages.

Local action to secure the Convair plant started officially in the latter part of 1941, when the City Council purchased 526 acres of land, at the time outside the city limits, for $99,750 and turned it over to the United States Army for a bomber-plant.[55] On the site the federal government built the plant which was operated by the Consolidated-Vultee Corporation. In April, 1942, the facilities were completed and, a month later, turned out the first B-24 bomber. Besides supplying the land for the site, the city provided or arranged for the necessary utilities and roads.

The influence of Convair on Fort Worth can be described in a variety of ways. Economically, its payroll has been vital to the city's business activity. Its manpower needs alone have varied from 15,000 to above 30,000 workers, but in addition it has drawn many airplane parts suppliers who have needed additional men. The fact of variation in manpower needs, however, has also been a significant result, leading to dislocation and shifts in employment. In terms of land-use, its location in the western part of the city has meant expanded settlement in the area, as well as the incorporation of several independent suburban towns.

Between 1940 and 1950 the population of Fort Worth increased 58.9 percent, from 177,662 to 278,778, an addition of 101,116 people during the decade. Since 1950 the population has grown to an estimated 357,000 as of February 1, 1956. In the chapter on economic development, the details of economic growth will be presented. At this point, we need only underscore the fact that such growth is the result of the addition of substantial primary economic activities. And while Convair is by far the largest single employer, there have been other industrial additions, many of whom were drawn to the city as suppliers for Convair, or because of the availability of a skilled labor force which Convair had helped train.

---

[55]Knight, *op. cit.*, p. 215.

CHAPTER III

URBAN POPULATION PATTERNS

Importance of Numbers. The size of a community has much to do with its functioning. Problems of only indifferent interest in the small town acquire major significance in the large city. The dirt or gravelled streets, individual wells, and outdoor toilet facilities of the small town are dangerous conditions in the city. Problems of recreation, health, traffic control, public transportation—to mention only a few—increase as the population grows larger. Institutional needs of a densely settled area are sharply different from those of a small town or rural area. The functioning of religion, education, and government in the large city relates to problems unknown in the small town. As one additional example, garbage disposal in the small town often involves merely dumping it in your own or a neighbor's chicken yard or turning it over to a nearby farmer. In contrast, a city government spends thousands of dollars for wages and equipment merely to collect garbage. Disposal is still another costly and often serious issue. The problems of numbers become even more pressing when the city is growing rapidly and increased needs and services cannot be ignored.

In addition, the make-up of any population is a matter of considerable importance in the community's functioning—the nature of the bi-racial situation, the number of males to females, the age distribution, ratio of children to adults, and so forth. Thus, for Fort Worth, in 1940, for every 100 adults between the ages 20 and 64, there were 33 children under the age 15, while in 1950 there were 38 children for every 100 adults. This helps to explain the need for new school facilities, and, given the current high birth rate and the probability of declining infant mortality and childhood mortality rates, this need will likely continue for some time.

In the following paragraphs some of the specific characteristics of the Fort Worth population in 1950, as well as for previous decades, will be considered in some detail. To make the
information more meaningful, comparisons will be made with
other selected Texas cities, and with still others throughout the
United States of a size similar to Fort Worth in 1950.[1]

Even though the emphasis herein is on Fort Worth, it must
be recognized that seldom do legal boundaries define the socio-
cultural area of a city. In recognition of the fact, the United
States Census Bureau, in its publication of 1950 population data,
reported information for the "Urbanized Area" of a central
city, and for its "Standard Metropolitan Area."[2]

General Population Trends. In general terms, the population growth of Fort Worth is related to the expansion of the
Southwest and of Texas because of the mutually related trends
of industrialization and urbanization. This fact is illustrated in
Figure 4, in which a semi-logarithmic scale is used to show the
rate of population change. From this figure it can be observed
that the rate of growth of the four Texas cities was slightly
greater than the rate for the total urban population in the United
States. Also of interest is the fact that Houston's growth has
been generally more steady than that of Fort Worth and Dallas. While Dallas has been consistently the larger city in comparison with Fort Worth, it can be observed that the rates of
growth by decades for the two cities are closely similar.

Additional explanations are necessary, however, in order
to understand why Fort Worth became one of the four leading
cities in the state. In Chapter I we have suggested some reasons
for its growth. Here we need only show the relationship between

---

[1]Unless otherwise indicated, the statistical data in this chapter are from: U. S.
Bureau of the Census, *U. S. Census of Population: 1950*, Vol. II, *Characteristics of
the Population*, Part 43, Texas. For cities in other states the source is the same,
except for the Part number. In each of the state reports the table numbers are
identical.

[2]Fort Worth's Standard Metropolitan Area includes all of Tarrant County. The
city's "Urbanized Area" includes the surrounding closely settled incorporated places
and unincorporated areas that comprise its "urban fringe."

the addition of a new primary economic activity and population growth. The major trends can be shown in outline form as follows:

Year	Population	Characteristics of Previous Decade
1856	67 (estimate)	Frontier settlement; supplying few needs of settlers in county and those moving westward.
1860	Less than 500 (estimate)	County seat; limited supply to settlers; considerable decline after beginning of Civil War.
1870	Less than 1,000 (estimate)	Supplies for settlers; stop-over place on cattle drives to northern markets.
1873	Possibly 3,000 (estimate)	Prospects of railroad; with shattered prospects, population dropped to probably less than 1,000.
1876	Possibly 3,000 (estimate)	Railroad completed to Fort Worth through local efforts.
1880	6,663	Railroad junction town; important supply station for West Texas settlement, and cattle shipment eastward.
1890	23,076	Additional railroads; fruits of location; increased West Texas settlement; minor industries.
1900	26,688	West Texas continues to develop, but Fort Worth no longer dominant; partly just another railroad town.
1910	73,312	Industrial development—stockyards, packing plants (important even though located outside city limits)
1920	106,482	Industrial development; center for West Texas oil explorations; results of World War I military installations.
1930	163,447	Industrial growth; annexation of already developed suburban areas, including packing area; internal development providing attractions for migrants desiring urban facilities.
1940	177,662	Depression.
1950	278,778	Aircraft manufacture; military installations; government office center; industrial expansion; annexation.
1955	345,000 (estimate)	Diversified industrial expansion; annexation of suburban areas.

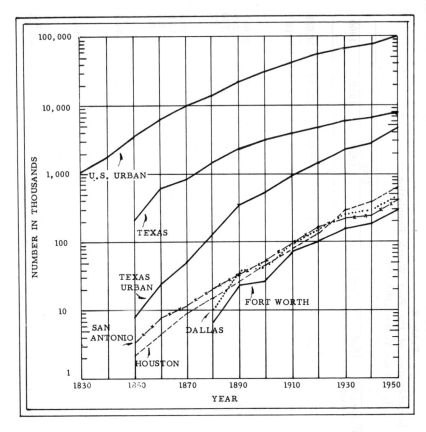

Figure 4. Growth of Population for Selected Areas, 1830-1950, logarithmic scale. (Original data from U. S. Bureau of the Census, decennial reports for corresponding years.)

Between 1940 and 1950 the city's population increased 56.9 percent. For the same period the Fort Worth Metropolitan Area increased 60.2 percent, and its percentage growth was exceeded by only two other Texas metropolitan areas—Lubbock, in West Texas (95.1) and Corpus Christi, on the Gulf coast (78.6). Selected details of the growth of the Fort Worth area are given in Table 3, which also provides comparative data for the city area from 1900 to 1950.

More specifically, the population growth of Fort Worth has been due to three factors, particularly since 1940. Of major im-

Table 3
Selected Characteristics of the Fort Worth Population
By Census Years: 1900-1950

Characteristic	1950 Metropolitan Area	1950 Urbanized Area	City 1950	City 1940	City 1930	City 1920	City 1910	City 1900
Total Population								
Number	361,253	315,578	278,778	177,662	163,447	106,482	73,312	26,688
Percent increase from previous decade	60.2	—	56.9	8.7	53.5	45.2	174.2	15.7
Race and Nationality								
Number								
Native White	316,561	272,919	237,502	148,805	136,282	83,107	55,751	20,651
Negro	39,675	38,102	36,933	25,254	22,234	15,896	13,280	4,245
Foreign-born White	4,794	4,358	4,149	3,540	4,870	7,359	4,209	1,766
Other races	224	199	194	63	61	120		22
Percent								
Native White	87.6	86.5	85.2	83.7	83.4	78.0	76.0	77.4
Negro	11.0	12.1	13.2	14.2	13.6	14.9	18.1	15.9
Foreign-born White	1.3	1.3	1.5	2.0	2.9	6.9	5.7	6.6
Other races	0.1	0.1	0.1	0.1	0.1	0.2	0.2	0.1
Sex Ratio								
Males per 100 females	97.0	95.6	95.0	91.9	95.9	112.5	113.7	104.3
Children								
Children Under 15 percent of total	25.8	25.5	23.3	21.3	25.5	—	—	
Child-Female Ratio								
Number of children under 5 per 100 females 15-44	44.4	44.4	41.7	23.3	27.9	28.8	35.2	38.6

*Source: U. S. Bureau of the Census, Decennial reports for corresponding years.

portance has been migration—persons who have moved to the city from elsewhere. Significantly, many of the new residents have come from outside Texas and from outside the "South." A second condition affecting growth has been the favorable balance of births over deaths. This alone has added approximately 9,000 to the total population annually for the last few years. Third, the city has more than doubled its land area since 1940, from approximately 56 square miles to slightly more than 102 square miles in 1950, and to over 130 square miles in July, 1955.[3]

Race and Nativity. In 1950 the population of the city of Fort Worth was 85.2 percent native-white, 13.2 percent Negro, and 1.5 percent foreign-born white, with 0.1 percent other races. Table 4 shows the 1950 population and the percentage distribution by race and nativity, as well as the same data for preceding census years back to 1900. It can be seen that the percentage for the native-white group is highest in 1950, with the percentages for the other groups being correspondingly lower. It should be recognized, of course, that the number of a particular group could increase, even though the percentage decreased. Thus, in 1900 there were 4,249 Negroes in the city, while in 1950 there was a Negro population of 36,933. Somewhat in contrast, the highest actual number of foreign-born white was in 1920, with a total of 7,359; in 1950 there were 4,149 foreign-born whites in the population. The other-races total (194) in 1950 was the highest actual number since 1900.

Table 4. Percentage Distribution of the Fort Worth Population by Race and Nativity, 1900 to 1950*

Year	Total Population	Percent			
		Native-White	Negro	Foreign-born	Other
1950	278,778	85.2	13.2	1.5	0.1
1940	177,662	83.7	14.2	2.0	0.1
1930	163,447	83.4	13.6	2.9	0.1
1920	106,482	78.0	14.9	6.9	0.2
1910	73,312	76.0	18.1	5.7	0.2
1900	26,688	77.4	15.9	6.6	0.1

*Source: United States Bureau of the Census reports for corresponding years.

---

[3]See Chapter I, Figure 3, for the expansion of the city limits from the time of incorporation, in 1873, to 1955.

Figure 5 shows the growth of the white and Negro population for both Fort Worth and Tarrant County from 1880 to 1950. In this graph the native-white and foreign-born white are combined.

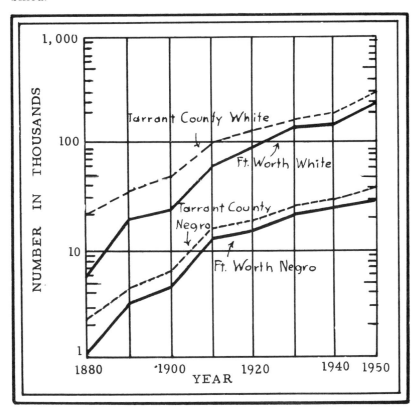

Figure 5. Growth of Population, Fort Worth and Tarrant County, by Race, logarithmic scale. (Original data from U. S. Bureau of the Census, decennial reports for corresponding years.)

Since 1920 the largest number of foreign-born has been from Mexico. Partly because of numbers, the "Latin Americans" function today in Fort Worth in many ways as a culturally separate group. The problem of assimilation is in part due to language and other differences, but also to the attitudes of the "Anglo" Americans. Whatever the reason, the "Mexicans" maintain somewhat separate ethnic communities in the larger com-

munity. There is not cultural isolation, but neither is there un-
qualified integration. In 1950 in Fort Worth slightly more than
36 percent, or a total of 1,509, of the foreign-born residents were
natives of Mexico. Certainly this figure represents only a part
of the total "Latin American" community.

To discover something of this situation, the United States
Census Bureau attempted in 1950 to enumerate those persons
with "Spanish Surname."[4] Even though this procedure is not
entirely adequate, and probably provides an under-representa-
tion, it does give some significant information. Using the "Persons of Spanish Surname" as a separate group, comparisons can
be made with the total Fort Worth population and the non-
white population.

In terms of age distribution, the Spanish-name group had
a higher percent in the younger age groups and a smaller percent in the middle and older age groups. The percentage distribution in 1950 for the three groups was as follows:[5]

Age-Group	Spanish-Name	Fort Worth	Non-White
All	100.0	100.0	100.0
Under 5	15.3	10.6	10.6
5-14 years	23.1	13.7	14.4
15-19 years	10.2	6.4	6.4
20-64 years	48.2	62.7	62.6
65 and over	3.2	6.6	6.0

Another way of considering the age distribution, as well
as providing some measure of the relative fertility, is in terms
of the number of children under five years of age per 100 females between the ages of 15 to 44. Such comparisons for the
city give the following:[6]

Persons of Spanish Surname	66.2
Total Fort Worth Population	41.7
Non-white Population	40.0

---

[4] U. S. Bureau of the Census, *U. S. Census of Population: 1950*, Vol. IV, *Special
Reports*, Part 3, Chapter C, "Persons of Spanish Surname." For an analysis of
the material in the Spanish Surname report, see Robert H. Talbert, *Spanish-Name
People in the Southwest and West*. (Fort Worth: Leo Potishman Foundation, 1955).

[5] U. S. Bureau of the Census, *Special Reports, ibid.*, Table 8; and *Characteristics of the Population, loc. cit.*, Table 33.

[6] *Ibid.*

Somewhat similar contrasts existed in 1950 with regard to education. For persons 25 years of age and over, approximately 20 percent (20.2) of the Spanish group had had no formal schooling, while for the total Fort Worth population and for the Negro population the percentages were 1.3 and 3.0, respectively. A more general measure of difference is provided by the median school year completed, which is a type of average and indicates that half of a group was above and half below the median figure. The median school year was completed for persons 25 years of age and over for the three groups was as follows:[7]

Total Fort Worth Population 11.1
Non-white Population 8.0
Persons of Spanish Surname 5.3

As would be expected, the Negroes form the most distinct and separate class or caste within the community. While they are not concentrated ecologically to the extent that is usually true in Northern cities, there are significant cultural and legal barriers which operate to make them a distinctively separate group without complete cultural isolation. On the one hand, there are among the Negroes distinct occupational and interest groupings, with typically American class consciousness, which are separate from the white group. Yet on the other, there are many situations in which the bi-racial pattern no longer exists.

In comparison with other urban areas in Texas, the percent of the total population of Fort Worth which was non-white in 1950 was just about average. For all urban areas (2,500 or more population) in the state the non-white group comprised 12.8 percent. For Fort Worth it was 13.2. Similar percentages for all the cities in Texas with 100,000 or more total population in 1950 were:[8]

Houston 21.1
Austin 13.4
Fort Worth 13.2
Dallas 13.2
San Antonio 7.2
Corpus Christi 6.6
El Paso 2.6

---

[7]*Ibid.*, Table 8; and Tables 33, 36.

[8]*Characteristics of the Population*, *loc. cit.*, Table 11. In Texas and the states in the South, Negroes comprise almost the total non-white population.

Moreover, the non-white population of Texas in 1950 was urbanized to almost the exact extent of the white population, with 62.6 percent of the non-white and 62.7 percent of the white group living in urban areas.[9] For proportion of non-white in the total population a somewhat different pattern is revealed in comparisons for cities of similar size throughout the country. This type of information is presented in Figure 6 for the 23 cities throughout the United States which in 1950 had total populations ranging from 250,000 to 500,000. In addition, Houston is included for Texas comparisons even though its population was above 500,000. Throughout this chapter and the remaining chapters this 24-city group will be used to provide comparisons and contrasts.

From the standpoint of community relationships and cultural adjustments, it is significant that the non-white population in Dallas, Fort Worth, and San Antonio comprised a smaller percent of the total population than was the case for some of the Northern, border, and far Western cities. The situation varies, however, with the Western cities having many Oriental peoples in their non-white population.

With some few exceptions, the foreign-born population of Texas cities has not been large. While the state received a number of the immigrants who came to America from Europe during the 19th and the early part of the present century, the actual number was small in comparison with the immigration to the Eastern cities and some of the states of the Middle West. In recent decades, particularly, most of the immigrants to Texas have come from Mexico. Thus, since 1910 over one-half of the foreign-born in Texas have been natives of Mexico.[10] For Fort Worth, however, it was not until 1920 that Mexico was the predominant source of the foreign-born population; for 1900 and 1910 the highest percent was from Germany. In 1950 the percent of the total population which was foreign-born was lowest

[9]Ibid., Table 15.

[10]Ibid., Table 24.

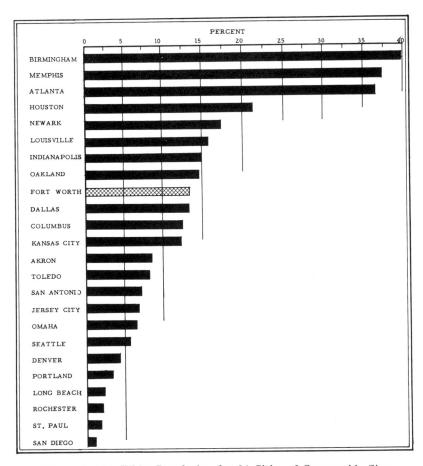

Figure 6. Non-White Population for 24 Cities of Comparable Size, 1950. (Original data from U. S. Bureau of the Census, *U. S. Census of Population: 1950*, Vol. II, Part 1, Table 86.)

for Fort Worth among the Texas cities with 100,000 or more population, as shown in the following tabulation:[11]

El Paso	16.8
San Antonio	8.0
Corpus Christi	4.6
Houston	2.9
Austin	2.7
Dallas	1.9
Fort Worth	1.7

[11]*Ibid.*, Table 34. These data are for white foreign-born only.

For the 24-city group the white foreign-born population as a percent of the total population varied from 16.1 for Newark, to 1.3 percent for Memphis. This information is shown in Figure 7.

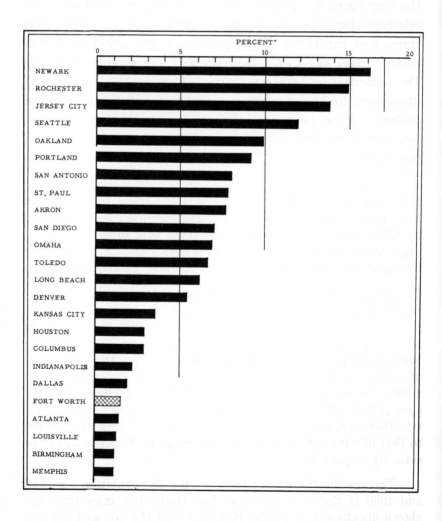

Figure 7. Foreign-Born White Population for 24 Comparable Cities, 1950. (Original data from U. S. Bureau of the Census, *U. S. Census of Population: 1950*, Vol. II, Part 1, Table 86.)

Age Distribution. One of the important factors in a community's functioning is its population distribution by age groups. In 1950 Fort Worth had, in comparison with 1940, as well as for earlier decades, a relatively high percentage of its population in the very young age groups, which is, in part, a reflection of the relatively low birth rates in the 1930's and the high rates throughout the 1940's. This is shown in the actual number of persons under age 15 for 1940 (37,901) and for 1950 (67,994). The numerical difference between 1940 and 1950 is even more pronounced for the age groups under 10; for 1940 this total was 23,668, and for 1950 a total of 51,254. Such increases mean more school facilities, and more goods and services needed for the young.

For the ages 65 and over the number has increased also. In 1930 there were 6,502 persons in this age-group in the city of Fort Worth. By 1940 the number had increased to 10,409, and by 1950 it was 18,364. This trend, along with other conditions, explains the increased demand for old age assistance, homes for the aged, and the newly developing medical field of geriatrics.

Another way of considering age distribution is in terms of the ratio of adults to the young and aged. This will tend to show the socio-economic burden of the adults. On this basis, in 1940 there were 42 persons, under age 15, and 65 and over, for every 100 persons between the ages of 20 and 65. By 1950, the ratio of youth and aged to adults had increased to 49 for every 100 adults. Thus, in 1950 the persons in the normally productive ages of 20 to 65 had, in terms of numbers, a heavier responsibility. However, this responsibility is relatively low in comparison to that of rural areas. For the rural areas of Texas in 1950 the ratio figure was 64.9.

The age distribution of the Fort Worth population for 1940 and 1950 is shown in Table 5. Essentially the same data are shown graphically in Figure 8, except that the age and sex figures are percentages of the total population. In both Table 5 and Figure 8 it can be seen that between 1940 and 1950 the very

Table 5. Population Distribution by Sex and Age Groups for Fort Worth
1940-1950*

Age-Group	1940				1950			
	Male		Female		Male		Female	
	Number	Percent	Number	Percent	Number	Percent	Number	Percent
Total	85,059	100.0	92,603	100.0	135,799	100.0	142,979	100.0
Under 10	11,858	13.9	11,810	12.8	25,861	19.0	25,393	17.8
10-19	14,807	17.4	15,532	16.8	16,500	12.2	17,757	12.4
20-29	14,675	17.2	17,705	19.1	25,748	19.0	27,765	19.4
30-39	14,726	17.3	17,055	18.4	23,052	17.0	23,576	16.5
40-49	12,555	14.8	13,277	14.3	18,449	13.6	19,335	13.6
50-59	8,719	10.2	8,629	9.3	13,363	9.8	13,993	9.8
60-69	5,113	6.0	5,537	6.0	8,300	6.1	9,164	6.4
70 and over	2,606	3.1	3,056	3.3	4,526	3.3	5,996	4.1

*Source: *Characteristics of the Population, loc. cit.*, Table 33.

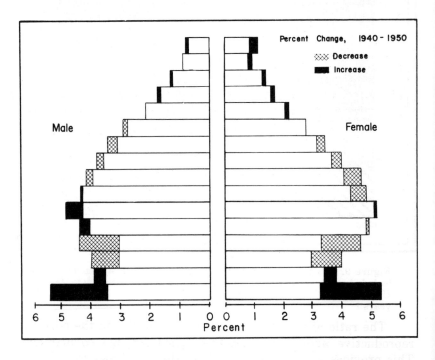

Figure 8. Population Change by Age and Sex Groups, Fort
Worth: 1940-1950. (Original data from U. S. Bureau of the Census, *16th Census of the United States: 1940*, Population, Vol. II,
Part 6; and *U. S. Census of Population: 1950*, Vol. III, Chapter
21.)

young and the older age groups increased not only in actual numbers but also as percentages of the total population.. While the increase in the younger age-group has occurred since 1940, with the rise in the birth rate after that time, the increase in the percent of persons 65 and over has been occurring over a longer period. This fact is shown in Figure 9, which gives the percent distribution of the Fort Worth population by decades from 1900 to 1950.

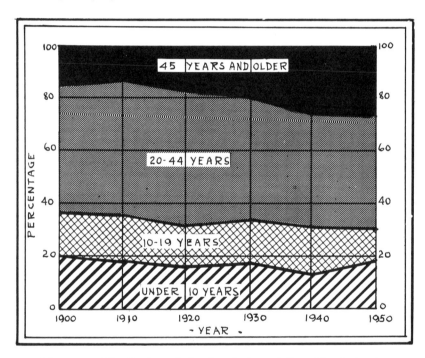

Figure 9. Distribution of the Population of Fort Worth for Selected Age Groups, by Decades: 1900-1950. (Original data from U. S. Bureau of the Census, decennial reports for corresponding years.)

The ratio of very young children to females in the normally reproductive ages is still another basis for age comparisons. This provides a rough reproduction rate and shows to a limited degree whether or not the population is reproducing itself. In 1950 in Fort Worth there were 417 children under the age of 5 for every 1,000 females between the ages of 15 and 44. This is

relatively meaningless until certain comparisons are made. In
1900 the number was 386. From 1900 there was a steady decline
to 1940, when there were only 233 children under 5 for every
1,000 females 15-44.

Essentially the same general trend is discernible for other
urban areas. For rural areas the ratio of children to females is
even higher. The high proportion of children in 1950 can be explained in terms of certain known conditions. First, the birth
rate has been relatively high since 1940, while the infant mortality rate has been declining. In contrast, there apparently has
been an important net in-migration of young adults with children to the city since 1940.

Several bases for comparing cities in terms of age are available. Each reveals something concerning the age distribution.
Together they indicate significant facts about a community's
population, and may help to explain something about social organization in the individual cities. For the larger Texas cities
the following information, ranked by median age, indicates some
important differences:[12]

City	Median Age	Percent 65 years and over	Number of children under 5 per 100 Females 15-44
Dallas	30.9	6.1	39.5
Fort Worth	30.1	6.6	41.7
Houston	29.4	5.0	41.2
San Antonio	27.4	6.2	54.0
Austin	27.2	6.6	40.6
Corpus Christi	26.3	3.7	54.2
El Paso	26.3	5.5	52.4

Perhaps most noticeable in this information is the small
percent of persons 65 and over for Corpus Christi, and the higher
ratio of children to females, for San Antonio, Corpus Christi and
El Paso. In all probability the latter variation is due, in part at
least, to the relatively large Spanish-name population in the
three cities.[13]

---

[12]*Ibid.*, Tables 10 and 34.

[13]The percent which the Spanish-name group was of the total population in
the three cities was in 1950: El Paso—49.0; San Antonio—39.3; Corpus Christi—
33.7. (See Talbert, *op. cit.*, p. 29).

Contrasts in urban age patterns can be seen more obviously by comparing two smaller Texas cities which show sharper variations. The two cities selected are Highland Park, which is an upper class residential suburb within the boundaries of Dallas, and Mercedes, located in Southern Texas near the border of Mexico, with a population which is 78.2 percent Spanish-name. Selected age information for these two cities in 1950 shows the following contrasts:[14]

	Highland Park	Mercedes
Median age	41.5	21.8
Percent 65 and over	10.3	4.4
Number of children under 5 per 100 females, ages 15-44	21.9	67.4

Such information would suggest community organization significantly different in the two cities.

The differences in age patterns for the 24-city group are given in Table 6, with the cities ranked by number of children under 5 years of age per 100 females between the ages of 15 and 44. Certainly the problems of the elderly would be greater in Long Beach (11.2 percent) than in Houston with only 5.0 percent of its population in the older age group. Similarly, the median age differences between San Antonio (27.4 and Portland (35.8) would suggest differences of some importance between the two cities.

Sex. Another factor of considerable importance in the functioning of a community is the number of males and females. This comparison is usually expressed as a sex ratio and numerically means the number of males per 100 females. A disproportion of either may importantly affect the community's moral tone, the degree and nature of family organization, and the degree to which the local population can be maintained through intra-city births. Within a city, areas of homeless men, or areas

[14] *Characteristics of the Population, loc. cit.,* Tables 10 and 33.

Table 6. Selected Age Data for United States Cities in the Population
Class 250,000-500,000, 1950*

City	Children under 5 per 100 females 15-44	Percent 65 and over	Median age
San Antonio	54.0	6.2	27.4
Akron	46.8	6.7	31.4
San Diego	46.6	7.7	29.3
St. Paul	45.5	8.8	31.9
Louisville	43.5	8.3	31.2
Omaha	42.7	8.6	32.1
Birmingham	42.7	6.3	29.4
Denver	42.6	9.4	32.1
Memphis	42.2	6.6	29.9
FORT WORTH	41.7	6.6	30.1
Indianapolis	41.6	8.7	32.3
Portland	41.2	11.0	35.8
Houston	41.2	5.0	29.4
Long Beach	41.1	11.2	34.8
Columbus	40.8	8.7	31.3
Seattle	40.6	10.2	34.4
Toledo	40.4	9.4	33.9
Rochester	39.8	11.0	34.7
Dallas	39.5	6.1	30.9
Oakland	38.8	9.5	34.6
Jersey City	37.7	7.3	32.5
Newark	36.9	7.1	32.5
Kansas City	36.4	9.2	34.0
Atlanta	36.1	6.7	30.6

*Sources: *Characteristic of the Population, loc. cit.*, Tables 10 and 33 in the corresponding state reports.

providing mainly housing for unmarried female workers are often sharply different kinds of areas from those in which the normal type of family relationship exists.

As was true of similar commercial-industrial cities, Fort Worth in 1950 had more females than males in its total population, but there was considerable variation for different age and race groups. For the total population, the 1950 sex ratio was 95.0; for the native-white, 95.3; for the foreign-born whites, 101.3; and for Negroes, 91.9. Combinations of selected age groups show some distinct differences. Table 7 gives these variations.

Table 7. Sex Ratios for Fort Worth in 1950 for Total Population and for Selected Age Groups, by Race (Males per 100 females)*

	Total Population	White	Non-White
All ages	95.0	95.4	92.2
Under 15	101.1	102.0	95.6
15-30	91.4	92.2	85.9
20-44	95.2	96.6	95.6
65 and over	80.5	79.1	91.8

*Source: Characteristics of the Population, op. cit., Table 33.

It can be seen that the lowest sex ratio is for the white age-group, 65 and over, with approximately 79 males for every 100 females. This probably indicates the general pattern of greater longevity for females. The non-white ratio for the middle age-group is significant because of the disproportionate number of females in the marriageable ages.

The trends in sex ratios for the city from 1890 to 1950 are shown in Figure 10. This information suggests the disappearance of Fort Worth as a frontier town with the usual larger number of males. The high ratio of males for the foreign-born whites before 1940 would indicate that immigrants who have come to this area have been predominantly male.

The number of males per 100 females for Fort Worth in 1950 was neither highest nor lowest among the Texas cities, and similar in-between status was the case in comparisons with cities of similar size throughout the United States. Among the Texas cities with 100,000 population or more, Corpus Christi had the highest ratio of males to females (97.1), while Dallas was lowest with 91.0. Ratios for the other Texas cities were: Austin, 96.2; El Paso, 93.7; Houston, 95.9; San Antonio, 91.9. For the selected United States cities the sex ratios varied from a low of 86.3 for Atlanta to a high of 103.7 for San Diego, which was the only one of the 24 cities with more males than females. Similar patterns existed for the non-white population of the 24 cities, except for the far-Western cities of Long Beach (117.8), Seattle (113.7) and San Diego (102.2). Possibly the predominance of males among persons of Oriental background would ex-

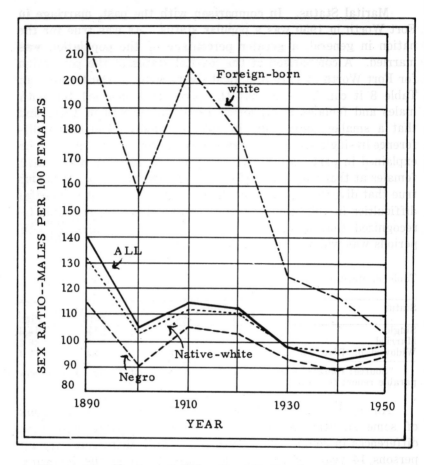

Figure 10. Number of Males Per 100 Females (Sex Ratio), Fort Worth, for Selected Population Groups, by Decades: 1890-1950. (Original data from U. S. Bureau of the Census, decennial reports for corresponding years.)

plain the high sex ratios in these three cities. Significantly, the non-white sex ratios for the Southern cities in the group are lower than those for the selected non-Southern cities. This is probably due to the greater opportunities for females to secure work in Southern cities, the industrial "pull" of the non-Southern cities for males, and the fact that it is easier for Negro males to migrate long distances.

Marital Status. In comparison with the past, marriage in Fort Worth in 1950 was a popular status. As was true for the nation in general, a greater percentage of the population was married. A comparison of the marital status of the population for Fort Worth in 1910 and 1950 shows some of the trends. In Table 8 it can be seen that the percentage married for both males and females is higher in 1950 than it was in 1910, and that a smaller percentage in 1950 is single. The sharp difference in single status between males and females in 1910 can be explained in part by the fact that there were more males than females at that time. For 1910 the sex ratio was 114. It is also true that divorce is more acceptable as an adjustment to marital difficulties in 1950 than it was in 1910. However, it should be recognized that a significant portion of the females in both periods was widowed rather than divorced.

Table 8. Marital Status of Fort Worth Population, 14 Years and Over, 1910 and 1950*

Status	Male		Female	
	1910	1950	1910	1950
Single	39.9	19.7	22.8	14.4
Married	54.6	73.2	62.8	68.2
Widowed or Divorced	5.5	7.1	14.4	17.4

*Source: *Characteristics of the Population, loc. cit.,* Table 34, and comparable report for 1910.

Among the larger Texas cities in 1950, there were variations of some significance in marital status, indicating important differences in community functioning, Such differences for all persons 14 years of age and over are shown in the following ranking by percent of persons single:[15]

	Single	Married	Widowed or Divorced
Austin	28.3	60.2	11.5
El Paso	24.6	64.0	11.4
San Antonio	21.1	66.3	12.6
Corpus Christi	18.7	71.4	9.9
Houston	17.6	70.5	11.9
Fort Worth	17.1	70.5	12.4
Dallas	16.3	70.4	13.3

[15]*Ibid.,* Table 34.

Probably the high percentage of "single" for Austin is due to its
location for state government offices and for the state university
(in 1950 the Census Bureau counted college and university students in the place where they were attending school). The
higher proportion of single in El Paso, and to a lesser extent in
San Antonio, is possibly related to the high percent of Spanish-
name people in the two cities.[16]

Among the comparable United States cities, Jersey City
ranked highest in population of single, with 28.0 percent, while
Dallas' 16.2 percent was lowest. Akron ranked highest in percent of married, with a figure of 71.8; Jersey city was lowest,
with 62.2 percent. For widowed and divorced, Akron was lowest
with 7.1 percent, and Portland was highest in this category,
with 15.0 percent.

Population Movement. As for many American cities, and
particularly the rapidly growing Texas cities, the Fort Worth
population has increased mainly because of net in-migration.
While the statistical evidence is not extensive, observation of the
most casual kind will show the influx of people into the city. The
best available evidence comes from the census reports. One of
the questions asked in the 1950 Census was (for persons one
year and over in 1949) "Where were you living in 1949?" The
results are revealing concerning the city's population in 1950.
Approximately 70 percent of the Fort Worth population was
"living in the same house" in 1950 as in 1949. Almost 18 percent
of the people was "living in a different house, but in the same
county." About 10 percent lived in a different county or abroad.

These data suggest two important conditions of an urban
area like Fort Worth. First, the fact that almost 18 percent of
the population was living in different houses suggests a high
degree of intra-county change of residence. The percent which
moved to the city from outside the county suggests that com-

---

[16]For a discussion of this somewhat surprising condition, see Talbert, *op. cit.*,
p. 55, ff.

munities like Fort Worth have important problems of integration and continuity.

The movement of population for Fort Worth between 1949 and 1950 was not unusual in comparison with the larger Texas cities as can be observed in the following percentages:[17]

	From out of county of location	Moved-within county of location
Austin	11.6	18.6
Corpus Christi	11.0	19.5
El Paso	10.5	15.2
Fort Worth	10.1	17.9
Dallas	8.9	20.5
Houston	7.0	19.6
San Antonio	6.9	14.6

While Fort Worth was only average among the larger Texas cities in terms of movement of people from outside its county of location, among the 24 comparable United States cities it was second only to San Diego in this respect. Such information for the 24-city group is shown in Figure 11.

Income Distribution. Certainly an important factor in the functioning of the urban community today is the distribution of income, since the individual family's income greatly influences the possibility of utilizing the great majority of available community facilities. Moreover, one's general status is largely circumscribed by income, particularly in a rapidly growing city like Fort Worth.[18]

In 1949 for Fort Worth, according to the United States Census Bureau, the annual median income for all families with in-

---

[17]*Characteristics of the Population, loc. cit.*, Table 34.

[18]This is not to deny the influence of family, education, occupation, and so forth, as indicated in the numerous studies of social class in America. It is, rather, merely an hypothesis which needs to be tested for cities like Fort Worth, 'where much of the "wealth" is first or second generation, and where the dynamic situation may lead to the use of money as THE measure of status.

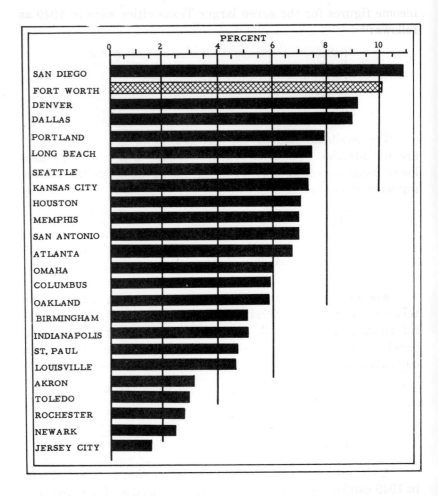

Figure 11. In-Migration for 24 Comparable Cities, 1950. Percent of Persons, One Year of Age and Over, Living in the City
in 1950, but Living Outside County of Location in 1949. (Original
data from U. S. Bureau of the Census, *U. S. Census of Population:
1950*, Vol. II, Table 34, in individual state reports.)

come was $3,308, and for families and unrelated individuals with
income it was $2,830. That is, half of the families with income
were above the median figure of $3,308 and half were below.
Among the larger Texas cities, Dallas families had the highest
median income and those in San Antonio the lowest. The median

income figures for the seven larger Texas cities were in 1949 as follows:[19]

Dallas	$3,526
Houston	3,389
Fort Worth	3,308
Corpus Christi	3,187
El Paso	3,109
Austin	3,098
San Antonio	2,685

The available figures for the non-white group separately are for families and unrelated individuals, and reveal a much lower median income. For 1949 for the seven cities the following were reported:[20]

El Paso	$1,836
Houston	1,700
Corpus Christi	1,369
San Antonio	1,602
Fort Worth	1,504
Dallas	1,486
Austin	1,165

Another way of considering the income pattern of a city is in terms of percent of population with low incomes. This type of information is provided by the Census Bureau for families and unrelated individuals with incomes below $2,000 in 1949. Such computations for the larger Texas cities reveal the following:[21]

Austin	46.8
San Antonio	40.9
El Paso	36.9
Fort Worth	33.8
Corpus Christi	32.9
Houston	32.2
Dallas	30.5

A clearer picture of the income distribution for Fort Worth in 1949 can be secured by separating the income of families and unrelated individuals into categories. In this manner at the lower extreme, 17.1 percent of the families and unrelated individuals had annual incomes of less than $1,000, while those with incomes of $10,000 and above comprised 2.8 percent. This type of pattern is shown graphically in Figure 12.

---

[19]*Ibid.*, Table 37.

[20]*Ibid.*, Table 37a

[21]*Ibid.*, Table 10.

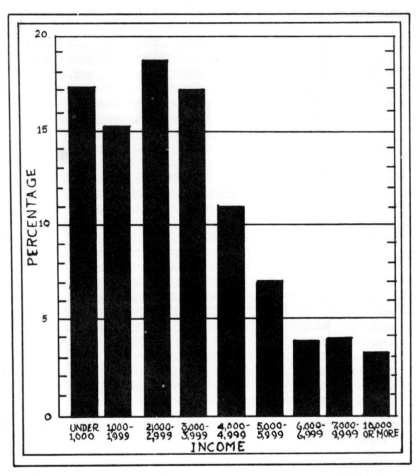

Figure 12. Distribution of Yearly Income for Families and Unrelated Individuals, Fort Worth, by Selected Income Groups, 1949. (Original data from U. S. Bureau of the Census, *U. S. Census of Population: 1950*, Vol. III, Chapter 21, Table 1.)

In the 24-city group the Texas cities ranked relatively low in median income, with Dallas ranking 11th, Houston 16th, Fort Worth 18th and San Antonio 22nd, but, with the exception of San Antonio, higher than the cities located in the Southeast. The ranking of the 24 cities in 1949 in terms of median income for families and unrelated individuals is presented in Figure 13. It may well be argued that the relatively low position of the

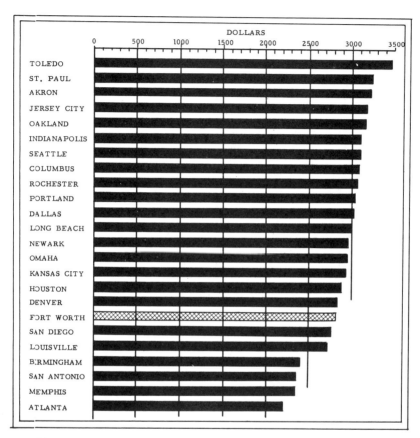

Figure 13. Median Income for Families and Unrelated Individuals for 24 Comparable Cities, 1949. Median figures from U. S. Bureau of the Census, *U. S. Census of Population: 1950*, Vol. II, Part 1, Table 92.)

Southeastern and Southwestern cities is due in part to the large Negro or Spanish-name populations, but it must be recognized that a family with low income and limited buying power is an ineffective part of an economy, irrespective of its racial or ethnic status.

Population Growth Since 1950. All the available evidence indicates that Texas cities have continued to grow since 1950, in some instances with a greater annual growth than was true for the previous decade. While the evidence is based on estimates, the fact of population growth seems to be obvious. For Fort Worth, three different approaches have been used. The writer developed estimates of the total population of the city, as well as census tract estimates, through the use of the annual school census enumeration;[22] Leland McCloud, of the Bureau of Business Research of Texas Christian University, has estimated the total and tract populations on the basis of building permits;[23] the Fort Worth Chamber of Commerce computes periodic estimates based mainly on utility connections.

Recently, the Associated Press collected estimates of population growth for Texas cities, which apparently were for July, 1955, and were secured from local Chambers of Commerce.[24] These estimates for the larger Texas cities are presented in Table 9. At the present, Houston is still the largest city in the state, but its estimated numerical and percent increase was less than that of Dallas and San Antonio. However, the metropolitan areas of these cities had a somewhat different pattern of growth,

Table 9. Growth of Population in Larger Texas Cities, 1940-1955*

City	1955	1950	Estimated Increase		Percent increase 1940-1950
			Number	Percent	
Houston	700,000	596,163	103,837	17.4	55.0
Dallas	575,000	434,462	140,538	32.3	47.4
San Antonio	518,488	408,442	110,046	26.9	60.9
Fort Worth	350,169	278,778	71,391	25.6	56.9
El Paso	182,000	130,485	51,515	39.5	34.8
Austin	180,000	132,459	47,541	35.9	50.6
Corpus Christi	155,000	108,287	46,713	43.1	89.0

*Sources: *Characteristics of the Population, loc. cit.*, Table 33, and Fort Worth *Star-Telegram*, July 17, 1955.

suggesting the importance of considering annexation policies of the individual cities. Thus, the estimated growth of the Houston Standard Metropolitan Area (Harris County) was 216,299, or 26.8 percent since 1950; for the Dallas area (Dallas County) the

---

[22]See the last section in Chapter IV.

[23]*Fort Worth Business Review*, 3 (June, 1954).

[24]Reported in Fort Worth *Star-Telegram*, July 17, 1955.

growth was 136,501, or 22.2 percent; for Fort Worth's (Tarrant County) the increase was 146,015, or 40.4 percent.

Reasons given by the Associated Press for the increase of Texas cities since 1950 included (1) new industries, (2) expansion of military bases—in 1950 the nation's military forces were numerically low, (3) oil and gas expansion, (4) new industries breed new businesses, (5) extension of city limits, and (6) prosperous agricultural areas. The sources of urban growth are given as (1) migration from other states—probably the largest source, (2) natural population growth, (3) migration from the farm and smaller towns.

While it must be recognized that the above figures are estimates, they do substantiate the fact of considerable growth. To continue such growth the cities of Texas must increase their job-producing opportunities. Also important, of course, is the necessity of expanding community facilities. Unless this is done, rapid population growth can be disastrous.

Chapter IV

AREA DIFFERENTIALS WITHIN THE CITY

Natural Areas Of The City

One of the consequences of urban heterogeneity is the development of significantly different areas of land-use, and socio-economic activities and interests. In one sense the urban area is a community with common interests, but in another there exist sharp variations in attitudes and practices, one manifestation of which is land-use. The "address of distinction," the "wrong side of the tracks," "Quality Row," "the slums," "row houses," and a host of similar terms are popular evaluations of differentiation in the use of land. While the topography (rivers, hills, ravines, and so forth) may have something to do with the value of the land and its use, probably more important in determining the value placed on a piece of property is the already existing or potential conditions surrounding it.

In the early development of American cities the diversification of land-use was the more or less natural product of the competitive struggle for favorable position. Land went usually to the highest bidder, to be utilized as the owner saw fit.[1]

In more recent years most American cities have attempted to control and do some planning with regard to the use of their land areas through the activities of zoning and planning boards.[2]

---

[1]In the study of communities a specialized division of research has developed to describe and explain "man-land" relationships which is called *human ecology*. The general emphasis of human ecology is, "the study of the spatial distribution of persons and institutions in the city, and the processes involved in the formation of patterns of distribution." Noel P. Gist and L. A. Halbert, *Urban Society* (New York: Thomas Y. Crowell Co., 1948), p. 95.

[2]In Fort Worth, use control and planning started in 1938, with the establishment of zoning and planning boards.

However, zoning and planning by the city government offer only general patterns of land control and development; also, zoning particularly is faced with the fact of an already existing pattern which cannot be changed without great cost. Moreover, zoning and planning by a city government cannot determine the quality of housing in a neighborhood,[3] or the specific uses of a building.[4]

A city such as Fort Worth inevitably develops areas which are differentiated in a number of ways. Some of the more obvious differences would be a central business district, areas primarily for industrial activity, low and high income residential areas, and racial and ethnic community areas. In significant ways these separate sections are somewhat distinctive "social worlds" within the general community organization.[5] In such social worlds one finds unique behavior patterns and attitudes, as well as distinctive levels of socio-economic activity. It is in this respect that we speak of "natural" areas of the city.

Certainly a factor of considerable importance in the development of natural areas in Fort Worth at the present time is zoning, since through city ordinance general categories of land-use are established. That is, zoning tends to establish distinct patterns for particular areas. Currently in the city, there are four broad categories which regulate the use of land, with areas for residential, business, light industry, and heavy industry. Each of these is sub-divided, so that in all there are 13 separate types of land-use.[6]

Changes in Land-Use. One of the inevitable consequences in a growing city is the fact that land-use varies in time. An area which at one time is an excellent residential neighborhood

[3]Recently private developers in Fort Worth, as well as elsewhere, have been able to do this to a considerable extent where they control an entire area.

[4]The city government can only establish health and safety standards. This phase of government activity will be discussed in later chapters.

[5]The writer is of the opinion that the social world concept as a functional entity is more useful in differentiating areas and groups within the urban community than is the concept of social class. While the use of the social world concept here is limited primarily to geographical areas, it can be applied just as readily to occupational, interest, religious and similar groupings.

[6]Zoning will be discussed in greater detail in Chapter VI.

usually later loses its desirability because of out-of-date structures, and or because of invasion.[7]   Other changes in land-use
occur because of the desire of particular businesses, professions,
or other activities to escape from the congestion of the central
business district.   Typical of this relatively recent trend is the
decentralization of doctors' offices, but certainly more important is the decentralization of business activity.   Within recent
years, Fort Worth, like other cities, has had an intensive development of suburban shopping centers.   While many of the
shopping areas outside the central business district have existed
for some time, a development since World War II of importance
is the integrated shopping center in which the entire development
may be planned and controlled by one company.

Types of Natural Areas.   Often in the study of a city like
Fort Worth, and the planning for community activities, there is
need for consideration of the city in terms of local neighborhoods.   The problem is primarily to divide the city into logical
areas.   Several divisions are available.   The voting precincts
could be used, but they are designed mainly for voting purposes
and nothing else.   Post office zones are available, but they tend
to follow natural land forms and barriers and do not take much
consideration of socio-economic conditions.   Then there are the
named neighborhoods in Fort Worth, such as Arlington Heights,
T. C. U., Stop Six, Rosen Heights, Meadowbrook, Morningside,
Riverside, and a host of others.   These have the advantage of
familiarity, but the areas are somewhat overlapping and not
specifically defined.

Census Tracts.   To overcome the limitations of the above
indicated area types, the common procedure in the United States
has been the division of a city into areas that are as homogeneous as possible in terms of land-use and social and economic

---

[7]An excellent example of this at the present time in Fort Worth is the area
around the intersection of Summit and Lancaster streets. At one time the homes in
the area were inhabited by some of the wealthiest families in the city; today their
homes are used mainly for business purposes, or have been demolished and new
business buildings constructed. If the city continues to grow, such areas will be an
integral part of the central business district.

characteristics. This procedure was adopted by the United States Census Bureau for the first time in 1910. In the Bureau's classification, each area of a city so divided is called a census tract.[8] Following each decennial census one or more special bulletins for each city is issued by the Bureau, which gives detailed population and housing data by census tracts. By 1950, 62 large cities in the United States, including Fort Worth, had been tracted.

Ideally, each of the tracts in a city will be a distinct and homogeneous area; actually, of course, this is not possible. However, it is believed that a properly designed tract is the best available area division.[9]

Prior to the 1950 Census, Fort Worth was divided into 48 tract areas, and, in addition, seven urbanized areas adjacent to the city were tracted. These areas for 1950 are shown in Figure 14. Since 1950 the remainder of Tarrant County has been tracted. Figure 15 shows the county tracts as of 1954.[10]

In the following section, the census tract will be used as the geographical base for intra-city comparisons. It will become apparent that there are important differences between the tract areas. And it can be seen that the socio-economic nature of the city cannot be understood without a recognition of area differences and contrasts.

Area Differentials of Fort Worth in 1950

As indicated in the preceding section, for the first time, in 1950, the United States Bureau of the Census tabulated and reported population and housing information for small areas with-

[8]For a more detailed description of the nature of census tracts, see *Census Tract Manual*, U. S. Bureau of the Census. In each city a local Census Tract Committee of citizens familiar with the local situation recommends the tract areas.

[9]For different conclusions concerning the validity of census tracts, see Jerome K. Meyers, "Note on the Homogeneity of Census Tracts: A Methodological Problem in Urban Ecological Research," *Social Forces*, 32 (May, 1954) 364-66, and Joel Smith, "A Method for the Classification of Areas on the Basis of Demographically Homogeneous Populations," *American Sociological Review*, 19 (April, 1954) 201-207.

[10]It is to be expected that the county tract areas will have to be altered before the 1960 Census because of annexations by Fort Worth and other county towns. For areas annexed to Fort Worth since 1950, see Figure 3.

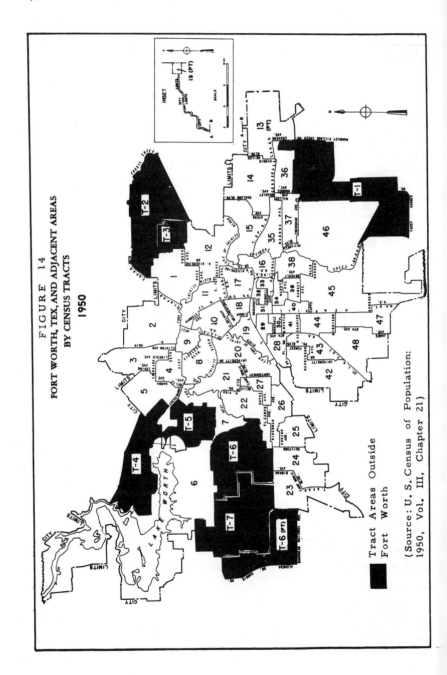

FIGURE 14
FORT WORTH, TEX, AND ADJACENT AREAS
BY CENSUS TRACTS
1950

Tract Areas Outside
Fort Worth

(Source: U.S. Census of Population:
1950, Vol. III, Chapter 21)

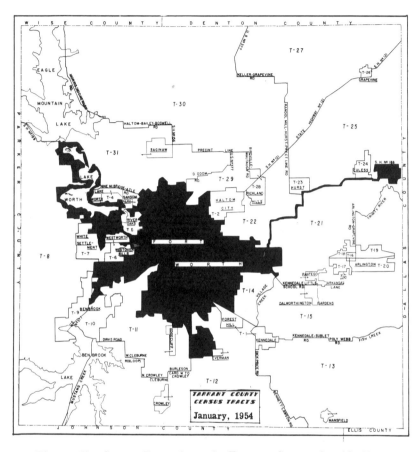

Figure 15. Census Tract Areas in Tarrant County Outside Fort
Worth: 1954. (As established by the Fort Worth Census Tract
Committee, and tentatively accepted by the U. S. Bureau of the
Census.)

in the city of Fort Worth. These tabulations have been published
in two special reports,[11] and provide population and housing

[11]U. S. Bureau of the Census. *U. S. Census of Population:* 1950, Vol. III, "Census Tract Statistics," Chapter 21 (Fort Worth); and *U. S. Census of Housing:* 1950 Vol. V, "Block Statistics," Part 67 (Fort Worth). These may be ordered from the Superintendent of Documents, U. S. Government Printing Office, Washington 25, D. C. for 20 and 35 cents, respectively.

data for the entire city, for 48 census tract areas within the city, and for 7 urbanized areas adjacent to the city.[12]

Perhaps the most obvious fact secured from observation, of the census tract data is the sharp variation in the socio-economic character of the different tracts. Certainly anyone familiar with the city is aware of this, but the tract reports tend to highlight the differences and provide measures of degree of variation. Such differences exist in quality of housing, population composition, attained educational level, median income, employment status, and in other similar ways. In. addition, sharp contrasts can be observed in crime rates, dependency rates, disease rates and other measures of socio-economic inadequacy. However, two cautions must be underlined. The various tract scores and indexes which will be presented in the following pages represent only the total tract picture. Within any one tract significant variations may exist. Thus, the general educational level of a tract may be below the city average, or the quality of housing may be low, even though certain blocks or neighborhoods within the tract are above the city-wide average. And secondly, it must be recognized that the reports of the Census Bureau for some of the characteristics are based on samples.[13]

The fact of important differences can. be illustrated by comparing two census tracts which represent opposite extremes of socio-economic status. Table 10 shows such contrasts. Tract 17, located just east of the downtown section, is an area generally low in. most of the measures of socio-economic status or high in measures of social inadequacy. Tract 42, in the southwestern section of the city and surrounding Texas Christian University, is fairly representative of a high level of socio-economic status.

---

[12]There is little evidence of important changes in the general character of the various tracts since 1950. There have been population changes, but little else. Over a longer period, however, significant changes in the social situation of the separate tracts can be expected.

[13]For an explanation of the reliability of sample data, see, "Census Tract Statistics," *loc. cit.*, p. 4.

AREA DIFFERENTIALS WITHIN THE CITY 79

Table 10. Area Contrasts: Selected Socio-economic Variables,
Tracts 17 and 42, 1950

	Tract	
	17	42
Income:		
Median yearly income	$1,553	$3,990
Percentage with incomes below $2,000	64.4	32.0
Percentage with incomes above $4,000	3.6	47.1
Housing:		
Median monthly rent	$21.33	$76.30
Median value of one-unit dwelling units	$3,478	$15,331
Homes with no private bath or dilapidated, percent	62.9	0.9
Homes with no running water or dilapidated, percent	47.3	0.9
Homes with mechanical refrigeration, percent	50.4	97.8
Occupation: (percent)		
Laborers,	21.0	1.0
Professional, Technical and kindred workers	1.9	26.0
Managers, officials, and proprietors	2.4	30.1
Education: (persons 25 years of age or over)		
Median school year completed	7.8	13.3
Percentage of persons with 4 or more years of college	8.1	27.2

Other data further emphasize the contrasts. Tract 17 had a high percentage of its population in the younger age groups, a high percentage of females in the labor force, a high percentage of its families receiving some type of welfare assistance, a high infant mortality rate, extremely high tuberculosis mortality and morbidity rates, and a high percentage of Negro residents. In contrast, Tract 42 was generally at the opposite extreme for each of these measures.

General Population Differentials. The areas of the city vary in population size in part because of the variations in square-mile area, but also because of density of land-use. In general, the tracts near the center of the city have a higher density of population, while the areas near the periphery more commonly have populations living in single or possibly duplex structures with some yard space. High density in the center of the city is particularly the case in the areas immediately south of the central business district. The 1950 population and population per square mile for each of the tracts are given in Table 11.

Table 11. Population and Population Per Square Mile, by Census Tracts, Fort Worth: 1950*

Tract	Population	Population Per Sq. Mile	Tract	Population	Population Per Sq. Mile
City	278,778	3,325			
			24	2,730	1,484
1	9,403	4,298	25	4,789	4,505
2	8,548	3,346	26	5,791	4,455
3	6,253	4,730	27	5,296	7,417
4	7,704	7,959	28	3,631	5,201
5	8,055	3,871	29	5,444	11,938
6	5,321	285	30	4,795	15,518
7	3,039	1,870			
8	6,231	5,509	31	4,082	8,952
9	4,859	7,263	32	4,236	11,236
10	4,517	3,417	33	5,040	14,441
			34	4,326	10,980
11	3,161	2,136	35	7,231	5,380
12	9,233	3,017	36	2,647	2,262
13	3,917	1,319	37	6,454	5,338
14	6,989	2,537	38	3,959	3,404
15	4,728	2,224	39	4,596	9,083
16	3,507	4,308	40	4,620	8,221
17	6,610	5,339			
18	6,379	8,714	41	6,321	12,203
19	4,513	4,451	42	9,148	3,259
20	6,312	4,233	43	5,726	5,117
			44	6,641	6,634
21	6,340	5,442	45	10,566	2,767
22	6,952	4,014	46	8,258	1,515
23	4,116	1,942	47	5,075	3,443
			48	10,635	4,048

Population of Tracted County Areas

T-1	3,757		T-5	7,097
T-2	6,531		T-6	874
T-3	3,930		T-7	10,827
T-4	4,788			

*Sources: Population figures from "Census Tract Statistics," *loc. cit.* (Square mile area and population per square mile computed by writer.) The population per square mile is based on the "net square miles," with land in parks and lakes being excluded.

Age-Sex Differentials. The differential character of the various census tracts can be seen also in terms of age and sex. In newly settled areas used primarily for residential purposes we would expect to find a sex ratio (number of males per 100 females), close to 100, a fairly high ratio of females in the re- productive ages in comparison to children under five years of age, and a relatively high percentage of the tract population under age 15. Tract 23 represents this pattern. Its sex ratio is slightly above 100; it has a high ratio of young children to females, and a high percentage of its population under age 15. Similar data for tract 18 offer a sharp contrast. As a downtown area it offers inadequate facilities for family residence, and tends to house the childless, the unattached adult, and more commonly the unattached adult male. Table 12 gives such information for these two tracts, as well as similar information for the other 46. In this table, as in those which follow, the tracts are arranged in rank order. To facilitate comparisons, in each table the upper and lower quartiles of tracts are indicated for the category ranked. Thus the first 12 tracts ranked represent the upper quartile, and the last 12 the lower quartile.

Table 12. Age-Sex Variations by Census Tracts, Ranked by Number of Children Under 5 Per 100 Females Ages 15-44, Fort Worth, 1950*

Census Tract	Ratio Children to females	Children under 15 percent	Ratio males to females	Census Tract	Ratio Children to females	Children under 15 percent	Ratio males to females
City	41.7	24.4	95.0	14	42.6	24.5	93.7
				12	41.3	26.2	94.3
20	62.9	32.4	103.1	32	41.0	23.8	91.6
23	60.5	35.6	102.3	19	41.0	21.6	95.6
36	56.9	31.4	88.8	39	39.1	23.8	85.8
11	55.4	32.1	94.8	47	39.1	24.3	90.9
6	54.7	17.9	89.7	15	38.8	24.6	86.9
2	54.3	32.1	99.4	21	38.1	23.4	89.4
48	54.2	29.7	96.7	1	37.8	24.6	95.0
24	53.6	32.2	92.4	35	35.6	20.6	86.2
46	51.9	30.4	98.5	22	34.9	22.2	89.5
7	51.5	30.2	99.8	4	34.3	22.0	92.4
5	51.4	30.9	99.5	8	34.1	20.6	91.6
45	49.9	28.6	96.0				
				33	32.1	20.6	87.4
3	49.6	30.1	95.6	28	31.7	18.4	86.5
17	48.8	28.8	89.6	42	31.2	21.0	93.6
10	47.1	26.1	97.5	31	30.5	17.2	86.6
9	46.8	27.0	97.2	27	30.3	20.5	88.4
25	46.0	28.3	90.8	40	29.9	16.3	81.9
13	45.7	26.1	99.3	44	29.5	19.2	80.4
16	45.0	24.3	92.9	41	29.2	16.0	76.4
26	44.7	28.3	95.8	29	28.2	15.7	79.3
43	44.6	23.0	89.4	34	26.8	19.2	86.8
38	43.5	24.9	94.3	30	26.0	14.4	78.2
37	43.2	25.3	91.5	18	20.4	196.7	8.8

*Number of children under 5 per 100 females ages 15-44; number of males per 100 females; percent of total population under 15 years of age. Source: "Census Tract Statistics," *loc. cit.*, Table 2 (ratios and percentages computed).

In Table 12 the data are ranked in terms of the number of children under the age of five years, per 100 females between the ages of 15 and 44. It can be observed that the ratio of children to females in Tract 20 was three times that of Tract 18. For percent of population under 15 years of age, Tract 23 was highest (35.6) and Tract 18 was lowest, with 8.8 percent. The greatest predominance of males (sex ratio) was found in Tract 18, with almost twice as many males as females, due to an abnormal number of unattached adult males. In contrast, Tracts 29, 30, and 41, had fewer than 80 males per 100 females, due most likely to a predominance of both unmarried and widowed adult females.

A more detailed picture of the age-sex pattern is shown in Figure 16, which represents the age and sex distribution for Tracts 18 and 23. The pyramid arrangement in this figure shows for Tract 18 a smaller percentage of the total population in the younger age groups, and a predominance of males in the upper age groups. The representation for Tract 23 is unusual because of the high percentage in the young and middle-age groups.

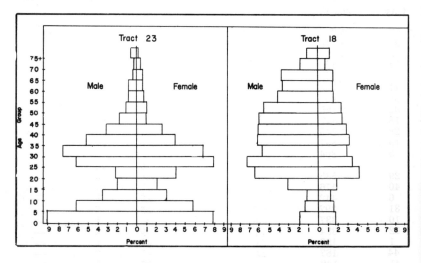

Figure 16. Distribution of Population by Age and Sex for Census Tracts 18 and 23, Fort Worth, 1950. (Original data from U. S. Bureau of the Census, *U. S. Census of Population: 1950*, Vol. III, Chapter 21, Table 2.)

Race and Ethnic Variations. As indicated previously, the only important non-white racial group in the city in 1950 was the Negro group. Other non-white persons totaled only 194. The only ethnic group of significance was the Latin-American or Spanish-speaking group.

In 1950 there were 36,933 Negroes in the city, comprising 13.2 percent of the total population. Negroes were living in all but one (Tract 7) of the 48 census tracts in the city, with 13 tracts having a total of 500 or more Negroes and 10 tracts with 1,000 or more. The 10 tracts contained 84.5 percent of the total Negro population of the city, and represent the major Negro neighborhoods. In many of the tracts with a few Negroes their status was that of servants. The Negro population for each of the tracts is shown in Table 13, with ranking by total number of Negroes. This table also indicates the percent which Negroes

Table 13. Distribution of the Negro Population by Census Tracts, Ranked by Number, Fort Worth, 1950*

Census Tract	Number	Percent of population	Census Tract	Number	Percent of population
City	36,933	13.2	42	104	1.1
			21	76	1.2
17	5,793	87.6	4	73	1.0
25	4,778	99.8	43	63	1.1
33	4,131	82.0	8	61	1.0
34	3,400	78.6	45	50	—
3	2,910	46.5	14	49	—
11	2,733	86.5	30	45	—
36	2,458	92.9	27	39	—
32	2,125	50.2	15	26	—
18	1,547	24.2	35	21	—
28	1,245	34.3	24	24	—
19	897	19.8	9	17	—
5	894	11.1			
			2	17	—
29	535	9.8	38	14	—
40	476	10.3	37	13	—
6	442	8.0	13	8	—
31	397	9.7	23	7	—
10	337	7.5	20	6	—
12	334	3.6	46	5	—
1	190	2.0	48	4	—
44	187	2.8	47	3	—
41	149	2.4	16	3	—
22	144	2.1	39	1	—
26	119	2.1	7	0	—

*Source: "Census Tract Statistics," *loc. cit.,* Table 1 (percentages computed).

were of the total population of each tract. Figure 17 presents
the tracts in which Negroes comprised 75 percent or more of the
total tract population.

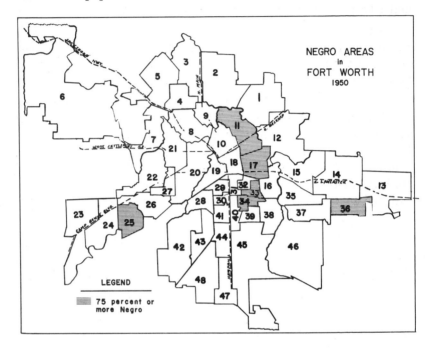

Figure 17. Areas of Concentration of the Negro Population,
Fort Worth, 1950. Census Tract Areas in which Negroes Comprised 75 Percent or More of the Total Population. (Original data
from U. S. Bureau of the Census, *U. S. Census of Population:
1950*, Vol. III, Chapter 21, Table 1.)

In 1950, there were 8,139 persons with Spanish surnames in
the city, or 2.9 percent of the total population.[14] Of this total,
1,509 were born in Mexico. While small in number, in terms
of the total city population, the Latin-American population is
still significant, primarily because a majority tend to live
and function together under conditions of at least partial
exclusion from the general life of the community. Although
spatially, persons of Spanish Surname resided in each of the 48

14U. S. Bureau of the Census, *U. S. Census of Population:* 1950, Vol. IV., Special Reports, Part 3, Chapter C, *Persons of Spanish Surname.*

tracts in 1950, their greatest concentration was found in 12 tracts around the center of the city and extending north along North Main Street. One other area of concentration was in the southern part of the city east of Hemphill Street.

The significance of the Negro and Latin-American groups is due to the fact that to some extent they were—and still are— groups set apart, think of themselves as being separate, and experience some degree of socio-economic discrimination because of their group membership.

Educational Differentials. The median school completed for all persons 25 years of age and over in 1950 for Fort Worth was 11.1. Similar measures for the individual tracts varied from a low of 7.7 for Tract 36, to 13.2 for Tract 42. In Tract 42 slightly more than 27 percent of the adult population had finished four or more years of college; in contrast, seven of the

Table 14.   Educational Differentials, Persons 25 Years of Age and Over. Percent with 4 or More Years of College, and Median School Year Completed, by Census Tracts, Fort Worth, 1950*

Census Tract	College percent	Median year	Census Tract	College percent	Median year
City	7.9	11.1	19	5.9	10.0
			34	5.9	8.9
42	27.2	13.3	23	5.6	12.3
24	22.2	12.9	46	5.5	10.7
43	21.0	12.7	37	4.9	11.4
48	18.1	12.3	40	4.8	10.1
21	17.6	12.6	31	4.4	9.8
22	16.7	12.6	45	4.4	10.7
27	14.7	12.6	8	4.1	10.9
44	14.1	12.4	18	4.1	9.2
26	13.9	12.4	12	4.0	10.4
41	10.8	12.2	36	2.6	7.7
28	10.4	11.6	33	2.5	7.9
35	9.1	11.6			
			39	2.5	10.3
29	8.3	11.6	9	2.5	8.5
17	8.1	7.8	25	2.2	8.3
15	8.1	12.3	32	2.2	8.1
14	7.7	12.1	10	2.0	8.5
13	6.8	10.5	5	1.9	9.2
30	6.8	12.1	38	1.7	9.7
33	6.5	8.8	2	1.6	8.6
20	6.5	11.1	11	1.5	7.9
47	6.4	11.0	16	1.3	8.9
1	6.4	12.0	7	1.3	9.8
6	6.1	11.9	4	1.3	9.6

*Source: "Census Tract Statistics," *loc. cit.*, Table 1. Reported data based on 20 percent sample. (percentages computed)

tracts (2, 4, 5, 7, 11, 16, 38) had less than two percent of the adult population with similar college experience.

Such variations in educational background would suggest significant differences in interests and attitudes. Table 14 shows the ranking of the tracts in terms of percent of persons with four or more years of college. In Figure 18 the location of the tracts in the upper and lower quartiles in this respect is shown. Also given in Table 14 is the median school year completed for each tract.

It can be observed that some of the tracts with a low percent of college persons had a relatively high median school year, indicating that many persons in such tracts had high school experience. In terms of the educational differentials, it is of

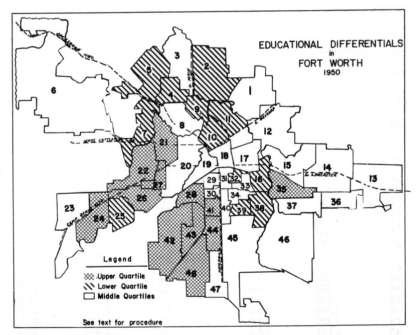

Figure 18. Census Tract Areas Ranking in the Upper and Lower Quartiles for Percentage of Persons, 25 Years of Age and Older with Four or More Years of College. Fort Worth, 1950. (See Table 14 for ranking of all tracts. Original data from U. S. Bureau of the Census, *U. S. Census of Population: 1950*, Vol. III, Chapter 21, Table 1.)

interest to note the similarities between the attained educational level and the occupational patterns and income distribution as presented below.

Income Differentials. The estimated median income in 1949 for families and unrelated individuals, for the several tracts, varied from a high of $5,685 in Tract 24, to a low of $1,388 for Tract 36. Tract 36 had over 60 percent of its families and unrelated individuals with incomes below $2,000, while for Tract 24 the similar percentage was only 9.5. For the entire city the median income was $2,830, with 32.2 percent of the families and unrelated individuals having incomes below $2,000.

The information for median income and for percent with incomes under $2,000, with ranking of the tracts by median income, is given in Table 15. Figure 19 shows the location for

Table 15. Median Income for Families and Unrelated Individuals and Percent with Incomes under $2,000, by Census Tracts, Fort Worth, 1949

Census Tract	Median Income	Percent Under $2,000	Census Tract	Median Income	Percent Under $2,000
CITY	$2,830	32.2	7	2,865	27.5
			20	2,859	23.2
24	5,685	9.5	41	2,848	29.9
21	4,355	14.9	2	2,848	27.2
22	4,313	18.6	38	2,679	31.6
43	4,301	16.5	5	2,675	31.2
27	4,293	15.4	28	2,659	35.2
26	4,146	18.5	16	2,615	35.7
42	3,990	32.9	30	2,508	33.7
1	3,835	14.1	9	2,335	39.2
14	3,750	16.5	40	2,310	39.8
15	3,698	15.3	29	2,272	39.6
44	3,500	24.2	3	2,147	43.6
37	3,476	18.1			
			31	2,120	44.3
47	3,354	19.4	19	2,044	47.2
23	3,426	13.7	32	1,818	54.1
46	3,352	17.8	33	1,794	52.6
13	3,276	20.9	10	1,750	53.8
8	3,230	24.2	25	1,711	59.8
12	3,222	22.5	11	1,679	57.6
45	3,187	26.3	34	1,637	57.0
35	3,102	29.2	17	1,553	64.4
39	3,049	25.0	18	1,479	57.3
48	2,936	28.2	6	1,464	51.0
4	2,936	26.6	36	1,388	62.6

*Source: "Census Tract Statistics," *loc. cit.*, Table 1. (Percentages computed).

those areas with median incomes in the upper and lower quartiles. From Table 15 it can be observed that there existed a close relationship between median income and percent under $2,000, with the percentages increasing as the median income decreased. The variations in this trend suggest that the tracts are not completely homogeneous. Local conditions help to explain some of the variations. Thus, in Tract 42, which includes Texas Christian University, the median income was below that of six other tracts, although in terms of value of housing this tract ranked first. The probable explanation here is that university students, living in the area and with income, were included in the computations.

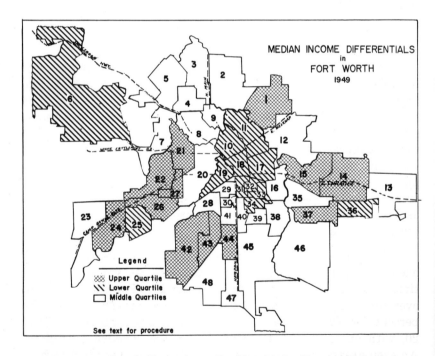

Figure 19. Census Tract Areas Ranking in the Upper and Lower Quartiles for Median Income, Fort Worth, 1949. (See Table 15 for ranking of all tracts. Original data from U. S. Bureau of the Census, *U. S. Census of Population: 1950*, Vol. III, Chapter 21, Table 1.)

Housing Differentials. Although housing is only one of the factors influencing the social life of a community, it is usually a significant one.[15] In Fort Worth, as in other large cities, the conditions of housing vary from area to area, and often from block to block. With some exceptions, however, the sharpest variations exist in Fort Worth between larger areas. Thus, in one census tract, Tract 24 in the Ridglea section, the average monthly rent in 1950 was $98.66, while at the other extreme Tract 17, just east of the central business district, had for the same period an average monthly rent of $21.36. Yet within these two tracts the variations were considerable. For Tract 24 the average monthly rent by blocks varied from $81.66 to $110.00; similar variations for Tract 17 were from $9.44 to $34.57. Other contrasts in housing (for Tracts 17 and 42) have been given in Table 10.

The contrasts in housing conditions throughout the city for 1950 are presented in Table 16. In this table the 48 census tracts are ranked in terms of average value of one-dwelling-unit structures; the other two measures included in the table represent relative degrees of housing inadequacy. It can be observed that in general there is a negative relationship between average value and the other two measures, with the percentages of dwelling units with overcrowded conditions and no running water increasing as the average value decreases. The exceptions, such as Tracts 28 and 29, indicate "pockets" of deficient housing in otherwise adequate areas.

Noticeable in Table 16 is the fact that the average value of one-dwelling-unit structures in Tract 42 was more than five times that of the average value in Tract 25. For units in which overcrowding (more than 1.5 persons per room) existed, the percent for Tract 42, and others, is in sharp contrast to Tract 20, with one fifth of its units having overcrowded conditions. An even greater contrast existed for dwellings classified as hav-

---

15In Chapter VI a general analysis of housing conditions in the city will be presented; here only selected contrasts between census tracts are given.

Table 16. Selected Characteristics of Housing in Fort Worth by Census Tracts, Ranked by Average Value of One Dwelling Unit Structures, 1950*

Census Tract	Average value	Percent Over-crowded	No running water or dilapidated	Census Tract	Average value	Percent Over-crowded	No running water or dilapidated
CITY	$ 7,246	7.3	10.1	12	$6,058	7.7	5.6
				45	5,990	9.2	9.8
42	16,037	0.9	0.8	31	5,877	13.7	16.9
24	12,593	0.5	0.8	40	5,765	5.7	5.4
21	12,483	1.6	0.6	19	5,601	18.0	25.2
43	11,315	2.5	0.8	4	5,473	4.9	6.4
22	11,080	2.0	1.2	39	5,437	4.6	1.9
27	9,844	1.5	0.8	6	5,428	10.7	8.3
44	9,403	2.6	2.8	33	5,386	9.2	14.6
28	9,090	7.8	17.0	34	5,328	9.4	22.4
1	8,954	2.3	1.8	7	5,257	11.6	4.5
14	8,792	2.6	2.3	9	2,250	16.1	17.4
15	8,640	2.6	2.3	18	5,100	17.2	37.2
26	8,168	1.9	2.0				
				10	4,803	14.6	21.2
41	7,777	4.4	3.5	20	4,558	11.0	11.8
29	7,332	8.1	10.5	38	4,364	7.6	10.0
30	6,906	4.8	5.7	32	4,364	17.2	33.5
35	6,582	2.4	4.1	2	4,133	16.2	14.4
48	6,484	3.6	3.5	5	4,123	14.0	18.5
46	6,478	6.5	5.6	16	4,105	8.7	10.6
23	6,469	5.9	4.7	11	4,091	20.9	44.6
37	6,413	2.6	1.1	36	3,540	13.7	40.0
13	6,385	3.9	2.8	17	3,470	17.0	47.3
8	6,281	4.6	2.9	3	3,227	17.1	38.9
47	6,127	4.5	2.2	25	3,182	13.4	28.4

*Source: "Block Statistics," *loc. cit.*, Table 2. (Percentages computed.) "Overcrowded" includes dwelling units with more than 1.5 persons per room. "Dilapidated" includes units which are beyond repair, of inadequate original construction, or in major disrepair.

ing no running water or in a dilapidated condition.[16] Five of the tracts had less than one percent of their units with this deficiency, while at the other extreme, in six tracts these conditions were found in more than one third of the units.

A more comprehensive picture of housing contrasts in the city is given in Table 17. In this table five measures of housing have been transferred into index scores to provide a combined

[16]"A dwelling unit is 'dilapidated' when it is run-down or neglected, or is of inadequate original construction, so that it does not provide adequate shelter or protection against the elements or it endangers the safety of the occupants." "Block Statistics," *loc. cit.*, p. 2.

Table 17. Housing Differentials in Fort Worth: Indices of Housing Adequacy, Based on Five Measures of Housing Quality, 1950*.

Census Tract	Composite Index	Census Tract	Composite Index
CITY	100	4	105
		40	102
24	417	45	93
42	400	29	91
21	303	28	89
27	278	6	88
22	278	7	88
43	256	38	82
26	238	20	81
1	208	16	74
14	208	33	70
15	196	31	64
44	189	34	62
37	169		
		2	61
13	151	5	61
47	149	9	57
41	145	10	56
48	143	19	53
35	141	18	45
23	132	25	45
8	130	32	44
39	128	36	42
46	122	3	41
30	115	11	37
12	108	17	36

*Scores above 100 indicate better than average housing conditions. Composite index based on scores for, "no private bath," "no running water," "overcrowded," "average rent," and "average value." In computing the composite scores, the scores for no private bath, no running water, and overcrowded were reversed. Source: "Block Statistics," *loc cit.*, Table 2. (Indices computed).

measure of housing adequacy. The five measures included are: "average rent," "average value," "no private bath or dilapidated" (reversed), "no running water or dilapidated" (reversed), and "overcrowded" (reversed).[17]

As thus presented the scores above 100 indicate better than

[17]The first step in computing index scores, as used herein, is to determine the percent or value for a particular characteristic for each tract, and for the city. Thus, using Table 16 for illustrative purposes, it can be observed that 7.3 percent of the dwelling units in the city were overcrowded. In computing index scores for overcrowding, the city-wide percent of 7.3 automatically has an index value of 100, since the index scores for individual tracts are percentage variations from the city pattern. The second step is accomplished by dividing each tract percent by the city percent. The same procedure is followed where rates or dollar values are involved.

the city-wide average in housing conditions, while those below 100 are below the city average.[18] The location of the tracts in the upper and lower quartiles in terms of the composite housing index is shown in Figure 20.

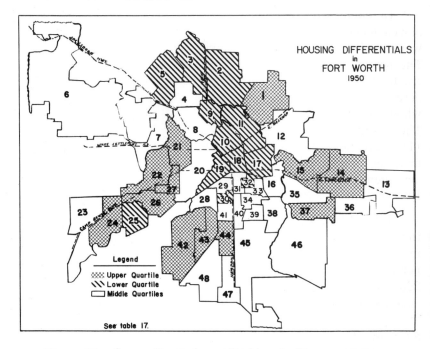

Figure 20.   Census Tract Areas Ranking in Upper and Lower Quartiles on Composite Housing Index, Fort Worth, 1950.   (See text for basis of index, and Table 17 for ranking of all tracts. Original data from U. S. Bureau of the Census, *U. S. Census of Housing: 1950*, Vol. V, Part 67, Table 2.)

Occupational Variations.   In Chapter V the labor force and its distribution by occupations and industries will be discussed. Here it may be worthwhile to consider some of the variations by census tracts in occupational patterns.   As would be expected, some of the tract areas are predominantly residential neighborhoods for professional and managerial workers; other

---

[18]For a more complete analysis of the 1950 Fort Worth housing data, see Robert H. Talbert, "Housing in Fort Worth," *Fort Worth Business Review* (July, 1952); also, "A Summary of Data on Housing in Fort Worth, Texas," prepared for the Program Scope and Research Subcommittee of the Mayor's Housing and Sanitation Board (October, 1953).

areas just as predominantly house laborers and other unskilled workers. While the homogeneity in such respects is not complete in any one tract, the contrasts between tracts are easily observed. This can be seen in combinations of occupations.

To emphasize the above, the census reports of the employed labor force by major occupation groups for each tract were used to determine the percent of workers in each group. The percentages for each occupational category for the 48 city tracts were transferred to index numbers, with the city-wide percent as a base. Next, combinations of categories were made which are intended to represent broad occupational differences. The result is three classifications which generally represent (1) Professional and Managerial workers, (2) Craftsmen, foremen and other skilled workers, (3) Unskilled workers. In this arrangement four of the occupation groups reported by the Bureau of the Census have been omitted.[19]

Table 18 presents the index scores for the three combinations, with the tracts ranked by proportion of professional and managerial workers. The ranking is from a high to a low proportion. Thus, Tract 42 ranking first, with an index score of 265, was 265 percent of the city-wide average; at the opposite extreme Tract 17, with an index score of 20, had professional and managerial workers equal to only 20 percent of the city average. In this respect, Tract 42 had 56.1 percent of its employed labor force so occupied, while for Tract 17 the percent was 4.3.

In general, there is a definite negative relationship between the scores for professional and managerial workers and for laborers. The tracts with high scores for the former had low scores for the latter, or the opposite. Thus, in terms of rank order, for the 12 tracts in the upper quartile for professional and managerial workers, nine were in the lowest quartile, for

---

[19]The groups included are: (1) "Professional, technical, and kindred workers," and "Managers, officials and proprietors, including farm," combined; (2) "Craftsmen, foremen and kindred workers," and "Operatives and kindred workers," combined; (3) "Laborers, except mine." Those omitted are: "Clerical and kindred workers," "Sales workers," "Private household workers," and "Service workers, except private household." See "Census Tract Statistics," *loc. cit.*, Table 2.

laborers, while 10 of the tracts in the lowest quartile, as shown in the ranking in Table 17, were in the highest quartile for laborers. It can be observed also from Table 17 that the tracts with relatively high scores for craftsmen and foremen are located, in the main, among the middle 24 tracts in the ranking. The exceptions to such generalizations indicate the lack of homogeneity of the tracts, and that in a city the size of Fort Worth such area divisions cannot be ideal.

Table 18. Occupational Variations by Census Tracts: Index Scores for Three Occupational Combinations, with Ranking of Tracts by Scores for Professional and Managerial Workers, Fort Worth, 1950*

Census Tract	Occupation Group*			Census Tract	Occupation Group*		
	(1)	(2)	(3)		(1)	(2)	(3)
CITY	100	100	100	8	92	116	42
				12	82	129	65
42	265	23	16	20	82	129	133
24	232	54	11	45	81	124	105
21	207	51	22	40	81	105	94
43	204	49	26	39	75	123	42
22	186	56	31	18	69	87	153
27	180	58	16	19	68	105	175
26	156	81	37	38	66	137	61
14	145	82	29	4	65	139	71
44	144	66	44	7	65	139	221
15	138	82	24	31	60	131	99
28	126	54	136	16	58	150	95
48	125	104	45				
				9	55	143	197
41	115	78	43	33	54	76	89
1	115	98	44	34	51	71	220
23	108	140	53	5	50	148	179
6	106	129	72	10	47	141	151
29	106	93	80	2	47	165	156
13	104	117	66	3	37	127	221
30	98	101	46	36	34	69	327
35	96	94	38	32	30	108	256
37	94	112	30	25	22	66	287
47	93	116	45	11	18	78	336
46	92	131	67	17	20	64	351

*(1) "Professional, technical and kindred workers," and "Managers, officials, and proprietors, including farm," combined; (2) "Craftsmen, foremen and kindred workers," and "Operatives and kindred workers," combined; (3) "Laborers, except mine." Source: "Census Tract Statistics," loc. cit., Table 2. (See text for method of computing indices).

Another method of emphasizing the occupational differences within the city is shown in Figure 21. In this figure the various tracts are classified in terms of the predominant occupational pattern, with each tract being classified in terms of the three combinations discussed above. The designation for each tract was determined by whether it was above the city average for one or more of the occupational combinations. In this instance

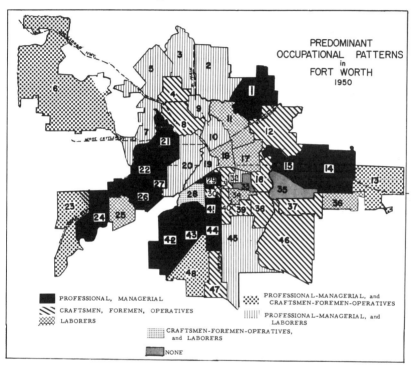

Figure 21. Predominant Occupational Patterns of Census Tract areas, Fort Worth, 1950. (See text for method used in classifying tracts and Table 18 for occupational indices for each tract. Original data from U. S. Bureau of the Census, *U. S. Census of Population: 1950*, Vol. III, Chapter 21, Table 2.)

two of the tracts were below 100 for each of the three combinations, indicating that they are mainly residential areas for one or more of the major occupational groupings which were omitted from consideration.

Area Stability. Two measures are available from the 1950 census reports which are revealing as to the relative stability of an area. Together, they show additional information about the nature of the various census tracts. These measures, percent of the population one year of age and over in 1950, not living in Tarrant County in 1949, and percent of unrelated individuals, are presented for the various tracts in Table 19.

Table 19. Measures of Residential Stability, by Census Tracts: Percent of Persons Living Outside Tarrant County in 1949, and Percent of Unrelated Individuals; Ranked by Percent of Unrelated Individuals, Fort Worth, 1950*

Census Tract	Percent		Census Tract	Percent	
	Unrelated individuals	Residence outside county in 1949		Unrelated individuals	Residence outside county in 1949
CITY	24.1	10.1	43	18.6	8.3
			21	17.0	10.3
18	73.8	18.3	25	16.7	5.0
6	69.3	24.1	39	15.8	8.6
29	41.5	16.0	16	15.6	8.5
34	41.4	6.0	4	15.5	6.9
19	39.2	13.8	8	15.1	8.2
42	36.0	12.9	36	13.5	4.4
30	33.5	15.0	45	13.4	8.7
31	32.3	15.2	26	13.2	10.7
41	31.0	10.2	15	13.2	10.0
33	29.0	6.6	38	13.0	8.6
40	28.5	11.5	7	12.4	16.6
17	28.4	4.8			
			47	12.2	9.5
32	27.9	8.5	20	12.0	19.2
10	27.5	8.5	2	12.0	7.8
44	26.2	9.5	14	11.8	8.8
22	25.2	11.1	12	11.5	10.4
35	23.5	9.0	13	11.4	8.6
28	23.4	18.7	5	11.0	8.3
27	21.5	9.5	37	11.0	6.6
9	20.9	8.3	46	10.1	6.2
11	19.6	13.7	1	9.7	5.8
3	19.5	7.9	24	8.3	10.1
48	19.1	11.6	23	3.0	18.7

*Source: "Census Tract Statistics," *loc. cit.*, Table 1.

The percent of unrelated individuals shows the relative predominance of organized family life, or the lack of it. The high percent in this respect for Tract 18 is a manifestation of its location (central business district) and a predominance of unattached males in the middle and older age groups (sex ratio: 196.7) without family connections. For Tract 6, the high score was due mainly to the location of Carswell Airforce Base in this area. In contrast, Tracts 29 and 34, with sex ratios of 79.3 and 86.8, respectively, ranked high for unrelated individuals primarily because of a predominance of unattached adult females. At the other extreme, Tracts 23 and 24, on the western edge of the city in 1950, were predominantly areas of family residence. Tract 23, particularly, is an area of recent settlement, given over almost entirely to relatively small, single-family dwelling units.

Relative mobility of the areas is expressed by the percent of persons not living in the county in 1949. Even though such figures do not measure intra-county or inter-tract movement, they do indicate some important differences. It is to be expected that Tracts 18 and 6 would have highly mobile populations because of the transitory condition of many of the residents of these areas. Similarly, the high percentages for Tracts 29, 28 and 20 suggest considerable mobility. The high percentages for Tracts 7 and 23, however, probably are the result of an influx of new residents. Low percentages for this measure suggest tracts with fairly stable and established households.

Additional Socio-Economic Variables. In addition to the data presented in the 1950 census reports, other information is available which helps to define the socio-economic nature of the various census tract areas within Fort Worth. Included are unpublished M. A. theses prepared by students in the Department of Sociology, Texas Christian University,[20] magazine art-

---

[20]L. D. Cain, "Ecological Patterns and Indices of Social Well-Being in Fort Worth, Texas," (1949); Jack Gibbs, "Five Years of Homicide and Suicide in Fort Worth, Texas, 1946-1950" (1952); Roy Moore, "Some Uses of Census Tract Data, With Special Emphasis on Some Health Problems" (1950); A. C. Youngblood, "Family Housing Conditions in Sub-Standard Areas of Fort Worth, Texas, in the Light of Ecological Factors, Social Values, and Functional Needs of Families" (1951). Earlier theses which were written before census tracts were established for Fort Worth, but which emphasized area differentials are: Robert E. Baker, "Areas of Social Disorganization and Personal Demoralization in Fort Worth, Texas" (1938); Floyd A. Leggett, "Social Antecedants of Slum Clearance in Fort Worth, Texas" (1940); and Fred B. Porter, "Indices of Social Organization and Disorganization in Fort Worth by Areas Related to the Problems of Youth" (1944).

icles,[21] a chapter in a source book,[22] and several pamphlets
and mimeographed materials.[23] Also available is a *Census
Tract Street Directory* for Fort Worth which was published in
1954.[24] This is a revision of an earlier directory published in
1950.

From the available materials, seven measures of tract differences have been selected and are presented in index form in
Table 20.[25] These are: infant mortality,[26] tuberculosis mor-

---

[21]Paul G. Hastings, "Suburban Banking in Fort Worth," Fort Worth *Business
Review* (November, 1953); Leland McCloud, "Housing Expansion in Fort Worth,
1950-1953," *Fort Worth Business Review* (August, 1953); also, "Housing Expan-
sion in Fort Worth, 1953-1954," *Fort Worth Business Review* (June, 1954); A. L.
Porterfield, "Suicide and Crime in the Social Structure of an Urban Setting, Fort
Worth, 1930-1950," *American Sociological Review*, 17 (June, 1952) 341-49; also
"Suicide and Crime in Folk and Secular Society," *American Journal of Sociology*,
LVII (January, 1952) 331-38; also, "A Study of Secularization and Depressed Folk
Populations: Suicide and Crime in the United States, With a Study of Fort Worth
as a more Intimate Local Situation," *Texas Journal of Science*, III (December, 1951)
516-30; R. H. Talbert, "Housing in Fort Worth," *Fort Worth Business Review* (July
1952); also, "Area Population Changes in Fort Worth, 1950-1954," *Fort Worth
Business Review* (March, 1954).

[22]"Crime and Suicide in the Social Structure of an Urban Setting," in A. L.
Porterfield and R. H. Talbert *Mid-Century Crime in Our Culture* (Fort Worth: Leo
Potishman Foundation, 1954).

[23]A. L. Porterfield, "Socioeconomic Correlates of Poliomyelitis by Census tracts
in Fort Worth: 1950-1952," paper presented at meetings of Texas Academy of Science,
December, 1952 (available from author); R. H. Talbert, et al., "Day Care in Tarrant County," prepared for the Tarrant County Society for Mental Hygiene, 1951;
also, "Tuberculosis in Fort Worth and Tarrant County," 1953, prepared for the
Fort Worth and Tarrant County Tuberculosis Society; R. H. Talbert, "Infant Mortality and Related Differentials in Fort Worth, Texas, 1954," (available from author); also, "A Summary of Data on Housing in Fort Worth, Texas," 1953, (available from author); "Fort Worth and Tarrant County Population Characteristics, Economic Indicators, Social Data, by Census Tracts," prepared by the Department of
Sociology of Texas Christian University and the Research Department of the Fort
Worth Chamber of Commerce.

[24]Prepared and published by the Department of Sociology of Texas Christian
University, the Fort Worth Chamber of Commerce, and the Council of Social Agencies (now the Community Council) of Fort Worth and Tarrant County.

[25]Note of reference number 17 in this chapter explains the procedure used to
compute index scores.

[26]Information on infant deaths, as well as births and total deaths, is tabulated
by the Fort Worth Health and Welfare Department, under the supervision of Mrs.
Nora Griffith, Director of the Bureau of Vital Statistics. The infant mortality rate
—Continued on Next Page

bidity,[27] juvenile delinquency,[28] aid to dependent children,[29] general welfare assistance,[30] executive residence,[31] and agency board member residence.[32] The first five are measures of relative socio-economic inadequacy; the latter two are representative of community leadership.[33] For eight of the tracts, scores

---

26 *Continued*—
represents the number of infant deaths per 1,000 live births. Intra-city contrasts are evidenced by Tract 18 which has a five-year average rate of 79.9, and Tract 8 which had a comparable rate of 14.1. For the same period the city rate was 28.5. In Table 20 such rates have been transferred into index scores.

[27]For source of tuberculosis data, see note of reference number 23 in this chapter.

[28]From a study carried out by students of the writer, from files of the Tarrant County Probation Office, with the assistance of Lynn Ross, Chief Probation Officer, and Mrs. Peggy King, who at the time was a case-worker in the probation office.

[29]Based on a study done by students of the writer, from the files of the Fort Worth office of the State Department of Public Welfare, with the assistance of Paul V. Reed, Field Representative and Mrs. Mamie Gelhausen, case supervisor.

[30]From a study by students of the writer, using the records of the Social Service Exchange (an agency of the Fort Worth-Tarrant County Community Council which is supported by the United Fund). The writer is of the opinion that this is a better measure of disorganization than crime, delinquency and other measures more commonly used for this purpose. The criminal may be "differently organized" rather than disorganized. The person taking *assistance* from an organized agency, at the time at least, is admitting that he cannot support himself or is unable to solve the problems of social adjustment.

[31]The executive residence index (1950) was developed by A. L. Porterfield and is based on the number of employers of 10 or more persons per 1,000 residences; it is derived from a periodic report of the Fort Worth Chamber of Commerce, "Employers of 10 or More Persons."

[32]The agency board index was developed by the writer from records of the Community Council.

[33]The measure of executive residence is closely related to income, and is almost as closely related to quality of housing. Of the nine tracts ranking above 100 for executives, all but Tract 28 were in the upper quartile in terms of median income, as shown in Table 15, and in the upper quartile for the composite housing index, as shown in Table 17. Quite probably, Tracts 21 and 24, in the upper quartile for both income and housing, would also be high for executive residence if such data for these two tracts were available. With one exception, similar patterns existed with regard to agency board membership. The exception is Tract 33, which is predominantly non-white (82.0 percent Negro in 1950) and was the residence for a number of the board members of the Negro welfare agencies.

Table 20. Indices of Socio-Economic Inadequacy and Leadership,
By Census Tracts, Fort Worth*

Census Tract	Infant Mortality 1951-55	Tuberculosis Morbidity 1948-52	Juvenile delinquency 1950	Aid to Dependent Children 1953	General Welfare Assistance 1936-46	Executive Residence	Agency Board members 1950
CITY	100	100	100	100	100	100	100
18	280	317	512	519	241	56	61
31	253	162	367	128	176	34	53
17	232	190	100	745	246	14	13
32	212	180	344	416	222	24	41
33	208	70	221	347	151	56	276
10	189	155	250	561	264	46	0
36	173	62	78	473	*	*	17
3	154	138	112	308	145	10	0
19	145	137	341	464	125	44	154
28	139	91	87	302	70	214	240
34	137	124	35	266	149	23	80
2	126	79	160	81	124	35	10
35	124	57	167	6	55	32	42
38	122	99	132	61	95	36	0
6	114	35	96	0	37	*	57
45	113	115	120	66	67	37	17
11	107	202	185	639	*	*	41
29	107	98	315	61	141	56	112
27	106	51	21	8	19	189	115
16	104	118	197	42	157	20	62
4	102	99	78	28	74	55	51
13	101	100	50	0	*	*	11
9	98	255	64	92	243	26	36
42	97	38	19	0	13	684	661
12	91	67	59	34	84	76	14
25	89	116	142	478	83	11	9
39	85	67	66	0	66	55	10
7	82	34	63	0	*	*	0
26	80	53	16	14	59	86	120
21	79	42	56	0	*	*	328
1	77	94	26	11	39	102	28
20	77	124	155	50	139	35	7
46	74	65	30	19	69	49	5
5	71	54	49	118	100	36	0
37	71	99	43	6	47	50	0
44	71	81	72	8	34	195	255
43	70	40	122	8	26	346	349
22	69	80	91	8	25	426	657
40	68	147	181	9	77	48	19
15	64	78	64	0	33	124	55
24	64	60	0	0	*	*	351
23	64	70	32	6	*	*	20
47	64	118	80	11	54	49	17
48	64	64	37	3	59	47	17
30	58	155	155	34	71	56	91
41	58	85	113	6	62	58	103
8	49	99	107	30	58	68	0
14	37	71	76	16	29	120	31

*Sources: See text.

for two of the measures are not given; these areas were either wholly or partially outside the city at the time of the original study. In Table 20, the census tracts are ranked by their scores for infant mortality, with the scores above 100 representing rates above the city-wide average. Figures 22 and 33 show the location of the tracts ranking high (upper quartile) for 4 of the measures of inadequacy.

Ideally, assuming the seven measures accurately differentiate socio-economic conditions in the various tracts, the score pattern of some of the tracts for the seven measures would be similar to the pattern for Tracts 18 or 17, with high scores for the measures of inadequacy and low scores for leadership; at the other extreme would be patterns such as those for Tracts 22 and 42, with low scores for inadequacy and high scores for leadership. In between these two extremes the expectation would be that some of the tracts would be low on all seven measures, suggesting a general pattern of middle-class status; Tracts 4 and 12 are representative of this pattern. Because of the nature of the statistical procedure, still other tracts would have score patterns which would vary above and below 100.

While the patterns of the tracts as shown in Table 20 reveal some exceptions to the above—indicating a lack of homogeneity of such tracts, or some deficiency in the measuring technique—similarities to the above defined ideal are apparent. Thus, using what is known about the eight tracts which were omitted from two of the studies, and including them, eight of the 48 tracts were above 100 on four of the five measures of inadequacy and low on the two measures of leadership. Six of the tracts were at the opposite extreme, with low scores on four of the measures of inadequacy and high for leadership scores. Fifteen tracts were low for both combinations. The remain-

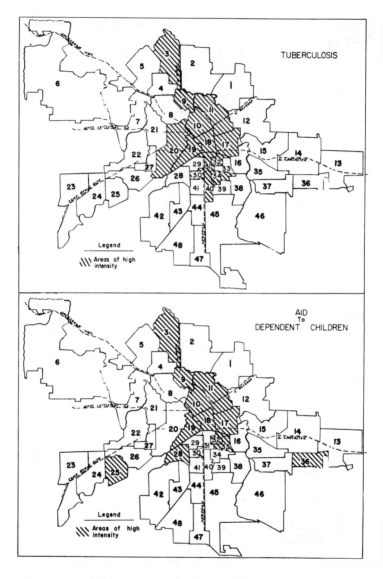

Figure 22. Census Tract Areas of High Intensity for Tuberculosis (1948-1952), and Aid to Dependent Children (1953), Fort Worth. (See text for method used in computing indices, and Table 20 for ranking of all tracts on each measure. Original data from Fort Worth-Tarrant County Tuberculosis Society, and from Fort Worth office of the State Department of Public Welfare.)

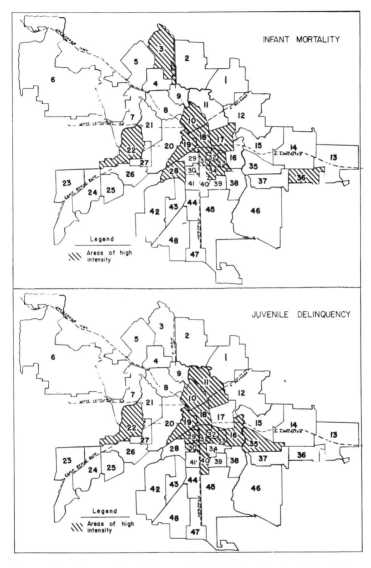

Figure 23. Census Tract Areas of High Intensity for Infant Mortality (1951-1955), and Juvenile Delinquency (1950), Fort Worth. (See text for method used in computing indices, and Table 20 for ranking of all tracts on each measure. Original data from Fort Worth Health and Welfare Department, and from Tarrant County Probation Office.)

ing 19 tracts had scores for the seven measures both
above and below 100.[34]   The tracts in each of these classifications are listed below:

High inadequacy Low leadership	High leadership Low inadequacy	Low leadership Low inadequacy		Mixed	
3	21	4	27	1	28
10	22	5	35	2	29
11	24	6	37	9	30
17	42	7	39	14	33
18	43	8	46	15	36
31	44	12	47	16	38
32		13	48	19	40
34		23		20	41
				25	45
				26	

A Composite of Differentials.   In the foregoing pages
we have sought to show something of the nature of the census
tract areas within the city of Fort Worth.   In this section a composite picture (index) of the tract areas will be given, based on
measures which are considered representative of the many factors making for differentiation.   Implicit in the information
which has been presented already is the fact that some areas are
better for residential purposes than others.   The composite index presented below is of a similar nature.   In fact, the various
measures included have been selected with this in mind, and are
intended to represent the standards which are considered important to the citizens of the community.

Standards of differentiation which are used show reference
to (1) the quality of housing, (2) level of health, (3) level of
education, (4) level of income, and (5) type of occupation.

For the measure of housing quality we have used the index
scores presented previously in Table 17.   However, the scores
as given in Table 17 have been reversed to provide the areas with
relatively few housing deficiencies with scores above 100. Health
is represented by combining the scores given previously for
tuberculosis morbidity and infant mortality in Table 20; in both
arrays the scores have been reversed for the composite index.
Indications of educational differences are provided by index

---

[34]In this classification, Tract 28 is representative of intra-tract contrasts and
lack of homogeneity, with high scores for leadership and a high score for "aid to
children."

scores based on the percent of persons, 25 years of age and over, with four or more years of college; the percentages for this measure are to be found above in Table 14. For the measure of income, the median income figures, as presented in Table 15, have been used, with the income figures above the city-wide median producing index scores above 100.

Occupational differences are represented by three measures —the percent of persons in the labor force in each tract classified as professional, technical and kindred workers combined with the percent classified as managers, officials and proprietors, and the percent of workers classified as laborers; the scores for laborers are reversed. In this instance the occupational scores as given in Table 18 have been used as shown.

The resulting composite index score for each tract is merely the mean (average) of the scores for the seven measures included. Table 21 provides the composite picture of tract differentiation. Figure 24 shows the same information graphically. With the caution given at the beginning of this chapter— that significant differences exist within tracts as well as between them—it appears valid to conclude that the composite index is a useful indication of tract differences. Whether it is a valid measure of socio-economic differences depends upon one's interpretation of what is important. In the writer's opinion the measures chosen to comprise the composite index are valid both in terms of what appear to be the standards of the community, and in terms of somewhat more objective standards of adequate facilities for meeting the basic needs of a society.

Even though there may be some question as to whether the combined index measures what it purports to measure, there can be little question concerning the consistency of the separate measures, with little evidence that any one of the measures has distorted the mean or composite scores. Thus the coefficient of correlation between the composite scores and the scores for housing is + .97; for the other separate scores the coefficients of correlation are: education, + .88; occupation, + .88; health, + .79 ;and income, + .88. The coefficient of correlation of + .97 for housing suggests that this measure alone measures almost the same thing as the composite index, and could be used by itself.

Ranking highest in socio-economic status on the composite index is Tract 24, located near the western periphery of the city limits in the Ridglea section. Four other tracts in the upper

Table 21. Ranking of Census Tracts for Combined Indices of Socio-Economic Status (High to Low): Composite Index Scores Based on Occupation, Housing, Education, Health, and Income; Fort Worth, 1950*

Census Tract	Composite Index	Census Tract	Composite Index
City	100	7	108
		30	107
24	282	29	99
42	275	28	98
21	222	20	94
43	220	5	91
27	203	45	89
22	187	4	88
26	179	40	87
14	163	38	80
15	156	33	80
44	151	16	75
41	138	2	74
35	132		
		34	66
37	130	19	65
23	127	31	64
48	126	36	63
8	124	25	58
47	122	9	57
6	117	10	53
46	117	3	53
1	114	17	52
13	114	18	46
39	111	11	45
12	108	32	45

*See text for sources of data and method of computation.

quartile (21, 22, 27, and 26) are located west of the central business district, on both sides of Camp Bowie Boulevard, and form something of a chain of upper-class expansion over a period of years. Also, located adjacent to Tracts 22 and 24 is the exclusive incorporated town of Westover Hills,[35] which has

---

[35]See Homer Hoyt, *The Structure and Growth of Residential Neighborhoods in American Cities*, Federal Housing Administration, 1939. Hoyt's "sector theory" of urban growth suggests that high rent areas tend to be located on the periphery of one or more sectors or quadrants of a city; as the city grows the new high rent areas are on the periphery in the same sector. In Fort Worth, this seems to be at least partly true with regard to the developments extending out from West Seventh Street and along Camp Bowie Boulevard, as well as for a similar type of expansion from the center of the city toward the southwest.

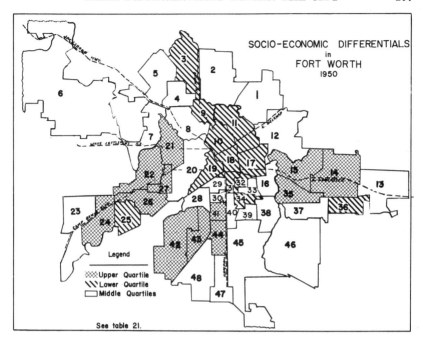

Figure 24. Census Tract Areas Ranking High and Low on Composite Socio-Economic Index, Fort Worth. (See text for bases used in developing index, and Table 21 for rank of all tracts. See text for sources of original data.)

probably the greatest concentration of wealth in the area. However, this pattern of upper status peripheral expansion is not unbroken. Located between Tracts 24 and 26 is the predominantly Negro area of Lake Como (Tract 25), which ranks in the lowest quartile of our composite index; also, an area of low income has developed on the southern edge of Tract 26, fronting on the Lancaster Yards of the Texas and Pacific Railroad.[36]

Just below Tract 24 in rank is Tract 42 in the southwest section of the city, in the TCU area. Two other tracts, 43 and 44, in the upper quartile, are adjacent, and roughly indicate a pattern of peripherical expansion in a given direction. At an

---

[36]Prior to World War I, the area comprising Tracts 25, 26, and 27 was plotted for an exclusive residential section, but little development occurred. During the war this area was leased to the military and Camp Bowie was established. After the war, residential construction occurred rapidly, in part probably because of the streets, sewer and water connections established for the camp. At an earlier time, Lake Como was an exclusive recreational area.

earlier time the areas between Tracts 42, 43, 44 and the central business district would have ranked high in socio-economic status, but the processes of invasion and succession have left them with a lower current status.

The remaining three tracts in the upper quartile (14, 15, and 35) are in the eastern section of the city, toward Dallas, and along East Lancaster Street. It should be understood, of course, that there are other areas in the city with above-average residential neighborhoods.

Ranking lowest on the composite index is Tract 32 located south of the central business district, and straddling the North-South Freeway just south of the point of interaction with the proposed East-West Freeway. In 1950 Tract 32 had over 11,000 persons per square-mile (3,325 per square-mile for the entire city), with its population almost equally divided between white and Negro residents (50.2 Negro). Eight of the remaining tracts in the lower quartile are a part of the central business district, or immediately adjacent to it. Only Tracts 25, 36, and 3, among the 12 lowest ranking tracts, are outside the central business area. Tracts 25 and 36 represent peripheral movements of the Negro population. Tract 3 borders on the stockyards and packing plants in north Fort Worth.

Area Population Changes, 1950-1956.

In the period from April, 1950, to February, 1956, the population of Fort Worth increased approximately 78,000 to an estimated total of 357,367, or an average yearly increase of approximately 13,000.[37]

---

[37]The Chamber of Commerce provides periodic estimates of the total population, based mainly on utility connections. The use of school census data as herein outlined has an advantage in that it provides area estimates. The population estimates presented here are based on the annual school census of the Fort Worth Independent School District. Previous estimates, using the same procedure, were attempted in 1952, 1953, 1954. For these three previous years the total estimates were 312,967, 322,845 and 331,435, respectively. The basis for the estimate is the annual school census, and the United States Census Bureau report by census tracts for the city in 1950. The procedure to use the school census reports for general population estimates was established through the cooperation of the Fort Worth Chamber of Commerce, Assistant Superintendent of School Elden Busby, and Mr. S. T. Willis, head of the Child Accounting Department of the Fort Worth Public Schools, and the Department of Sociology, Texas Christian University. Actual estimates were made by the writer.

Table 22. Population Change For Fort Worth by Census Tracts, 1950-56, and 1956 Estimates of Population for Areas Annexed Since 1950

Census Tract	Population 1950	Population 1956	Increase Number	Increase Percent	Natural Increase*
City	278,778	357,367	78,589	28.2	34,520
1	9,403	10,342	939	10.0	1,115
2	8,584	11,760	3,175	37.0	1,302
3	6,253	6,592	339	5.4	780
4	7,704	7,251	— 453	— 5.9	668
5	8,055	9,080	1,025	12.7	1,317
6	5,321	6,177	856	16.1	322
7	3,039	3,469	430	14.1	584
8	6,231	5,450	— 781	—12.5	526
9	4,859	4,408	— 451	— 9.2	455
10	4,517	2,344	—2,173	—48.1	320
11	3,161	3,629	468	14.8	595
12	9,233	9,453	220	2.4	769
13	3,917	7,188	3,271	83.5	551
14	6,989	11,611	4,622	66.1	1,290
15	4,728	4,505	— 223	— 4.8	275
16	3,507	3,676	169	4.8	238
17	6,610	5,764	— 846	—12.8	399
18	6,379	6,508	129	2.0	—208
19	4,531	4,248	— 283	— 6.2	358
20	6,312	3,987	—2,327	—36.8	928
21	6,340	6,268	— 72	1.1	467
22	6,952	6,422	— 530	7.6	414
23	4,116	8,708	4,592	111.5	999
24	2,730	6,109	3,379	123.8	629
25	4,789	6,972	2,183	45.5	712
26	5,791	5,946	155	2.6	661
27	5,296	5,695	399	5.6	257
28	3,631	3,500	— 131	— 3.6	204
29	5,444	4,882	— 562	—10.3	405
30	4,795	3,865	— 930	—19.4	397
31	4,082	4,205	123	3.0	306
32	4,236	3,265	— 971	—22.9	538
33	5,040	5,286	246	4.8	287
34	4,326	3,675	— 651	—15.0	244
35	7,321	7,838	607	8.4	493
36	2,647	8,638	5,991	226.3	999
37	6,454	9,426	2,972	46.0	781
38	3,959	3,806	— 151	— 3.8	319
39	4,596	4,681	85	1.8	357
40	4,620	4,257	— 363	— 7.8	340
41	6,321	6,217	— 104	— 1.6	428
42	9,148	9,568	420	4.6	595
43	5,726	7,444	1,718	30.0	350
44	6,641	5,545	—1,096	—16.5	396
45	10,566	13,136	2,570	24.3	1,355
46	8,258	19,956	11,698	141.6	2,235
47	5,075	7,848	2,773	54.6	826
48	10,635	14,498	3,863	36.3	2,198

Table 22 Continued—

Annexed Areas

A	2,754
B	800
C	2,339
D	750
E	8,551
F	4,895
G	1,680
H	9,300
I	1,200

*The natural increase represents the balance of births over deaths. In those tracts where the total population increase is greater than the natural increase, the difference is assumed to be due to net-migration (the difference between in-migration and out-migration.

Although the city as a whole has grown since 1950, significant area variations of population change have occurred. For some areas, the percentage growth has been far greater than that of the city, while other areas showed a population decrease.

At the two extremes, Tract 36 increased in population by an estimated 226 percent, while Tract 10 decreased approximately 48 percent. In all, 29 tract areas increased in population, and 19 areas showed a population decrease.

Table 22 shows the estimated population changes for each of the 48 census tracts in the city, as of 1950, and the estimated population of areas annexed since 1950. Table 22 gives also the natural increase, which is the balance of births over total deaths for the years 1951-1955, as tabulated by the city Health Department. It can be observed that several of the tracts, which had an increase in population between 1950 and 1956, would have declined without the surplus of births. Figure 25 shows the location of the 1950 census tracts, and the areas annexed to the city limits since 1950.

Another way of observing the area variations can be shown by comparing logical combinations of census tracts. This information is presented in Table 23. Thus, the areas including, and immediately adjacent to, the central business district had a decrease in population of 8.8 percent, while the areas on the

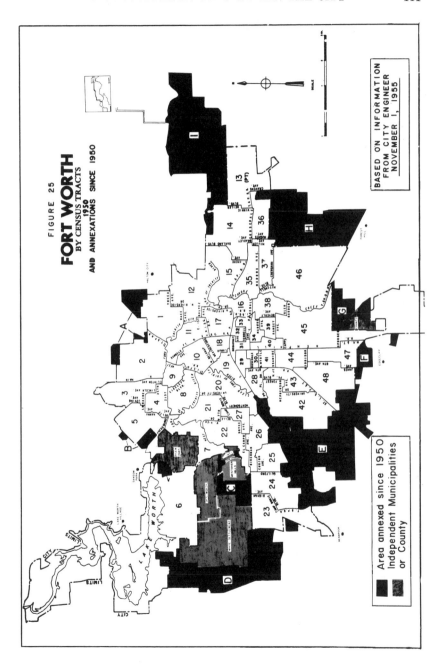

FIGURE 25

FORT WORTH
BY CENSUS TRACTS
1950
AND ANNEXATIONS SINCE 1950

BASED ON INFORMATION
FROM CITY ENGINEER
NOVEMBER 1, 1955

Area annexed since 1950
Independent Municipalities
or County

outer edge combined had an estimated increase of 26.1 percent. As can be seen in Table 23, when these peripheral areas are separated into directional groups some significant differences appear. It should be recalled, however, as shown in Table 22, that a part of the increase of these areas was due to the balance of births over total deaths. In the main, Fort Worth has tended

Table 23. Sectional Population Variations, 1950-1956, by Tract Combinations

| | Total Population | | Change | |
	1950	1956	Number	Percent
Central	29,280	26,698	— 2,582	— 8.8
Periphery	115,600	152,464	31,542	26.1
North	32,295	37,774	5,479	17.0
West	22,168	30,885	8,717	39.3
South	43,682	65,006	21,324	48.8
East	13,553	27,437	13,884	102.4
Annexed areas		32,269		

*Census tracts included in areas: Central—10, 11, 17, 18, 19, 31; *Periphery*—all tracts on outer edge of city; *North*—1, 2, 3, 5; West—6, 7, 22, 23, 24; South—42, 45, 46, 47, 48; East—13, 14, 36.

to grow horizontally rather than vertically. This fact can be observed in areas annexed to the city since 1950, as shown in Figure 27. However, a few areas, densely populated in 1950, continued to grow.[38]

It must be recognized, of course, that areas outside the legal limits of Fort Worth but in Tarrant County have grown in population also. This is particularly observable in the county towns East of Fort Worth in the direction of Dallas.

[38]For a discussion of some of the consequences of horizontal growth, see Chapter VI, herein, and particularly Table 47 for contrasts with other comparable cities.

Chapter V

THE ECONOMIC LIFE OF THE COMMUNITY*

As suggested earlier, the general culture of a city is influenced significantly by its economic activity. In a very real sense there exists the "long arm of the job." A city which is primarily a trading center will differ sharply from one which is predominantly engaged in manufacturing. Then too, the type of trading, or manufacturing, or wholesaling will influence the local socio-cultural situation.

Of major importance is the nature of the primary economic activities, that is, the ways in which money is brought into the local area. With current standards of living, there is a constant need for goods and services from outside the locality, and these can be secured solely by a city's "producing" something locally.

Thus, in manufacturing, although the necessary raw materials may be imported, local people supply their labor and provide a "value added by manufacture." The net return resulting can be paid to local people in the form of salaries and wages, which in turn can be used to purchase goods produced elsewhere. In this sense, manufacturing is a primary economic activity. Such inter-community trading can be achieved only through the production of something locally which can be traded.

In this sense, then, a city's primary economic activities would include the following:

1. Manufacturing—by producing a "value added by manufacture," a part of which is a net return accruing to the locality.

2. Wholesale trade—by producing a service and charging a fee which adds to the locality's purchasing power.

3. Retail trade—directly through sales to customers from outside the community.

4. Banking—through lending money to persons or companies outside the community.

*Mr. James E. Bunnell, Manager of the Research Department, Fort Worth Chamber of Commerce, read this chapter and made suggestions as to content.

5. Professional services—that portion of medical, hospital, legal or other services supplied to persons outside the community.

6. Recreational services—that portion supplied to outsiders.

7. Educational services—that portion of the income added by colleges, universities, technical schools and consolidated schools which draw students from elsewhere.[1]

8. Transportation and Communication services—through money spent locally by both travelers and employees.

9. Government—from the county government in the sense of money drawn from agriculture in the county, and from state and federal agencies with regional headquarters in the city.

10. Other activities—in similar ways many other capital-increasing activities are performed. Here could be included such services as those provided for conventions.

Limited evidence is available in the form of estimates concerning the consequences of the addition of a new primary economic activity. The Michigan Department of Economic Development has concluded that an industry employing 50 persons would produce the following consequences:

support from 300 to 400 people
require 75 to 100 homes
put 200 children in school
require six teachers
cause the purchase of 100 automobiles
enable eight professional people (dentists, ministers, doctors, lawyers, etc.) to live in the community
pay about $175,000 annually for transportation
buy the products of 1,800 acres of land
produce a payroll of $180,000[2]

The above, of course, does not mean that every new industry will create the indicated increase, since a community's already established economic base may be underemployed, and can therefore absorb new demands; yet normally the introduction of new activities would create a need, even though grad-

---

[1]For a statement emphasizing the economic importance of educational services at the college level, see Fort Worth *Star-Telegram*, February 9, 1956 (morning edition), p. 22. The statement is the published account of a speech made by T. J. Harrell, co-chairman of a campaign to raise $1,500,000 to construct dormitories for married students at Southwestern Baptist Seminary. In the statement, Mr. Harrell seeks to show how much "new money" the Seminary students bring into the community.

[2]*The First Step in Community Industrial Development*, Michigan Department of Economic Development, October, 1949, quoted in L. W. Casaday and N. H. Ringstrom, Jr., "The Community Investment in New Industry," *New Mexico Business*, 5 (October, 1952) p. 4.

ual in nature, for additional services and facilities. In the last section of this chapter a brief analysis will be presented of some of the other consequences.

The purpose of the emphasis in the preceding paragraphs is to distinguish between inter-community and intra-community economic activity, and to suggest that intra-community ex· change of goods and services alone is effective only if the people of a community desire no goods from elsewhere.

General Nature of Economic Growth. The growth of Fort Worth reveals the story of a frontier settlement which became an established community, then a city, and today is a metropolitan center with an important and related hinterland. In Chapter II it was suggested that the city has passed through different and somewhat distinct stages, and that each new stage in the development has been achieved through the addition of new and significant socio-economic activities. The importance of these additions has been that in each instance the economic base of the city has become broader and of a more diversified nature. Thus, after the early period of frontier settlement, the location of the courthouse gave the community a permanence which it ctherwise would not have had. In a similar fashion, the movement of cattle from the South and West Texas ranges through Fort Worth to the railroad junction in Kansas gave to the town new business activity. With the coming of the railroad a superior means of transporting people and goods in and out cf the community was achieved. The railroad, however, did not assure Fort Worth the metropolitan status which it later achieved. This came about through the later addition of a variety of big and little job-producing primary economic activities. In Figure 26 the relationship between the major primary economic additions and growth of population is emphasized.

In a general way the economy of Fort Worth grew and expanded as Texas and the Southwest developed. This can be observed in the information presented in Table 24, which gives the population by decades for Texas and for the four largest cities in the state.[3]

---

[3]The same information is shown in Figure 4 in Chapter III.

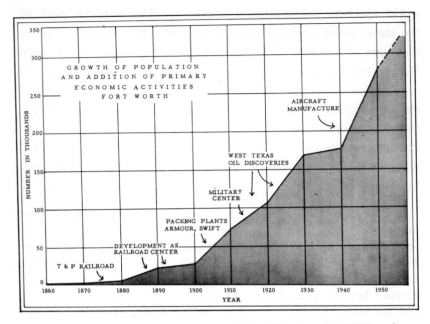

Figure 26. Growth of Population of Fort Worth and Addition of Major Primary Economic Activities, 1860-1950.

Table 24. Population by Decades for Texas, and for Houston, Dallas, San Antonio, and Fort Worth, 1850-1950*

Year	Texas	Houston	Dallas	San Antonio	Fort Worth
1950	7,711,194	596,163	434,462	408,442	278,778
1940	6,414,824	384,514	294,734	253,854	177,662
1930	5,824,715	292,352	260,475	231,542	163,447
1920	4,663,228	138,276	158,976	161,379	106,482
1910	3,896,542	78,800	92,104	96,614	73,312
1900	3,048,710	44,633	42,638	53,321	26,688
1890	2,235,527	27,557	38,067	37,673	23,076
1880	1,591,749	16,513	10,358	20,550	6,663
1870	818,579	9,382	—	12,256	—
1860	604,215	4,845	—	8,235	—
1850	212,592	2,396	—	3,488	—

*Source: U. S. Bureau of the Census, *U. S. Census of Population: 1950*, Vol. I, "Number of Inhabitants," Ch. 43, Texas, pp. 9-12.

Following the Civil War, Texas moved rapidly from an agricultural frontier, in which farming had self-sufficiency as its goal. By 1900, farm products from Texas were entering the world markets in increasing numbers. The western part of the state, which originally had practiced cattle-raising as merely a part of a self-sufficient agriculture, turned after the Civil War to raising cattle for the market. Manufacturing of a local nature existed early in Texas towns, but only after the era of railroad-building did Texas industry become a part of the national economy. Certainly the coming of the railroads is not the only explanation which can be given for the drastic economic changes in Texas in the latter part of the Nineteenth Century, but their coming was vitally important.[4]

The economic development of Fort Worth, however, was not automatic. In addition to the fact that there was little economic validity for the development of two cities as close together as Fort Worth and Dallas (approximately 30 miles), there was the fact of no particular advantage of site location (no navigable rivers,[5] harbor, or closeness to mineral deposits), and the town did not have the advantage of priority in the region. In terms of location, any of a dozen other communities in the area could have achieved metropolitan status, or the metropolitan needs of the area could have been served by Dallas.[6]

---

[4]For an intensive analysis of the changes which occurred in Texas from 1870 to 1900, see John S. Spratt, *The Road to Spindletop: Economic Change in Texas, 1875-1901* (Dallas: Southern Methodist University Press, 1955). (Spindletop was the name of the first major oil discovery in the state, coming in 1901).

[5]The Trinity River, with its West Fork and Clear Fork flowing from the west and southwest, and Sycamore Creek entering the city from the south, have had, however, considerable influence on the internal development of the city, both ecologically and as sources of water for industrial and human consumption. At times, these streams, which normally are sluggish and of creek size, have reached flood stage and have caused considerable damage, as in 1949. Flood control for the West Fork was partially accomplished with the completion of Lake Worth Dam in 1913 (built mainly to create a dependable source for water). Attempts to control the Clear Fork were started in 1947, with the Benbrook Dam project (completed in 1952), and the Fort Worth Floodway projects, begun in 1950 and officially completed in 1956. A future possibility for the Trinity River is that envisioned by the Trinity River Improvement Association (a regional organization), to make the Trinity navigable as it flows south to the Gulf of Mexico.

[6]As indicated previously, there is no intention here to imply that growth is necessarily desirable. Nor is there the intent to imply for Fort Worth continuous effective leadership. At times, the community seems to have been lethargic and without effective leadership.

In the following section the general development of the economy of Fort Worth will be emphasized. Although no exhaustive presentation is given, there is the attempt to suggest the representative, and sometimes unique, economic conditions prevalent during particular periods. The economic trends in the city are briefly traced through the various stages, as outlined in Chapter II, to the current economy and the present institutional patterns in the area of economic behavior.

Economic Trends

The beginning of Fort Worth as an economic center has been duplicated dozens of times throughout the land. Probably the first economic activity began when the military traded with the few hardy settlers of the area. Historical records indicate that the first business establishment in the vicinity was a sutler's store for military personnel only. In the next year a store was opened for use of the settlers. After the military moved farther westward in 1853, the abandoned buildings of the fort were used to open other business establishments. Understandably, the business activity of the time was limited because the number of people alone (approximately 650 in Tarrant County in 1850)[7] would have set limitations on the economic activity; but in addition, the settlers had little or no money, and the means for transporting salable goods to the area were limited. They practiced what one writer has called a "simple economy of independent self-containment."[8] As elsewhere, the early settlers produced their own food and most or all of their clothing. Their purchasing, or bartering, involved such things as coffee, sugar, and salt. In addition, the stores of the time sold coffee grinders, bolts of cloth, thread, hammers, picks, oxen yokes, and huge chunks of solidified sugar for the children.[9]

---

[7]Oliver Knight, *Fort Worth: Outpost on the Trinity* (Norman: University of Oklahoma Press, 1953), p. 29.

[8]Spratt, *op. cit.*, p. 3. His chapter I, "A Frontier Economy," describes in detail the living conditions of the Texas frontier before the railroad.

[9]For a more complete account of early merchandising, see Fort Worth *Star-Telegram*, "Fort Worth's First 100 Years" (October 30, 1949), "Merchandising," p. 2. See also, Knight, *op. cit.*, p. 29.

In spite of its small population in 1860, Fort Worth did have some importance as a stop-over place for settlers moving West, and, according to Knight, even at that early date the rivalry between Fort Worth and Dallas existed. He records that it was a fairly common occurrence for Fort Worth runners to meet settlers east of Dallas and try to lure them around Dallas to Fort Worth.[10]

If the location of the army post on the forks of the Trinity and its later abandonment was the first step in the development of Fort Worth, the second was the moving of the county courthouse from Birdville to Fort Worth in 1856. Today, Birdville is an unincorporated hamlet a few miles from the northeast boundaries of the present Fort Worth city limits.

As elsewhere, the Civil War had serious effects on the economy of Fort Worth. The population of Tarrant County had increased during the decade 1850-1860 from 664 to 6,022, as the area had ben made relatively safe for settlers; but during the war the number declined to around 1,000. Merchants had extreme difficulty getting supplies. Mail service was provided by a pony courier from Waxahachie. Little or no "hard" money was in circulation. County authorities issued certificates, which for a time substituted for money, but this procedure was of little value. While the area was not subject to the devastation of war, the effect on Fort Worth was temporarily disastrous.

After 1865 there apparently was some recovery. Some of the businesses which had been closed during the war reopened, and some new ones were started, but even by 1870 the county had not regained the population size of 1860. Also, businss activity of the day was far different from the present. This was true in part because money was still scarce; also, the settlers of the time had relatively few needs.

Each store was a log structure with a rear and front door and a window on each side of the main entrance. There were no streets, only roads around the courthouse. Log residences were scattered here and there east of the square.[11]

---

[10]Knight, *op. cit.*, p. 28.

[11]*Ibid.*, p. 57.

The period from 1870 to 1880 was an important one in the economic development of Fort Worth and Tarrant County. The movement of cattle from the South and West Texas ranges, and the use of Fort Worth as a stop-over place, meant considerable business for the community, and the beginning of the continued interest in the cattle industry.[12] A second development of importance during the decade was the coming of the railroad. Even before its arrival in 1876 the possibilities attracted people and business activity.

> In 1873, Fort Worth rumbled with an excitement, an eagerness that transcended even the natural bumptiousness of the ebullient frontier. Merchants hurried to the town, rushed buildings to completion, flung merchandise on the shelves, and waited for the golden horde. For the railroad was on the way! Sure signs of empire, twin strands of rail were like magnet drawing men by the score from the older states.[13]

The interest aroused by the potentialities of the railroad attracted not only merchants but also those interested in wholesale trade and manufacturing, who saw in the railroad possibilities to service the West Texas area of settlement. The greater stability of the town during the decade 1870-1880 is indicated by the fact that in 1873 incorporation was achieved and the first town government established. In 1876 Dun's Report listed 59 business concerns in the town of Fort Worth; by 1880 there were 460 retail and wholesale firms.[14] In Tarrant County, according to the census report of 1880, there were 58 manufacturing plants, employing 163 wage earners, and with a plant value of $467,087.00.[15] Certainly these were not large factories in any sense of the word, but such evidence does indicate a movement away from the frontier type of settlement. Further evidence of community and county stability is shown by the population figures of 6,663 for 1880, for Fort Worth, and 24,671 for

---

[12]For a map showing the cattle drives, see "Ranch and Farm," Fort Worth *Star-Telegram, loc. cit.,* p. 2.

[13]Knight, *op. cit., p. 66.*

[14]"Merchandising," Fort Worth *Star-Telegram, loc. cit.,* p. 2.

[15]*Tenth Census of the United States: 1880,* Vol. II, "Manufacturers," p. 179. The total wages figure reported for the year was $56,832, or an average annual wage of $348.66 per worker. Of the 58 manufacturing establishments listed, 15 were classified as flour and/or grist mills.

Tarrant County. It must not be assumed, however, that the coming of the railroad meant that Fort Worth became the center of a thriving trade territory. Much of the area of West Texas was at that time unorganized and had few settlers. In most of the area of Texas west of Fort Worth in 1870 there were less than two people per square mile.[16] In the entire area which at the present comprises 84 counties in West Texas and is considered the "Fort Worth trade territory,"[17] the total population in 1870 was approximately 40,000, including the 5,788 people living in Tarrant County.[18]

Between 1880 and 1890 the city improved its economic position. This is shown by the increase in manufacturing for the ten year period. By 1890, the census reports for Fort Worth showed an average of 2,368 employees, and total wages of $1,618,073.[19] The city population increased 246 percent, to 23,076. By this time Fort Worth was no longer on the frontier. Certainly much of the frontier tradition must have persisted, but the area to the west was being rapidly settled, with a total population in 1890 of well over 400,000.[20] A part of this growth, at least, must be attributed to the railroad building, which was important in the growth of Fort Worth. And significantly, with one exception, the trunk line railroads which spread through West Texas at a time when highways were unknown, moved west from Fort Worth. In this sense, as well as in other respects, there is some logic to the present-day claim that Fort Worth is the "gateway to the West"—at least to West Texas. This fact is emphasized in Figure 27, which shows the present-day Fort Worth trunk line railroads. It can be observed that as

---

[16]See *Tenth Census of the United States: 1880*, Vol. I, map, opposite p. xx.

[17]As designated by *Sales Management*, May 10, 1952. See Figure 33 in this chapter for a map of the area.

[18]Computed from *Ninth Census of the United States: 1870*, Vol. I, pp. 63-64

[19]*Twelfth Census of the United States: 1900*, Vol. III, "Manufactures," Part II, p. 994.

[20]In the Fort Worth Trade Territory, mentioned previously, the total population was 356,465 (Computed from *Abstract of the Twelfth Census of the United States: 1900*, pp. 170-2).

far as railroad transportation is concerned, Fort Worth is the
gateway to West Texas and the Panhandle.

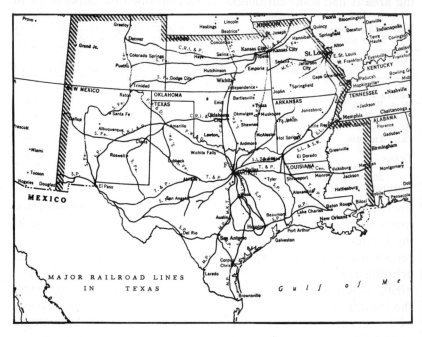

Figure 27. Major Railroad Lines in Texas, 1955. (Note that lines
serving West Texas and the Panhandle extend westward from
Fort Worth.)

However, the promise of the 1880-90 decade was not fulfilled in the next ten years. The population had increased to 26,-
688, but economically the picture was not bright. While manufacturing was growing in other leading Texas cities and in the
state, Fort Worth suffered a considerable decrease. Between
1890 and 1900 the average number of employees declined 38.8
percent, and the total wages and value of products decreased
47.7 and 21.9 percent, respectively. Comparable percentages
for Fort Worth and the other leading cities and for the state
are shown in. Table 25.

Apparently, by 1900 Fort Worth was just another town
along the railroad lines. It was an established community, but

with not too many prospects of much greater economic growth. As a county-seat town and as a trading center for the surrounding area it had some influence. It had retained its importance in

Table 25. Percent Change for Selected Manufacturing Measures Between 1890 and 1900 for Five Leading Texas Cities and For the State*

City	Number of Establishments	Average Number Employees	Total Wages	Value of Product
	Percent Change, 1890-1900			
Dallas	19.6	5.7	8.1	26.8
Fort Worth	—33.9	—38.8	—47.7	—21.9
Galveston	55.3	22.6	2.1	—12.4
Houston	142.4	69.2	78.0	55.7
San Antonio	1.0	52.2	44.2	21.3
Texas	133.3	38.4	35.7	69.5

*Source: *Twelfth Census of the United States: 1900*, Vol. III, "Manufactures," Part II, p. 866.

the cattle industry in the sense of providing a stop-over place for cattle moving from the range to the Northern and Eastern packing plants, but it had not been able to establish a local meat-processing plant. Its largest single manufacturing activity was printing and publishing, with the manufacturing establishments hiring only an average of seven employees.[21] Without exception, the "manufacturing" of the time was small and of the type needed to service only the immediate area. Fort Worth's business community was substantial, housed, in part at least, in brick and stone buildings, with some of them rising to four stories. Its wholesale jobbing activity apparently was considerable, providing a necessary service for the small towns and villages in West Texas; but as the railroads were extended, and as towns in that area developed, Fort Worth was no longer the only junction-point for wholesale trade.[22]

Certainly Fort Worth had come far since its early days as an isolated frontier settlement, and the change had been rapid from the almost disastrous Civil War period. It had a city government, including organized fire and police departments; a

[21]*Twelfth Census of the United States: 1900*, Vol. III, "Manufactures," Part II, p. 994.

[22]The 84-county Fort Worth "Trade Territory" had by 1900 increased 39.8 percent during the decade, to a total population of 498,245. Fort Worth's population increase during the same decade was 15.7 percent.

publicly controlled water system; the beginnings of a sanitary sewer system; 50 miles of graded streets, and macadamized streets in the business section; home delivery of mail; approximately 32 miles of electric street car lines; congregations of all the major religious denominations; a public tax-supported school system; two privately supported colleges; a variety of fraternal, educational and social clubs; and two daily newspapers.[23] It had been working to develop a public library since 1892—and was to achieve it in 1901[24]—and had just organized a Fort Worth Board of Trade, which was the forerunner of the present Chamber of Commerce.[25]

It seems apparent that by 1900 Fort Worth had achieved a new level as an established community. As a railroad town, county seat, and as a wholesale and retail trade center for the immediate area, it could have continued to grow gradually as the area developed. Any but gradual growth, however, was impossible without the introduction of important new manufacturing activity.

Evidently, the limitations of the existing economic base were recognized by many of the community leaders of the time. Earlier, attempts had been made to establish meat-processing plants with local capital, but with no lasting success. A stock yards which could handle an estimated 12,000 head of cattle was in operation[26], but its influence was probably limited as an income-producing activity. Most needed were new industries of more than local size.

This fact, plus active interest on the part of local community leaders, led to the location in 1902 and actual operation in 1903 of branch plants of the Armour and Swift meat-packing companies. The effect of this new primary activity, which was

[23]Andrew Morrison, *Fort Worth and Texas*, (St. Louis: George W. Engelhart and Co.), (no date).

[24]B. B. Paddock, *Fort Worth and the Texas Northwest Chicago* (The Lewis Publishing Company, 1922), p. 640.

[25]*Ibid.*, p. 651.

[26]Morrison, *op. cit.*, p. 89.

Fort Worth's first major industry, and the related drawing power were felt locally almost immediately. Referring to the effect of the packing plants, Knight writes,

> They drew practically all of the West Texas cattle into Fort Worth for either sale or reshipment at the stockyards, or for sale to the packers. When the cattlemen came to market, they naturally did their shopping. Their wives came along, and the money spent magnified the boon the packing houses were to the city.[27]

The importance of the packing plants can be observed in the report of receipts of the Fort Worth Stock Yards Company, which had been established earlier. In 1902 the total number of animals handled was 226,106.[28] By the end of 1903, the number had increased threefold, to 732,741, and in the following year to 1,045,179. By 1909 the total receipts were ten times those of of 1902. Thereafter a slight drop occurred, but with the increased demand for American meat during World War I, the receipts increased sharply. The total annual receipts of all types of livestock received in the Fort Worth market for the period from 1902 to 1954 are shown in graphic form in Figure 28.

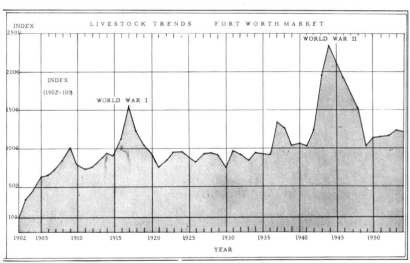

Figure 28.   Indices of Trends of Total Livestock Receipts, Fort Worth Stockyards, 1902-1954.   1902 Total Receipts (head of cattle) = 100.   (Original data supplied by the Fort Worth Chamber of Commerce.)

---

[27]Knight, *op. cit.*, pp. 174-5.
[28]Paddock, *op. cit.*, p. 680.

The influence of the packing plants on the Fort Worth economy is evident also in the growth of manufacturing. This fact can be observed in Table 26, which provides manufacturing data (for the city only) for 1899, 1904, and 1909. The improvement in manufacturing as revealed in Table 26 is particularly signifi-

Table 26. Trends in Manufacturing for Fort Worth, 1899-1909*

Year	Wages	Salaries	Value added by Manufacture
1909	$1,285,000	$484,000	$3,395,000
1904	843,000	213,000	2,479,000
1899	565,000	131,000	1,341,000

*Source: *Thirteenth Census of the United States*, 1910, Vol. IX, "Manufactures," p. 1214.

cant, since the manufacturing activity of the packing plants is not included, both the stockyards and packing plants being located just outside the Fort Worth city limits.[29] In 1909, for the city, "printing and publishing" was still the most important single "manufacturing" activity, but apparently other manufacturing activities had been developed since 1899, at least partially because of the "pulling" power of cattle processing. Manufacturing data for the county were not available until 1920, but the information based on 1919 reports reveals the importance of the packing plants; at that time Tarrant County was the leading county in the state in terms of "value added by manufacture."[30] Another measure of the change in the city's economic activity can be observed in the increase in population. From 1900 to 1910 there was an increase of 175 percent. By 1920 the population of the city had passed the 100,000 mark (106,482). In addition, areas which today are a part of the city, such as Riverside, Sycamore Heights, Polytechnic, Mistletoe Heights, Arlington Heights, Niles City, and Diamond Hill were, in 1920, suburban areas outside the city limits. According to Paddock, these areas combined had a population of approximately 30,000 in 1920.[31]

---

[29]The packing-plant area (Niles City) was not annexed to Fort Worth until 1922.

[30]*Fourteenth Census of the United States: 1920*, Vol. IX, "Manufactures," pp. 1449-1450.

[31]Paddock, *op. cit.*, p. 656.

There were several reasons for the population growth of Fort Worth during the decade 1910-1920. Retail and wholesale trade expanded, in part because of some improvement in transportation facilities. From 1909 to 1919 manufacturing was expanded, with an increase in persons employed, from 2,641 to 4,452, and a four-fold increase in "value added by manufacture," from $3,391,822 to $12,389,566. One factor in the increase in manufacturing during this decade was the expansion of flour mill production and grain storage, influenced in part by the expanded demands of World War I.[32] Also, there was a sharp demand for processed meat, but, as indicated above, this did not show in the Fort Worth tabulations. Apparently, too, there was expansion in other ways. During this period local steel production was established, and for a time Fort Worth had a sizable automobile assembly plant.[33]

Another factor of significance was Fort Worth's interest in providing facilities for war-time military training. These included an army cantonment (Camp Bowie), which was located in the area currently known as Arlington Heights, and three airfields, located near Hicks, Everman, and Benbrook. The leadership in securing these military installations was taken by the Chamber of Commerce. The owners of the land needed for the camps permitted free use of their property or received only a small rental, and the city government and the Chamber of Commerce provided water, sewer, light and telephone connections, all without cost. Also provided without cost to the Federal Government were hard-surfaced roads, and street-car and railway connections. The value of physical improvements alone of the Camp Bowie area was estimated to be approximately $2,225,-000.[34]

While the military influence was mainly of a temporary nature, it seems apparent that some of the men who trained in

---

[32]For a brief statement concerning Fort Worth as a grain market, see *ibid.*, p. 667.

[33]*Ibid.*, p. 665. In 1916 the Chevrolet Motor Company established an assembly plant in Fort Worth, and by 1920 was employing approximately 500 workers. This plant was later closed. For an account of the manufacturing activity in the city around 1922, see pp. 657-79.

[34]*Ibid.*, p. 680.

the Fort Worth area returned later to become residents. Probably, also, the success in securing the military installations demonstrated again what could be accomplished through cooperative effort.

Still another influence which began in the second decade, but not of major importance (for Fort Worth) until later, was the discovery of oil in the Ranger Field (Eastland County) in 1917, and the discoveries at Burkburnett (Wichita County) in 1918. This influence has been discussed in some detail in Chapter II. The importance of Fort Worth's location can be seen in Figure 29. Although this figure presents only current crude oil production (1953), it does suggest reasons for the city's continuing interest in oil operations.

In the early period of the development, Fort Worth received benefits mainly because of its railroad connections and because it was the closest city of any size to the oil fields.[35] Many of the operators made their temporary headquarters in the city and got their supplies from it. Later, some of the wealth accumulated in oil developments became a part of the Fort Worth economy, since many of the companies and independent operators established permanent headquarters in Fort Worth. Oil equipment suppliers also became an important part of the local economy.[36]

During the next two decades (1920-1940) Fort Worth continued to grow in population, to 177,662 in 1940. Its 84-county West Texas trade area increased in population from 919,017 in

---

[35]Most of the present cities in North and West Texas developed into urban areas after the oil discoveries.

[36]Oil refineries had been established in Fort Worth prior to the Ranger and Burkburnett discoveries, but following these developments, the number increased, and by 1922 there were nine operating within the Fort Worth area. Currently there are only two refineries in Tarrant County, but their combined crude input capacity (barrels per day) ranks the county 7th in Texas, although considerably below the production capacity of such leaders as Harris (Houston), Jefferson, and Nueces counties. In terms of total crude oil production to the present (1954), the Ranger and Desdemona fields (Eastland County) cannot be considered major producers. As of January 1, 1954, 40 other Texas counties had so far produced more crude oil. In contrast, the operations in Wichita County (Burkburnett) ranked 6th in total production to January 1, 1954. See Texas Mid-Continent Oil and Gas Association, "Texas Oil and Gas," (no date) p. 30.

1920, to 1,218,524 in 1940. In both instances most of the growth occurred during the 1920's. During the Depression years of the 1930's, Fort Worth and its trade territory suffered along with the rest of the country.

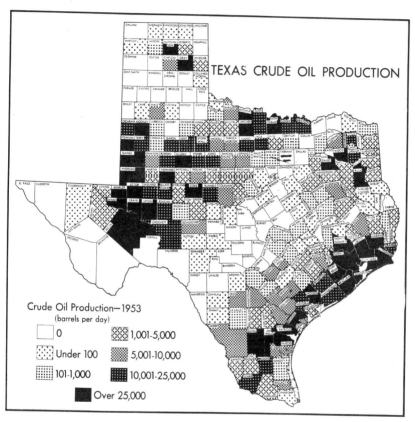

Figure 29. Texas Crude Oil Production (barrels per day), 1953, by Counties. (Prepared by Texas Mid-Continent Oil and Gas Association.)

After 1920, the city acquired many of the permanent benefits of oil exploration. Manufacturing was expanded, although apparently some of the development was not permanent. Between 1919 and 1929 the "value added by manufacture" increased from $12,389,000 to $27,693,000, but part of this increase was probably due to "boom" values. More important is the fact that Fort Worth annexed many of the adjacent and already established industrial areas. This fact is indicated by data on manufacturing in the county. Figure 30 shows the lack of significant change in manufacturing in the county between 1919 and 1939, as well as the sharp increase thereafter.

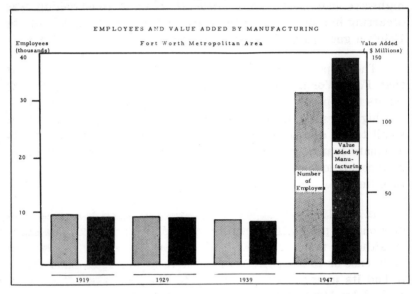

Figure 30. Growth of Manufacturing, Tarrant County, 1919-1947. (Prepared by the Bureau of Business Research, Texas Christian University.)

One factor of permanent importance in this period was the intensified interest in highway construction. Interest in road building in Tarrant County began soon after the Civil War, when the establishment of farms destroyed the "natural" paths of overland travel.[37] Interest increased around 1900 when the state put pressure on the counties to build roads.[38] but real in-

---

[37]Spratt, *op. cit.*, p. 24.

[38]Each county had its own independent system, although state law required coun-:y commissioners to build a "first class road" from county seat to county seat. For some time, all able-bodied male citizens between 18 and 60 were required to work on the road five days annually, furnishing their own tools. In 1904, a system of trunk line roads was started in the state, with the adoption of a constitutional amendment authorizing counties to issue bonds for road building. See "Automotive," Fort Worth *Star-Telegram, loc. cit.*, p. 17.

terest was not developed until after the wider use of the automobile and the pressure of the automobile associations.[39] In 1926 hard-surfacing of the present U. S. highway 80 through Tarrant County to Dallas was completed. By 1933 all of the present U. S. highways in the county, and some of the state highways had been hard-surfaced.[40] Similar construction was occurring in other parts of the state, so that by the middle of the 1930's a good part of Texas was "out of the mud"—or sand.

The importance of highway construction, of course, was that Fort Worth was no longer dependent upon the railroads for its transportation contacts with the outside world; and while the highways often paralleled railroad lines, in many instances small towns and whole areas achieved for the first time fairly adequate transportation connections. As elsewhere, permanent road construction soon led to the establishment of bus and truck facilities.

In the 1930's Fort Worth experienced much the same kind of economic problems found in other cities throughout the county although there is some evidence that the suffering was not as intense as in the more industrialized areas. Like other cities, it had its unemployed. According to Knight, "Conditions were so bad by 1932 that on November 30, the (city) council appropriated one hundred dollars a month for the operation of a soup kitchen."[41] And like other cities, it applied for and received relief money and secured PWA and WPA projects from the Federal Government. Many of these projects led to the construction of public buildings and transportation facilities which are still in use today.[42] From an economic standpoint the Depression period was essentially a time of "holding on." Little of permanence was added to the economy. It was not, however, a period

---

[39]In 1917 the state highway department was organized, and thereafter began an intensive state-wide road-building program.

[40]Letter to writer from the Texas Highway Department.

[41]Knight, *op. cit.*, p. 210.

[42]Additional information on the influence of the Depression of the 1930's as it affected Fort Worth is given in Chapter VII in the section on welfare.

of general catastrophe. In the latter part of the decade the city slowly recovered economically. And when the time came for the industrial expansion of World War II, Fort Worth was ready to go after its share. In the following sections some idea of the share it got, and some of the consequences of the changes resulting will be discussed.

Recent Economic Trends. Between 1940 and 1950 the population of Fort Worth increased by over 100,000 (101,116), an increase of 56.9 percent for the decade, to a total population in 1950 of 278,778. While some of this increase was due to natural increase and annexations, the major factor in the city's growth was the development of manufacturing, and the major industrial addition to the city was aircraft manufacture. Without question, a new economic level began with the opening of the Convair plant of the Consolidated-Vultee Corporation in 1942. This one plant has employed from 15,000 to 30,000 persons. In addition, its drawing power has probably been decisive in bringing in new aircraft-parts manufacturing to supply the needs of Convair, and its influence has probably been important in the development or re-location of other aircraft manufacturing companies in the metropolitan area. Also, aircraft manufacture led to the development of skills which would be attractive to other manufacturers seeking a skilled labor force. As one writer has described the influence,

> The aircraft industry has provided an initial impetus toward the industrialization of the Fort Worth area after a twenty-year period of relatively static industrial activity. This intense concentration, despite its drawbacks, has been beneficial in providing rapid development and upgrading in the skills of the area's labor force. The basis of a highly skilled labor force for the future development of a diversified industrial economy has been provided. Thus the area is in a more favorable position to attract additional industries than during the pre-war period when the greater part of manufacturing activity in the area was limited to food processing plants which, in general, do not require a highly skilled labor force.[43]

Some idea of the economic influence of the Convair plant can be secured from the data on yearly payrolls which are presented in Figure 31. If the information given in this figure is

---

[43]Leland McCloud, "The Economy of Fort Worth," *Fort Worth Business Review,* 2 (October, 1953), p. 6. (The *Review* is published monthly by the Bureau of Business' Research, School of Business, Texas Christian University).

compared with the Census Bureau reports previously shown for 1947, in Table 25, as "Wages and Salaries," it can be observed that in that year the Convair plant accounted for approximately 30 million of the total 78 million dollar manufacturing payroll in the city. Also, it can be observed from Figure 31 that Convair reached its peak of payrolls after 1947.

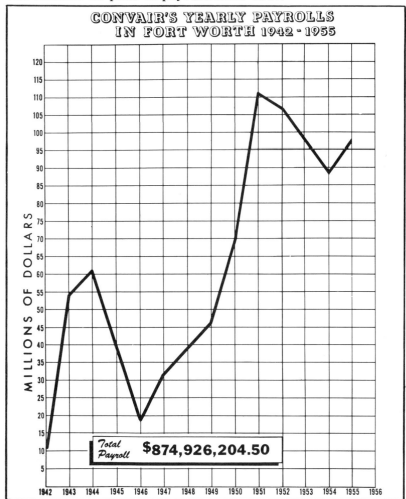

Figure 31. Annual Payroll of Convair Plant, (Airplanes), Fort Worth, 1942-1955. (Prepared by Convair, A Division of General Dynamics Corporation—Fort Worth.)

Since 1940 other economic activities besides Convair have been important in providing jobs and expanding the local economy. The additions have included manufacture and/or assembly facilities for airplanes, airplane parts, clothing, oil-well equipment, steel processing, plastics, chemicals, food processing, boxes and cartons, roofing materials, and air conditioning. Probably most important of these were the Container Corporation in 1950 (boxes), the Southwest Corrugated Box Company in 1940 (now the Horner Corporation), the Thornton Steel Company in 1945, the Lenox Furnace Company in 1946 (which also manufactures air-conditioning units), the ARA in 1949 (auto refrigeration), International Minerals and Chemicals Corporation in 1950 (fertilizers), General Motors Corporation, Bell Aircraft in 1951, Chicago Pneumatic Tool Company in 1952 (rock drilling bits), and the Dairy-Pak Corporation in 1954 (milk cartons). In this group the leaders are Bell Aircraft, which currently has approximately 3,500 workers, and General Motors, with between 2,000 and 2,500 workers. Of major economic importance also was the establishment of Carswell Airforce Base in 1942. This base trained airmen during World War II and since has been the home base of the 8th Airforce and the B-36 bomber. A major addition to transportation facilities was the completion in 1953 of the Fort Worth International Airport and Amon G. Carter Field. This $15,000,000 installation is equipped to provide Fort Worth with all needed air transportation facilities in the foreseeable future.

Various indices are available which indicate the recent economic developments. In 1870, the present Fort Worth Metropolitan Area (Tarrant County) was not included in the ten leading manufacturing counties in the state[44]; by 1950 the Fort Worth Metropolitan Area ranked fourth in the state in "value added by manufacture," and second in terms of percent of labor force engaged in manufacturing. In 1948 the city ranked 36th in the nation in total volume of retail sales; in 1939 it ranked 46th.[45]

---

[44]Spratt, op. cit., p. 300.

[45]United States Bureau of the Census, United States Census of Business, "Retail Trade, United States Summary" p. 42. Other Texas cities ranked as follows in 1948; Dallas—18th; San Antonio—35; Houston—16.

Between 1939 and 1948 retail sales in the city increased 270.6 percent. For the same period net wholesale sales increased 365.4 percent, and "value added by manufacture" increased by 383.7 percent. These and other related data are shown in Table 27. Employment figures show the degree to which Fort Worth has become an industrial city. In 1950, almost 25 percent of the labor force was employed in manufacturing. This was an increase from 17.4 percent in manufacturing in 1940.

Table 27. Economic Activity in Fort Worth, 1929, 1939, 1948*

Type	1929	1939	1947 or 1948	Percent increase 1939-48
Retail Trade				
No. establishments	1,981	2,603	3,142	48.6
Sales entire year	$99,859,347	$92,976,000	$370,077,000	270.6
Avg. no. employees	9,103	11,394	22,181	143.7
Wholesale Trade				
No. establishments	141	**	562	298.6
Net sales	$139,174,383		$647,795,000	365.4
Avg. no. employees	2,448		7,010	186.4
Manufacturing				
No. establishments	228	284	382	67.5
Value added by manufacture	$27,693,891	$25,542,000	$133,952,000	383.7
Avg. no. employees	8,212	8,339	30,495	271.3

*Sources: U. S. Bureau of the Census, separate reports for "Retail Trade," "Wholesale Trade," and "Manufacturing" for corresponding years.
**Data not available.

The recent economic growth of the city can be seen also in the trends for postal receipts, bank debits and similar measures. Such trends since 1936 are shown in Figure 32.

Probably manufacturing reflects the economic growth of the city better than other factors, since, in most instances, a major portion of the manufactured products is "traded" with the outside world for products desired locally. Table 28 shows the growth of manufacturing from 1909 to 1947.[46]

[46]These data were presented graphically in Figure 3, Chapter I. In this figure index numbers were used. In this instance, the 1909 data were used as the base (100), with the information for the succeeding years being merely percentage variations from 1909. In this manner, the increase between 1909 and 1947 for "value added by manufacture" was 3,949 percent.

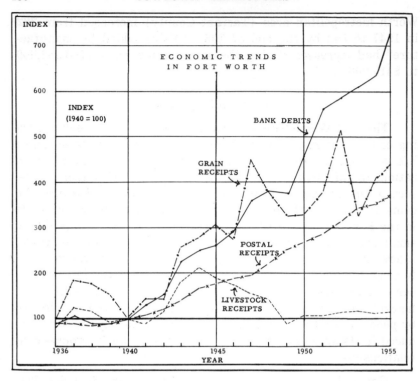

Figure 32.   Indices of Trends for Selected Economic Measures, Fort Worth, 1936-1955.   (Original data from Fort Worth Chamber of Commerce.)

Since 1947, as indicated above, a number of new manufacturing plants have been added to the Fort Worth economy, and some of those already established have increased their production. According to estimates of the Fort Worth Chamber of Commerce, the number of manufacturing plants in the Fort

Table 28. Summary of Manufacturing in Fort Worth, Texas, 1909-1947*

Year	Number of Establishments	Total Employees	Total wages and salaries	Value added by manufacture
1947	382	30,435	$78,902,000	$133,952,000
1939	284	8,339	10,160,806	25,542,000
1929	228	8,412	12,466,024	27,693,891
1919	229	5,505	7,724,202	12,502,858
1909	147	2,641	1,768,834	3,391,822

*Source: Bureau of the Census, "Census of Manufacturers" for corresponding years.

Worth metropolitan area (Tarrant County) increased from 382 in 1947 to 652 by the end of 1954. "Value added by manufacture" had increased during the same period from $133,952,000 to $415,000,000.[47]

The Current Economy

The Fort Worth Trade Territory. Essential to an understanding of the economy of Fort Worth is the fact that its economic life is intimately related to an area far beyond its county of location. In this sense the city is a metropolis. This fact can be seen in the number of people from smaller cities and towns who come to Fort Worth to shop and who maintain charge accounts in the Fort Worth stores, or in the retail establishments in the small towns which get their supplies from Fort Worth wholesalers; it can be seen also in the number of people who regularly come for medical care, and for entertainment, or in the number of ranchers who bring their cattle and sheep to the local market. Thus, the city is a supplier of goods and services desired by people in its trade area, but it is also a receiver of goods produced in its area. In a very real sense this is an interdependent relationship.

Generally, the trade territory of Fort Worth includes Tarrant County, most of West Texas, and a part of the Panhandle, although its extent will vary somewhat, dependent upon the type of trade or activity under consideration. This fact can be seen in the Fort Worth trade territory, as defined by *Sales Management,* and the newspaper coverage of the Fort Worth *Star-Telegram,* which is defined as the "Star-Telegram Market." These two area designations are shown in Figure 33. A somewhat different pattern is provided by the home addresses of persons with charge accounts with 11 Fort Worth retail stores. Evidence of this type is provided by a study made jointly by the Bureau of Business Research of Texas Christian University and the Fort Worth Chamber of Commerce.[48]

---

[47]"Fort Worth in Brief", (1955) prepared by the Fort Worth Chamber of Commerce. Similar information from other sources will be presented in a later section of this chapter.

[48]*Fort Worth Business Review,* 1 (May, 1952), p. 3.

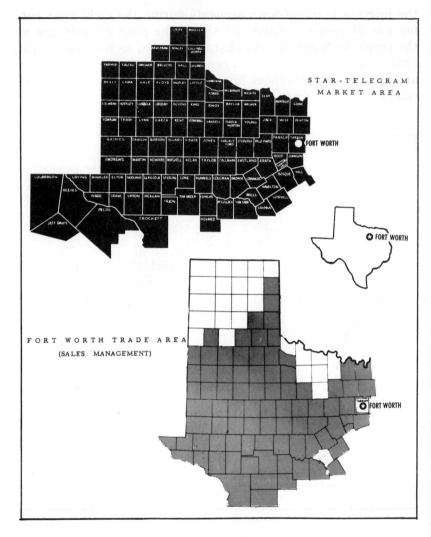

Figure 33. The "Fort Worth Trade Territory," as defined by *Sales Management,* and by the Fort Worth *Star-Telegram.* (From *Sales Management,* May, 1952, and Fort Worth *Star-Telegram.*)

This study revealed that the 11 stores had a total of 40,746 out-of-town charge accounts, which was 26 percent of all the accounts of these stores in 1952. A comparable survey which was completed in 1946 revealed 21,899 out-of-town accounts;

the increase in out-of-town accounts during the eight year period was 86 percent. Figure 34 shows the place of residence of the people with Fort Worth charge accounts, as revealed by the 1952 study. From this map it can be observed that the accounts are distributed throughout the state, but that the greatest concentration is in West Texas.

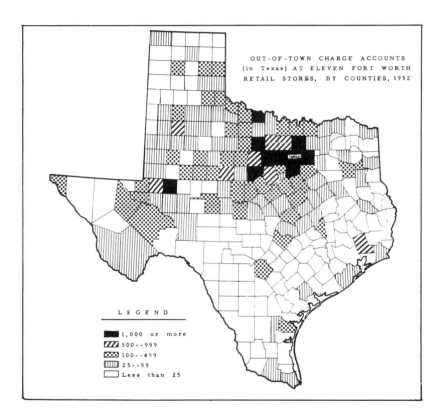

Figure 34. Out-of-Town Charge Accounts of Eleven Fort Worth Retail Stores, 1952. (Original data from Bureau of Business Research, Texas Christian University.)

Fort Worth's importance in the cattle industry, and its drawing power for cattlemen is suggested by Figure 35, which shows the origin of the cattle entering the Fort Worth market. This geographic pattern does not correspond, however, to the area of the city's major dominance; rather, it emphasizes that Fort Worth's contacts are not limited to West Texas.

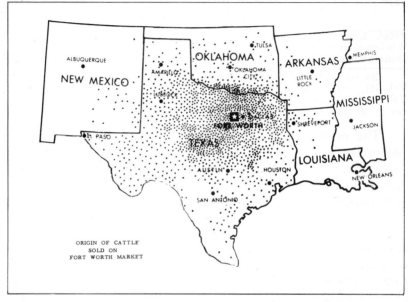

Figure 35.   Origin of Cattle Shipped to the Fort Worth Livestock Market, 1954.   (Prepared by Continental National Bank, Fort Worth.)

Fort Worth's Economic Dominance in Tarrant County. The Fort Worth metropolitan area, according to the United States Bureau of the Census, includes all of Tarrant County.[49] In terms of numbers, 77.6 percent of the county population lived in the city of Fort Worth in 1950. In terms of business and industry, the city provides an even greater share of the economic activity. As of 1948, 92.0 percent of the total county retail sales were made in the city of Fort Worth. For wholesale trade, the Fort Worth percentage was 98.1, and for manufacturing (value added by manufacture in 1947), it was 91.4. These percentages and similar comparisons for number of establishments and number of employees are given in Table 29.

---

[49]In the 1950 Census Bureau reports, the Bureau used tht term, "Standard Metropolitan Area" and reported population, housing and other data for such areas. The Standard Metropolitan Area of Fort Worth is Tarrant County.

Table 29. Fort Worth's Economic Dominance in Tarrant County
Fort Worth's Percentage of County Economic Activity*

Type	Sales or Value added by Manufacture	Number of Establishments	Average Number Employees
Retail Trade (1948	92.0	81.0	93.8
Wholesale trade (1948)	98.1	95.7	90.7
Manufacturing (1947)	91.4	89.6	95.2

*Sources: U. S. Bureau of the Census, *U. S. Census of Business: 1948*, Vol. III, "Retail Trade-Area Statistics,' Table 103 in state report, and Vol. V, "Wholesale Trade-Area Statistics, Table 103 in state report; *Census of Manufactures: 1947*, Vol. III, Table 2 in state report.

The evidence suggests that Fort Worth's dominance has decreased since 1948. As new industries have come into the area, many have located outside the city limits. This in turn will influence the percentage distribution of retail trade and, to a lesser extent, wholesale trade.

Composition of the Labor Force. Another way of understanding the recent economic changes, as well as the present economic situation, is in terms of the composition of the labor force. The available data from 1940 to the present reveal the changes which have occurred. In the main, the trend has been in terms of increased numbers of workers, but because of general changes in the economy there have been a number of changes in specific occupational and industrial patterns.[50]

In 1940 there were 66,866 persons in the labor force in Fort Worth, and approximately 97,000 workers in Tarrant County. At the time of the census of 1950 (April) the total labor force for the county was 156,231, and for the city, 125,742; the civilian labor force figures were 151,060 and 121,507, respectively. The employed civilian labor force for Tarrant County totalled 146,698; for Fort Worth the comparable figure was 117,821.

[50]The numerical data in the following paragraphs are derived from: United States Bureau of the Census, *U. S. Census of Population: 1950*, Vol. II, *Characteristics of the Population*, Part 43, Texas, Chapter B, p. 112 (Fort Worth data), p. 26 (Tarrant County data); and, *16th Census of the United States: 1940, Population, Vol. II, Characteristics of the Population*, Part 6, p. 1040 (Fort Worth data), p. 585 (Tarrant County data).

Approximately one third (32.1 percent) of the employed civilian. workers in Fort Worth in 1950 were female. Slightly more than one third (34.1) of all females, 14 years of age and over, were in civilian employment. In 1940, the female employed workers comprised 31.2 percent of the employed labor force.

Unemployment was lower in 1950 than in 1940 in Fort Worth. In 1940 there were 12,776 workers seeking work or employed on public emergency work; this was 8.4 percent of the total labor force. The number unemployed in 1950 was 3,686, or 2.9 percent of the civilian workers.

Some idea of the distribution of the labor force in terms of occupations and of industry can be secured from two sets of data collected by the United States Bureau of the Census. Table 30 provides one of these and shows the classification of civilian employed workers in Fort Worth for 1940 and 1950 in terms of occupations.

Table 30. Employed Civilian Labor Force by Type of Occupation
Fort Worth, 1940, 1950*

Type of Occupation	Number		Percent	
	1950	1940	1950	1940
TOTAL	117,821	66,866	100.0	100.0
Operatives and kindred workers	20,679	10,474	17.5	15.7
Clerical and kindred workers	18,826	10,369	16.0	15.5
Craftsmen, foremen and kindred workers	17,939	7,428	15.2	11.1
Managers, officials and proprietors, inc. farm	12,899	8,627	10.9	12.9
Professional, technical and kindred workers	12,117	5,881	10.3	8.8
Service workers, except private household	11,861	7,784	10.1	11.6
Sales workers	10,441	6,832	8.9	10.2
Laborers, except mine	7,017	4,070	6.0	6.1
Private household workers	4,296	4,985	3.6	7.5
Not Reported	1,746	416	1.5	0.6

*Sources: Bureau of the Census, *U. S. Census of Population: 1950*, Vol. II, *Characteristics of the Population*, Part 43, Texas, Chapter B, p. 112; *16th Census of the United States: 1940, Population*, Vol. II, *Characteristics of the Population*, Part 6, p. 1040 percentages computed).

It can be observed from this table that during the decade an increase occurred in each of the occupational types except in the category "private household workers." The decline in household workers probably reflects the decreased "pulling" power of home employment for the available workers. Significant also is the numerical and percentage increase for "operatives and kindred workers" and "craftsmen, foremen and kindred workers," apparently reflecting the increase in manufacturing.

Another way of classifying workers is in terms of industry, business, profession. Table 31 gives this information.

Table 31. Distribution of Fort Worth Labor Force by Industry, Business, Profession, and Similar Economic Activities: 1940, 1950.*

Industry Group	Number		Percent	
	1950	1940	1950	1940
TOTAL	117,821	66,866	100.0	100.0
Manufacturing	28,347	11,955	24.1	17.9
Retail trade	22,986	14,332	19.5	21.4
Personal services	11,153	10,180	9.4	15.2
Professional and related services	9,730	5,762	8.2	8.6
Construction	8,821	3,747	7.5	5.6
Transportation	7,318	5,071	6.3	7.6
Wholesale trade	6,874	3,844	5.8	5.7
Public administration	5,328	2,760	4.5	4.1
Finance, insurance and real estate	5,174	3,178	4.4	4.8
Business and repair services	3,232	1,762	2.7	2.6
Utilities	1,987	937	1.7	1.4
Agriculture, forestry and mining	1,984	1,171	1.7	1.7
Communication	1,620	761	1.3	1.3
Entertainment and recreation	1,415	729	1.2	1.1
Not Reported	1,852	657	1.6	1.0

*Source: Bureau of the Census, *U. S. Census of Population: 1950,* Vol. II, *Characteristics of the Population,* Part 43, Texas, Chapter B, p. 112; *16th Census of the United States: 1940, Population,* Vol. II, *Characteristics of the Population,* Part 6, p. 1040 (percentages computed). (For an explanation of the industrial groups, see the 1950 reference).

Of major significance in the above comparisons is the increase in manufacturing. Retail trade also increased numerically during the 1940's, but by 1950 had been supplanted by manufacturing as the leading industrial group. In terms of numbers, the greatest percentage changes from 1940 to 1950 (not shown in Table 31) were for manufacturing (137.1) percent), and for construction (135.4 percent).

In connection with the "manufacturing" total in Table 31, it is well to remember that the data for the table were tabulated by residence of worker. Thus, although the Convair plant is located within the city limits, many of the workers live outside the city. This is suggested by the evidence given previously in Table 29, which showed that manufacturing plants located in Fort Worth employed 95.2 percent of all workers in the county engaged in manufacturing, while the number of workers for the manufacturing group as given in Table 31 (by place-of-residence) represents only 77.7 of the total county workers so engaged in 1950.

Such data as presented in Tables 30 and 31 can be even more meaningful if comparisons are made with other cities. Table 32 provides comparisons for three other Texas cities by industrial group, and is similar to Table 31.

Table 32. Percentage Distribution of the Labor Force for Four Texas Cities by Industry, Business, and Similar Economic Activities: 1950*

	Fort Worth	Dallas	San Antonio	Houston
		Per Cent		
Total	100.0	100.0	100.0	100.0
Manufacturing	24.1	17.8	11.7	20.4
Retail trade	19.5	20.7	21.9	18.5
Personal services	9.4	9.3	10.0	10.4
Professional and related services	8.2	7.4	8.2	8.0
Construction	7.5	8.3	8.8	9.6
Transportation	6.3	6.0	5.5	8.2
Wholesale trade	5.8	6.8	5.5	5.8
Public administration	4.5	4.3	14.2	2.8
Finance, insurance and real estate	4.4	7.3	4.4	4.8
Business and repair services	2.7	3.3	3.4	3.2
Utilities	1.7	1.8	1.3	1.9
Agriculture, forestry and mining	1.7	1.8	1.4	2.4
Communication	1.3	2.5	1.5	1.6
Entertainment and recreation	1.2	1.5	1.4	1.0
Not Reported	1.6	1.2	0.8	1.4

*Source: United States Bureau of the Census, *U. S. Census of Population: 1950*, Vol. II, *Characteristics of the Population*, Part 43, Texas, Chapter B, pp. 111-116.

The data in this table emphasize the differences in the economic patterns in the four major Texas cities. Particularly important are the percentage differences in "manufacturing," and in "finance, insurance and real estate." For manufacturing, however, Houston and Dallas ranked above Fort Worth in actual number of workers, with totals of 51,477 and 35,698, respectively. The importance of Dallas as a financial center is emphasized in the higher percentage of workers engaged in "finance, insurance and real estate." Significant for San Antonio is the high percent for "public administration," which in part reflects the number of military installations there.

Labor Force Trends, 1950-1955. Indicative of the growth of population since 1950 in Fort Worth and Tarrant County are the reports of the Texas Labor Commission. According to the Commission, there were 194,838 persons in the civilian labor force in the county in April, 1955.[51] In April, 1950, the Census Bureau reported 151,060 civilian workers. These two totals are not entirely comparable, however, since the Census Bureau report for number of workers in 1950 is by place-of-residence, while the Commission estimate is by place-of-work. Using the Commission procedure (estimates of workers by place-of-work), the total number of civilian workers in the county as of April, 1950, was 158,693. On this basis, the 1955 estimate of 194,838 represents an addition of 36,145 workers, or an increase of 22.8 percent.

During the five-year period (using Texas Labor Commission estimates) manufacturing employment has shown the most significant variation from month to month, with the greatest contrasts in transportation equipment (primarily airplanes). The peak of employment in the transportation category was reached in October, 1951, with an estimated 32,641 workers. This can be compared with the estimates of 18,257 in April, 1950, and 23,475 in April, 1955. In contrast, "nondurable manufacturing" has shown a relatively steady increase from an estimate of 16,276 workers in April, 1950, to 19,208 in April, 1955. Also of importance is the fact that while there were

---

[51]Estimates of the Fort Worth Office of the Texas Employment Commission for the Fort Worth Market Area are based on information obtained regularly from over 900 local employers, representing approximately 60 percent of the total employment, from Texas Employment Commission office records and activities, and from other agencies and organizations. April, 1955, is used as the "break-point" for data given in this section, since it is halfway between the 1950 and 1960 census enumerations.

considerable shifts in manufacturing employment during the
five-year period, total employment maintained a generally constant increase. The above mentioned trends are summarized
for selected months for the "Fort Worth Labor Market" (Tarrant County) in Table 33. Figure 36 presents graphically
through the use of index scores representative trends for the
five year period. In this figure the estimated employment data
for April, 1950, represent index scores of 100.

Table 33. Estimated Total Civilian Labor Force, Estimated Total Employment, and Estimated Employment for Selected Categories: Fort
Worth Labor Market, For Selected Months, 1950-1955*

| Year | Total | | | Manufacturing | | | |
| Month | Civilian Labor Force | Employed | Total | Durable | | Non-durable Total | Trades Total |
				Total	Trans. Equip.		
1955							
April	194,838	185,338	52,324	33,116	23,475	19,208	45,436
1954							
October	193,438	184,138	53,481	33,375	24,412	20,106	44,217
April	189,217	179,917	52,460	33,425	24,368	19,035	42,717
1953							
October	186,873	179,373	51,988	32,649	24,448	19,339	41,445
April	185,675	177,875	53,982	34,888	26,350	19,094	40,269
1952							
October	186,252	180,552	56,821	36,419	28,944	20,402	40,392
April	183,595	177,395	56,318	37,593	30,366	18,725	39,750
1951							
October	181,627	177,027	57,308	39,545	32,641	17,763	39,335
April	173,230	168,430	52,937	35,889	28,885	17,048	37,021
1950							
October	166,182	161,081	45,875	29,087	22,762	16,788	36,958
April	158,693	153,193	40,684	24,408	18,257	16,276	36,034

*Texas Labor Commission, Fort Worth Office (Transportation equip-
ment is one of several types of durable manufacturing; the trades total
includes both wholesale and retail trade; all of Tarrant County is included in the Fort Worth Labor market).

The estimated labor force for Tarrant County for the first
four months of 1955, as classified by the Texas Employment
Commission, is shown in Table 34. This table shows much
about the current composition of the economy of the Fort Worth
Metropolitan Area. It can be seen that transportation equipment (airplanes: Convair, Bell) accounts for almost half of the
total manufacturing employment; but it can be observed also
that nondurable manufacturing, with food products the most

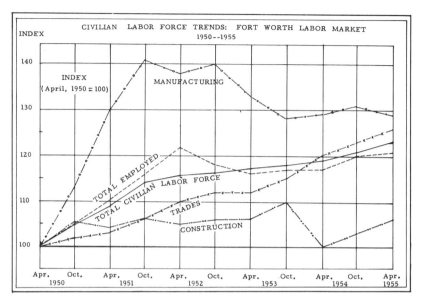

Figure 36. Indices of Civilian Labor Force Trends, for the Fort Worth Labor Market (Tarrant County), for Selected Categories and for Selected Months, 1950-1955. (Estimated employment for each category for April, 1950 represents an index score of 100. Original data from Texas Employment Commission, Fort Worth Office.)

important (meat, candy, bread), is also important to the economy. Among the nonmanufacturing categories, transportation and wholesale trade are significant, since in part they represent primary economic activities. Also important is the number of women in the labor force.

Among the four largest metropolitan areas in Texas, the Fort Worth area has shown the greatest percentage increase in employment since 1950, although currently Fort Worth still ranks below Houston and Dallas in total employment, and until April, 1955, ranked below San Antonio. The estimated nonagricultural employment figures for the four cities for selected months for the period 1950-1955 are presented in Table 35. In Figure 37 the trends for the five years are presented as index scores, with the actual estimated nonagricultural employment in each city for April, 1950, represented by an index score

Table 34. Estimated Civilian Labor Force, Fort Worth Labor Market Area By Industrial Categories, January-April, 1955*

Category	1955			
	January	February	March	April
Civilian labor force	193,946	194,282	194,083	194,838
Unemployed	10,000	9,800	10,000	9,500
Employed	183,946	184,482	184,083	185,338
Agricultural	5,000	5,000	5,300	5,400
Nonagricultural	178,946	179,482	178,783	179,938
Manufacturing	52,931	53,578	52,003	52,324
Durable Goods	33,017	33,759	33,007	33,116
Wood products	540	540	550	589
Furniture	1,017	971	996	996
Stone, clay glass	841	852	851	851
Primary metal	1,055	1,079	1,097	1,093
Fabricated metal	1,457	1,492	1,540	1,534
Machinery	3,446	3,566	3,766	4,016
Transportation equip.	24,222	24,794	23,657	23,475
Other durable	439	465	550	562
Nondurable goods	19,914	19,819	18,996	19,208
Food products	11,371	11,248	10,461	10,665
Apparel	2,785	2,759	2,704	2,674
Paper products	965	960	958	991
Printing	2,646	2,660	2,660	2,666
Chemical products	987	989	998	983
Petroleum products	630	651	661	673
Rubber products	82	82	85	84
Leather Products	448	470	469	472
Nonmanufacturing	126,015	125,904	126,780	127,614
Mining	2,708	2,708	2,717	2,712
Construction	12,800	12,800	13,000	13,200
Transportation	10,353	10,344	10,404	10,440
Communication	2,302	2,294	2,265	2,240
Utilities	2,183	2,182	2,182	2,199
Wholesale Trade	10,247	10,262	10,288	10,343
Retail trade	34,925	34,714	34,878	35,093
Finance, Ins., Real Est.	6,967	7,014	7,024	7,071
Service Industries	14,557	14,527	14,646	14,752
Medical, professional	12,242	12,240	12,251	12,255
Private household	7,800	7,800	8,000	8,000
Government	8,931	9,019	9,125	9,309
Women, nonagricultural	55,191	54,991	55,203	55,563
Manufacturing	9,901	9,952	9,858	10,031

*Source: Texas Employment Commission, Fort Worth Office.

of 100. These data suggest a greater expansion of the general economy in the Fort Worth metropolitan area. However, of equal importance, would be the purchasing power of employment in the four areas.

Table 35. Estimated Nonagricultural Civilian Employment in the Metropolitan Areas of Fort Worth, Dallas, Houston and San Antonio, For Selected Months, 1950-1955*

Year Month	Fort Worth	Dallas	Houston-Baytown	San Antonio
1955				
April	179,900	312,700	372,400	178,900
1954				
October	177,900	309,300	365,900	179,000
April	172,800	305,000	355,200	175,300
1953				
October	172,400	308,300	354,400	180,800
April	162,800	292,300	356,100	194,400
1952				
October	164,400	288,000	351,100	196,600
April	162,200	280,400	343,800	192,300
1951				
October	160,300	276,300	340,200	190,800
April	148,900	269,000	335,900	168,900
1950				
October	142,700	260,000	328,900	157,200
April	133,100	246,400	321,700	151,200

*Texas Employment Commission, "Texas Labor Market," monthly reports prepared by the state office of the Commission, Austin, Texas. The labor market areas of the four cities are: Fort Worth—Tarrant County, Dallas—Dallas County, Houston-Baytown—Harris County, San Antonio—Bexar County.

The Current Economy 1955.[52] Since the United States Bureau of the Census reports of 1947 (Manufacturing), 1948 (wholesale and retail trade), and the population and general economic data published for 1950, there is every indication from the available data of further growth of the Fort Worth economy. The population of the city on April 1 was an estimated 345,000, and the estimate for the county for the same date was 500,000.

At the present time, manufacturing is considerably diversified, although aircraft manufacture is still the "blue ribbon." industry. Currently, the Convair plant is at a low point in employment, yet the working force of Convair and Bell Aircraft totals more than 20,000 persons. Meat processing is still im-

[52]In this section, as in the previous one, the base-point for the analysis of the "current" economy is April, 1955. This time is used mainly because it is the mid-point in the decade in terms of population reports of the U. S. Bureau of the Census.

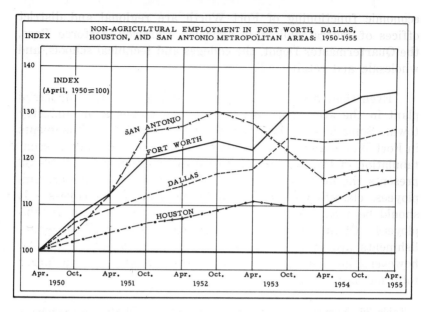

Figure 37. Indices of Non-Agricultural Employment in the Fort Worth (Tarrant County), Dallas (Dallas County), Houston-Baytown (Harris County), and San Antonio (Bexar County) Labor Market Areas, for Selected Months, 1950-1955. For each area the estimated employment for April, 1950, represents an index score of 100. Original data from Texas Employment Commission, "Texas Labor Market," for corresponding months.)

portant, with the Armour and Swift plants having a total employment of slightly less than 5,000. A newcomer to the economy of the county is the General Motors plant at Arlington, and although it is located about 15 miles from Fort Worth, its employment of between 2,000 and 2,500 workers has an important influence on the Fort Worth economic pattern. Other industries of major importance are grain storage and milling; the manufacture or assembly of boxes and cartons, work clothing, candy, air conditioning units for home and car, and industrial trailers, and the fabrication of steel. Besides such major industrial activities, there are many smaller ones. Currently there are an estimated 427 manufacturing plants in the county.[53] Basic also to the

---

[53]Fort Worth Chamber of Commerce.

economic functioning of Fort Worth are regional and district offices of federal and state agencies, Carswell Airforce Base, the Quartermaster Depot, the colleges and technical schools, and wholesale and retail trade.

Even, though Convair is by far the largest single industrial plant in the area, Fort Worth is by no means a one-industry town. Some idea of the diversity and number of establishments in Fort Worth and Tarrant County can be secured from a recent tabulation of the Fort Worth Chamber of Commerce. Table 36 presents the number of firms in the area with 10 or more employees, classified by type and by number of employees. It should be recalled that many firms have fewer than 10 employees. Of importance is the fact that over half of the establishments are in the category of 10-25 employees. Probably, however, the firms in the 251 or more category have a larger total number of employees.

Table 36. Number of Firms in Tarrant County Classed by Average Number of Employees, March, 1955*

	10-25	26-50	51-100	101-250	251-500	501 or more	TOTAL
Manufacturers	205	100	41	41	9	10	406
Wholesalers	120	36	19	9	2		186
Retailers	231	42	29	16	4	6	328
Financial Organizations	21	12	2	2	2		39
Transportation	28	17	6	9	4	2	66
Professional	117	31	13	7		2	170
Oil Producers	16	5	2	5	2		30
Utilities	3	1	2			3	9
Government	13	10	5	7	3	8	46
Construction	108	44	9	3	1		165
Service Organizations	271	60	30	15	3		379
TOTAL	1,133	358	158	114	30	31	1,824

*Source: Fort Worth Chamber of Commerce, "Employers of Ten or More in Fort Worth and Tarrant County, By Functions and Number of Employees." March, 1955.

Evidence of recent growth is provided also by the annual reports of *Sales Management*. According to the estimates of this magazine, the Fort Worth economy has increased in retail sales, and in effective buying power since 1950. The tabulation below provides their estimates since 1950 and earlier figures for comparison for Tarrant County:[54]

Year	Efective buying income	Retail sales
1940	$174,127,000	$ 99,469,000
1945	420,237,000	185,437,000
1950	604,109,000	453,695,000
1953	791,119,000	585,990,000
1954	819,294,000	610,477,000

Sales Management's estimate of manufacturing in the area for 1954 suggests a decline from the activity during 1953, yet considerably higher than that for 1947, when the last United States Census of Manufacturing was compiled. The Census Bureau's tabulation for 1947 and Sales Management's estimates are:[55]

	1947	1953	1954
Employment	30,435	55,900	52,600
Number of establishments	382	427	427
Value added by manufacture	$133,952,000	$350,000,000	$329,000,000

Today, the Fort Worth economy rests on considerable industrial diversification. In its brief history the city has expanded because of the railroads, the processing of agricultural products, its role in the oil industry, and most recently because of aircraft manufacture. In the future any expansion will probably occur because of diversified manufacture. Agriculture and oil will continue to be of importance but not to the degree that they were in the past. Fort Worth will continue also to secure benefits from its wholesale and retail trade territory, and from other established primary economic activities, but any considerable future growth will be dependent upon industrial expansion. This fact is emphasized by Leland McCloud of the Texas Christian University School of Business:

> It is likely that the future development of the Fort Worth area rests more heavily upon further industrial expansion than upon the agricultural and petroleum elements of its economy. The oil development activity which centered around Fort Worth has passed its peak and as the focal point of this development activity

[54]"Survey of Buying Power," *Sales Management,* annual report for years indicated.
[55]U. S. Bureau of the Census, *loc. cit.,* and *Sales Management, ibid.* (Information for 1954 is latest available from this source).

continues to move farther and farther west, its direct influence on the economy of Fort Worth will become of less importance in the overall picture. Similarly, with the increasing urbanization of the state, the relative importance of the agricultural economy will decline. Thus as agriculture and the petroleum industry have in the past successively provided the basis for growth, now the extent of further industrialization provides the key to the area's future economic development.

Today, Fort Worth again finds itself a youthful city in terms of its industrial development. The industrial development of the past decade in itself makes further growth more feasible. Further, the growth of capital and the development of banking and credit facilities which accompanied the area's past growth are now even more indispensable. As the basis for the area's economy progressed from agriculture to agriculture and extractive industries, and now to manufacturing industries, the capital requirements for further development have multiplied many times. These and many other factors will affect the future growth of the area and determine the extent of its ultimate development; however, what is certain is that the Fort Worth metropolitan area has the greater part of its growth still to come.[56]

Comparative Economic Position. In previous sections some reference has been made to the economic position of Fort Worth in comparison with that of other Texas cities. Here such relationships, and Fort Worth's position in comparison with cities in other states will be considered in greater detail.

As indicated earlier in Table 27 in this chapter, the retail sales in Fort Worth in 1948 totaled $370,077,000 for the year, giving the city a national ranking of 36th among all cities of 250,000 or more population. In 1939, Fort Worth had a similarly determined ranking of 48th.

Among cities in its population class (250,000-500,000) Fort Worth ranked 18th in total retail sales and 7th in per capita retail sales. In this latter respect, Fort Worth ranked above Houston and San Antonio and below Dallas; in total sales, however, it ranked below the other three large Texas cities. The information for per capita retail sales and national rank in 1948 is given in Table 37. Included are selected data for all the United States cities (23) which in 1950 had populations between 250,000 and 500,000; in this table and those following, information for Houston is included for Texas comparisons, even though Houston's population in 1950 was above the 500,000 mark (596,163).

[56]*Fort Worth Business Review*, 1 (May, 1952), p. 3.

Table 37. Per Capita Retail Sales and National Rank in Total Retail Sales for 1948, U. S. Cities with Population between 250,000-500,000 in 1950, plus Houston, Ranked by Per Capita Sales*

City	Per Capita Sales	Population 1950	National Sales Rank, 1948
Kansas City	$1,661	456,622	14
Atlanta	1,616	331,314	25
Portland	1,549	373,628	23
Oakland	1,441	384,575	—
Dallas	1,436	434,462	18
Indianapolis	1,380	427,173	21
FORT WORTH	1,336	278,778	36
Newark	1,333	438,776	22
Seattle	1,327	467,591	20
St. Paul	1,315	311,349	32
Toledo	1,306	303,616	33
Long Beach	1,272	250,767	43
Omaha	1,247	251,117	44
Rochester	1,242	332,488	30
Denver	1,236	415,786	26
Columbus	1,228	375,901	29
Akron	1,184	274,605	41
Houston	1,173	596,163	16
Memphis	1,172	396,000	28
Birmingham	1,146	326,037	39
San Diego	1,144	334,387	37
Louisville	1,119	369,129	31
San Antonio	929	408,442	35
Jersey City	784	299,017	53

*U. S. Bureau of the Census, *U. S. Census of Business: 1948*, Vol. III, Retail Trade-Area Statistics," p. 42 and *U. S. Census of Population: 1950*, Vol. II, *Characteristics of the Population*, Part 1, U. S. Summary, Chapter B, p. 140. (National sales rank is for all cities of 250,000 or more total population).

More recent information (for 1954) suggests that Fort Worth's retail sales position in the 24-city group is approximately the same, although the available reports indicate that the Fort Worth metropolitan area has had a greater increase in retail sales volume since 1948 than all but one of the 24-city group.*[57]

In terms of retail sales for cities only, Fort Worth had an estimated sales per family of $4,119 in 1954. In this respect Fort Worth ranked below Dallas, Kansas City, Indianapolis,

[57]"Survey of Buying Power," *Sales Management*, Annual Report (May 10, 1955).

Toledo, and Memphis in that order.[58]   Similar estimates for the
four large Texas cities were:[59]

Dallas	$4,484
Fort Worth	4,119
Houston	3,963
San Antonio	3,831

In terms of metropolitan retail sales growth since 1948,
Fort Worth ranked second in the 24-city group, just below San
Diego.   Using the 1948 total sales as an index of 100, *Sales
Management* provides an estimated index value of the total 1954
sales for counties.   In this respect, the 1954 sales for the Fort
Worth metropolitan area (Tarrant County) had an index value
of 151.7.[60]   Similar values for the four large Texas metropolitan
areas and for selected metropolitan areas of the 24-city group
are:

San Diego	157.4
Fort Worth	151.7
Dallas	146.6
Houston	146.5
San Antonio	141.1
Denver	137.1
Indianapolis	132.1
Seattle	127.0
Omaha	124.4
Toledo	124.4

A second type of information which is revealing as to the
relative economic position of a city is the volume of wholesale
trade. And while the volume of activity is in general related to
city size, it is also closely influenced by a city's general location
and its competition for business from other cities. Thus, Denver,
Colorado, with a 1950 population close to that of San Antonio,
had a volume of wholesale trade over three times more than that
of the latter city, while Dallas, with only a few thousand more
total population, had twice the wholesale trade volume of Denver, and almost five times that of San Antonio. Factors which
influence a city's wholesale trade volume include nearness of
other large and competing cities, size of "natural" trade area,

---

[58]*Ibid.*, p. 158, ff.

[59]*Ibid.*

[60]*Ibid.*, p. 92, ff.

facilities for transportation, and probably tradition, in the sense of established businesses which have given good service in a territory.

In 1948 the wholesale trade of the city of Fort Worth totalled $647,795,000. This business was done by 562 establishments, with an employment (November) of 7,010 workers.[61] In terms of total sales, Fort Worth ranked 16th among the 24-city group. Information on wholesale activity for all the 24 cities is given in rank order by volume in Table 38. Shown also are the number of establishments and the number of employees as of November, 1948. It can be observed from this

Table 38. Selected Wholesale Trade Information for 1948 for 24 Cities With 1950 Populations in the 250,000-500,000 Population Group, Ranked by Volume of Sales*

City	Sales	Establishments	Employees (November)
Kansas City	$2,897,110,000	1,807	24,953
Dallas	2,195,991,000	1,699	25,197
Atlanta	2,100,478,000	1,474	25,228
Memphis	1,965,255,000	896	15,111
Houston	1,683,286,000	1,261	21,618
Seattle	1,456,250,000	1,784	20,045
Indianapolis	1,443,105,000	1,085	14,395
Omaha	1,433,609,000	790	11,720
Denver	1,235,789,000	1,292	19,222
Portland	1,209,987,000	1,085	15,777
Newark	1,178,831,000	1,499	19,667
Louisville	949,371,000	752	13,539
Birmingham	817,744,000	816	11,590
Columbus	653,934,000	661	9,777
St. Paul	651,099,000	597	8,846
FORT WORTH	647,795,000	562	7,010
Oakland	639,070,000	824	10,140
Toledo	510,803,000	616	8,187
San Antonio	477,796,000	680	9,113
Jersey City	470,296,000	424	5,903
Rochester	465,482,000	762	8,223
Akron	318,678,000	390	4,445
San Diego	230,080,000	413	4,769
Long Beach	208,204,000	307	3,226

*Source: U. S. Bureau of the Census, *U. S. Census of Business: 1948*, Vol. V, "Wholesale Trade-Area Statistics," Table 103 in state reports.

[61] U. S. Bureau of the Census, *U. S. Census of Business: 1948*, Vol. V, "Wholesale Trade-Area Statistics," Table 103 in state report.

table that the volume of wholesale trade for Dallas was considerably greater than that of Fort Worth. This difference is apparently related to the factors mentioned above.

The growth of Fort Worth as a manufacturing city has been n,oted previously. Prior to 1940 the city was essentially a trade-commercial center, but by 1950 approximately 25 percent of the total working force was engaged in manufacturing, which in this respect ranked the city second among larger Texas urban areas. But in terms of "gross manufactured product" or "value added by manufacture" Fort Worth ranked third below Houston and Dallas. In the nation, Fort Worth ranked below most of the cities in its population class. This fact is indicated by the available data for 1947. While there is some evidence that Fort

Table 39. Selected 1947 Manufacturing Information for all Cities With 250,000-500,000 Population in 1950, Plus Houston, Ranked by Total "Value Added by Manufacturing"*

City	"Value Added by Manufacture"	Average Number of Total Employees
Newark	$525,540,000	92,291
Rochester	486,322,000	99,934
Indianapolis	431,028,000	79,805
Akron	367,844,000	76,534
Louisville	350,199,000	55,575
Toledo	330,666,000	59,500
St. Paul	272,751,000	40,631
Kansas City	266,342,000	46,683
Houston	257,050,000	40,563
Jersey City	248,598,000	37,347
Seattle	242,640,000	50,214
Columbus	222,072,000	41,367
Dallas	209,201,000	34,245
Oakland	207,569,000	31,998
Portland	195,164,000	33,803
Atlanta	190,127,000	36,172
Memphis	189,940,000	33,160
Denver	162,391,000	30,876
Omaha	157,479,000	25,399
FORT WORTH	133,952,000	30,495
Birmingham	129,972,000	26,484
San Diego	91,062,000	18,553
Long Beach	70,201,000	8,116
San Antonio	62,828,000	14,411

*U. S. Bureau of the Census, *U. S. Census of Manufacturing: 1947*, Vol. III, Statistics by States, (Table 2 in individual state reports).

Worth is improving its relative position, in 1947 it was considerably below, in volume and for other measures, the manufacturing status of the industrial cities of the North, and some of the cities in the South. In "value added by manufacture" it ranked 20th in the 24-city group, and had the same ranking in average number of employees. This information is presented in Table 39. When the "value added" figures are related to total population, Fort Worth's position changes slightly, but still 16 of the 24 cities had a higher per capita production in this respect. Table 40 shows this relationship. This table also gives the per-

Table 40. Selected Manufacturing Information for all U. S. Cities with 250,000-500,000 Population in 1950, plus Houston, Ranked by Per Capita Value Added by Manufacture; and Percent of Total Employed Engaged in Manufacturing*

City	Value Added Per Capita	Employed in Manufacturing Percent	Employed in Manufacturing 24 City Rank
Rochester	$1,463	44.3	2
Akron	1,339	48.4	1
Newark	1,198	38.8	3
Toledo	1,089	38.2	4
Indianapolis	1,009	32.4	6
Louisville	949	31.1	7
St. Paul	876	26.0	8
Jersey City	831	32.8	5
Omaha	627	20.5	14
Columbus	591	25.3	9
Kansas City	583	22.2	13
Atlanta	574	16.8	21
Oakland	540	19.8	17
Portland	522	17.4	20
Seattle	519	18.5	18
Dallas	482	17.9	19
FORT WORTH	480	24.1	11
Memphis	480	20.4	15
Houston	431	20.4	16
Birmingham	399	25.1	10
Denver	391	16.7	22
Long Beach	280	22.5	12
San Diego	272	15.4	23
San Antonio	154	11.7	24

*"Value added per capita" computed from 1947 manufacturing figures and 1950 population figures; "employed in manufacturing" percentages are for 1950. From U. S. Bureau of the Census, *U. S. Census of Manufacturing: 1947*, Vol. III, Statistics by States, Table 2 in individual state reports; and *U. S. Census of Population: 1950*, Vol. II, *Characteristics of the Population* (Table 10 in individual state reports).

cent of total employed engaged in manufacturing in 1950. This latter information is shown graphically in Figure 38.

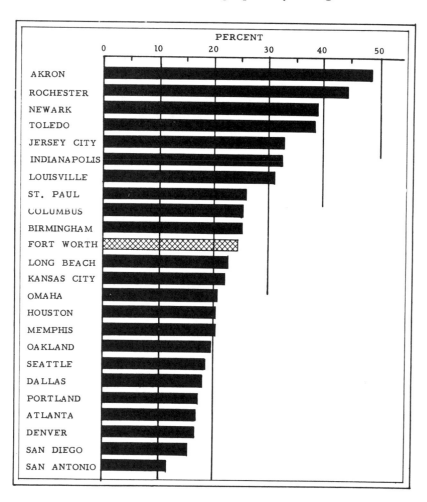

Figure 38.   Percent of Employed Persons Engaged in Manufacturing for 24 Comparable Cities, 1950. (Original data from U. S. Bureau of the Census, *U. S. Census of Population: 1950*, Vol. II, Part 1, Table 91.)

As suggested previously, the available evidence shows that Fort Worth is improving its relative status as a manufacturing area.   By 1954 the available estimates indicated that it had

moved ahead of Denver, Portland, and Omaha in "value added
by manufacture" to rank 17 in the 24-city group.[62] In this
respect, the Fort Worth metropolitan area (Tarrant County)
ranked 69th among the 100 leading manufacturing counties in
the nation. Similarly, Harris County (Houston) ranked 31st,
and Dallas County 39th.

In growth of manufacturing since 1947, Fort Worth's rank
was 3rd, behind San Diego and Dallas in the 24-city group.
Following the procedure of computing index scores, and using
the 1947 "value added by manufacture" figures for each city
separately as 100, Fort Worth's index of manufacturing for
1954 was 224.[63] Similar indexes for the 24-city group are given
in Table 41 in rank order.

While such data as presented indicate that Fort Worth does
not have the volume of industrial production found in many of
the nation's more industrial cities, other information may indicate considerable growth in the future. Certainly as a manufacturing city, Fort Worth is in its infancy, in comparison
with cities of the Northeast region, but it, along with other
metropolitan areas in the South and Southwest, is growing rapidly. Possibly the Fort Worth and Dallas Chambers of Commerce are right when they contend that in the future the two-
county area is destined to become one of the leading industrial
complexes of the nation, as it already is in the South.[64]

Fort Worth's recent industrial developments, however, have
not obliterated interest in the cattle industry. The city is still
proud of its "cowtown" status. And in terms of livestock receipts such pride is logical, since the city continues to be the

---

[62]*Sales Management, loc. cit.,* p. 77. The information given is for county areas
only. In several instances where the figures for the city's metropolitan area included more than one county, the major county was used.

[63]Computed from figures reported in *Sales Management, loc. cit.* The available
information is for county areas only.

[64]While the rivalry between Fort Worth and Dallas is still a factor in the
functioning of the two cities, and particularly at the present concerning air transportation facilities, there is also considerable cooperation between the two cities.
For an opinion as to the possibilities for economic interdependence in the future,
see the final chapter herein.

Table 41. Indexes of Manufacturing Change, 1947 to 1954, For Selected
Counties*

County	City	Index of Change
San Diego	San Diego	320
Dallas	Dallas	264
TARRANT	FORT WORTH	224
King	Seattle	195
Harris	Houston	192
Fulton	Atlanta	179
Jackson	Kansas City	178
Franklin	Columbus	175
Shelby	Memphis	167
Marion	Indianapolis	161
Jefferson	Birmingham	159
Lucas	Toledo	158
Denver	Denver	156
Summit	Akron	153
Alemeda	Oakland	152
Multnomah	Portland	145
Monroe	Rochester	144
Jefferson	Louisville	144
Ramsey	St. Paul	138
Essex	Newark	138
Hudson	Jersey City	134

*The counties selected comprise the metropolitan areas of the 24-city
group, or the major county. The indices are computed from data reported in U. S. Census Bureau, *Census of Manufactures: 1947*, Vol. III,
Statistics by States, Table 2 in individual state reports and, *Sales Management*, "Survey of Buying Power," May 10, 1955, p. 77. (See text for
method of computation.) Information for the San Antonio and Omaha
areas was not available for 1954. Long Beach has been omitted from the
above tabulation because of its location in Los Angeles County.

leading livestock center of the South and Southwest.[65]   In the
nation in 1954, Fort worth ranked 10th in total livestock receipts, behind Chicago, Omaha, St. Paul, St. Louis, Sioux City,
Denver, Kansas City, St. Joseph, and Indianapolis, in that order.

[65]"There is, however, one fundamental trend in Texas agriculture which nobody can stop, and which plays straight into Fort Worth's hand. That is the continuing movement in Texas away from cotton and corn and toward cow, sow and
hen. And every North Texas farmer who switches to ranching has his thinking and
business reoriented to fall within Fort Worth's orbit. In fact, the first two things
a man wants to know when he is buying a ranch in this region are: (1) the annual local rainfall and (2) the distance to Fort Worth's one hundred acres of stockyards, where daily, a thousand truckloads of livestock arrive at their last roundup.
To live farther than a night's haul away from these yards means an expensive and
troublesome stop-over at some intermediate pasture, with all that implies of vexa-
tious unloading and reloading." George Sessions Perry, *Cities of America* (New York:
Whittlesey House, 1947), p. 63.

As might be expected, the rank of Fort Worth varied by type of livestock. For hogs, the city ranked 16th, for cattle its rank was 8th, while for calves its rank was 5th, and for sheep and lambs it was 3rd.[66]

In a general way Fort Worth's economy appears to be rather well balanced at the present time. Just as it is not a one-industry community, so it is not solely or mainly dependent on one type of economic activity. This fact is shown by a tabulation of percentage distribution of employment by industry group compiled by the Richmond, Virginia Chamber of Commerce for 1950.[67] Using United States Census Bureau data, they determined the percent of workers employed by type of industry (manufacturing, wholesale and retail trade, construction, and so forth) for 58 Standard Metropolitan Areas which in 1950 ranged in population from 250,000 to 1,000,000, and ranked each of the areas by least deviation from the average for all the 58 areas. The ranking so derived is suggested as a measure of "balance and diversification." In this manner the Fort Worth metropolitan area ranked third from the top, below Louisville and Columbus. Houston ranked 12th, Dallas 27th and San Antonio was 46th.

The same procedure was followed in ranking the 58 areas by occupations (professional, clerical, laborers, and so forth). Here too the Fort Worth Metropolitan Area ranked third, but below Louisville and Cincinnati. Houston had a ranking of 9th, San Antonio 11th, and Dallas 31st.

The Meaning of Economic Growth. One final emphasis is perhaps pertinent in this chapter, having to do with the consequences of economic growth, and generally, with what happens to a city when its population increases rapidly—when it moves from a cowtown to a metropolis.

Previously, it has been suggested that a city grows through the introduction or expansion of primary economic activities, and that in some cases such additions require local effort in the

---

[66]"Total Receipts at Public Livestock Markets, 1954," United States Department of Agriculture, Agricultural Marketing Service, Livestock Division.

[67]"Richmond Data Sheet," No. 53:12, Research Department, Richmond Chamber of Commerce.

form of subsidies or other inducements. Here an examination will be made of some of the consequences.[68]

In an earlier section in this chapter reference has been made to the consequences of industrial additions in terms of new jobs, homes, business growth, and the increased demand for professional and similar services. That is, a new industry or other primary economic activity brings "new" money into the community and into circulation.

Often less obvious and sometimes overlooked in the search for new industries is the fact that such additions may require new capital investments in utility services, in streets, in sewers, and will intensify traffic and parking problems. The rapidly growing city is faced with increasing demands for police and fire protection, and for expansion of its welfare, health, and sanitary facilities. Educational and recreational resources are inevitably taxed and require expansion. Religious denominations are faced with the problem of expanding existing plants or establishing new neighborhood units. These are but a few of the consequences of the rapid addition of primary economic activities.

Certainly there is the possibility that the increase in wealth and tax resources may eventually offset the additional costs of community expansion, but in many instances the requirements are for immediate capital expenditures, which necessitate a sharp rise in taxes or contributions, or extensive borrowing. Whatever the situation, the growing city finds itself with new requirements which may be met eventually with increased wealth, but which at the time place a heavy burden on the existing community structure. The community which works to secure new industries but fails to plan for the expansion of general services and facilities is merely postponing the inevitable, and will have to pay a terrific cost in "catching up."

There is some evidence that modern industry, as it seeks new plant locations, is today looking for something more than a plot of ground, an adequate labor supply and a favorable tax

[68]For an intensive analysis of this subject, see L. W. Casaday and N. H. Ringstrom, Jr., *op. cit.*

structure. Many industries want to know about the schools, churches, efficiency of city government, quality of health, and so forth, which the community already has.[69] That is, they want to know whether a particular community is ready and sufficiently "established" to receive them.

Important in such considerations is the composite community attitude. Is it interested in new industry but reluctant to expand its educational, health, welfare and similar facilities? More specifically, there is often found a "progressive" attitude toward economic expansion, but extreme conservatism and a "hold the line" philosophy toward an increase in school expenditures, or expansion of public services; and there is often a failure to recognize that the welfare needs of a large city are different and more costly than those of a small city or town.

In the case of Fort Worth, a great amount of effort is being expended at the present time to develop new sources of water supply.[70] There is a keen awareness that future growth is in part dependent upon additional water resources. Similarly, various groups are working and planning for future needs for streets, and highways.[71] The Fort Worth Independent School District has recently completed a study of the educational needs of the school district for the next ten years.[72]

In sharp contrast, the attitude of some agencies and organizations in the community seems to be to "hold the line" on ex-

---

[69]*Ibid.*

[70]One of the difficulties, with even planning and foresight, is that the future may bring developments unthought of at a particular time. When the current water supply of Fort Worth (Lake Worth, Lake Bridgeport, and Eagle Mountain Lake) was completed, it was thought the water needs could be met for an indefinite period. The fact that less than 40 years later the city must seek additional water resources is not, however, proof that planning and foresight are useless.

[71]For the State Highway Department's most recent master plan for future highway and freeway construction in Tarrant County, see Fort Worth *Star-Telegram*, (evening edition) July 6, 1955. Included is a map of the proposed plan.

[72]"Population Trends and School Building Needs in the City of Fort Worth, Texas, 1954-1955 to 1965-66: A Report to the Board of Education, Fort Worth Independent School District" (Available in the office of the Superintendent, or in the Fort Worth Public Library).

penditures. Rather than "swimming ahead," they are mainly trying to keep "their heads above water."

And the community in general at time seems to be following such a procedure. As an illustration of this, the voters of Tarrant County recently rejected by majority vote a proposal to create a county hospital district with separate taxing rights, even though it appears evident that the city and county governments can no longer provide adequate support for the county's public hospitals. Possibly the vote was due to inadequate information, but apparently a strong argument against the proposal was in terms of the possible increased taxes which would result.

Chapter VI

HOUSING IN THE URBAN ENVIRONMENT

Housing in the Urban Community. Basic in the American philosophy has been the belief that housing should be a matter of individual concern. With some notable exceptions, throughout the development of the United States the community has, until rather recently, assumed no responsibility for the kind of housing which individual families secure and maintain. Partially as a result of this attitude, and partially because of the functioning of natural socio-economic forces, urban areas in the United States have developed mainly in an unplanned fashion. An inevitable consequence has been the production of blighted areas, deteriorated housing, and slums.

Although inadequate and deteriorated housing is to be found in widely scattered rural sections of the country, blighted areas and slums are essentially the product of urban-industrial living. On the one hand, there has been the tendency for business and industry to invade residential neighborhoods, with the resultant decline in their desirability; on the other, there has been the standard in the United States of wanting the newest and latest in homes. These two influences have meant that certain older neighborhoods have become dilipidated for lack of care and repair.

In the United States the slum was "discovered" in the latter part of the 19th century, following the development of humanitarianism after the Civil War, and because of the search of journalists for human interest stories. The result was an era of journalistic "muckraking" and the development of wide-spread interest in the problems of the slum.[1]

Attempts to do something about the slums followed two patterns. One involved various programs to help the people in such areas, leading to the establishment of settlement houses,

---

[1] See Nels Anderson, "The Slum. A Project for Study," *Social Forces* (September, 1928), pp. 87-90.

missions, and various types of recreational and service clubs. Another approach which gained popularity in this country after the Chicago World's Fair of 1893, and the resultant publicity given to the idea at the Fair, was city planning and zoning. Gradually, city planning and zoning regulations were established in most American cities, although even today some urban areas in the United States have zoning regulations but no comprehensive city plans. Apparently, however, many cities produced comprehensive plans—and then proceeded to forget them.

As a result of the discovery of the slum, American cities began to consider the question of health and safety in their tenement areas. Laws were passed concerning the construction of buildings; space requirements were created, and health standards were established. But in spite of such standards, or probably because the laws were seldom enforced, American cities, and particularly their residential sections, continued to grow mainly in a *laissez faire* fashion. Periodically, committees would be organized to do something about slums and blighted areas, but blight continued to develop. Apparently, the stumbling block was the unwillingness to pass the necessary rigid laws required, and/or the unwillingness to rigidly enforce the laws which were available. This was mainly the situation at the time of the depression which began in 1929.

Partially as a financial measure and as an attempt to create jobs, but also because of a desire to eliminate blighted housing, the Federal Government after 1933 inaugurated a series of programs designed to clear slums; closely related were programs to maintain home ownership, for housing construction, and for housing rehabilitation. Although each of these programs was at least partially successful, they did not eliminate all housing blight, nor did they make any provision to prevent blight development.

More recently, programs for the prevention of housing blight have been developed by both the Federal Government and by interested private groups. The private approaches have varied somewhat, but the core of each of the current private programs is an attempt to sell the idea of housing rehabilitation in terms of dollars and cents.[2] The interested groups have sought to have passed by city councils more stringent laws regulating housing construction and maintainence, and the creation of the necessary machinery for rigid enforcement. In addition, programs of education are being attempted to sell home owners and renters in blighted neighborhoods on the money value of home rehabilitation and proper maintenance.

A more recent development, representing a new interest of the national government in local housing, is that provided by the United States Housing Act of 1954. This Act makes provision for cooperation between the Federal Government, the local government, and private groups for what is popularly called "Urban Renewal." To qualify for federal assistance under the Housing Act of 1954, the community must develop a "workable program" approved by the local government and by the Housing and Home Finance Agency, the administrative agency for the Act.[3] More specifically "Urban Renewal" emphasizes the following seven objectives:

1. Adequate local codes and ordinances, effectively enforced.

2. A comprehensive plan for development of the community.

3. Analysis of blighted neighborhoods to determine treatment needed.

4. Adequate administrative organization to carry out urban renewal programs.

5. Ability to meet financial requirements.

------

[2]Typical of such programs is the approach of the National Association of Home Builders, and a group which uses the name of ACTION (American Council to Improve Our Neighborhoods). The emphasis of the NAHB is presented in a pamphlet entitled, "A New Face For America: A Program of Action Planned to Stop Slums and Rebuild Our Cities." (No date).

[3]A "workable program," prepared by the Fort Worth Housing and Sanitation Board, was approved by the Federal Housing and Home Finance Agency on May 15, 1956.

6. Responsibility for rehousing adequately families displaced by urban renewal and other governmental activities.

7. Citizen participation.

Trends in Fort Worth. As in most frontier settlements, the first homes in Fort Worth were of log construction, of the simplest design. Not until after the Civil War was the first house of clapboard constructed. With the growth of the community during the late 1870's and thereafter, housing became a matter of status as well as utility, and by 1890 Fort Worth could point with pride to the homes of the elite, made of finished lumber and following the construction patterns popular throughout Eastern cities. Brick and stone were also commonly in use by this time.

From the time of the community's inception, until 1928, housing in Fort Worth was almost entirely a matter of individual concern. Earlier, health ordinances existed which prohibited obvious dangers to the public health,[4] but not until 1928 did the city government provide for a building code. Later ordinances provided for electrical and plumbing codes. Then in 1938, zoning, with its emphasis on space and safety requirements and land-use control, became a part of local government activity. Yet in spite of such regulations, blighted areas have continued to exist in the city.

As one approach to the problem of blight, the City Council in 1938 created the Fort Worth Housing Authority to operate under the provisions of the United States Housing Act of 1937,

---

[4]In the opinion of some of the local leaders who are currently interested in procedures to improve standards of housing in the city, ordinances that were passed by the city council or incorporated in the 1906 charter are sufficient (if enforced) to maintain adequate housing standards. Moreover it is contended by some that if these existing ordinances had been adequately enforced much of the current housing blight in the city would have been prevented. See *Charter and Revised Ordinances, 1906* (Fort Worth: Texas Printing Company), 1907, Chapter VII, (Available in the Fort Worth Public Library). A later ordinance (1927) which was a revision of an earlier ordinance, required, among other things, that in all instances sewer connections must be made where housing is located within a distance of 100 feet of a public sewer. See *Fort Worth City Code*, Chapter 18, Article XIV, Section 270.

which had made provisions for grants to cities for slum clearance. By 1940 two housing projects built under this Act were
in use locally.[5]

The most recent concerted local attempt to do something
about blighted housing conditions in the city occurred in 1953,
at least partially at the instigation of the local branch of the
National Association of Home Builders. At that time, the
mayor appointed a Housing and Sanitation Board to investigate
housing conditions in the city and make recommendations to
the City Council. The report of this citizens' committee was
made to the mayor and the City Council in March, 1954. The
recommendations were as follows:

> 1. The immediate introduction and passing of ordinances, to es-
> tablish minimum housing standards and to create a new Housing
> Commission with power to enforce minimum housing standards
> and accomplish complete neighborhood reconstruction.
>
> 2. Establish the Housing Commission with a citizens' council as
> specified in the ordinance to be completely responsible for the ac-
> complishment of the program.
>
> 3. Make available the necessary funds for the operation of the
> rehabilitation program of the Housing Commission.

While the report of the Housing and Sanitation Board was
received favorably, no positive action was taken by the council,
apparently because of doubts about the legality of some of the
recommendations in the report. Since its first report, the
Board has continued studying the local problem, and particularly
in terms of developing revised recommendations.

Except for the local government action mentioned above,
residential development in Fort Worth followed the usual competitive struggle for space. Local conditions, such as the topography of the land, rivers, the early pattern of dispersion of
railroad lines, and the already existing industrial and business
locations, as well as the existing racial and ethnic neighborhoods,
have all been influencial in residential development.

Upper-income residential areas have been located generally
on the periphery of the existing community; as the city grew in

---

[5]See a later section in this chapter for additional information about public
housing in Fort Worth.

population, with the expansion mainly horizontal, new elite areas were established, and usually extending in the same general direction from the center of the city.[6]

Apparently one factor influencing the development of such areas was the early location of the stockyards, and the prevailing winds. With the prevailing summer winds from the south it was logical that upper income areas should be located south of and away from the odor of the yards.

The Trinity River and its forks have had little drawing power for elite residential neighborhoods, probably mainly because of the sluggish condition of the streams most of the year. In the early history of the city, the bluffs of the river near the central business district were choice locations, but today such areas are too close to business activity. The railroad lines have not been a particularly negative influence, since the manner in which the various lines slice through the different sections of the city leaves few residential areas free from railroad noise.

Certainly an important factor in residential development in Fort Worth, in recent years at least, has been the high degree of mobility. Instances where two generations have successively lived in the same house would be hard to find. Commonly, children after marriage, even when they remain in the city, are seldom willing to "inherit" the homestead of either parents. Usually the second generation wants a new house. Even within one generation there seem to be few families who buy a house with the idea that it will be a permanent house. Probably partly because of the attitude of lending agencies, but also because of the attitudes of home buyers, an important factor in the average home purchase is the probable resale value. Of similar importance is the above indicated desire for a new house with the latest gadgets. As a result, few families start out early in life to plant permanent roots in a particular neighborhood.[7]

---

[6]As suggested in Chapter IV, the pattern of development in Fort Worth tends to substantiate the sector theory of urban growth. See Homer Hoyt, *The Structure and Growth of Residential Neighborhoods in American Cities*, Federal Housing Administration, 1939.

[7]This is suggested by the fact that in 1950, at the time of the census, 17.9 percent of the population, one year of age and over, had changed residences within the county between 1949 and 1950.

In a general way, housing construction in the city in recent decades has kept pace with population growth; but because of the nature of the housing industry, and particularly in the past, construction of new dwelling units has been influenced by general economic conditions, and by the availability of materials. This fact can be seen in the construction figures for the city which are available from 1920 to the present. A year-by-year picture of residential construction is given in Table 42. The same information is shown graphically in Figure 39. These data

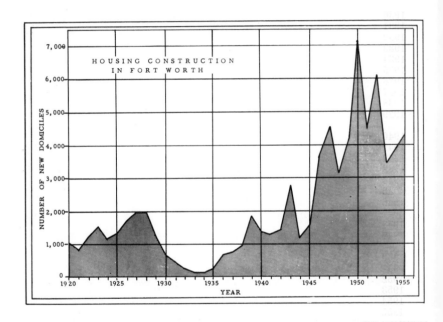

Figure 39. Trends in Housing Construction in Fort Worth: Domiciles Provided by New Construction, 1920-1955. (Original data from City of Fort Worth, Public Works Department.)

can be summarized for ten year periods as follows:

Year Period	Increase in Population	New Residences	Reported Value of New Residences
1920-1929	56,965	14,210	$ 46,842,793
1930-1939	14,215	6,181	14,511,580
1940-1949	101,116	25,042	77,994,024
1950-1955	5,490	29,434	157,594,506

Table 42. Number of New Dwelling Units in Fort Worth by Years*

Year	Total Dwelling Units	Total Value
1920	1,049	$ 3,812,642
1921	870	2,055,271
1922	1,210	2,917,175
1923	1,534	4,513,633
1924	1,134	3,408,104
1925	1,358	4,956,000
1926	1,770	6,566,419
1927	1,989	6,521,978
1928	1,998	7,845,753
1929	1,298	4,245,818
1930	611	1,823,587
1931	493	1,658,720
1932	233	524,784
1933	145	309,150
1934	110	208,100
1935	293	733,550
1936	671	1,464,886
1937	772	2,184,984
1938	995	2,396,478
1939	1,858	3,207,341
1940	1,385	3,280,683
1941	1,301	3,876,143
1942	1,415	3,583,193
1943	2,765	2,825,729
1944	1,128	1,105,382
1945	1,568	4,376,364
1946	3,651	14,202,124
1947	4,493	15,268,188
1948	3,205	13,025,314
1949	4,131	16,450,904
1950	7,131	31,117,302
1951	4,494	19,819,989
1952	6,185	30,071,936
1953	3,453	19,520,749
1954	3,864	24,688,210
1955	4,307	32,376,320

*Source: Building Inspection Division, Public Works Department, City of Fort Worth.

During the 1920's a new residence was constructed for every 4.0 persons added to the population; in the 1930's the ratio was one new house for 2.3 new residents. Between 1940 and 1950 the ratio was 4.0; from 1950 to 1955 the estimated ratio was 2.2. In terms of value, the average (mean) value per residence during the first decade was $3,948, in the second it was $2,869; during the 1940's it was $3,615, and from 1950 it was $5,821

These differences should be considered with some caution, however. The reported value probably is an underestimate, since the cost of a construction permit is determined by the reported value of the construction. Moreover, such data fail to show the number of demolitions. These have been considerable in the near-downtown area as the central business section has expanded along the radial streets, and even in other areas as community shopping or industrial areas have developed.

Another important trend of recent years has been the development of incorporated residential suburbs around the city. As can be seen from Figure 3 in Chapter I all the suburbs immediately adjacent to Fort Worth, except Westover Hills, were incorporated after 1940. While some of these were residential areas sometime before incorporation, and some even at least partly distinct and separate towns, their main growth has occurred since incorporation and because of the growth of Fort Worth. Where separate incorporation has not been achieved, the development of residential areas on the outskirts of the city usually has led to the expansion of the city limits to include such areas. Thus, the city limits of Fort Worth have expanded from 65 square miles in 1940 to approximately 138 square miles in November, 1955.[8]

A significant aspect of the rapid post-war construction of residences in Fort Worth has been the planning and completion of whole areas by one private development company. While the individual homes may be actually built by many different contractors, an over-all plan is followed, thus providing considerable homogeneity in the type of construction.[9] An integral part of most such developments has been the provision for community shopping centers.

---

[8]Table 47 in a later part of this chapter provides comparisons of the land area of the cities in the 24-city group.

[9]This raises a question about land development, particularly since in Fort Worth most of the new houses are being built by developers. Do developers build houses of a type and in a location to meet the desires of purchasers, or do people buy houses where they are available? In part at least, the developer has an important influence on city growth, because he tends to build houses where plenty of space is available and land is relatively cheap. The influence of the developer is particularly important in cities like Fort Worth, where until recently the demand has been greater than the supply.

Another picture of recent housing trends and conditions in the city can be secured by observing available census data. Between 1940 and 1950 the number of dwelling units in the city increased from 54,483 to 89,380, according to reports of the United States Bureau of the Census.[10] This was an increase of 64.1 percent for ten years. In the same period, the population of the city increased by 56.9 percent, suggesting a greater increase in the number of separate families than in the total population. Of the total number of dwelling units in 1950, 56.8 percent were owner-occupied, 38.9 percent were renter-occupied, with the remaining percent vacant. In contrast, in 1940 only 40.3 percent of the dwelling units were owner-occupied, while 54.4 percent were renter-occupied. In terms of the condition of the housing, the number with no private bath or in a dilapidated condition decreased from 35.7 percent in 1940, to 24.3 percent in 1950.[11] A summary of general housing characteristics in 1940 and 1950 is given in Table 43.

Table 43. Characteristics of Housing, Fort Worth, 1940 and 1950*

Category	1940	1950
Dwelling units:	54,483	89,380
Renter-occupied, percent	54.4	38.9
Owner-occupied, percent	40.3	56.8
Vacant, and other, percent	5.3	4.3
Condition and plumbing facilities:		
No running water or dilapidated, percent	**	10.0
No private bath or dilapidated, percent	35.7	24.3
Non-white dwelling units, percent	14.9	12.5
Dwelling units with 1.51 or more persons per room, percent	10.5	7.3
Average contract monthly rent		$44.24
Average value owner-occupied	**	$7,246.00
Contract or estimated monthly rent	$21.76	**

*Under "condition and plumbing facilities" the two categories for 1950 are not mutually exclusive. For a more detailed presentation of housing deficiencies, see Table 45 in this chapter. For source of data, see note of reference 10 in this chapter.
**No comparable data available.

[10]U. S. Bureau of the Census, *Sixteenth Census of the United States: 1940*, Report on Housing, Vol. I, Supplement, "Fort Worth Block Statistics," and, *U. S. Census of Housing: 1950*, Vol. V. "Block Statistics," Part 67 (Fort Worth).

[11]According to the Census Bureau, "a dwelling unit is 'dilapidated' when it is run-down or neglected, or is of inadequate original construction, so that it does not provide adequate shelter or protection against the elements or endangers the safety of the occupants."

Public Housing. As seen above, the Fort Worth Housing Authority was created in 1938, following passage of the United States Housing Act of 1937. The primary purpose of the Authority has been to work toward the elimination of slums and the construction of permanent low-rent housing. In addition, it has constructed and supervised temporary housing for war workers, and projects for veterans and servicemen, and their families.

Following the intent of the Housing Act of 1937, the local Housing Authority soon after organization started plans to demolish existing sub-standard housing in two areas, and in the same place construct adequate permanent housing, to be restricted to low-income families. The first two developments were completed and ready for occupancy in 1940. These were the Ripley Arnold Place, with 252 units, located just west of the county courthouse on Belknap Street, for white occupants, and the 250-unit H. H. Butler Place, north of Lancaster Avenue on Harding Street for Negro occupants.[12]

In 1949, an additional 500 units were authorized by the Fort Worth City Council. One development of 300 units for Negroes (J. A. Cavile Place) has been completed in the Stop-Six area, just south of the 4900 Block of East Rosedale Avenue. A development of 200 dwelling units for white occupancy is currently being considered.

The general purpose of the permanent housing program has been to provide adequate housing for low-income families, with the rent charges being at least partly determined on the basis of individual family income. Some idea of the income of families

---

[12]One of the requirements of the United States Housing Act of 1937 was that a housing project be located in an area from which slum housing had been cleared, and that the number of new units constructed should be limited to the number of slum dwelling units eliminated. According to information collected by the Fort Worth Housing Authority, the area covered by the Ripley Arnold and H. H. Butler projects comprised approximately 43 acres of land. At the time the projects were started, there were 1,481 people in the two areas, a total of 324 families, and living in 326 buildings containing 483 dwelling units. In 1937, total city and school taxes assessed on the two sites were $6,690; only $2,183 had been collected. In 1939 there were many housing vacancies in the two areas, but in individual dwellings overcrowding was the rule rather than the exception. For additional information about public housing in Fort Worth, see Annual Reports of the Fort Worth Housing Authority.

admitted to the two projects can be secured from reports of the Housing Authority. In 1951, the average (mean) income of families admited was $1,413.99. For the eleven-year period of 1941 through 1951, the average annual income was $1,194.17.[13] This and other information about the permanent program is given in Table 44.

Table 44. Selected Data for Permanent Low-Rent Housing Program, Fort Worth, Texas, 1941-1951

Total number of applicants taken	8,083
Total number of new families admitted	1,633
Average annual income per family	$1,194.17
Total amount placed on books for collection	$1,583,931.92
Amount charged off as uncollectible (less than 1 percent loss)	$6,752.84
Average annual payment in lieu of taxes (city of Fort Worth and School District)	$8,429.24

In 1942 and 1943, the Authority, acting for the Federal Government, constructed and then managed two housing developments, originally built for war-worker occupancy, located near the Consolidated-Vultee aircraft plant. One was known as Liberator Village and had 1,500 dwelling units; the other, Victory Apartments, had 399 units. After the end of World War II, the units in these two developments were turned into housing for veterans and their families. In 1950, upon recommendation of the local Authority, the Victory Apartments project was turned over to the United States Army. In 1953, 500 units of the Liberator Village project were deeded to White Settlement Village; the remainder were demolishd.

In 1947, the Authority as agency for the city of Fort Worth, cooperated with the Federal Government in the development of an additional 444 temporary dwelling units, to be used by veterans and servicemen and their families. In 1950 this property was given to the city of Fort Worth. Included were 282 dwelling units for white occupants, located on city property at University Drive and Crestline Road; 32 units for Negro occupancy, located on the site of the Butler Place project; and 130 units for white occupancy, on city property near the Southwestern Baptist Theological Seminary. During 1951 the 444

[13]Fort Worth Housing Authority, "Annual Report for 1951," p. 5.

units showed a profit of $99,656.51; this amount was paid or accrued to the city of Fort Worth. In line with the legal requirements under which these temporary units were constructed, the Authority concluded that the emergency for which they had been constructed had ended, and in 1954 demolition of the three projects was authorized.

Private Housing Construction. As mentioned previously, one of the most significant developments in post-war housing is that the greater part of such construction has been done by large developers and construction companies. Prior to World War II, it was a common practice for a developer to open a piece of land and sell lots to individuals, who then, at their own convenience, contracted for individual houses. This meant that each house might be built by a separate contractor, and it often meant that within any one block several of the lots would be vacant for some time.

In contrast, in the post-war period, the common practice has been for a developer to sell land in large plots to one company, which proceeds to build houses either through its own company or by sub-contracting of some type. Also, in some cases the developer has opened an area, and has controlled, or actually built the houses, in that area. In other instances a whole block would be sold to one contractor who would proceed to fill the lots with houses. Another consequence of this general practice has been that the houses constructed within one block have been of similar design and within a similar size and price range; the result has produced what is commonly called a block-by-block price area. That is, the price range of houses would vary from block to block, but within any one block the type of houses would be similar.

Another of the consequences of large-scale housing construction has been the development of a highly cooperative procedure. Such construction requires adequate financing by banks and loan companies, and careful planning in order to keep the work going without loss of time or money. Rather commonly the developer or the large companies have followed a practice of sub-letting contracts for the construction of certain parts of the house or of the houses in part of a certain area. Thus, one company will be given one contract to put in the plumbing in twenty or more houses; another might be given the contract to do the roofing, another the painting, still another the brick or stone work. These companies in turn may sub-let in a variety of ways so that actually for any one house dozens of crews may have a part in the construction.

An outstanding example of this type of development in Fort Worth has been the opening of the area southwest of Texas Christian University and in the southwest part of the city. The present residential subdivisions included are the Westcliff, South Hills, Kellis Park, and Wilshire additions. The development of these subdivisions was planned and controlled by one company (J. E. Foster and Son).[14] The development process has involved acquisition of land, lot and street lay-out, building of streets, installation of sewage facilities, and installation of all utilities. In addition, provisions were made for shopping centers, schools, and neighborhood parks, and some planning was done for neighborhood churches.

A second basic feature of the development was control over housing construction. This was done through restrictions in property deeds which retained for the developer the right to supervise blueprints (and the actual construction) of individual houses. In this way it was possible to maintain a block-by-block similarity in price range, style and quality of dwelling units.

Local Government Housing Regulation. Regulations established by the city government of Fort Worth affecting housing have been of three types. The earliest regulations were related to health, with specified standards for the construction of septic tanks, the necessity for using sanitary sewers when available, and requirements for the removal of trash and garbage. Another type has been regulation of building construction, which currently is provided by the Building Code, the Plumbing Code, and the Electrical Code. In general, this type of regulation is designed to establish standards of health and safety. The third

---

[14]Information used herein was secured from Alvin E. Soniat and Jack Howell of the Foster organization and R. B. Billings, formerly with J. E. Foster and Son.

type of municipal control has been an attempt to maintain the residential character of certain neighborhoods through a system of zoning.

Within the past 30 years almost all of the large cities and many of the smaller ones in the United States have developed some system of zoning. Briefly stated, zoning involves local governmental control of land-use. A city is divided into districts in terms of functions. Although a particular city may create a dozen or more zoning classifications (Fort Worth currently has 13), there are four general categories which are considered basic: (1) heavy industry, (2) light industry, (3) business and commercial, and (4) residential. As suggested, within each of these it is the common practice to define sub-districts. In general, the residential areas have been the most restricted, and the heavy industrial zones the least limiting. That is, in a heavy industrial zone, residential, business, or light industrial land-use is permitted; while in a strictly residential area none of the other uses are allowed. In addition to land-use, zoning ordinances commonly regulate height of buildings, space covered by buildings, and place some limitations on type of architecture.

In a general way, "zoning ordinances represent the legal recognition that the community as a whole has a right to protect land against encroachments that would depreciate property values or be inimical to health, morals or safety of the residents."[15] In actual practice, all cities, with the exception of a few which started with complete plans, have had to start zoning in terms of the existing conditions at the time. This has meant that in only newly-developed sections of a city can any large area be set aside for a single land-use purpose.

The reasons for zoning in Fort Worth can be seen in the original ordinance which established zoning locally, as shown in the following statement of purpose:

Whereas, the City Council of the City of Fort Worth deems it necessary in order to lessen congestion on streets, to secure safety from fire, panic, and other dangers; to promote health and the

---

[15]Gist, N. P. and L. A. Halbert, *Urban Society* (New York: Thomas Y. Crowell Co., 1948), p. 512.

general welfare; to provide adequate light and air; to prevent the over-crowding of land; to avoid undue concentration of population; to facilitate the adequate provisions of transportation, water, sewerage, schools, parks, and other public requirements; to conserve the value of property and encourage the most appropriate use of land throughout the city, all in accordance with a comprehensive plan . . .[16]

The procedure can be seen in the introduction to the zoning ordinance. It is defined as,

An ordinance to regulate and restrict the location and use of buildings, structures, and land for trade, industry, residence, or other purposes, the height, number of stories, and size of buildings and other structures, the size of yards and other open spaces, the density of population, and for said purposes to divide the municipality into districts of such number, shape and area as may be deemed best suited to carry out these regulations; to prescribe penalties for the violation of its provisions and to provide for its enforcement.[17]

When the first zoning ordinance was established, the entire city was divided into zones, primarily in terms of the existing land-use. Eleven types of zones were established. The ordinance also provided for a zoning commission, and a system for the enforcement of the zoning regulations. The most recent revision of the zoning ordinance (1952) follows the general procedure of the original ordinance. Probably the most significant addition is the creation of two new types of districts, and the requirement for off-street parking facilities for all new or reconstructed buildings. The amount of parking space required is defined in terms of the floor space or number of persons regularly using the building. The requirements apply to all new or reconstructed buildings, including residences.

Probably the statement "too little and too late" may be applied to construction and zoning regulations in Fort Worth. Thus, as of 1950, approximately 47 percent of the dwelling units in use had been built before 1930, or prior to the establishment of city construction regulations. And over 65 percent of the 1950 dwelling units had been built (before 1940) prior to the establishment of zoning regulations.[18] Certainly the desirability of housing

16See City Ordinance No. 2082.

17Ibid.

18For 1950 housing "Year Built" figures, see U. S. Bureau of the Census, *U. S. Census of Housing: 1950*, Vol. I, *General Characteristics*, Chapter 43, *Texas*, p. 45.

construction and zoning regulations may be questioned, but if we assume that such regulations are needed in a large urban area, the fact remains that in Fort Worth roughly half of the housing was built, and a significant portion of the land area was utilized, before construction and zoning regulations went into effect. As a result, the zoning pattern of the older part of the city is essentially a patchwork arrangement. In the case of the older housing, only the extreme cases of dilapidation would be considered dangerous to the health and safety standards of the city and therefore subject to condemnation.

Here is another instance of confusion in our thinking. A hole in the street or a broken sewer main can be recognized as a danger to our health or safety, and we are generally in agreement that it is the responsibility of the city government to eliminate such dangers. In contrast, sub-standard housing is not so easily recognized as dangerous to the general welfare, and we are in disagreement, when we do see its dangers, as to whether such is an individual deficiency to be eliminated in an individual way, or a proper matter of public responsibility and control. Something of this type of disagreement can be seen in the fact that public housing is a controversial issue, while public education, as a tax supported activity is no longer so.

The Problem of Housing Blight. There are many different and varied forces operating to produce slums or blighted areas, and the blame for their existence cannot be placed on any one individual or group of individuals. Perhaps the most obvious fact concerning a blighted area is the general appearance of deterioration. This includes unpainted or poorly painted houses that are dilapidated and in disrepair, streets which may lack paving or are spotted with chuck holes, a general cluttering of paper, old cans, and other trash, and the haphazard use of scrap lumber or other discarded building materials. Less obvious is the general condition of overcrowding of individuals and families in limited space, and gross deficiencies in the available sanitary facilities. Blighted conditions may develop in houses which were once adequate, or in relatively new structures of shoddy construction, or in areas where shacks are permitted.

For the houses which were once adequate, the onset of blight occurs when, for one reason or another, they are not kept in a state of repair. Often associated is the dividing and subdividing of a structure to house more people, and the somewhat makeshift addition of toilet and cooking facilities. Thus, a house which was once adequate for one family becomes inadequate because of deterioration and overcrowding. Moreover, this pattern is not restricted to one or two houses; quite soon it affects whole blocks and larger areas.

In the past, blighted areas and slums were considered the inevitable consequences of city growth and change. Particular areas were thought of as zones in transition. More commonly today, it is realized that with proper laws and inspection, and with some care on the part of the owners and users of property, blighted areas can be prevented. Awareness of this fact is shown in an editorial of the Fort Worth *Star-Telegram*:

> The mass exodus of population to the suburbs has speeded the decay of large sections of cities into slums. They constitute a liability for municipal government, which still is required to render services for such low tax areas.
>
> Slum clearance under government auspices proved too limited for dealing with the problem adequately, and now citizen groups in several cities have been sponsoring efforts to improve urban living so as to stem the flow of residents to outlying sections. The urban renewal idea is being applied by such cities as New York, Philadelphia, Detroit, Pittsburgh, Albany, Baltimore and Stamford.
>
> ... The infusion of stability into residential sections of cities would lead to many beneficial results, ranging from the strengthening of local government to the economy gained by conserving existing housing.[19]

Housing Blight in Fort Worth.[20] In Fort Worth in 1950, according to the Bureau of Census reports, approximately 28 percent of the dwelling units were rated as having some type of serious deficiency. This information is summarized in Table 45. Certain limitations of the Census data need to be indicated, how-

---

[19]Fort Worth *Star-Telegram* (evening edition), March 2, 1956.

[20]For a more inclusive report on dilapidated housing in Fort Worth, as well as the nature and cause of slums in general, see Daisy Brown, "Slums: Their Causes and Suggested Cures, With Special Reference to Fort Worth, Texas," (Unpublished M. A. Thesis, Texas Christian University, 1956.)

ever. Probably the standard used for "dilapidated" was rather low. A house in need of paint, minor repairs, or even major repairs was not considered dilapidated if the construction was sound. Then too, lack of screens and garbage cans, the prepon-

Table 45. Housing Conditions, Fort Worth, 1950, By Type of Deficiency*

Category		Number	Percent
Total dwelling units		89,380	100.0
Not dilapidated, with hot water, private bath, and toilet		62,448	70.0
Deficiencies (number):			
Not dilapidated:			
With running water, but lacking private toilet or bath	12,354		
No running water	1,940		
No hot water heater	3,671		
Dilapidated:			
Lacking hot water, private bath or toilet	5,803		
With hot running water, private bath, and toilet, but dilapidated	1,111		
Total units with some deficiency		24,879	27.8
Not reported		2,053	2.2
Dwelling units "overcrowded" (1.51 or more persons per room)		6,193	6.9

*Source: U. S. Bureau of the Census, *U. S. Census of Housing: 1950*, Vol. I, *General Characteristics*, (Texas) Tables 18 and 19.

derance of debris, trash, broken fences, and similar hazards, or the need for sewer and street construction and street lighting were not considered. In this connection, many of the conditions which impair the health and safety of local residents can be eliminated at relatively little cost. And for those dwelling units rated as "dilapidated" (needing major repairs) the census reports show that the great majority of such dwelling units were small houses. Among the owner-occupied units so rated, 70.7 percent consisted of 4 rooms or less. For the renter-occupied and owner-occupied units combined, 82.5 were 4 rooms or less.[21]

It should be remembered, however, as shown in the section on housing by census tracts in Chapter IV, that sharp variations exist within the city in terms of condition-of-housing. Some tract areas are relatively free from blight and housing deficiencies, while in others, and particularly in neighborhoods within

[21]U. S. Bureau of the Census, *U. S. Census of Housing: 1950*, Vol. II, "Nonfarm Housing Characteristics," Chapter 58 (Fort Worth), p. 7.

certain tracts, housing blight and even slum-like conditions are
commonly found. Although the contrasts between Tracts 17 and
42 given in Chapter IV highlight intra-city differences, housing blight is not restricted to one or two tract areas.

Comparisons. It is of considerable importance to know how
Fort Worth compares, as to housing characteristics, with other
cities of similar size throughout the United States. Such comparisons for 1950 are given in Table 46 in which the cities are
ranked by the characteristic, "No private bath or dilapidated."
The first three columns in this table provide common measures
of sub-standard housing. These three characteristics, however,
are not mutually exclusive. That is, a particular dwelling unit

Table 46. Selected Housing Characteristics for Cities in the 250,000 to
500,000 Population Group and Houston, Ranked by Percent of Dwelling
Units with "No Private Bath or Dilapidated," 1950*

City	No Private Bath or Dilapidated	No Running Water or Condition	"Over-Crowded"	Non-White	Average Rent	Average Value
	Percent					
Birmingham	38.5	16.4	10.3	36.1	$27.50	$ 6,707
Memphis	38.5	18.8	11.7	34.4	33.78	8,613
Atlanta	34.4	17.9	10.9	33.1	32.10	9,874
San Antonio	31.7	18.9	14.4	7.3	38.54	6,930
Louisville	31.1	10.6	9.1	15.5	36.37	7,681
Indianapolis	25.9	9.5	4.8	13.2	41.00	8,412
Kansas City	25.5	7.4	5.7	12.0	42.03	8,426
FT. WORTH	24.3	10.1	7.3	12.5	44.24	7,246
Denver	21.2	4.6	4.8	3.6	43.42	10,371
Newark	19.9	10.2	4.4	14.7	38.25	10,945
St. Paul	19.8	4.8	3.4	1.9	40.20	9,956
Houston	18.4	9.6	6.6	19.7	47.63	9,215
Columbus	18.0	5.3	3.6	10.7	39.86	8,964
Dallas	17.8	8.0	5.4	11.7	49.31	9,324
Akron	16.0	3.0	2.1	6.6	40.01	9,223
Jersey City	15.5	5.7	3.3	5.7	37.38	7,855
Omaha	16.6	4.6	3.6	6.0	46.59	8,424
Oakland	11.6	3.8	3.2	11.1	59.65	11,070
Seattle	11.6	3.6	1.9	4.8	43.11	10,070
Portland	11.4	2.9	2.4	2.6	41.26	8,677
Toledo	10.6	4.1	1.8	6.2	40.46	8,709
Rochester	9.2	3.5	1.5	1.8	42.03	9,143
San Diego	6.5	3.1	1.9	4.4	44.04	10,630
Long Beach	4.2	1.5	1.5	1.8	46.16	10,121

*Source: U. S. Bureau of the Census, *U. S. Census of Housing: 1950,*
Vol. V, *Block Statistics,* for the individual cities.

may be without private bath, have no running water, be in a
dilapidated condition, and contain "overcrowding." It can be
seen that Fort Worth has a slightly higher percent of housing
classified as sub-standard than Dallas and Houston, but much
lower than San Antonio, and lower than the other Southern cities
included.

Another comparison among the 24 cities which is revealing
as to land-use in Fort Worth, and generally related to the nature
of housing, can be observed in information on population per
square-mile. Data on this are shown in Table 47. It can be seen
that Fort Worth ranks lowest among the comparable cities in
population concentration. This tends to substantiate the conclu-

Table 47. Population Per Square Mile and Per Square Mile Area for 24
Cities of Comparable Size, Ranked by Population Per Square Mile, 1950.

City	Population Per Square Mile	Square Mile Area
FORT WORTH	2,975	93.7
San Diego	3,364	99.4
Houston	3,726	160.0
Memphis	3,800	104.2
Dallas	3,879	112.0
Birmingham	4,993	65.3
Akron	5,114	53.7
Kansas City	5,665	80.6
Portland	5,829	64.1
San Antonio	5,877	69.5
Average	5,887	
St. Paul	5,965	52.2
Omaha	6,170	40.7
Denver	6,224	66.8
Seattle	6,604	70.8
Long Beach	7,227	34.7
Oakland	7,256	53.0
Indianapolis	7,739	55.2
Toledo	7,927	38.3
Atlanta	8,979	36.9
Rochester	9,236	36.0
Louisville	9,251	39.9
Columbus	9,541	39.4
Newark	18,592	23.6
Jersey City	23,001	13.0

*Source: U .S. Bureau of the Census, *County and City Data Book,
1952*, Table 4.

sion that Fort Worth's growth has been predominantly horizontal. Such information suggests also, what observation indicates is a fact, that the city's blighted areas are composed mainly of one and two story dwelling units, rather than being the intensive concentrations of dilapidation found in other cities.

Future Trends and Needs. It appears evident that the population of Fort Worth will continue to grow, with the general need for additional housing. And unless significant cultural changes occur in attitudes and values, the goal of most families will be a house and yard space. This general trend of population settlement outward, rather than upward, has occurred both because of intra-city migration and because of the extension of the city limits, and of course, because space for expansion was available.

Such horizontal growth raises serious tax and public service problems. New schools must be built, police and fire protection extended, and health and sanitation facilities expanded, to mention only a few; and such problems are somewhat unique to peripheral development. If for any future population growth the existing land area were more intensively utilized, the costs of public service might increase, but not to the extent that will result with peripheral development.

Since this intense utilization seems unlikely, with the current desire for yard and living space, the probability is that present trends will continue; as the population increases, new housing developments will be established in the peripheral areas of the city, or the city limits will be extended to include newly developing areas, with resulting increased costs of public services.

The future housing needs of the city consist mainly in liminating the deficiencies of the past. In general, as new houses are constructed, they will be adequate, if present construction regulations are enforced, for human habitation for many years to come. The major problem is the discovery of an acceptable method of eliminating present sub-standard housing, and the prevention of dilapidation of currently adequate dwelling units.

In, the prevention of housing blight and slum conditions, it seems apparent, Fort Worth has not had the kind of leadership found in other areas of community development. The notable exception, has been the local leadership provided in the slum clearance and low-income housing program of the Fort Worth Housing Authority. As suggested earlier, the main difficulty has been disagreement as to where the responsibility should rest for the elimination and prevention of dilapidated and over-crowded housing, which endangers the health and welfare of the community.

The writer is of the opinion that there is still time in Fort Worth to make major headway in the elimination of existing blighted housing and prevent its development in the future. Fort Worth does not have the type of concentrated slums found elsewhere. Because of its essentially dispersed land utilization, the city has few areas of intensive dilapidation. Although Fort Worth has a relatively high proportion of deficient housing, most of such deficiencies are found in small single or duplex structures.

To achieve the goals suggested as possible, there will be required, first, intelligent leadership and action with regard to zoning. That is, the community must be made aware that zoning can be a highly useful tool to protect land values and the over-all growth of the city. Secondly, community planning must play a more vital role in future developments, unless there is a willingness to accept the excessive costs of haphazard growth dictated by individual whim.

To this writer, there are real possibilities in the general approach recommended by the Mayor's Housing and Sanitation Board. It is believed that there will remain the need for further extension of the publicly sponsored slum-clearance program such as that sponsored by the Fort Worth Housing Authority, but the approach of public control and restriction, plus private initiative, as advocated by the Housing and Sanitation Board, can, with proper leadership, do much to eliminate existing housing dilapidation and prevent its further extension.

Chapter VII
ORGANIZED HEALTH AND WELFARE

In this chapter two additional institutional patterns will be considered. Each has developed as the community has grown and as new standards and goals have been established. In the main, however, new institutional procedures have developed locally not because of local invention, but rather because of the influence of national and world-wide trends. Thus, there has occurred a sharp reduction in Fort Worth's infant mortality rate during the past fifty years, partially as the result of certain types of local action; yet the knowledge which made the reduction possible was the product of general cultural change. Local adaptation of general cultural trends, moreover, has often meant local variations. New general cultural patterns have been adjusted to the already existing local cultural forms.

Community Health*

Importance of Health in the Urban Community. Because of the congestion of living, and because of numbers, the condition of health is vital to the welfare of the modern urban community. In a variety of ways the present-day city attacks the problems of disease, and positively promotes the desired goals of health. The intensity of the effort, and the amount of success, is shown in the reduction of the danger, or complete elimination, of certain diseases, and in the decline in certain specific death rates. Today, in contrast somewhat with the past, it is generally accepted that diseases have causes which can be discovered, with control or eradication accepted as logical goals. This has not always been the case. In fact, during the life-span of Fort Worth, attitudes toward health and disease in the United States have changed drastically.

---

*Suggestions as to content in this section were made by Dr. W. V. Bradshaw, director of the Department of Health and Welfare of the city of Fort Worth and by Mrs. Phoebe M. Hommell, director of Nursing Services, Miss Gladys Pittenger, Director of Welfare Services, and by Miss Florence Gregg.

The most important trends in this respect—besides the vastly increased knowledge concerning the nature of disease, and the rapid development of medical techniques—are mainly in terms of changes involving attitudes. Of major significance here would be the following: (1) change from private, individual responsibility in the area of health and disease, to large-scale public and organized private interest and responsibility; (2) from the concept of disease as almost inevitable, to a point of view which emphasizes control and prevention; (3) the growth of institutionalized patterns; (4) from charitable medical assistance for certain needy persons, to the necessity of preventive health-care for low income groups as a protection for the general public; and (5) the growth of public controls.

Health Trends in Fort Worth. Like other American cities, Fort Worth has made startling improvements in its condition of health in the last several decades. Part of the improvement is due to the general increase in medical knowledge, but it is due also to local improvements in sanitation, to increased hospital facilities, and to improvements in related facilities for maintaining health or curing the ill.

The frontier village of Fort Worth acquired its first physician in 1853, when Dr. Carroll M. Peak settled in the community. He had started practice in the more established village of Dallas, but, because of the urging of Fort Worth citizens, decided to move. For a time he was the only doctor in Tarrant County. He made his calls on horseback and, like other frontier doctors, he compounded his own prescriptions. Peak became not only a successful physician, but also a leading citizen of the frontier community. He was a leader in the fight to move the courthouse to Fort Worth, was instrumental in the establishment of a public school system, for a short time was a member of the city council, and took an active part in other enterprises which changed the frontier settlement into an established community.[1]

---

[1]See Fort Worth *Star-Telegram*, "Fort Worth's First 100 Years" (October 30, 1949), "Homes," p. 6.

Other doctors followed Peak into the area, but apparently the next important development affecting health in the settlement resulted from incorporation of the town by the state legislature in 1873. Following the organization of a government in that year, the new city government gradually faced the question of its responsibility in the field of health.[2]

One of the first acts of the first City Council was the appointment of a Board of Health, composed of two aldermen and the city marshal, with instructions to clean and disinfect the city. A city physician was appointed soon afterwards.[3] An early ordinance regulated the cleaning of slaughtering pens. A sanitary committee was appointed in 1877, and immediately recommended the prohibition of swimming in that section of the Trinity River from which city drinking water was obtained. Quarantine regulations were established in 1878, and a physician was appointed to look after patients quarantined. In 1880, the office of city scavenger was created; in 1882 a smallpox guard was appointed. At about the same time ordinances were passed regulating the construction and location of privies, and requiring the use of removable containers. In 1889, additional regulations of privies were provided, and a sanitary policeman was appointed to enforce such regulations. In 1886, a site for a pesthouse was acquired, with its establishment to be jointly financed by the city and county. In 1888, the city council provided for a board of health to be composed of citizens who were not city officials. In 1889, the office of city meat inspector was created.

2W. J. Hammond, "History of Municipal Departments of the City of Fort Worth, 1873-1939," Federal Security Agency Radio Project 705-3-9 (available in Fort Worth Public Library and Library of Texas Christian University), pp. 44-54.

3Concerning the early development of local health activity throughout the United States, one authority concludes, "There were two principal situations that precipitated early action in the interest of the public health. The first of these was the epidemic, the second the necessity for providing some sort of medical care for those who through age, poverty, or misbehavior had become wards of the community. Epidemics brought brisk but temporary action in the nature of a board of health. The need for medical care was met by a fairly continuing but limited and somewhat grudgingly provided physician for the poorhouse and jail." Harry S. Mustard, *Government in Public Health* (New York: the Commonwealth Fund, 1945), p. 116.

In the efforts outlined above we see the early development of the city government's responsibility for the regulation of certain conditions affecting the health of local citizens. In all probability there were considerable gaps between the regulations and effective enforcement, yet such actions do indicate an awareness of community needs. In the main, of course, as already suggested, the local community was merely following patterns already established elsewhere, but with local adaptations.[4]

Aftr 1900 new regulations were established, including the office of city garbage officer in 1907, and in the same year the office of city milk inspector. In 1913, the board of health, which prior to this time had been operating by order of the city council, was established by ordinance. In the following year a sanitary survey of the city by a firm of sanitary engineers was ordered. A 1915 ordinance provided for the licensing of sellers of milk. With the location of Camp Bowie near the city limits in 1917, additional regulations of conditions affecting health were established.

Among the factors influencing health in the early community were the lack of hard-surfaced streets, sanitary sewers, and safe sources of water. Early newspaper editorials complained of hogs and other animals being allowed to run wild and burrow holes in the dirt streets, the lack of an adequate water supply, and the desperate need for a sewer system. These are, of course problems which confront any growing community, and are never completely eliminated. In the case of Fort Worth the first hard-surfaced roads were constructed in 1882, in what was then the business district; not until much later—in the present century—were even the majority of residential streets

---

4"The public health work of local communities, especially of the smaller ones in the nineteenth century, may with fairness be described as desultory. A number of factors contributed to this. Public health was concerned only with the communicable diseases, and, except in vaccination against smallpox, knowledge as to their control rested upon two procedures, quarantine and environmental sanitation. The latter was general rather than specific, aesthetic rather than scientific. There was a tendency to judge the danger of a situation in terms of unsightliness and smells, an inclination manifested even today . . . The local boards of health were unlikely to take any action except in the face of an epidemic; and the continuing high endemic and mortality levels of ordinary diseases, particularly those of childhood, did not as a rule cause any activity on the part of local authorities." *Ibid.*, p. 120.

hard-surfaced. Even today, as in other large cities, Fort Worth has many streets in certain sections of the city which are either dirt or gravel.

The first sewer system was installed in 1882, but with some sections having only open ditches to carry refuse to the Trinity River.[5] Here too, an adequate system has been a continuing problem, and closely related has been the problem of getting residents to use the available facilities. At the present time, there are still many residences in the city which do not have running water and have only outdoor privies, although water and sewer connections are available.

A sufficient and sanitary water supply has been a particularly difficult problem for Fort Worth. Originally water was used untreated from the Trinity River. In a few instances springs were available. Later, shallow wells were constructed, but it was not until 1878 that the first artesian well was completed.[6]

Apparently, the first concerted public demand for a safe water supply came as a result of a smallpox epidemic in 1882. For various reasons, however, the new city government did nothing immediately to meet the problem. As a result, a private company, the Fort Worth Water Works Company, was organized, and secured a franchise in 1882. By 1883, a water plant had been completed to draw water from the Trinity River and pipe it untreated through six miles of pipe which were installed at the time.[7]

In the following years, water continued to be a major problem, both with regard to adequacy and safety. Various methods for purifying the available water were developed, but it was not until 1912 that the city built the first filtration plant.

---

[5]Oliver Knight, *Fort Worth: Outpost on the Trinity* (Norman: University of Oklahoma Press), 1953, p. 155.

[6]"Citizens obtained water from cisterns, shallow wells, and the Trinity, or bought it at twenty-five cents for two barrels from peddlers who hauled water in tarred tank wagons from springs near Birdville. Whether directly from the ground or from tank wagon, the water was used untreated." *Ibid.*, p. 75.

[7]*Ibid.*, p. 154.

Closely related to the above trends, which are mainly of a public health nature, are the developments in private medicine, the establishment of hospitals, and the organization of private agencies with a special interest in some phase of health.

In general, the number of physicians and surgeons increased in the city with population growth; in addition, there has been a gradual expansion of provisions for specialized medical services. Along with the continued importance of the general practitioner, there has occurred an important increase of various kinds of medical specialties, partly due to advancing medical knowledge, but also as a result of community growth and the numerical and financial ability to utilize the services of a variety of specialists. Moreover, the services available in the city are used by both city residents and by many people in th larger metropolitan, region. In this sense, and with regard to hospital facilities, Fort Worth is the leading medical center of West Texas.[8]

Hospital development began soon after incorporation of the city, when the City Council in 1877 agreed to join with the county government to build a hospital building for the indigent poor. Apparently this was not a large structure, since the county contribution of $600.00 was two thirds of the total cost. The building was completed in 1879, and a hospital committee was appointed.[9] However, its public nature was short-lived, apparently because the city and county could not agree on its operation. In 1883 the property was deeded free to the Sisters of Charity, a Catholic organization, under an agreement to treat destitute cases.[10]

Possibly smaller private hospitals existed earlier, but the first of the present-day major hospitals was St. Joseph's, originally known as St. Joseph's Infirmary, which was started in

---

[8]For a short time Fort Worth had its own medical college. In 1894 a medical school was organized and connected with Fort Worth University. It was staffed mainly by doctors living in the city.

[9]See Hammond, op. cit., pp. 45-8.

[10]Ibid., p. 48.

1885 in a frame structure on the site of the present property. Later, in 1896, a three-story brick building was constructed.[11] The next of the present-day hospitals was All-Saints Hospital which was started in 1896 by a group of women who were members of Trinity Protestant Episcopal Church, with the purpose of caring for the indigent sick. In 1907, the city and county governments combined again to provide a tax-supported hospital, under the name of City-County, only recently changed to John Peter Smith Hospital.

The next surge in construction of hospitals came in the 1920's, and was probably related to the growth and prosperity of the city in that decade.[12] Pennsylvania Avenue Hospital was started in 1920, and during its history has varied from first a privately owned unit, to an open-staff, church-controlled hospital, and back to private ownership. Harris Hospital was next, beginning in 1922 as Harris Clinic Hospital; in 1937 a consolidation with Methodist Hospital, which has been opened in 1930, was completed. More recently the name was changed to Harris Hospital.[13] Cook Memorial Hospital was opened in 1929, as the result of an endowment by Mrs. W. I. Cook. Other smaller hospitals, most of them privately owned, existed for a time, but disappeared when their owners died. The most recent hospital

---

[11]"Homes," Fort Worth *Star-Telegram, loc. cit.,* p. 6. Knight, *op. cit.,* p. 201, gives the founding date as 1889.

[12]For a time, around 1920, the United Charities and later the Fort Worth Welfare Association operated a health clinic as a part of its services. Visiting nurses traveled throughout the city providing nursing service. Local doctors gave their services free to the clinic.

[13]Dr. Charles H. Harris, for whom Harris Hospital is named, first opened the Harris Sanitarium in the city in 1912. During the same year he, along with two other doctors, secured a charter for the Harris School of Nursing. In 1922 Dr. Harris secured additional medical personnel and formally opened the Harris Clinic Hospital. At about the same time he was able to convince the Central Texas Conference of the Methodist Church that there was a need for additional hospital facilities in the city. A fund raising campaign was started in 1923 and in 1930 facilities were sufficient to admit the first patient. However, partly because of the depression, the Methodist hospital was not able to maintain itself financially, and in 1937 the property was sold at public auction. Dr. Harris bought the property and combined it with his own to form the Harris Memorial Methodist Hospital. In 1948 the property was deeded back to the Methodist church, and the name changed to Harris Hospital. (Information supplied by Miss Mabelle Hudgins, Records Librarian, Harris Hospital).

addition is the Fort Worth Osteopathic Hospital, which was chartered in 1945 and opened in 1950, with a 25-bed capacity.[14]

Along with the development of hospitals in the city, there has continued the essential need for the training of nurses. In the early history of the community, nursing skills were acquired through practcial experience, although some of the nurses working in the early city received professional training elsewhere. Not until the second decade of the present century did the need for a local school of nursing become sufficiently great to lead to the necessary organizational interest.

The three present-day schools were established during this period. The Harris School of Nursing, as mentioned above, was chartered in 1912, and since has become the Harris Colllege of Nursing, affiliated with Texas Christian University. The School of Nursing of City-County Hospital (now John Peter Smith Hospital) was chartered in 1914. The St. Joseph's Hospital School of Nursing was chartered in 1917.[15]

An additional element in the development of present-day health and medical practices was the establishment of specialized private agencies. The first of the national organizations established locally was a tuberculosis association, started in 1916.[16] More recently similar local groups have been established. In general, such organizations have as their main purpose the promotion of understanding of specific diseases or afflictions, and the discovery of individuals so affected.

A major step in the promotion of community health by the local government was the creation of the City Health and Welfare Department in 1925, following the establishment of the

---

[14]A new Osteopathic Hospital building was opened July 30, 1956, with 75 adult beds, five pediatric beds, and 15 bassinets. In an emergency the new building can provide 115 beds. For a brief history of Osteopathy in Texas and Fort Worth, see "Homes," Fort Worth Star-Telegram, loc. cit., p. 12.

[15]Specialized nursing training at St. Joseph's Hospital was started in 1906. During the 1920's the city had three additional schools of nursing. All-Saints Hospital had a school until World War II; a school was connected with Baptist Hospital, which is now the privately owned Pennsylvania Avenue; a third school was connected with a hospital which closed during the depression.

[16]The National Tuberculosis Association was organized in 1904 and the Texas Association in 1909. Houston had the first city association in the state.

present council-manager form of government. Although no sharply different health regulations were immediately created, the provision for a separate department did make possible the grouping of all the various health activities of the city government under one responsible official, and the possibility of unified control and planning.[17]

Current Community Program to Promote Health and Control Disease. Today, in cities like Fort Worth, as well as in larger and smaller communities, the promotion of health, the eradication of disease, and the prolongation of life are generally considered possible and desirable. Such standards, reflecting basic community attitudes, are in sharp contrast with the past, when health and disease were mainly considered a matter of fate. The proof of the value of present-day activities can be observed in decreased infant and maternal death rates, in the almost complete eradication of certain diseases, in the sharp drop in the death rate for many diseases, and in the significant prolongation of life. As indicated earlier, such changes have been made possible through increased medical knowledge, a sharp increase in medical and related facilities, more intensive training for professional workers, an increased awareness on the part of the public as to the desirability of promoting health and controlling disease, and a willingness to provide the necessary money for such improvements.

In Fort Worth today the attack against disease includes (1) the work of private medicine, (2) the work of the public, tax-supported, health and related departments, (3) the private and public sponsored hospitals, and professional training provided

---

[17] As suggested previously, public activity in Fort Worth in the field of health began soon after the city's incorporation, but apparently the early boards of health did not meet national standards with regard to the collection of mortality and morbidity information, since it was not until 1922 that the city was first listed as a part of the United States Registration Area for vital statistics. For the first listing, see U. S. Bureau of the Census, *Mortality Statistics*, 1922, p. 99. To be accepted into the Registration Area, a city or state had to have established acceptable procedures for the collection and tabulation of vital statistical information. Health procedures and conditions were not involved. Significantly, San Antonio was listed as in the Registration Area as early as 1900 (see *Mortality Statistics*, 1905, p. 67). The annual report for 1912 listed vital statistics for El Paso, Galveston and San Antonio; in 1917 Beaumont, Cleburne, Dallas, El Paso, Galveston, Houston, and San Antonio were included.

for nurses, and (4) the activities of the privately sponsored health agencies. Results of the varied attack on disease can be shown by comparing two time periods and noting the differences in specific death rates.[18] This is done in Table 48 for the years 1925 and 1954.

Table 48. Births, Total Deaths, Deaths By Specific Causes For Fort Worth, Texas, 1925 and 1954*

Type	1925		1954	
	Number	Rate	Number	Rate
Population, estimated	148,043		310,774	
All births	2,566	17.3	8,564	25.2
All deaths	1,497	10.1	2,328	6.9
Infant deaths	203	79.1	258	30.1
Maternal deaths	24	9.4	4	.5
Tuberculosis deaths	104	70.2	15	4.4
Typhoid fever deaths	8	----	0	0.0
Diphtheria deaths	9		0	0.0
Pneumonia deaths	149	100.6	42	12.4
Influenza deaths	30	20.3	0	0.0

*Rates for total births and total deaths computed on basis of per 1,000 total population; infant and maternal deaths per 1,000 live births; specific disease death rates per 100,000 population. Source: Health and Welfare Department, Bureau of Vital Statistics, City of Fort Worth. (The deaths for tuberculosis are for deaths by "place of occurrence." If "deaths by residence" were included the number and rate would be higher.)

In the field of private medicine, Fort Worth has become a focal point for a variety of medical services, and, according to the American Medical Association, is one of the 88 "Prime-Primary Medical Service Centers" in the United States, and one of nine in Texas.[19]

Public health work in the city is the responsibility of the city health department. Its major duties include the prevention or control of contagious diseases, the promotion of better health facilities, the development of a program of health education, and

---

[18]In contrast, death rates for other diseases, such as those involving the heart, have risen. It must be recognized, however, that many of the major causes of death today are not closely related to the quality of public health measures or medical knowledge. In the main, medical and public health controls have provided effective controls over most of the contagious diseases. Moreover, with regard to the current major causes of death (such as cancer and diseases of the heart) a basic dificulty lies in getting individuals to utilize available knowledge.

[19]Frank G. Dickinson and Charles E. Bradley, "Distribution of Physicians by Medical Service Areas," Bulletin 94A, Bureau of Medical Economic Research, American Medical Association, 1953, p. 64. Such centers have been so designated because every type of medical care and surgery is available. Other centers in Texas are: Houston, Dallas, San Antonio, Galveston, Temple, Amarillo, Lubbock, and El Paso.

the prohibition of conditions considered dangerous to the health of the community. More specifically, it provides well-baby clinics and home nursing services; laboratory services; venereal disease control and treatment; milk and meat inspection; inspection of food establishments, nursing homes and beauty and and barber shops; supervision of lake sanitation; typhus and pest control; and the collection of vital statistics.[20] In addition to the above, the city government shares with Tarrant County the cost and operation of John Peter Smith Hospital, Elmwood Sanatorium for tuberculous patients, and shares with Tarrant County a portion of the cost of the Fort Worth-Tarrant County Guidance Clinic.

The city government also provides many other services which in part, at least, are for the promotion of better health conditions. Included here would be street cleaning, storm sewer maintenance, supervision of the construction of sewers, plumbing inspection, provision for building construction standards, weed cutting, and waste disposal.[21] Some idea of the current activity of the city government along these lines can be seen in the amount of money allocated for health and related services as presented in Table 49.

Table 49. Fort Worth City Government Allocations for Health and Selected Related Services, Fiscal Year 1955-56*

Service	Allocation	
Health Department	$375,510.00	
Lake sanitation	18,492.00	
V. D. Clinic	11,646.00	
Weed cutting	27,288.00	
City-County Hospital	312,000.00	
Elmwood Sanatorium	68,250.00	
Guidance Clinic	5,000.00	
		$ 818,186.00
Waste Disposal		1,416,689.00
		$2,234,875.00

*City of Fort Worth, "General Budget," fiscal year Oct. 1, 1955—Sept. 30, 1956, pp. 70, 102. It is estimated that the return from fees will more than cover the cost of waste disposal (see p. 10).

[20]Department of Public Health and Welfare, City of Fort Worth, "Organization Chart."

[21]With regard to many of the services listed, the individuals directly benefited are charged a fee. Thus, each household is assessed a charge for garbage and waste collection.

Hospital facilities in the city are currently provided by seven open-staff hospitals; in addition there are a number of privately owned facilities available. The following information shows the status of the seven open-staff hospitals in 1953:[22]

Hospital	Beds	Bassinets	Births	Total Admissions	Average Census
Harris	310	78	3,895	15,216	282
St. Joseph's	295	53	2,828	12,231	226
John Peter Smith	200	24	1,180	4,701	139
All-Saints	110	25	1,710	6,651	107
Cook Memorial Children's	36	—	——	2,022	30
Fort Worth Children's	32	—	——	274	12
Fort Worth Osteopathic	25				

Because the available facilities are considered inadequate for a city the size of Fort Worth, and because of the city's future possibilities of growth, there was organized in 1951 the Greater Fort Worth Hospital Campaign, with a goal of $3,965,000. The original plans called for an addition of 400 beds to the existing hospitals (at an estimated $10,000 per bed) as follows:[23]

	Beds	Percent Allocation Available Funds
Harris	150	37.6
All-Saints	100	2.15
St. Joseph's	86	21.5
Children's Group	50	12.9
Osteopathic	50	6.5
	436	100.0

---

[22]Three of these—Harris, John Peter Smith and St. Joseph's—are approved by the "Council on Medical Education and Hospitals for Training of Interns" of the American Medical Association. Harris, John Peter Smith, St. Joseph's and All-Saints are approved by the "Council for Training of Residents," and these four are approved by the "Joint Committee on Accreditation of Hospitals" of the American Medical Association. For information given in this tabulation (except data for Fort Worth Osteopathic Hospital) and for record of accreditations, see "Hospital Service in the United States: The 1953 Census of Hospitals," *Journal of the American Medical Association*, Supplement, May 15, 1954, p. 78. The Fort Worth Osteopathic Hospital is approved for both treatment and "intern" training by the American Osteopathic Association. Besides the above hospitals, the American Medical Association lists the following hospitals in the city:

Hospital	Beds	Bassinets	Births*	Adimssions*
Dorsey	28	6	67	336
Medical and Surgical Clinic	10	(recently established)		
Pennsylvania Avenue	68	10	335	4,444

*(Births and Admissions figures are for year 1953).

[23]Information from Mrs. Barton Roberts, General Manager of the Fund.

Earlier in this section, it was suggested that Fort Worth has become a medical and hospital center of major importance, serving a considerable portion of West Texas. Some evidence of this fact is found in a study of admissions to Harris Hospital in 1953. During the year the admissions totalled 19,339. Of this total, 3,350 persons, or 17.3 percent, resided outside Fort Worth, with 143 individuals from outside Texas. The distribution of the out-of-city admissions is shown in Figure 40.[24]

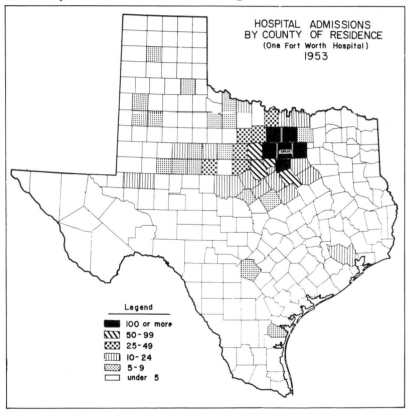

Figure 40.   Home Residence of Persons Admitted to Harris Hospital, Fort Worth, 1953. (Original data supplied by Harris Hospital.)

[24]Fort Worth is also the site of the United States Public Health Service Hospital, with 1,000 beds. Currently this hospital provides care mainly for narcotic patients. Of some importance locally is the Carswell Airforce Base Hospital, which gives medical care for service men attached to the Base, and some care for their wives and families.

A fourth major factor in the current community health program revolves around the work of a number of private health agencies, most of which are local branches of national organizations. Funds for these local organizations are derived from individual contributions, either through the United Fund Campaign or through individual agency campaigns. Among this group are local units of the National Tuberculosis Association, American Cancer Society, National Foundation for Infantile Paralysis, American Heart Association, Crippled Children's Society, Lighthouse for the Blind, National Multiple Sclerosis Society, and Alcoholics Anonymous.

The work of these agencies includes an educational program to inform the public as to the dangers of the particular diseases, the sponsoring of clinics, a program to discover afflicted individuals, a program of research or contribution of money to the national organization for research, and assistance to other agencies carrying on similar work. Typical of all of these is the work of the Fort Worth and Tarrant County Tuberculosis Society. Its funds are secured independently of the United Fund Campaign through an annual Christmas Seal Campaign. All individuals who contribute at least $1.00 are members of the society. The program of the society is determined by a board of interested citizens and administrated by a full-time staff. This program includes, health education, case-register, case-finding, emergency medical care, medical social work, rehabilitation assistance, an information service, and research.[25] More specifically, the society has co-operated with official agencies and private physicians in the operation of a Central Case Register, periodically sponsors a free X-ray program, which in 1955 reached approximately 29,800 persons,[26] and currently employs a trained med-

---

[25]See "Tuberculosis in Fort Worth and Tarrant County: A Progress Report," Fort Worth-Tarrant County Tuberculosis Society, April 1953. This report was prepared by the present writer.

[26]The 1955 program was sponsored by the Tuberculosis, Heart, and Cancer societies. Of the number given X-rays, approximately 900 were referred to private physicians for further investigation.

ical social worker who seeks to coordinate the work of the various agencies with patients, their families, and the hospitals. In recent years it has been instrumental in arousing interest in securing improvements for Elmwood Sanatorium, and has provided several thousand dollars of its own funds to buy needed equipment for the sanatorium.[27]

Besides the work of the above listed agencies, the city has a number of privately operated homes for the aged, and rest homes. Important also, in the field of rehabilitation, is the Goodwill Industries, which provides useful employment for physically handicapped persons.

Comparisons with Other Cities. It is, of course, difficult to make valid comparisons of the general level of health between two or more cities, since any two cities taking the same steps to improve health conditions will arrive at different results because of other related conditions; yet with such limitations in mind, it seems proper to compare and contrast certain commonly used indices of disease and health.

In general, Fort Worth is a relatively healthy city. It has had no serious epidemics in recent years, and has shown significant decreases in those rates of disease which are commonly used to measure a community's level of health. In comparison with other United States cities, and particularly in the population class (250,000-500,000) used herein, Fort Worth is neither the best nor the worst.

One measure of the general health of the community is the infant mortality rate, which represents the number of live-born babies who die under one year of age per 1,000 live-born babies. This is a useful measure because it shows in a general way the availability and level of medical and hospital care, the level of knowledge and interest of parents, and the level of knowledge and interest of the community. For this measure, Fort Worth is about average for the 24 cities in the United States of comparable size. During a period of five years—1945-1949—the

---

[27] $8,276 in the past three years.

average infant mortality rate for the 24 cities was 32.6; for Fort Worth the average rate was 32.9.[28] Such information for the 24 cities is shown in Figure 41. It can be observed that among the Texas cities included, the rate for Fort Worth was lower than that for Houston and San Antonio, but higher than

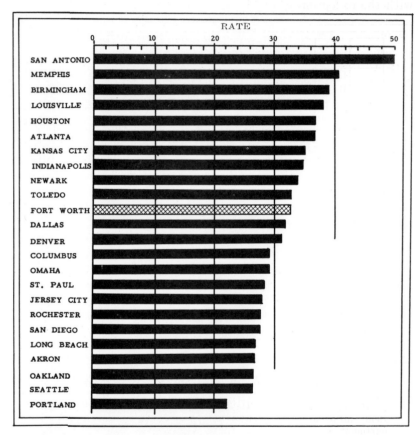

Figure 41. Infant Mortality Rates for 24 Comparable Cities: Average Rate for Five Years, 1945-1949. (Original data from *Vital Statistics of the United States* for corresponding years.)

[28]Rates are computed from, Bureau of the Census, *Vital Statistics of the United States*. The Bureau publishes these reports annually. However, since 1951 the Bureau has not published the necessary information for city areas. The rates for counties can be computed, but since some of the 24 cities are merely a part of a larger population constellation and not the dominant unit, county rates were no included.

the Dallas rate. The trends for an eleven year period (1945-55) for the four Texas cities can be observed in the yearly rates as represented in Figure 42. Of some importance is the fact that in 1949 the Fort Worth rate rose slightly from 31.5 for the previous year, to 33.6; but in 1950 it dropped to 31.5 again, and, with the exception of 1954, has been below 30 since.[29]

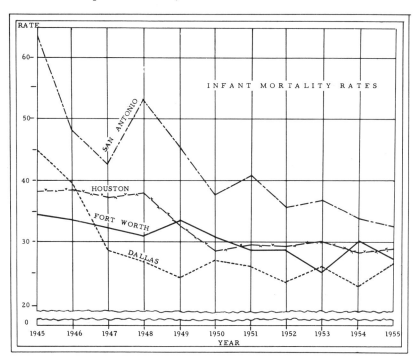

Figure 42. Trends in Infant Mortality for Four Texas Cities: Annual Rates for Eleven Years, 1945-1955. (Original data from *Vital Statistics of the United States*, annual reports for 1945-1950; information for 1951-1955 from respective city health departments.)

Another measure of community health standards is provided through the use of tuberculosis morbidity and mortality data. Although TB is in many respects considered an individual matter, and generally there are no laws requiring confinement

---

[29]Information on births and infant deaths since 1950 secured from departments of health of the four cities.

of the individual so infected, there is the fact that tuberculosis is an infectious disease. The reduction of the incidence, and the cure of those in the early stages, is closely related to community and individual awareness and interest, and to the willingness of the community to utilize its resources to prevent the spread of the disease. The fact is that with the present medical knowledge, tuberculosis is susceptible to control. It is also a fact that throughout the United States the tuberculosis death rate (number of deaths per 100,000 total population) has declined,[30] but it is equally true that the rates for some cities have been and still are much higher than the rates for others. Thus, among our 24 cities the average tuberculosis death rate for a five-year period (1945-1949) varied fom a high of 83.0 for San Antonio, to a low of 19.1 for St. Paul.[31] Such information is shown in Figure 43.

Other measures would reveal somewhat different patterns, but it appears evident that, whatever the reasons, the health level and protection against unnecessary disease and sickness is better in some cities than in others.

Current and Future Health Needs of the Community. If Fort Worth continues to add to its population in the future, it seems apparent that the community will have to expand its facilities for the promotion of health. In a sense, this is one of the costs of growth, but more realistically, such expansion is an investment which can reap rewarding dividends. Growth will require expansion of the activities of the city health department, expansion beyond the present hospital building program, an increase in the number of private physicians and nurses, and,

---

[30]Between 1933 and 1951 the rate for the United States declined from 59.6 to 20.1. For the same period the rate for Texas dropped from 72.0 to 24.8. The rate for Tarrant County dropped from 48.6 to 15.6. From, "Tuberculosis in Fort Worth and Tarrant County," *loc. cit.*, p. 16.

[31]It may be argued that San Antonio's high rate is due to its large population of Mexican origin, and to a sizeable Negro population, but there is no evidence that a particular ethnic or racial group is more susceptible to a particular disease. The fact is that tuberculosis is more prevalent among low income groups and in slum and dilapidated housing areas with their overcrowding, poor water supply and general poor conditions of sanitation. Such conditions are economic and related to education.

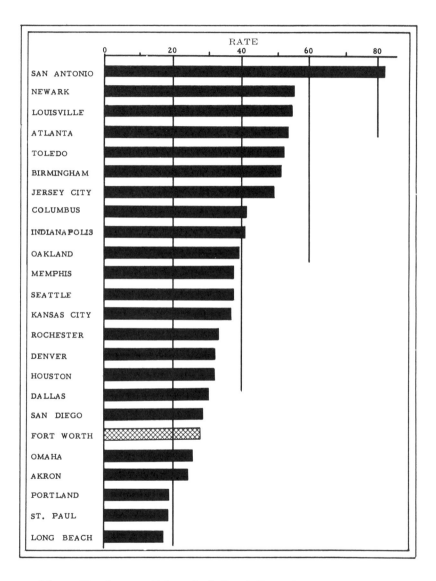

Figure 43. Average Tuberculosis Death Rates for 24 Comparable Cities, 1945-1949. (From "Tuberculosis in Fort Worth and Tarrant County: A Progress Report," Fort Worth-Tarrant County Tubeculosis Society, April, 1953.)

in the opinion of many (including the writer's) a pressing need for more stringent public regulations and private interest in eliminating the dangerous health conditions found in slum and sub-standard housing areas of the city.

The most important deficiency, however, in the community's program of health, and certainly the most pressing need, is a program for the care of the mentally ill. At the present time, there is no psychiatric hospital or any psychiatric services available in any of the general hospitals in Fort Worth for the psychiatrically ill patient who requires maximum, medium, or minimal treatment or care. There is no place in the general hospitals for the temporary care of patients who have been or are awaiting commitment to one of the state hospitals. In the case of patients dangerous to the welfare of others, the only facilities available where they can be held, pending commitment to a state institution, is either the city or county jail.[32]

Closely related to the requirements for psychiatric care is the need for a re-examination of the community's attitude and program for the alcoholic and the narcotics addict, both types of which are generally lodged in jail, and a re-examination of the community's attitude and treatment of the first offenders among juveniles.[33] Additional pressing needs are domiciliary facilities for Negroes (the Tarrant County Home will take only white persons), a growing need for facilities for chronic and incurably ill persons—John Peter Smith Hospital or the private hospitals will not take such persons, regardless of financial status—and the need for more and better rest or care home facilities for the aged.

The community has made a start in providing psychiatric services. Mainly through the interest and pressure of the Tarrant County Mental Health Society, there was established the Fort Worth-Tarrant County Guidance Clinic, which is currently supported by the City and County governments, the United Fund, and the Fort Worth Independent School District. Although

---

[32]From "Minutes of the Joint Meeting of the Family and Child Welfare Division and Health Division, Community Council," October 25, 1955.

[33]*Ibid.*

not the sole aim, the primary goal of the clinic is to discover and correct the first emotional imbalance among children.

Summary. In this section some of the highlights in the development of the present health standards of the community have been presented. As suggested earlier, Fort Worth has generally followed standards established elsewhere. It must be recognized, however, that the achievements are important, and required the interest of local citizens. A hospital, a clinic, city ordinances regulating conditions affecting health, an agency promoting health education, or psychiatric facilities, do not just happen. They emerge out of the interest and work of hundreds of citizens. An integral part of the process is the necessary leadership to arouse the people and emphasize the needs. In a very real sense, Fort Worth has reached its present level of health because leaders have been able to see the needs and translate ideals into action.

Organized Social Welfare*

The Nature of Social Welfare. In an agricultural or small-town environment, welfare needs and activity exist, if at all, at a minimum. Organized social welfare at the local level in such situations was, in the past, almost unknown. The only exception was the county relief to the indigent, sporadic help to needy children, and some help for the physically handicapped. Individual families, or church groups might help individual families, but little of a planned welfare nature existed.

Welfare activity as it is known today and particularly private welfare activity, is a product of, (1) the complex urban environment with its heterogeneity and uncertainty of living, and (2) a change in attitudes in recent decades as to what can and should be done. As conceived today, organized welfare activity is much more than relief to the needy. The current approach is to help people help themselves. This point of view is based on the belief that rehabilitation of human beings is possible, that with proper guidance such individuals can become assets to the community.

---

*Mrs. Ann Twiss, Executive Secretary of the Fort Worth-Tarrant County Community Council read this section and made suggestions as to content.

In the past, the common attitude was one of responsibility to the less fortunate. Today the approach is more positive. There is first the realization that some individuals are unable to care for themselves, or need some kind of assistance for a time because of fortuitous circumstances beyond their control. But there is also the firm belief in the value of rehabilitation— that many of the persons in need at a particular time can, with assistance and guidance, become independent and contributing members of society. Modern urban welfare activity, however, is much more than aid and rehabilitation given to certain persons in need. Today an integral part of the total program involves emphasis on prevention and on the development of integrated and adjusted adults. Thus, such groups as Boy Scouts, Y. W. C. A., Camp Fire, and Panther Boys Club, to mention only a few, aim not so much at rehabilitation, but rather toward the development of physically healthy and socially adjusted individuals. This change in emphasis is symbolized in the change from "charity" to "welfare services." Ideally, welfare activity is an investment, with the dividends accruing in organized self-supporting adults.

The Growth of Local Welfare Activity. As is true of other cities, organized welfare activity has grown in Fort Worth in a somewhat piece-by-piece fashion. In the main, a new service or activity has developed because some individual or group has recognized a specific need, or through the introduction into the local picture of a branch of a national organization. Until recently, little has been done in terms of an over-all planning approach.

In its beginning, charity activity was confined entirely to helping the widows, orphans, and the destitute, and was an individual matter. Possibly the first organized effort in Fort Worth was that of the Independent Order of B'nai B'rith in 1878. The stated purposes were to "alleviate the wants of the poor and needy, to visit and attend the sick, and to provide and assist the widow and orphan."[34] At about the same time, the

---

[34]Quoted in Fort Worth *Star Telegram*, "Fort Worth's First 100 Years" (Oct. 30, 1949), "Automotive," p. 23. Much of the information in this section is secured from this source.

city and county developed a program of charity. The city made direct grants to indigents, and the county established a pauper farm.

The first community-wide solicitation of funds for charity occurred in 1880 under the leadership of the churches of the city. This led to the organization, in 1867, of the Fort Worth Benevolent Association, whose main purpose was to supply food and clothing to the needy. Similar organizations came into being in the following years, but with special purposes, such as the Women's Benevolent Institution for the care of "outcast children and abandoned women." Apparently the overlapping created some problems, because in 1907 an attempt at consolidation was made with the organization of the Fort Worth United Charities. This was followed in 1912 with the Fort Worth Relief Association, which in turn gave way to the Community Chest organization in 1923. The Community Chest lasted until 1927, when it failed to raise its quota of funds. "Once more the relief agencies were scattered, each on its own in the raising of money. Continuous drives and tag days led harried businessmen to call for reorganization of the Community Chest".[35] As a result, in 1929 the Community Chest was reorganized with 17 member agencies, and remained as the central fund-collecting agency in the city until 1952, when a reorganization occurred which included additional agencies. Currently the central fund-raising group is the United Fund organization. After 1929 the number of agencies included in the yearly campaigns increased in the next few years to 28, so that from 1934 to 1951 there were either 27 or 28 agencies included, although not the same agencies throughout. In 1952, because of the inclusion of agencies which had previously carried on separate fund-raising campaigns, the number of agencies for which funds were raised increased to 43. The additions since 1951 are: American Red Cross, American Heart Association, American Cancer Society, Arlington Community Chest (four agencies), Children's Museum, Crippled Children's Society, North Fort Worth Day Nursery, Multiple Sclerosis Society, and the Fort Worth Safety Council. At the present time,

---

35*Ibid.*

the United Fund Group includes 16 agencies which were members of the Community Chest in 1932.

Financially, the Community Chest and United Fund present a picture of growth from 1930, when the goal was $248,930.74, to 1955 when the goal was $1,570,595.14. Table 50 provides selected information concerning the campaigns from 1930 to 1955. It can be observed that the general trend has been toward increased demands for funds. Part of this increase has been due to the addition of new agencies, but much of the increase has been considered necessary because of the growing population, and the changing needs of the community. Part of the information in

Table 50. Community Chest—United Fund Campaigns
Fort Worth, 1930-1955*

Campaign Year	Goal	Secured	Number Subscribers	Agencies
1930	$248,930.74	$254,857.26	18,940	17
1931	277,780.47	277,780.53	16,731	22
1932	277,639.36	284,421.12	21,934	23
1933	285,826.68	211,329.50 —	18,824	26
1934	249,891.76	221,422.53 —	20,132	26
1935	264,872.73	218,364.68 —	20,646	27
1936	304,744.17	235,320.56 —	21,317	27
1937	312,595.17	254,725.59 —	22,677	27
1938	344,176.17	257,872.50 —	26,900	28
1939	316,322.21	259,097.68 —	27,000	28
1940	292,103.06	298,273.01	27,933	27
1941	308,925.00	314,600.00	27,726	28
1942	315,163.00	312,040.00 —	33,372	28
1943	479,157.00	528,540.77	43,621	28
1944	649,457.00	683,939.84	48,664	28
1945	655,107.59	680,600.87	49,441	28
1946	590,364.00	542,710.00 —	35,321	28
1947	543,029.58	487,505.19 —	37,312	28
1948	481,777.43	492,081.87	35,068	28
1949	511,422.22	514,953.15	42,688	27
1950	564,860.81	565,389.65	51,557	28
1951	583,897.07	585,124.91	59,203	28
1952	1,359,069.53	1,440,000.00	74,493	38
1953	1,420,395.41	1,449,208.47	98,764	42
1954	1,470,611.20	1,485,355.22	95,965	43
1955	1,570,595.14	1,574,105.04		43

*Source: Records of Council of Social Agencies and Community Council. For the years 1943 through 1946 the drive was called "War Chest." (—indicates the years in which the goal was not reached).

Table 50 is shown graphically in Figure 44. From Table 50 and Figure 44 it can be seen that World War II had an important influence on the "giving" practices of the local citizens. Also, as a general trend, the contributions on the basis of the total population have shown some increase. Thus, in 1930 the per capita figure was $1.56 per person; in 1940 it had increased to $1.68, and by 1950 to $2.03. The mean average contribution (total contributions divided by total number of contributors) has also shown some change. This can be seen from the following:

Average Contribution per subscriber

1930	$13.46	1945	$13.76
1935	$10.58	1950	$10.97
1940	$10.68	1954	$15.48

Closely paralleling the trend in private charitable and welfare activity has been that of the city and county governments. Beginning in the 1880's, the city started a plan of grants in cash

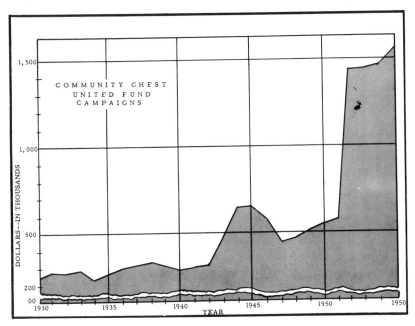

Figure 44. Trends in Welfare Giving: Yearly Total Amount of Money Pledged for Community Chest and United Fund Campaigns, Fort Worth, 1930-1955. (Original data from United Fund office.)

and kind to indigents, and during the same period the county (in 1867) assisted financially in the starting of a home for children, which today is known as the Tarrant County Children's Home. At about the same time the county established a home for paupers, which more recently has become the Tarrant County Home for the Aged. In 1927, after the failure of the Chest organization, the city took over for a short time some of the financial responsibilities of that group. In addition, the city and county governments entered the area of health care for the indigent with the establishment of the City-County Hospital in 1907, and Elmwood Sanatorium for tuberculosis patients in 1915.

A new phase of public welfare activity developed during the depression years of the 1930's. As both economic and welfare measures, the Federal government set up nation-wide programs, which had their local units, to reduce unemployment, as well as for other purposes. The first such attempt was made with the establishment of the Civil Works Administration in the fall of 1933. This was hurriedly followed by the Federal Emergency Relief Administration, which in turn was followed in 1935 by the Works Progress Administration, later changed to the Works Projects Administration. Of a slightly different character, but with the same general purpose, was the Public Works Administration which began in 1935. Each of these programs provided job opportunities for certain persons who were unemployable in private industry.

A sharply different emphasis was made with the passage of the Federal Social Security Act in 1935. With some revisions, the act has remained in force to the present time. This act provides for public assistance programs, for "Old Age and Survivers Insurance," and for improvement of child welfare services. The public assistance part of the act includes, "Aid to Dependent Children," "Aid to the Blind," and "Old Age Assistance."

Aid to children, the blind, and the aged under this program is given on the basis of need and financed by matched state and federal funds; the insurance phase of the program is based on contributions by individual workers and their employers. In the public assistance and child welfare phases of the Social Security program both the state and federal governments share in the cost and supervision. Trends for the state-federal public assistance program in Tarrant County (1942-1945) are shown in Table 51. This table gives the number of cases and the average monthly grant for the three types of programs as of September 1 for each year.

Table 51. State-Federal Public Assistance Program in Tarrant County 1942-1955; (Status as of September 1 for Each Year)*

| | Old Age Assistance | | Aid to Dependent Children | | | | Aid to Blind | |
| | Number of Cases | Average Monthly Grant | Number of Cases | Average Monthly Grant | | | Number of Cases | Average Monthly Grant |
Date			Fam-ily	Child-ren	Per Fam-ily	Per Child		
1942	7,336	$23.12	811	1,646	$10.50	$ 5.18	133	$25.05
1943	7,338	22.73	223	481	21.01	9.74	166	27.08
1944	6,888	23.22	156	324	20.69	9.96	164	25.46
1945	6,887	25.44	182	414	21.00	9.23	151	26.03
1946	7,328	25.49	219	557	23.40	9.20	193	29.72
1947	7,969	32.12	422	1,085	40.21	15.64	211	36.15
1948	8,648	34.19	554	1,427	39.46	15.32	230	37.46
1949	9,217	37.27	707	1,825	43.09	16.69	271	41.25
1950	9,580	36.50	823	2.123	39.70	15.39	297	40.45
1951	9,176	35.68	813	2,112	44.98	17.31	288	40.43
1952	8,982	36.47	618	1,697	50.07	18.23	264	41.61
1953	8,954	40.69	751	2,099	62.85	22.49	284	46.04
1954	9,045	41.15	1,004	2,891	58.38	20.27	298	47.32
1955	8,848	43.58	1,092	3,179	55.89	19.20	305	47.95

*Source: Division of Research and Statistics, State Department of Public Welfare, Austin, Texas.

The Current Pattern of Health and Welfare Activities. Health and welfare services in the city of Fort Worth are provided currently by a large number of public and private agencies, organizations and groups. These are so numerous, and their activities are so varied, that it is only possible here to give the broadest outlines of the current pattern. This includes work by governmental agencies, by private agencies and organizations, and by private organizations having other major purposes.

In the area of public or governmental responsibility, all four of the basic government units—federal, state, county, and city—

engage in welfare activity in the city. At the federal and state levels, the State Department of Public Welfare office supervises locally the administration of the welfare part of the federal Social Security Act.[36] This dual action involves contribution of money by both units, and the actual administration by state employees. The Division of Public Assistance of the State Department of Public Welfare (Fort Worth office) supervises grants for Old Age Assistance, Aid to the Blind, and Aid to Dependent Children in Tarrant County. In each instance, eligibility is restricted to those persons meeting the specified requirements of age, residence and need. The Child Welfare Division of the Department also supervises the licensing, according to state law, of child-caring facilities and child-placing agencies. A financial picture of the public assistance program as it functions in Tarrant County has been presented in Table 51. Comparisons of Tarrant County with other areas are provided in the annual report of the Texas Department of Public Welfare. For Tarrant County, Texas, and the United States, the average payments for June, 1955 were as follows:[37]

Type of Assistance	Average Grant, June, 1955		
	Tarrant County	Texas	United States
Old age assistance	$41.21	$39.10	$52.30
Aid to dependent children, per family	55.70	56.38	86.78
Aid to the blind	47.61	44.22	57.41

In this connection, according to the State Department's report, Texas ranks 38th among the states in average old age assistance payments, 37th in average payments to the blind, and 43rd in average payments to families receiving aid to dependent children, grants.[38]

---

[36]The Insurance phase of the Social Security Act—Old Age and Survivors Insurance—is administered locally by a separate office. Old age and survivors insurance is, of course, a welfare measure also, since it is designed to produce an annuity for individuals after they reach a specified age, or for their survivors. Through this part of the Act, the individual is forced to save for his old age. In contrast with the assistance phase as defined herein, eligibility for Old Age and Survivors Insurance is determined by age and at least partial retirement, as well as the contributions made by the individual and his employer, rather than need.

[37]Annual Report of the Texas State Department of Public Welfare, Austin, November 1, 1955, Charts 7, 8, and 9.

[38]Ibid., pp. 3-4.

The welfare program provided by Tarrant County includes family and individual aid for indigent persons who are residents of Tarrant County outside the city of Fort Worth. An integral part of the county program includes the work of the County Probation Department, which supervises the care of delinquent, dependent and neglected children throughout the county. Tarrant County also maintains the Tarrant County Children's Home for dependent children. In Fort Worth, the Welfare Division of the Department of Public Health and Welfare provides necessary direct relief to residents of Fort Worth, and financial provision for certain children placed in foster homes or institutions.

In addition to the welfare activities, both the county and city governments, as previously mentioned, have health departments, with many of their services designed primarily for low-income groups. In fact, welfare and health services are often so closely interrelated that it is difficult to differentiate between the two. This interrelationship is even more apparent with regard to some of the private agencies.

The area of private welfare activity can be divided roughly into four separate categories, three of which constitute full-time organized work, while the fourth includes aid by certain groups with other purposes. This classification includes (1) agencies in the United Fund, (2) other non-profit private agencies not in the United Fund, (3) commercial facilities, and (4) welfare aid given by service clubs and associations. Table 52 provides a listing of the agencies included in the first two categories, and suggestions as to the type of commercial services available (the fourth category is discussed in a later paragraph.) [39]

Central in the area of private health and welfare are those agencies which form the United Fund group. This group is composed of independent agencies, each with its own governing board, who receive all or a part of their financial support from a single fund-raising program. For some of the agencies, addi-

---

[39]For a complete list of the agencies in the general field of health and welfare service, see "Directory of Social Health and Welfare Agencies Serving Fort Worth and Tarrant County," The Community Council, Fort Worth. This directory gives the name of organization, officers, nature of financial support, and general program.

Table 52. Health and Welfare Activity in Fort Worth: Private Agencies
1955

United Fund Group	Independent Agencies
All Church Home	Alcoholics Anonymous
American Cancer Society	Association for Childhood
American Red Cross	Education
Arlington Community Chest	Children's Opportunity Center
(4 agencies)	Classes for Exceptional Children
Babyland	(Fort Worth Public Schools)
Boy Scouts	Crime Prevention Society
Camp Fire Girls	Cumberland Rest Home for Aged
Community Council	Women
Crippled Children's Society	Eastern Star Home
Family Service Association	Edna Gladney Home
Fort Worth Boys' Club	Fannie C. Brown Nursery
Fort Worth Children's Hospital	Farmer Foundation—Grove Home
Fort Worth Children's Museum	Fort Worth Good Neighbor Council
Fort Worth Day Nursery	Fort Worth-Tarrant County Men-
Fort Worth Heart Association	tal Health Society
Fort Worth Safety Council	Fort Worth-Tarrant County
Fort Worth-Tarrant County	Tuberculosis Society
Guidance Clinic	Home for Aged Masons
Fort Worth Urban League	Idella McDonald Home (Negro)
Girl Scouts	Legal Aid Clinic
Girls' Service League	Listening Eye School
Goodwill Industries	Masonic Home and School
Jewish Social Service Agency	Masonic Service Bureau
Lena Pope Home	Nationl Conference of Christians
Lighthouse for the Blind	and Jews
National Multiple Sclerosis Society	National Foundation for Infantile
North Fort Worth Day Nursery	Paralysis
Panther Boys' Club	Saint Ann's Business Women's Club
Planned Parenthood Center	Salvation Army Men's Social
Saint Teresa's Home	Service Center
Salvation Army Emergency	Tarrant County Association for
Relief	the Handicapped
School Lunch Program	Tarrant County Day Care
Servicemen's Center	Association
Travelers Aid Society	Tarrant County Parole Board
United Defense Fund—USO	Union Gospel Mission
Veterans' Affairs Council	Variety Club Boys Ranch
Volunteers of America	
Wesley Community House	
YMCA (9 Branches)	
YWCA	
YWCA (Negro Branch)	

Commercial

Convalescent and Rest Homes
Day Nurseries
Homes for Unwed Mothers
Sanitariums

tional needed funds are secured by membership dues, or through
assistance by persons interested in the agency's program. With
regard to a few of the organizations, a portion of the funds col-

lected locally are sent to their national headquarters for use in needed areas throughout the country. This is particularly true for the American Heart Association, the American Cancer Society, and the American Red Cross. For the Heart Association and the Cancer Society, the money going to national headquarters is used for research and care of victims of the diseases. In the case of the Red Cross, the money contributed to national headquarters is used mainly for the Red Cross disaster program and for its services to the Armed Forces. In this connection, in 1949, the Red Cross collected through contributions in Tarrant County approximately $289,000,000, but the National Chapter spent in the county approximately $1,750,000.00 for disaster relief because of the flood that year.

The non-profit agencies outside the United Fund group are different mainly in the manner in which they secure their financial support. Like the Fund agencies, each seeks to provide one or more services thought to be necessary in the community.

Possibly one emphasis made earlier needs to be reiterated. This refers to the nature of the present-day agency services, and the distinction between welfare and charity. Certainly a portion of the work of some of the current private agencies involves charity in the older sense, but in the main, these agencies today are much more generally engaged in rehabilitation and prevention. Today, most of the direct relief—of money or supplies— is provided by public agencies, although they too do much more than merely provide charity or relief.

In addition to the full-time agencies working in the field of health and welfare, many organizations and clubs give service or financial aid of one kind or another. In this connection, many of the churches maintain regular programs of aid. Typical are Catholic Charities, the Jewish Social Service Agency,[40] the Beth-

---

[40]Saint Teresa's Home, which is sponsored by Catholic Charities, Incorporated, and the Jewish Social Service Agency secure part of their funds from the United Fund.

lehem Center (Methodist Church), and the Baptist Goodwill Center. Also, certain church groups give aid in special cases. Most of the service clubs make some provision for welfare assistance of some type. The Fort Worth *Star-Telegram* and the Fort Worth *Press* maintain special funds for assistance to the needy. Some idea of the scope of the special activities can be secured from the following list of groups with welfare programs:

Health and Welfare in Fort Worth: Special Activities

Clubs, Organizations

Convair Contrib Club
Rotary
Optimist
Kiwanis
Civitan
Lions
Junior League
Civic Leagues
Council of Jewish Women
Women of Rotary
American Legion
Parent Teacher's Association

Newspapers	Churches
Fort Worth *Star-Telegram:*	Baptist Goodwill Center
Milk and Ice Fund	Catholic Charities, Inc.
Goodfellow Fund	Jewish Social Service Agency
Fort Worth *Press:*	Bethlehem Center
Santa's Pals	Aid to church affiliated
	organizations
	Aid for individual cases

Community Council. An integral part of the community welfare idea is the desirability of having some central co-ordinating and planning agency to work toward removal of duplication of effort, and to promote assistance in areas of the community's life where unmet needs are discovered. In Fort Worth this central agency is the Community Council which was organized as the Council of Social Agencies in 1939.[41] Currently it is composed of representatives from each of the United Fund group, as well as representatives from other voluntary agencies, from governmental agencies, and from cooperating organizations. In addition, individuals may become a part of the Council organiza-

---

[41]For a history of Fort Worth Council, see Frances Allen, "Study of the Council, Fort Worth, Texas, 1929-1947" (available in Community Council office).

tion. At the present time the Council represents 96 organizations. Its work includes operation or supervision of the Social Service Exchange, the Volunteer Center, and the Yuletide Program, formerly the Christmas Clearing Bureau. In its promotion of health and welfare in the community the Council's program is divided into three divisions—the Family and Child Welfare Division, the Health Division, and the Group Work and Recreation Division. In addition to promoting agency and organization co-operation to meet common needs, the divisions regularly organize conferences which deal with special welfare problems of the city. The divisions also assist in bringing attention to unmet needs of the community.[42] An example of this has been the Council's interest in day care for children of working mothers.[43]

Comparisons. Inter-city comparisons of welfare activity and effort are certainly to be desired. Such questions as which community is making the best effort to meet its responsibilities, which communities are getting good returns from their investments, and which communities are ignoring or under-supporting basic welfare needs, to mention only a few, require answers. Answers are difficult, however, because of the variety of local patterns.

---

[42]As suggested elsewhere, a community often does not develop an adequate awareness of a problem when it arises. Commonly, a situation becomes a problem only after the community has been made aware that something needs to be done, and only after the presentation of evidence that something can be done. In this context, a distinction is made between a condition and a problem. To the former we make the necessary adjustments. A situation becomes a problem when (1) we decide it is undesirable, and (2) when we come to believe that action can be taken which will lead to reduction or eradication. An example would be the approach to such diseases as typhoid fever, which was for a long time a condition, but which in the twentieth century became a problem because of the discovery of effective controls. In other instances there is not even a general awareness of danger.

[43]An interesting sidelight here is the belief on the part of many working mothers that a nursery or day care center must have been approved in order to stay open—otherwise it would be closed by the authorities. In Fort Worth, at least, at the present this is not the case. Apparently also, many parents merely "hope" that a place is all right for their children; or they decide that the person in charge "loves" children and that is enough. Certainly love of children is a desirable attribute for persons working with children, but possibly something else is needed—understanding as to the needs of children, techniques of learning and so forth. In a doctor who specialized in diseases of children a love of children is desirable, yet a knowledge of disease and treatment techniques is also to be desired!

One procedure which has been used to provide comparisons is based on the funds collected through Community Chest or United Fund campaigns.[44] Such studies show that welfare effort varies considerably from city to city. There seems to be little question but that this conclusion is generally correct. However, there are some limitations in the results. That is, such standardized reporting as that compiled by the Community Chests and Councils, Incorporated,[45] only gives information on fund raising by united groups such as the United Fund in Fort Worth. In Fort Worth the Red Cross illustrates the limitations. Before 1952 this organization raised its funds independently and quite successfully. At the present this organization is in the United Fund group in Fort Worth, while in Dallas the Red Cross still raises its funds in a separate campaign. Thus, any index of effort for Fort Worth before 1952 would under-rate the city, while comparisons based solely on United Fund totals of the present between Dallas and Fort Worth would under-estimate the welfare effort of Dallas. One other example may suffice. In one state a particular service may be provided through public agencies while in another through private agencies. An example of this would be the day care facilities financed publicly in California cities, and the private support provided in cities in other states.

Summary. In the development of the social welfare approach in cities like Fort Worth the change in attitudes has been a gradual one, and considerable evidence exists that charity is still the dominant theme in the minds of many citizens. In a region where individualism has been particularly prominent it has been difficult for many people to recognize the demoralizing nature of urbanism, or that man is not always the complete mas-

---

[44]See Robert C. Angell, "The Social Integration of American Cities of More Than 100,000 Population," *American Sociological Review*, 12 (June, 1947) 335-42, and "The Moral Integration of American Cities," *American Journal of Sociology*, 57 (July, 1951) Part 2. See also, C. Arnold Anderson, "Community Chest Campaigns as an Index of Community Integration," Social Forces, 33 (October, 1954) 76-81.

[45]The studies cited in the previous note of reference used this source for their basic information.

ter of his fate. There is still the wide-spread assumption that the individual can make of himself what he will, and if he fails it is his fault and he must suffer the consequences.[46]

Local citizens believe strongly in character-building organizations, yet there is the insistent belief that the home is the real place to build character. Thus in juvenile delinquency the blame is placed first on the home. This is all very well if the home is a functioning entity; where this is true successful changes can be made in the home which produce a juvenile delinquent;[47] in other homes which are themselves disorganized, adjustments are impossible because the parents have problems too. It is all well and good to blame the products of such homes on the parents, but such blame does little to produce useful adults.

Also, because of the confusion between the welfare approach and the idea of charity, there is a common assumption that one should give for the less fortunate, but that the aid should not be too agreeable for the recipients lest it corrupt them, or lead others into seeking aid. This is true even though a great proportion of private welfare funds is allocated for such activities as scout work. Possibly a basic need here is public education; and while words alone cannot accomplish miracles, it might be rewarding to change the "Give the United Way" to "Invest the United Way," on the assumption that welfare activity provides protection for the community and is an investment for the future.

---

[46]The writer would not subscribe to the opposite—that man is merely a creature of fate. Rather, there are areas of action, varying with individuals, within which individual decisions can be made. Such decisions, however, are related to previous conditioning. In the writer's opinion, the problem of understanding human behavior and the nature of causation is the basic dilemma of welfare activity. In contrast, the need for such things as highways can be observed; that good highways are desirable is an acceptable goal which can be achieved. Also, their construction at public expense is generally accepted without question. In highway development we have technical and financial problems, whereas in social welfare, there are ideological, as well as technical and financial aspects.

[47]The writer was one of a group "haled" into court as a delinquent. The charge was "jerking" trollies on street-cars. There was no question about guilt, since we were caught "red-handed." However, after impressing us with the gravity of our offense, the judge let us off, probably because our parents were respected citizens—mine was a minister—or possibly because the ringleader of the gang was the judge's son!

Finally, it may be suggested, in spite of the great amount of time and effort expended by thousands of local citizens, that local welfare is mainly trying either to catch up or hold the line. There seems to be little concerted planning to meet the future needs of a growing city in which welfare needs will become increasingly complex. If this is a correct evaluation, it is due not so much to the present leadership as to the lack of general community awareness concerning the consequences of rapid urbanization and industrialization.

Chapter VIII

THE ORGANIZATION AND FUNCTIONS OF MUNICIPAL GOVERNMENT

The growth of municipal government is obvious to anyone familiar with the history of American cities; the reasons are less obvious but still observable. First, for any one city, such as Fort Worth, the increase in operations is related to population and area growth. Thus, in 1873, when Fort Worth was incorporated, it had a population of approximately 4,000[1] and an area of 4.3 square miles. By 1950 the population had increased to 278,778, with the area of the city comprising approximately 102 square miles. Secondly, there have been, significant changes in the expectations of local citizens. Whether this can be labeled a movement from rugged individualism to collectivism is debatable, but the fact is that local citizens are today demanding services from local government which in the past were matters of individual concern. A third factor, closely related to the second, is the increase in understanding as to what can be done to improve the lot of the average citizen. An obvious example here is to be found in the field of public health.

Other factors related to the growth of municipal government are industrialization, and the increased heterogeneity and complexity of American cities, with the resultant requirement of more rigid formal controls. Whereas in 1873 the municipal government of Fort Worth was charged mainly with keeping the peace, today it not only attempts to keep the peace, which incidentally is an exceedingly more costly task, but it also provides such services as fire protection, health protection, traffic control, the operation of parks, playgrounds and other recreational facilities, library facilities, public works, and many other services. Illustrative of the increased complexity of urban living is the change in modes of transportation from the horse to the

---

[1]This was the situation when the Texas and Pacific Railroad was expected any day; when that hope was temporarily extinguished, late in 1873, the population probably dropped to around 1,000.

automobile. Hard-surfaced streets and some traffic control were desirable in the horse-and-buggy era, but in the era of the automobile, paved and wider streets and traffic control are absolutely essential demands, and much more costly.

Development of Government. The development of government in Fort Worth has not been particularly different from that found in other metropolitan centers. Within particular municipal departments there has been some attempt to foresee future needs, but in general the approach has been one of meeting and trying to adjust to new requirements after they have arisen.

For almost a quarter of a century after its inception, Fort Worth remained an unincorporated frontier settlement. In 1856 it became the county seat of Tarrant County, but legal status did not come until 1873. Apparently, incorporation in that year was pushed by local citizens because of the expected arrival of the railroad. The municipal charter granted by the state legislature provided for a mayor-council form of government, and for the election of a mayor, five aldermen, marshal, assessor-collector, treasurer, and secretary.

The railroad did not come in 1873 as expected, and for a while, because so many people moved away, there was doubt concerning the need of government, but optimism was revived when the railroad actually arrived in 1876; and with it came a conglomeration of adventurers, settlers, gamblers and the like.

The early days after incorporation were mainly ones of stumbling and trying to determine what a government should do. The first council in 1873, among other things, provided for regulation of gambling, bawdy houses, and shooting galleries; restricted the carrying of deadly weapons; requested the construction of sidewalks; created a police force; and arranged for an accurate survey of the town's limits.[2] Other problems facing the new government included the need for a sanitary water supply; action to make the streets passable; some control over hogs and other animals; means to control the disposal of gar-

---

[2]Oliver Knight, *Fort Worth: Outpost on the Trinity* (Norman: University of Oklahoma Press, 1953), p. 74.

bage and other waste matter; and some means to control contagious disease. Probably typical of the attitude of the time was the appointment of a health officer (in 1881) with power to quarantine and vaccinate, only after a smallpox epidemic seemed imminent.

Apparently the major issue of the first few years, and particularly after the railroad came, was whether Fort Worth should be a wide-open town for gambling and other entertainment, or should lay the foundations for a stable community. According to Knight:

> Vice and lawlessness were virtually unchecked by 1878. Gamblers set up their games on sidewalks. Because the town was full of prostitutes, respectable women could not walk down the street without danger of being accosted. Thugs infested dark streets. Professional men dared not return from work after dark unarmed. Reform was imperative.[9]

A reform ticket appeared in the election of 1876, but aroused little interest among local citizens. By 1878, however, the reform group had gained strength and was able to elect a new mayor and city council. Reforms initiated included more strict regulation of gambling and brothels, and reorganization of city finances. Saloons and beer halls were ordered closed on Sunday. The new council also ordered the grading of Main Street, and passed an ordinance regulating the construction of theaters and other public buildings. Hogs were banished from the main streets, but only after securing a special vote from local citizens. An anti-hog law was barely favored by a vote of 377 to 324.[4] Another major problem of the time was the danger from fires. The first organized effort to combat fires was entirely voluntary, with the voluntary fighters owning their own equipment. In 1875 the city council made its first investment in fire fighting by voting $1,000 for equipment; then in 1877, at the insistence of the local newspaper, the council set aside money to dig cisterns for firefighting purposes. It was not until 1893, however, that a professional fire department was created, and not until 1905 that all wooden buildings on Main Street were condemned.

---

[3]*Ibid.*, p. 112.
[4]*Ibid.*, p. 116.

By 1880 Fort Worth was taking on the appearance of an established city. It had a population of 6,663, and was looking forward to future growth. Some of the lawlessness of the frontier had disappeared, but the town still had many problems. In municipal affairs there was still the question of what the government should or should not do. But by 1886, according to Knight, "The municipal government was on solid footing for the first time. The hand-to-mouth days of government by expediency were over."[5] This had been accomplished through the administration of John Peter Smith, who was mayor from 1882 to 1886. The major contributions of Smith's administration were (1) a municipal water system was provided for the first time, (2) the fire department was reorganized and modernized, (3) the first street-paving program was instituted and carried through, and (4) the first sanitary sewers were built.[6]

In the years following, the city government was changed and its activity enlarged to meet the needs of population growth, area growth, and the changing standards of the community. New services were added or new controls created almost entirely through pressure from community groups. One example of new services to meet the changing standards of the community is found in the field of recreation.

Growth of Public Recreation. For several reasons recreation has become important in the urban area. Today, in contrast with the past, urban people normally have more time away from their jobs, and they have need for release from the tensions of urban living. Then too, their standards have changed in recent years. They demand more opportunities to relax and are willing to pay for such opportunities.

Like any other community, recreational activities have existed in Fort Worth since its inception. Even as a frontier settlement, in spite of the ruggedness of life, the early residents took time to play. But their play was different from present-day recreation. Probably many had heard of Poor Richard's admoni-

---

[5]*Ibid.*, p. 150.

[6]*Ibid.*

tion that "all work and no play makes Jack a dull boy," but few took it seriously. Recreation was an incidental rather than an institutional part of the daily life of the frontier.

Later, as cattle became a more important part of the economy of West Texas, unattached men who were drawn to cattle raising found considerable need for "recreational facilities." Apparently quite early the settlement of Fort Worth provided some kind of leisure-time activity for such men. And when the cattle drives began to the Northern markets immediately after the Civil War, and Fort Worth became a resting place on the drives, opportunities for recreation were greatly increased. The pattern which was established prior to the incorporation of the city in 1873 continued for some time thereafter. "Hell's Half Acre" became a place of considerable reputation throughout West Texas.[7] Early newspapers of the time record the struggle between the forces of "good" who wanted to establish a stable community, and those whose main interest was in providing places of fun for travellers, cattlemen, and others of the region. In some respects, this conflict has continued down to the present. Fort Worth is still faced with something of a dilemma. That is, there is the question as to whether the city can be both a "recreational" center for the people of West Texas bent on pleasure, and at the same time a stable, law-abiding moral city.

With some exceptions, the early recreational facilities of the community were predominantly of a commercial nature. Organized, non-profit facilities developed only after the community had become firmly established, and after the development of a point of view that recreation was a justifiable goal of life.

The city acquired its first park in 1892, when Trinity Park (earlier known as City Park) was set aside for public use,[8] but it was not until 1922, when a recreation department was created

---

[7]In 1884 the city directory of that year listed 35 saloons, which would be one for every 379 estimated population of that year. See Fort Worth *Star-Telegram*, "Fort Worth's First 100 Years" (October 30, 1949), Commerce," p. 30, for story of saloons.

[8]Circle Park was created earlier, in 1888, but at the time in the independent municipality of North Fort Worth.

in the city government, that the use of tax money to promote leisure-time activities became generally acceptable to the local community.[9]

The community's present system of parks represents probably one of the best examples of the foresight of early citizens. As indicated above, land for Trinity Park (originally 31 acres) was purchased in 1892; in 1897 a Board of Park Commissioners was appointed by the city council. Apparently, however, this was not sufficient in the opinion of many local people, since soon after 1900 a park league was organized to press for a larger park system; probably as a result of the pressure exerted by this league, the city council created a Park Board in 1907. Two years later an expert on city planning was retained to draft a master plan for park development. This plan, according to Knight, has been the continuing guidepost for park development in the city.[10] At about the same time (1911) the city's zoo was started. After the creation of Lake Worth and Eagle Mountain Lake the land around these lakes was set aside for recreational purposes, and by 1914 a definite plan had been started.

Before 1922 there had existed organized, non-profit recreation programs, but all of them were privately supported by either churches or other interested organizations.[11] A tax-supported recreation program was provided through a charter amendment voted by local citizens in 1922, and reaffirmed three years later when the council-manager form of government was adopted. Even before voter approval, the city government had in 1920 built the first municipal swimming pool (Forest Park Pool). In 1923 Worth Hills became the first municipal golf course in the city.

---

[9]The development of a system of parks must be differentiated from the development of a recreational program. The former involves the acquisition of suitable land and its development; a recreational program involves the planning for games and other recreational facilities. This distinction is observable in Fort Worth, with its separate park and recreation departments.

[10]Known as the Kessler Plan. See Knight, *op. cit.*, p. 185.

[11]*Ibid.*, p. 208. In 1915 a part of the Texas and Pacific Reservation was donated for use as a public playground. Equipment was purchased from money given privately.

In the field of recreation, two of the more recent additions to the city government's tax responsibility were acquired, when in 1951, through inclusion in a bond issue of that year, the voters approved allocation of public funds to construct the Art Museum and Children's Museum. At present a part of the funds for the operation of these museums is secured from the United Fund Campaign, and from other private sources.

In such ways the current community program of recreation was developed. Space does not permit the proper description of the work of various boards, private and public, and individuals who worked to provide the present facilities. Considerable space would be required to describe properly the time, effort and interest expended to secure such present facilities as the Will Rogers Auditorium and Coliseum,[12] the zoo, the botanic gardens, and similar facilities.

As suggested several times, few of the present facilities, for recreation or for other purposes, were purely local innovations. Almost invariably there was the fact of developing locally what had been observed elsewhere; yet such additions did not come automatically. Also, almost without exception, the initial interest was created by some private group which sensed an unmet need. In Fort Worth, at least, the evidence indicates that city governmental activities have expanded not because of "bureaucrats grasping for more power," but rather because of the pressure of private groups. In the main, the city government as such has been extremely hesitant to take on any new duties and responsibilities.

---

[12]The auditorium can handle large conventions and meetings, and has complete facilities for plays and operas. The rodeo, which is an integral part of the annual Southwestern Exposition and Fat Stock Show, is held in the coliseum. The coliseum is also used for the annual Shrine Circus. Adjacent, are smaller buildings which are used for the housing and showing of stock during the Southwestern Exposition. The city's new Children's Museum and Art Museum, housed in separate buildings, are located in the same area.

Possibly the most significant features of current public recreation in the city are the diversity of opportunities, and the importance of recreation, in the daily lives of residents.[13]

At the present, the city has 48 parks, with a total of 4,752 acres (including municipal golf courses), five municipal golf courses, six swimming pools, and five recreation buildings; an all-year recreation program, with an intensified summer supervised playground program, (there were 34 supervised playgrounds in 1955); baseball diamonds, tennis courts, and other planned play spaces in many of the parks. The geographic location of the publicly maintained parks and play areas in the city can be seen in Figure 45. Besides the considerable amount of land area so allocated, it can be observed that the city's park area is rather widely dispersed throughout the community. In addition, play space and equipment are available at each of the city schools. Other facilities at least partially recreational in nature include a zoo, botanic gardens, an art museum, a children's museum, Will Rogers Municipal Auditorium and Coliseum, and a public library.

In the growth of recreational facilities we see, possibly most obviously, the tremendous changes in attitudes of citizens with regard to what they expect from their local government. Probably expenditures for most of the present activities would have been considered fantastic by the majority of citizens at the turn of the century. Today, however, such services come within the normal expectations of the average resident. Moreover, it seems apparent that the considerable change in attitudes, and the related changes in recreational practices, have been strongly influenced by effective local leadership.

[13]Since 1925 the Park and Recreation departments, have had a semi-independent status, with their funds provided by separate tax income. Currently the tax rate for parks is $0.09 per $100.00 evaluation; for recreation the rate is $0.04. (See City of Fort Worth *General Budget*, 1955-1956, p. iii). Members of the Park and Recreation boards are appointed by the City Council. For a more complete statement of the current program of the city recreation department, see, "The Fort Worth Recreation Department," September 30, 1955 (available from the department).

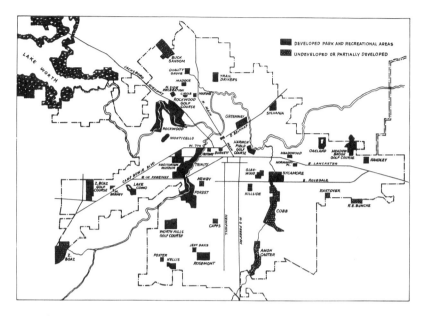

Figure 45. Public Park and Play Areas in Fort Worth, 1955 Prepared by Winston Croslin, *Star-Telegram* artist, Fort Worth *Star-Telegram*.)

In the preceding paragraphs some of the details of the development of recreation as a public responsibility have been presented. This has been done both to show one way in which government grows, and also because the growth of recreational facilities represents a good example of the influence of local interest. It must be recognized, however, that other phases of municipal government could have been selected. This cannot be done because of space limitations, but it does seem appropriate to consider selected features of the current structure of the local government in order that we may understand the product of the processes of growth. This is done in the following sections.

Present Form of Government. The mayor-council form of government as originally established in Fort Worth, remained the basic pattern of government until 1907.[14] In that year the voters adopted the Commission form of government, and this type of organization remained as the local pattern until 1925.[15]

At the present, Fort Worth has a Council-City Manager form of government. This was adopted by the voters in 1924 and became operative in 1925. The City Council, composed of nine members, is the legislative and policy forming body of the government. Councilmen are elected at large from the city and serve for a period of two years. The Council elects one of its members as mayor; he presides at its meetings, is the official head of the government, and represents the city on all ceremonial occasions. By law, the Council "is empowered to carry out the provisions of the City Charter, including supervision and control of all departments of the city government . . . ; it passes city ordinances, and adopts the annual city budget."[16] The council appoints the city-manager, various other city officials, and members of boards and commissions, as required in the Charter.

---

[14]See W. J. Hammond, *History of Municipal Departments of the City of Fort Worth, Texas, 1873-1939*, Federal Educational Radio Project 705-3-9, pp. 1-8, and appendex for amendments to original charter. As one type of amendment, in the original charter provision had been made for the election of two aldermen from each of three wards. As the town grew new wards were created, so that by 1891 there were nine wards and 18 aldermen.

[15]One of the common criticisms of the commission form is that, since the commissioners are usually elected to head specific departments, such as fire and police and are responsible only to the voters, there is no strong pressure to cooperate with each other. Also, each commissioner has considerable administrative responsibility, but is selected by popular vote rather than because of any technical skill. The council-manager form is intended to overcome some of the weaknesses of both the mayor-council and commission forms of city government. Commonly, in the council-manager form, the council, elected by the voters, is charged with determining general policy. The manager who ideally is chosen by the council for his technical and professional skill is the administrative head of the city government; he in turn chooses department heads who are skilled in their particular field. Ideally, a council may change, but the manager and his staff continue to function. Again ideally, this form provides the democratic control through council election, but recognizes the fact that the large city government today requires technical and professional skills, and a well-defined line of responsibility.

[16]Most of the information concerning the organization of the city government has been secured from, "Know Your Community; Facts About Fort Worth City Government," issued August 15, 1951, by the League of Women Voters of Fort Worth.

The city manager is charged with the proper administration of all the departments under his supervision. He appoints the heads of certain departments, and recommends the appointment by the council of others. Certain of the departments are under the direct control of boards or commissions, the members of which are appointed by the council. The pattern of organization and responsibility of the various departments can be seen in the organization chart which is presented as Figure 46.

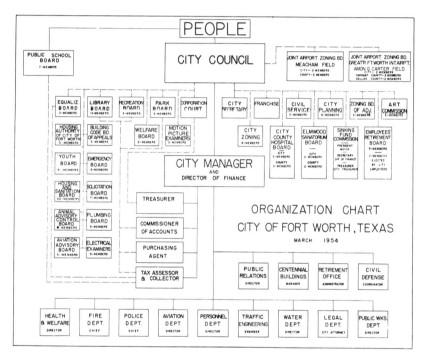

Figure 46. Organization of the Fort Worth City Government. (From Annual Report, Public Works Department, February, 1955.)

Logically, at this point, it would be desirable to consider the various departments and their separate duties, but such emphasis is considered beyond the scope of this work. The reader can, however, secure a fairly adequate picture of the city government through consideration of selected information concerning the nature of city finances. Such information can reveal the broad outlines of governmental policy.

City Finances. The cost of government in Fort Worth has increased from a yearly expenditure of around $30,000.00 in 1881, to appropriations of $21,193,034.00 for the fiscal year of 1955-56.[17] As was stated previously, this increased cost of municipal services has been due generally to the growth in population and size of the city, and to the increase in activities performed by the city government. Obviously, however, the assessed value of property in the city has increased also. Thus, in 1881 the listed value of property produces assessments of $29,886.33, while for the fiscal year 1955-56 the estimated value of local property for tax purposes is $475,000,000.00, which according to local estimates is approximately 55-60 percent of the current market value.[18]

A general picture of the fiscal operations of the city government of Fort Worth is given in Table 53, which shows the estimated receipts and appropriations for the fiscal year 1955-56.

Table 53. Summary of Estimated Receipts and Appropriations, City of Fort Worth: Fiscal Year 1955-1956*

	Estimated Receipts	Appropriations	Unappropriated Balance
General Fund	$14,277,034.00	$14,205,817.00	$ 71,217.00
Water Works General Fund	5,431,335.00	5,361,726.00	69,609.00
Park Department	916,790.00	734,259.50	182,530.50
Recreation Department	430,474.50	430,474.50	—0—
Public Library	300,486.00	300,486.00	—0—
Municipal Airports	163,525.00	160,271.00	3,254.00
Gross Total	$21,519,644.50	$21,193,034.00	$326,610.50
Less Water & Sewer Payments on General Obligation Bonds included in both the General Fund and the Waterworks General Fund	746,965.12	746,965.12	—0—
Budget Net Totals	$20,772,679.38	$20,446,068.88	$326,610.00

*City of Fort Worth, General Budget (1955-56), p. 1.

[17]See Hammond, *op. cit.*, p. 267, for the 1881 figures, and the City of Fort Worth, General Budget for the 1955-56 figures. Hammond's study gives the tax assessments for each year from 1881 to 1938.

[18]The current tax rate is $1.67 per $100 assessed value. Of the total rate, $1.49 goes into the General Fund, $0.09 for parks, $0.05 for the library, and $0.04 for recreation.

More than half of the city's revenue is from the General Property Tax. The remainder comes from fees, licenses, and other charges for particular services.[19] Thus, the estimated receipts for the Water Works General Fund as shown in Table 53 will be derived mainly from charges for water, sewer service, and waste disposal.

In 1955-56, approximately half of the city's budget was for salaries of city employees. The next largest expenditure was for debt service.[20] Evidence of the percentage distribution is seen in the allocations from the General Fund only, as given in Table 54.[21] A slightly different way of considering city expenditures is shown in Table 55. This shows the services provided by the revenue dollar. It should be recognized that part of the expenditures for specific purposes is balanced by income from those particular services.

Table 54.   General Fund Appropriations by Types of Activities
Fort Worth: 1955-1956*

Type	Amount	Per Cent
Salaries and wages	$7,850,215	55.3
Debt Requirements	3,448,259	24.3
Unclassified	743,360	5.2
Sundry charges	553,494	3.9
Supplies	511,309	3.6
Miscellaneous services	394,639	2.8
Maintenance of equipment	304,023	2.1
Maintenance of structures	171,009	1.2
Replacement of equipment	124,857	0.9
Capital outlay	104,652	0.7
	$14,205,817	100.0

*City of Fort Worth, General Budget (1955-56), p. 14. Percentages computed.

[19]Revenue for school purposes is collected by the city government, but is administered entirely by the school board.

[20]A relatively high debt is a fairly common condition of rapidly growing cities. Rapid growth requires large amounts of money for new capital improvement. In Fort Worth this has meant construction of new sewers, streets, park and recreational facilities, and similar permanent improvements. Few cities have the resources to pay for such additions as they are made.

[21]Note that the General Fund is only one of the funds of the city government. See Table 53 for the others.

Table 55. The Revenue Dollar: Percentage Allocated by Type of Service: 1955-1956*

Activity	Per Cent
Water Works	25.3
Public safety	22.7
Debt requirements	16.3
Health and sanitation	8.7
Highways	7.3
General administration	4.9
Miscellaneous accounts	3.5
Park department	3.5
Donations and charities	2.9
Recreation Department	2.0
Library	1.4
Municipal airports	0.8
Capital improvements	0.6
City planning	0.1
	100.0

*City of Fort Worth, General Budget, (1955-56).

Capital Improvements. Capital improvements have been an important part of municipal financial activity within recent years. And like most American cities, Fort Worth has found it necessary to finance its major capital improvements through bond issues. As already stated, additions have been thought necessary because of the growth of the city, and partly because of new services wanted by citizens.[22] Since the beginning of World

Table 56. Improvements Authorized in Bond Elections in Fort Worth 1942, 1945, 1951*

| Improvement | Amount Authorized | | | |
	1942	1945	1951	Total
Street Construction	—	$ 9,000,000	$23,450,000	$32,450,000
Airport	—	2,500,000	1,750,000	4,250,000
Water Works	—	3,000,000	—	3,000,000
Sewage, Waste Disposal	75,000	2,000,000	800,000	2,875,000
Park and Recreation	—	1,700,000	500,000	2,200,000
Exhibit Buildings	—	1,500,000	—	1,500,000
Museum Building	—	800,000	200,000	1,000,000
Fire Protection	—	—	500,000	500,000
Police Station & Jail	—	300,000	—	300,000
River Control	275,000	—	—	275,000
TOTALS	$350,000	$20,800,000	$27,200,000	$48,350,000

*Does not include bonds voted for school purposes.

[22]The first local bond issue was for $1,500, in 1875, to gravel Main Street. Since that time the city has had 81 bond issues. See "Historical," Fort Worth *Star-Telegram, loc. cit.,* p. 21.

War II (to December, 1955) the citizens of the city have approved through three separate elections the issurance of bonds, the money to be used for certain capital improvements. The amounts approved in recent elections and purposes are shown in Table 56.

Financial Comparisons. General comparisons between governments, as well as comparisons for particular departments, which would measure qualitative differences would be quite valuable, but in the main the necessary information to make such distinctions is not available. With some exceptions, the information which is accessible provides only financial comparisons. Even mere comparisons must be made with considerable caution. It is often difficult to determine when one city is getting more for its money than another. That is, the per capita expenditure for a particular service may be high, but the value of actual services rendered may be relatively low. Thus, one city may spend a large portion of its park budget on a complicated formal

Table 57. Per Capita Expenditure of Public Funds for Selected Services Cities in Population Group 250,000 to 500,000*
1950

PUBLIC SAFETY		LIBRARIES		SANITATION	
Jersey City	$20.68	Newark	$2.29	Rochester	$9.19
Newark, N. J.	20.31	Seattle	1.80	Newark	8.61
Oakland	16.31	Long Beach	1.67	Toledo	5.74
Portland, Ore.	15.51	Oakland	1.66	Memphis	5.04
Seattle	13.30	Rochester	1.64	Long Beach	5.04
Indianapolis	12.93	Louisville	1.53	Jersey City	4.93
Long Beach	12.80	Jersey City	1.48	Dallas	4.78
Rochester	12.17	St. Paul	1.40	FORT WORTH	4.59
Toledo	11.72	Denver	1.33	Atlanta	4.51
Denver	11.41	San Diego	1.19	Columbus	4.49
San Diego	11.18	Atlanta	1.16	Akron	4.17
St. Paul	10.99	Columbus	1.01	Seattle	4.02
Dallas	10.97	Birmingham	.67	Denver	3.88
Atlanta	10.61	FORT WORTH	.63	San Diego	3.82
Omaha	10.12	Omaha	.62	Houston	3.72
Kansas City	9.98	San Antonio	.56	Louisville	3.35
FORT WORTH	9.86	Dallas	.52	St. Paul	2.76
Columbus	9.25	Memphis	.38	San Antonio	2.63
Louisville	8.92	Houston	.32	Kansas City	2.41
Birmingham	8.88			Birmingham	2.36
Houston	8.74			Portland, Ore.	2.19
Memphis	7.76			Oakland	2.14
Akron	7.18			Indianapolis	1.24
San Antonio	5.95				

Continued on Next Page—

Table 57 Continued—

HEALTH		GROSS DEBT		GENERAL EXPENDITURE	
Newark	$3.57	Seattle	$232.26	Jersey City	$122.46
Toledo	2.68	Houston	189.15	Newark	122.16
Seattle	1.99	Dallas	180.70	Rochester	108.43
Atlanta	1.92	Jersey City	141.02	Denver	102.86
Rochester	1.85	FORT WORTH	135.31	Louisville	78.43
Oakland	1.68	Louisville	135.24	Atlanta	76.33
Indianapolis	1.38	Newark	133.30	St. Paul	74.95
Long Beach	1.28	San Antonio	132.60	Seattle	66.90
Denver	1.18	Denver	107.15	Memphis	60.18
Houston	1.16	Kansas City	86.60	Dallas	58.13
Jersey City	1.13	Atlanta	85.29	Toledo	57.14
San Antonio	1.09	St. Paul	82.58	Houston	56.22
Portland, Ore.	1.07	Memphis	78.42	Portland, Ore.	56.18
San Diego	1.06	Rochester	74.62	Long Beach	56.17
Akron	1.03	San Diego	70.21	Akron	56.05
Columbus	.96	Long Beach	69.54	Oakland	51.32
Kansas City, Mo.	.94	Birmingham	68.84	San Diego	48.90
Dallas	.92	Akron	68.52	Birmingham	42.74
Omaha	.84	Portland, Ore.	63.70	FORT WORTH	42.17
FORT WORTH	.78	Columbus	62.04	Kansas City	42.01
St. Paul	.72	Oakland	47.60	Columbus	41.28
Memphis	.66	Omaha	46.58	Omaha	39.15
Louisville	.46	Toledo	45.38	San Antonio	33.41
		Indianapolis	14.61	Indianapolis	33.37

Source: U. S. Bureau of the Census, "Compendium of City Government Finances in 1950," Table 13, for information on Public Safety, Libraries, and Health (per capita figures computed): and Bureau of the Census, "Large-City Finances in 1950," Table 21, for per capita figures for Sanitation, Gross Debt, and General Expenditures.

rock garden, while another city may use a smaller amount for playing fields; moreover, one city may maintain adequate swimming and boating facilities, through the construction of a few docks and roped-off areas on a lake, river or ocean, while, to secure similar facilities, another city may need to spend thousands of dollars.

With such limitations in mind, consideration can be given to Table 57 which provides comparisons for specific expenditures for the cities in our 24-city group for 1950. In all probability changes have occurred in these figures since 1950, but most likely the changes have been in the same general direction.

Summary. No attempt has been made here to evaluate the city government of Fort Worth and its functioning in its day-by-day activities. Such an analysis would require intensive study, and is considered beyond the scope of this work. It is well to remember, however, that city governments maintain high levels of efficiency and honesty generally when the bulk of the citizens are intelligent in their demands and interested in the city's activities. In a sense, citizens get the kind of government they deserve.

Other generalizations can be presented. Certainly it is obvious that city government has grown, but possibly less obvious is the fact that the growth has occurred mainly because of the increased complexity of urban life and the demands of citizens. With the greater complexity of urban living, there has developed in the realm of government, as elsewhere, the need for trained and skilled personnel. No longer is it safe or economical to employ persons in purely administrative jobs whose main qualifications are popularity and the proper connections. This certainly is not a denial of democratic ideals, since policy is still determined by elected representatives (council). Rather, it is the recognition that to achieve true representative government, there is the necessity that the functions of government must be performed efficiently.

Chapter IX

THE EXPANSION OF EDUCATION*

As was usually true elsewhere, and particularly in the South, the early schools in Fort Worth were operated privately, on a subscription basis. At the time, many people believed that education should be a private matter, and hence favored private schools. Others felt that education should be the responsibility of the church. Still others were generally indifferent and considered formal education unnecessary for their children. Certainly many felt they should not be taxed to pay for the education of children other than their own.

Not until 1882 was public education established in Fort Worth, first with grade school training, and then a year later with high school training. Since that time tax-supported education through the high school level has continued and has grown to be an important phase of the community's functioning. Along with public schooling, private schools have continued and have provided a significant portion of the community's total educational program. At the present, privately supported schools include parochial schools at the grade, high school, and college level; privately operated kindergartens and nursery schools; one liberal arts college, one university, and two seminaries— as well as many business and other specialized technical training schools and colleges.

Fort Worth has come a long way since the early opposition to public, tax-supported schooling. Gradually, education has become an increasingly important part of community life. Tax support has become an accepted and expected part of the community's education program. Good schools, both public and

---

*Dr. Eldon B. Busby, Assistant Superintendent in the Fort Worth schools, and Mr. S. T. Willis, head of the Child Accounting Department, read this chapter and made suggestions as to content.

private have become a desired goal of local citizens, and they have been willing to pay for such, as witnessed by widespread support for school bond elections. In a very real sense, because of widespread popular support, and as a result of the professionalization of workers, education in the community has become strongly institutionalized.

Early Development of Education. The first private school in the city was opened in 1854 by John Peter Smith. Tuition at the time cost about five dollars per month, with board and room for the teacher being provided by parents. Smith taught a school for three years and then closed it because of poor health. Before the Civil War started, several classes were conducted by wandering tutors, and a few "male and female" schools were established by community action; with the war, all educational activity in the communiy ceased. At the time Smith came to Fort Worth the population of the town was something less than 100. After the war, local residents again thought of the need for schools. The Masonic Hall, built in 1855, was available, but it was in a dilapidated condition. To repair it three local citizens raised seventy-five dollars, bought flour and traded it for East Texas lumber. A Confederate soldier stranded in Dallas was hired as the schoolmaster.[1] Other private schools were soon opened, and in 1878 the first "high school" was started. At about this time the state government entered the field of education, with the payment to the City Council of $2.25 per pupil per year. This money was used for tuition for students who otherwise could not attend the private schools.

As mentioned above, public, tax-supported education was begun in the city in 1882, but not without considerable opposition. According to the Fort Worth *Star-Telegram,*

Tough pioneers founded Fort Worth's present free public school system in 1882. They had to be tough to do it. Not everyone

---

[1] For accounts of early private education in the city, see, Fort Worth *Star-Telegram,* "Fort Worth's First 100 Years," "Community Life," (October 30, 1949); Elden B. Busby, *A Study of Trends and School Building Needs in the City of Fort Worth, Texas* (Fort Worth Board of Education 1951): Anne L. Goerte, *Some Phases of the Development of the Fort Worth, Texas School System* (M. A. Thesis, University of Colorado 1934) available in Texas Christian University Library; Oliver Knight, *Fort Worth: Outpost on the Trinity* (Norman: University of Oklahoma Press, 1953.)

wanted the city, still hardly more than a dusty frontier town, to educate children free . . . The battle started in 1874 and raged eight years. It was fought on street corners, in the city council chambers and in the courts.[2]

The main problem of the time, apparently, was that comparatively few parents could afford to send their children to the private schools. The above quoted source reports a survey of 1878 which showed 1,266 children between the ages of 6 and 17 years, with 409, or nearly one third unable to read or write. Another issue of the time was the widely held belief in the South that education was an individual family responsibility. Between 1830 and 1860 the battle for public schools had been fought and won in the Northern states, but it was not until after the Civil War that a similar struggle occurred in Southern states. However, it should be emphasized that at the state level the fostering of education was recognized as a responsibility. At the time of the Fort Worth struggle for free schools, the state already had laws providing for the establishment of local public schools. The state law permitted localities of 10,000 or more population to operate schools if two thirds of the residents voted for a school tax.[3]

The first school tax election occurred in 1877, with 85 votes for the tax and 5 votes against, but the opponents of public schools argued that two thirds of the property owners had not voted. Another election was held the same year and again the result was in favor of public schools. The first city ordinance establishing public schools was passed August 20, 1878, and on September 1, 1879 six rented school buildings were opened. However, the opponents of the plan appealed to the state attorney-general, and he ruled, because of errors in election procedure, that public funds could not be used for school purposes. A third election to meet the legal objections was held in 1880, with a vote of 425 to 45 in favor of public schools. The final attempt of the opponents occurred when they charged that the population of Fort Worth was less than the necessary 10,000. This question was taken to court, and it was ruled that proof of the city's size would have to be presented. When the City

---

2"Community Life," Fort Worth *Star-Telegram, loc. cit.,* p. 17.
3*Ibid.*

THE EXPANSION OF EDUCATION

245

Council failed to provide the necessary funds for a census, two local men raised the money. The count showed a population of over 11,000, and the citizens readily voted a one percent school tax.

The development of college-level training in Fort Worth, like the lower-school work, followed the pattern fairly common in the South. This pattern included church control and support, plus local financial assistance. This local support developed in part because of the felt need for education, but also because of local pride. At the time, just about every town with any self-respect had at least one college or academy. Since a "college" could be, and often was, opened in a vacant building, it was not too difficult for many communities to have their own colleges. If the school desired its own building, the necessary land usually could be secured from local donors. Certainly this is in sharp contrast to the present financial requirements for maintaining a first-class college or university.[4]

Fort Worth's first college was established in 1881 by the Northern Methodist church and was named Texas Wesleyan College. It later (1889) became Fort Worth University; at its peak it had a student body of 900, and a faculty of 47, with schools of medicine, law, art, music, oratory, pedagogy, and a liberal arts college. Apparently because of a decline of students and financial support, it was closed in 1911 and moved to Oklahoma. The present Texas Wesleyan College was started in 1891 by the Southern Methodist Church, and was first known as Polytechnic College. In the beginning it was co-educational; but with the founding of Southern Methodist University in Dallas in 1911, the name was changed first to Wesley Woman's College and then to Texas Woman's College. In 1935 the col-

---

[4]The present Texas Christian University was started at Thorp Springs in a three-story rock building, which was sold to the founders for $9,000, including the adjoining land. In contrast, two of the newer buildings on the present Texas Christian University campus cost over $2,000,000 each.

lege again became co-educational, and the name was changed to the present Texas Wesleyan College. Throughout the changes in name and function the college has maintained its same geographical location, which at the time of founding was approximately 4 miles from the city limits. The surrounding area has long since become a part of the city, but is still called Polytechnic or "Poly," locally.

Other colleges soon followed. By 1910 Fort Worth was a thriving metropolis. Its population had increased from 26,668 in 1890 to 73,312 in 1910. Apparently, community leaders were looking for new ways to expand the city. This ambition included not only the search for new industries, but also, further expansion of the community's facilities for higher education. At least partly through local efforts, three schools at the college level were opened in the city in 1910. These were Texas Christian University, the Southwestern Baptist Seminary, and Our Lady of Victory Academy. Texas Christian University was started in Thorp Springs, later was moved to Waco, and then after a disastrous fire in 1910, was moved to Fort Worth, in part at least because Fort Worth promised 56 acres for a campus, $200,000 in cash, and the assurance that necessary utility and street car connections would be extended to the campus.[5] A similar pattern occurred with the Southwestern Baptist Seminary. Founded in 1906 in conjunction with Baylor University at Waco, the seminary's move to Fort Worth was made partly because of a desire for greater independence, but also because of gifts of land and money from Fort Worth residents. Our Lady of Victory Academy and College was opened in 1910 by the Sisters of St. Mary of Namur to provide teacher training and college work for girls. This same Catholic order had started St. Ignatius Academy for girls in 1885. After the beginning of Our Lady of Victory, St. Ignatius concentrated on grade school work. More recently, in 1937, under the leadership of the First Baptist Church, the Fundamental Baptist Bible Institute was organized. Later, the name of the school was changed to its present one, Bible Baptist Seminary. In addition to the above, Fort

[5]See Colby D. Hall, *History of Texas Christian University: A College of the Cattle Frontier* (Fort Worth: Texas Christian University Press, 1947), p. 144, ff.

Worth has had the more or less usual number of business and other specialized colleges, many of which lasted only a few years.

Recent Development of Public Education.[6] Like other large cities, Fort Worth has been faced for a number of years with a growing school-age population, an increase in educational needs, and increasing costs. Since 1930 four bond issues have been voted to meet the increased building needs.[7] In 1933, the value of school property, based on original cost, was $7,025,458. By June, 1955, the total value, based on original cost, had increased to $31,788,278.00. From 1931 to 1955 the number of scholastics increased from 36,796 to 62,036.[8]

During recent years comparisons between total number of scholastics, total school enrollment, and average daily attendance show considerable variations.[9] These trends are shown in Figure 47. The variations between total enrollment and the school census counts can be explained in part by the fact that from 8 to 10 percent of the scholastics attend parochial and private schools; then too, many of the seventeen-year-olds who are counted in the census have already graduated from high school. Probably the recent increase in the ratio of scholastics enrolled and in average daily attendance, as compared to total

---

[6]Statistical material in this section has been secured from Busby, *op. cit.*, Chapters III, V; and, *A Study of Population Trends and Schools Building Needs in the City of Fort Worth, Texas. 1954-55-1965-66*, prepared under supervision of Eldon B. Busby. Dr. Busby is assistant superintendent of the Fort Worth Public Schools. The information for the school year, 1954-55 was supplied by Mrs. Margaret Duncan, of the administrative staff.

[7]The amount of these issues and the year in which the bond election was held are as follows: 1935—$4,000,000; 1948—$8,500,000; 1952—$14,990,000; 1956—$20,000,000.

[8]The number is determined by a house-to-house canvass, as required by state law.

[9]"Total scholastics" refers to all youths between the ages of six and under 18, as revealed by the annual school census; "scholastic enrollment" includes all youths enrolled in the public schools; "average daily attendance" figures are determined on the basis of the number of students actually in the classroom. Each student absence for each school day is excluded in average daily attendance computations. Thus, since school expenses are fixed (determined by total enrollment), and since part of the school system's allocation from state funds is based on average daily attendance, it is advantageous to have the students who are enrolled, in actual attendance.

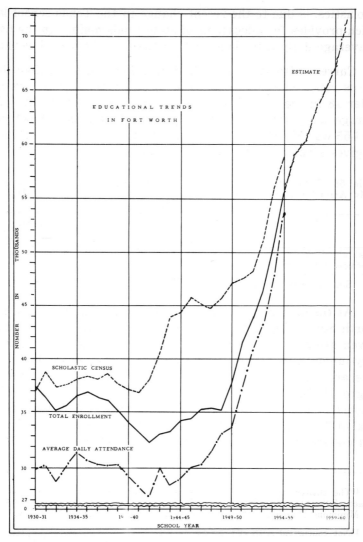

Figure 47. Trends in Total Enrollment, Scholastic Population, and Average Daily Attendance, 1930-31 to 1954-55, and Estimates of Total Enrollment, 1955-56 to 1960-61, Fort Worth Independent School District. (Original data from "A Study of Population Trends and School Building Needs in the City of Fort Worth, Texas," 1951, and "Population Trends and School Building Needs in the City of Fort Worth, Texas, 1954-1955 to 1965-1966," both reports prepared by the adminitrative staff of the school district for the Board of Education.)

scholastics, is due to the recent change in the Texas school law, which provides for allocations of state funds mainly on the basis of average daily attendance rather than on the school census.[10]

Current Structure of Public Education. In 1955, the school census reported 62,036 scholastics between the ages of six and under 18 in the Fort Worth Independent School District.[11] The average daily attendance for all students for the school year 1954-55 was 50,656, or 90.8 percent of the total enrollment. Table 58 gives similar information by race.

Table 58. Total Public School Enrollment, and Public School Average Daily Attendance, by Race for Fort Worth Independent School District: 1954-1955*

	White		Negro	
	Number	Percent	Number	Percent
Total enrollment	48,106	100.0	7,650	100.0
Average daily attendance	44,132	91.7	6,524	85.2

*Source: See note of reference 6 in this chapter.

At the present time, there are 93 public schools in the Fort Worth School District. Sixty-eight of the total are elementary, eleven are at the junior high level, two are classed as elementary-junior high, three as elementary-junior-senior high, and nine are senior high schools. Of the total number, 13 are for Negro students, one of which is a senior high school.[12] The schools in use at the present time (January, 1956) provide a total of 2,199 classrooms. The information for number of schools and classrooms in current use by race is given in Table 59. In

[10]The change in methods for the allocation of state funds was established by an act of the State Legislature in 1948. The new provisions were incorporated in the Minimum Foundation Act, popularly known as the Gilmer-Aikin law.

[11]Not concurrent with city limits.

[12]There are eleven state-approved parochial and private schools. Nine of the parochial schools are Catholic. These are: St. Mary's, St. Alice, St. Ignatius, Holy Name, San Jose, Mt. Carmel, Our Lady of Victory, Laneri, and Our Lady of Mercy for Negroes. Our Lady of Victory provides training from the first grade through two years of College; Laneri provides high school training. The remainder give only grade school training. There is one Seventh Day Adventist school, and one private, non-sectarian school—the Brous Private School—the latter providing training through the second grade. There are also many facilities which give training and care below the first grade level.

Table 59. Schools and Classrooms in the Fort Worth Public School District by Type and Race, January, 1956*

Type	White		Negro	
	Schools	Classrooms	Schools	Classrooms
Elementary	62	1,213	6	86
Junior high	11	373	—	—
Senior high	8	311	1	40
Elementary-junior high	—	—	2	80
Elementary-junior-senior high	—	—	3	96
Totals	81	1,897	12	302
UNDER CONSTRUCTION:	1	20	3	42

*Source: See note of reference number 6 in this chapter.

addition, four schools are currently under construction and will provide an additional 63 classrooms.

By combining information given in Tables 58 and 59, a clearer picture of the ratio of students to classrooms can be secured. This is shown in the following tabulation, which provides the average number of students per classroom in terms of total enrollment and in terms of average daily attendance:

	White	Negro
Total enrollment per classroom	28.1	28.8
Average daily attendance per classroom	23.3	21.6

To manage its school system the qualified citizens of the Fort Worth Independent School District elect a Board of Education of seven members who serve without pay for a period of six years. The board is charged with planning and supervision of the school system. It selects a Superintendent of Schools, and must approve his selection of administrators, assistants, and the teachers of the system. For the school year 1955-56 the total number of classroom teachers in the school ystem is 2,088.

Teaching Staff (1955-1956). Approximately 60 percent of the employees in the Fort Worth school system are classroom teachers. Their salaries account for approximately 77 percent of the school budget. As is true elsewhere, the actual salary of the individual teacher is determined by amount of education and teaching experience. For classroom teachers, the salary schedule ranges from $3,252 to $5,052, for teachers with a B. A. degree, and from $3,452 to $5,252 for those with an M. A. degree. For a Ph.D. degree the maximum is $5,452. Normally, it takes 18 years in the system to move from the minimum to the maximum salary, at $100.00 per year increment. In terms of educational training, 36 percent of the teaching staff have completed graduate training with either Master of Arts or Master of Education degrees. Only 20 teachers in the local system hold no collegiate degrees.[13]

The Financial Picture. Although it is obviously true that money alone will not produce a school system which successfully meets the needs of children and of the community, it is also true that the level of achievement of a particular school system is related to availability of money for equipment (including teaching aids), salaries, and for capital development (buildings).[14] One of the measures commonly used to measure the financial pattern of a school system is the per capita expenditure for current expense based on average daily attendance.[15] For all students in the Fort Worth system in 1954-55, the per capita expenditure was $238.59. For the same school year the per capita expenditure for all Negro students was $254.33. The higher per capita expenditure for Negro students was in part due to fixed expenditures in areas of low student enrollment. In contrast, the per capita expenditure for all students in 1937-38 was less than $80, and for Negro students, less than $50. As is generally true, the per capita expenditure for senior high school students was higher than for the other two levels. For

---

13Trades and industries teachers.

14There is a tendency on the part of some people to develop considerable nostalgia about the "little red schoolhouse" of the past, with its limited equipment and its "dedicated" teachers, and to point to the great men who received their formal education in that way. There is the question here as to whether men became great because of, or in spite of, the kind of training they received. Certainly most people would agree that the "little red schoolhouse" could not meet present-day educational needs.

15For limitations of this measure, see note of reference number 17 in this chapter.

the 1954-55 school year in the Fort Worth system, the variations in per capita expenditures for all students by levels were as follows:

Senior high $286.51
Junior high 241.00
Elementary 221.95

Another way of considering school finances is in terms of sources of income, and ways of expenditure. For the 1954-55 school year, the total expenditures of the Fort Worth School District were approximately $13,000,000. Almost half (46.8 percent) of the total budget was secured from the state Minimum Foundation Act program; local taxes accounted for 39.9 percent of the total school budget. Information on the income, and the basis for expenditures is presented in Table 60.[16]

Table 60. Estimated Income and Expenditures for Fort Worth Independent School District, 1954-55 School Year*

INCOME:
Local taxes ....$ 5,336,951.00
Misc. sales, rentals, tuition, fees 310,000.00
State foundation program fund 6,253,034.28
Federal grant, children of federal employees 350,000.00
Budget surplus 1,114,790.69

$13,364,775.97

EXPENDITURES:
General instruction $10,284,762.00
Auxiliary services 196,041.00
Administration 348,919.00
Physical plant operation 1,076,244.00
Physical plant maintenance and repair 557,635.00
Equipment 243,648.00
Fixed charges, insurance 35,336.00
Debt services, interest 3,750,00
Unallocated balance 618,440.97

$13,364,775.97

*Source: see note of reference number 6 in this chapter.

Level of Current Education. Perhaps the most significant educational fact about Fort Worth is that, in comparison with the past, more persons are getting more formal educational

[16]Currently (January, 1956), local school taxation is based on a levy of $1.17 per $100 assessed valuation. The total net assessed valuation of the school district currently is $567,000,000, with approximately $20,000,000 assessed valuation outside Fort Worth city limits.

training, either through the local schools or elsewhere. In the ten years from 1940 to 1950, the median school year completed for persons 25 years of age and over increased from 9.9 to 11.1. That is, in 1950, half of the persons 25 years of age and over had completed 11 or more years of schooling, and half had completed less. For persons under the age of 25 the median school year would be higher. Table 61 shows the distribution of the

Table 61. Years of Schooling Completed, Persons 25 Years of Age and Over, Fort Worth, 1940, 1950*

Years Completed	1940		1950	
	Number	Percent	Number	Percent
None completed	1,879	1.7	2,240	1.3
1 to 4 years	8,394	7.8	10,370	6.2
5 or 6	12,824	11.9	14,035	8.4
7 or 8	23,886	22.2	29,660	17.8
1 to 3 years high school	22,628	21.0	36,015	21.6
4 years high school	21,131	19.0	38,905	23.3
1 to 3 years college	9,961	9.2	18,365	11.1
4 or more years college	6,544	6.1	13,140	7.9
Not reported	545	0.1	5,080	2.4

*Sources: U. S. Bureau of the Census, *16th Census of the United States: 1940* Vol. II, *Characteristics of the Population,,* Part 6, p. 1038, and, *U. S. Census of Population: 1950,* Vol. II, *Characteristics of the Population,* Part 43, Texas, Chapter B, Table 34.

Fort Worth adult population by years of school completed for 1940 and 1950. In Fort Worth, as in most other large cities, the median school year completed was higher for adult males. Indicative of this was the fact that in 1950 more than nine percent of the adult males had completed four or more years of college, as compared with 6.8 percent of the adult females.

Comparisons. While financial and other comparisons between cities have certain obvious advantages, certain limitations to such comparisons must be recognized. The usefulness and limitations of the available per capita data are summarized in a publication of the Federal Security Agency:

Data on per-pupil expenditures in city school systems may be looked at from a fiscal viewpoint—considering the figures merely as amounts spent per pupil in average daily attendance—the figures for the different city school systems in this report are reasonably comparable, to the extent that the different systems make use of standardized accounting definitions and procedures. From an educational point of view, however, the figures are less comparable. Such circumstantial factors as the following affect the current expenditure per pupil in average daily attendance: Climate; local living costs; age and state of repair of school buildings; stability of the number of children in attendance daily; proportion of children in elementary vs. secondary grades; and proportion of teachers in lower vs. upper portions of the salary scale. Despite the influence of such factors (which should always be taken into account in evaluating the expenditures of any particular city), it still remains true that, by and large, the level of educational expenditure in the typical city school system is determined chiefly by the *scope* and *quality* of its educational facilities, and services. Naturally, a school system that offers kindergarden facilities, a well-diversified curriculum (including the fine arts, and vocational or pre-vocational opportunities), special classes for exceptional children, appropriate playground and gymnasium facilities, a well-trained counseling service, a sanitary cafeteria, and adequate health services, will require more funds than a school system without such advantages. Similarly, a school system which attracts and retains the services of competent, experienced teachers, and makes use of the best teaching aids (such as educational films, excursions, and summer camps) must expend more than other school systems. In general, then, it is fair to say that the current-expenditure figures in this circular have some value as a guide to the scope and adequacy of the educational programs in the various city school systems.[17]

With such limitations in mind, we can use several sets of measures which indicate inter-city differences. The first is the median school year completed as of 1950, for persons 25 years of age and over. This, of course, shows the educational level of only the adult population, and because of widespread migration and changes from past patterns, reveals little as to the level of current school systems. A similar measure gives the percent of the adult population which had four or more years of college.[18] A third measure which is revealing as to current attitudes towards education provides the percent of persons in the 14-17 age group enrolled in school in 1950. A fourth measure, and probably the most widely used for comparative purposes, is the per capita expenditure (current expense) per student in average daily attendance.

---

[17]"Expenditure Per Pupil in City School Systems, 1950-51," Federal Security Agency, Office of Education, Circular 337, p. 3.

[18]If it is assumed that there is a significant relationship between level of formal education of the adult population and awareness of the problems of urban living, then these first two measures are of importance. That is, it would be expected that college graduates would have a greater awareness of the need for protection against disease than would a group with little or no formal education.

Among the larger Texas cities, Dallas ranked highest for median school years completed, with a median of 11.6; San Antonio was lowest, with 9.0. For percentage of adult population with four or more years of college and for percentages of youths, ages 14-17, in school, Austin and San Antonio ranked highest and lowest respectively. Such information for the seven largest Texas cities in rank order by median school year completed is as follows:[19]

City	Median school year	4 or more years college	Percent 14-17 in school
Dallas	11.6	8.2	79.2
Austin	11.5	14.1	83.3
Fort Worth	11.1	7.9	81.0
Houston	10.4	8.2	82.4
Corpus Christi	9.8	7.8	77.4
El Paso	9.5	7.5	79.6
San Antonio	9.0	5.8	73.8

Among the comparable cities in the United States, in terms of median school year completed, Seattle, Long Beach, and Denver ranked highest, with figures of 12.1, Newark, New Jersey was lowest, with 8.7. For percent of the adult population with four or more years college, Denver was highest, with a percentage of 10.9, and Jersey City lowest, with 3.7. Long Beach had the highest percentage of its youth, ages 14-17 in school, with a figure of 95.5, while San Antonio was lowest, with 73.8. Table 62 gives these three types of data for the 24 comparable cities.

Per capita yearly expenditure based on average daily attendance for the school year 1951-52[20] varied among the 24 comparable cities from a high of $355.02, for Newark, New Jersey, to a low of $136.80, for Memphis, Tennessee. Fort Worth ranked 18th in the group, with a per capita expenditure of $208.86. Such information for all the cities is shown graphically by rank order in Figure 48.

---

[19]U. S. Bureau of the Census, *U. S. Census of Population, 1950*, Vol. II, *Characteristics of the Population*, Part 43, Texas, Chapter B, Tables 10, 34.

[20]Latest year for which data are available.

Table 62. Selected Educational Data for Comparable United States Cities
1950*

| City | Persons 25 years and over | | Persons 14 to 17 |
	Median school year	4 or more years of college percent	Percentage in school
Denver	12.1	10.9	85.2
Long Beach	12.1	7.2	95.5
Seattle	12.1	10.5	91.3
San Diego	12.0	8.2	85.2
Portland	11.8	8.5	94.1
Dallas	11.6	8.2	79.2
Oakland	11.5	7.8	92.7
Kansas City	11.4	7.0	82.3
Omaha	11.4	7.0	87.6
Columbus	11.1	8.0	86.8
FORT WORTH	11.1	7.9	81.0
Indianapolis	10.6	7.8	84.2
St. Paul	10.6	7.7	89.6
Akron	10.4	6.0	91.4
Houston	10.4	8.2	82.4
Toledo	9.9	5.4	91.5
Memphis	9.7	5.6	81.9
Rochester	9.6	5.8	89.3
Atlanta	9.5	7.1	78.5
Birmingham	9.4	5.4	84.1
San Antonio	9.0	5.8	73.8
Jersey City	8.9	3.7	81.3
Louisville	8.9	5.5	82.9
Newark	8.7	3.9	83.4

*Sources: For median school year, and 14-17 age group, U. S. Bureau of the Census, *U. S. Census of Population: 1950*, Vol. II, *Characteristic of the Population*, Part 1, U. S. Summary, Table 86: for college percentages, see respective State reports, Table 34.

Future Development. All the evidence available suggests that Fort Worth will continue to grow for a number of years. While the current high birth rate may not be maintained, the inescapable conclusion is that the city's educational needs will continue to grow. One estimate suggests that between 1955 and 1960 the total enrollment will increase from 55,551 to over 72,000. For the same period it is estimated that 517 additional classrooms and the same number of additional teachers will be needed.[21] Essentially the same information, for a year later,

21A Study of Population Trends and School Building Needs in the City of Fort Worth, Texas, 1954-55 to 1965-66, *loc. cit.*, pp. 18-19.

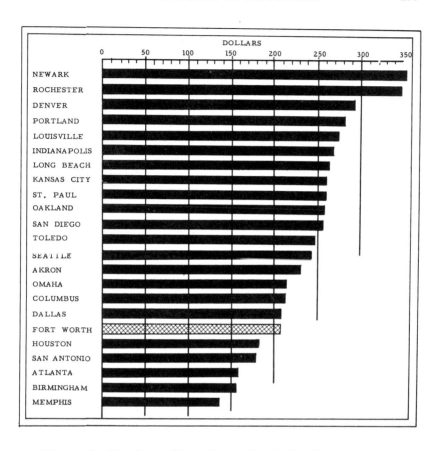

Figure 48. Per Capita Expenditures for Public Education in 24 Comparable Cities, 1951-52. Per Capita Expenditure Based on Total Expenditures for Current Expense, and Number of Students in Average Daily Attendance. (Original data from U. S. Office of Education, "Current Expenditures Per Pupil in City School Systems, 1951-52," Circular 371, 1953.)

is shown in graphic form in Figure 49. One of the difficult aspects of the problem is the determination of where the growth will occur. Wrong guesses mean a surplus of classrooms in one district and a lack of them in another. Moreover, the district which needs additional elementary classrooms at one time may have a surplus six to eight years later. One illustration will suggest the kind of problem. Peter Smith Elementary School, built several years ago and located in the downtown business district,

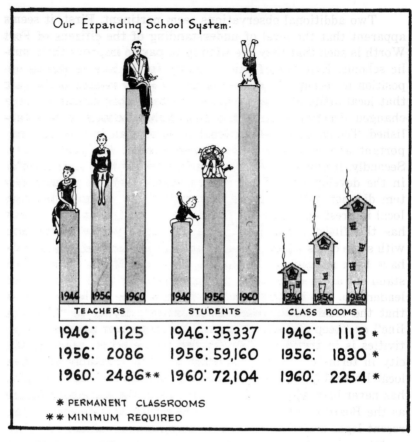

Figure 49. Educational Trends in Fort Worth: Number of Students Enrolled, Number of Classrooms, and Number of Teachers for 1946 and 1956, and Estimated Needs in 1960. From *Fort Worth*, official publication of the Chamber of Commerce, March, 1956, p. 22.)

has 18 classrooms and can handle over 500 students. At the present time, the average daily attendance is under 300. There is no evidence that the student load will increase in the future. To meet this type of problem, the school board is today planning not in terms of a peak load, as was the case in the past, but in terms of a long-time average student load. For short-time needs which are considered excessive, the school board has adopted a policy of using temporary construction, which can be moved elsewhere once the excessive need disappears.

Two additional observations seem pertinent. First, it seems apparent that the level of understanding of the citizens of Fort Worth is such that they are willing to pay to improve their public schools. Evidence of this is shown in the lack of strong opposition to recent school bond issues. Closely related is the fact that local attitudes toward tax-supported public education have changed drastically since the first public schools were established. Today, public education has become an increasingly important and generally unquestioned part of the local culture. Secondly, it appears that local leadership has been instrumental in the development of the local system—that the present system did not merely emerge, but rather was nurtured through local interest and support. This is not to imply that Fort Worth has the finest school system in the land; yet in comparison with some cities where, through lack of local interest, the schools have been allowed to deteriorate, the Fort Worth system does stand out as an example of the importance of local interest and leadership. An integral feature of this type of leadership is that the local school board is not merely trying to "hold the line" or "keep the schools open;" an important part of its activities is in trying to plan for the future school needs of the city in terms of future population growth. Probably effective local leadership, with the necessary intelligence and foresight, has never been so essential as it will be in the immediate future as the Board of Education seeks the proper adjustments to the recent legal decisions relating to segrgation in education. And an integral part of the necessary leadership will be an informed public opinion.

CHAPTER X

WHAT MAKES A CITY GOOD?

"Our Fair City."[1] Possibly since the beginning of urban life men have pointed with pride to their own town. Local pride and patriotism have been a common belief of urban dwellers from time immemorial, and many have agreed with Saint Paul in concluding, "I am a citizen of no mean city." In the United States today one hears from the lips of the residents of almost every city something similar to the following summary statement:

> Our city is noted as a city of fine residences, good schools, and strong churches—a good place to live. From thousands of sources one hears this theme is some form. Local citizens point with pride to their fine school buildings, their beautiful new auditorium, their expensive stadium. Or they take their visitor along tree-lined streets of magnificent residences, through their spacious parks.[2]

Certainly the characteristics mentioned in the above statement are desirable and may be visible evidence of a community's awareness for the welfare of its citizens. But those who are interested in an objective evaluation of community life must go further. They must determine whether the fine buildings are merely a facade behind which lie less desirable conditions. For citizens interested in the nature of their community, there must be the recognition that the welfare of the whole community is affected by the living conditions of each part of it. Conversely, individual human welfare is a function of the general welfare.

---

[1]See Robert S. Allen, ed., *Our Fair City* (New York: the Vanguard Press, 1947), for what the editor believes is a true picture of the vice and corruption of American cities. The defect of such "muckraking" is the danger that the uninformed reader will assume that an entire city functions at its lowest level.

[2]A. L. Porterfield and R. H. Talbert, *Crime, Suicide and Social Well-Being* (Fort Worth: Leo Potishman Foundation, 1948), p. vii.

The evidence which is available suggests that in reality some citizens do live in mean cities. As one writer has concluded:

> But as a matter of fact many of our cities are mean in their provisions for health, comfort, education, recreation and other features of a good life. This is partly because of lack of resources, but it is partly because their citizens do not know what a city can be and should be, and what some American cities have made themselves and do not know their own city in comparison with others.[3]

Other students of American community life have come to the same conclusion, that there are in reality significant differences in the quality of living available in different urban areas.

Basic Questions. Such conclusions as to the nature of American cities lead logically to at least three basic questions. First, is it correct to conclude that some areas are in reality better places to live? Second, is it possible for individual citizens or groups of citizens to improve their city, or is improvement or degeneration a function of basic influences beyond the control of the individual community? And finally, is it possible to agree as to what makes a city good? The writer is of the opinion that the answer to each of these three questions must be given in the affirmative. However, it must be recognized that objective measures are essential in working toward an adequate answer to the third question.

The Need for Objective Measures. An adequate understanding of a city's functioning, and proper consideration of its potential for growth and development, require objective measures which will reveal present conditions and future possibilities. That is, the study of community life must seek to create an honest balance sheet of accomplishments and failures for the present, and an awareness of future needs. While many surveys of this type have been attempted for individual cities, there are relatively few studies which provide the basis for comparative analysis. Three such attempts can be briefly considered. The oldest of the three comparative studies was done by E. L. Thorndike and published under the title, *Your City*.[4] Thorndike stud-

---

[3]E. L. Thorndike, *Your City* (New York: Harcourt, Brace and Company, 1939), p. 7.

[4]*Ibid.*

ied 310 cities in the United States, and used some 297 measures to arrive at what he calls the "general goodness of cities." Although Thorndike's approach emphasized material accomplishments, it does reveal significant differences between cities in terms of such basic needs as education, health, library facilities, and similar basic institutional needs. Most recently Robert C. Angell has attempted to measure the relative "moral integration of cities."[5] For Angell, the major factors differentiating cities revolve around the quality of local leadership and the willingness of citizens of individual cities to work together for their general welfare.[6]

Still another attempt to provide qualitative differences between cities has been made by Austin L. Porterfield in developing what he calls an Index of Urban Integration.[7] Basic to Porterfield's index of community quality is a composite measure labeled ACID. Each of the letters refers to a combination of several series of data. The A portion of the composite index measures the degree of anomie; the C is composed of various sub-series and provides a measure of conflict between rival groups; the I provides a relative measure of interpersonal disaffection; and the D gives a measure of the influence of depressed classes. Porterfield thinks of the composite ACID index as representing a continuum along which individual cities would fall. In each of these attempts to differentiate between cities, although each has utilized different measures, there is the common purpose of seeking to determine the relative goodness of cities.

The differences between the measures briefly outlined above suggest some of the difficulties in arriving at general agreement as to what a city should have. A great majority of citizens would agree as to the necessity of good streets, sanitary

---

[5]Robert C. Angell. "The Moral Integration of American Cities," *American Journal of Sociology*, 57 (July, 1952), part 2 (140 pages).

[6]Angell's concept of leadership is presented at the end of this chapter.

[7]Austin L. Porterfield and Robert H. Talbert, "Crime in Southern Cities," in Rupert B. Vance and Nicholas J. Demerath, (eds.), *The Urban South*, (Chapel Hill: University of North Carolina Press, 1954), pp. 180-203.

sewers, and similar material accomplishments. Less general agreement would be achieved in deciding what other roles the city government should play in community improvement. Thus, there would be serious disagreement as to whether public authority has certain types of responsibilities, such as that of providing low-rent housing units for low-income families. In a less obvious way, there would be some disagreement as to the proper asthetic goals for the community, or what should be the goals in the field of morality.

Even so, while such disagreements do exist, they do not make impossible the task of urban improvements. In line with this idea, the following list of desired goals is presented. This listing is intended to suggest the basic needs which will make the urban community a fit place in which to live.[8] The basic needs would include the following:

1. A stable economy.

2. An educational system which successfully transmits the necessary skills and understanding for mature living in our society.

3. A program of health and sanitation which successfully utilizes the current knowledge of medicine and science.

4. Stable family life.

5. Effective religious experiences.

6. A program of recreation which is both re-creative and conducive to the development of mature adults.

7. A physical structure which maintains maximum standards for safety, convenience, and the aesthetic needs of the people.

8. A program for housing the population which will recognize the needs of people.

Admittedly, these are only broad generalizations. Yet they are believed to be the basic requirements for effective community life. They are intended to provide goals which will give direction to action somewhat as a map shows us which way we want to go. And like a map, they suggest ways which can be

[8]The editors of *Life* Magazine take an extreme point of view and seem to condemn American cities in general. They conclude, "Belatedly, U. S. cities are waking up to the fact that they are scarcely fit to live in. Not even counting slums, cities have become so rundown that few areas are inviting enough to keep residents from fleeing to the suburbs." See "A City Shows How to Fight Decay" (March 12, 1956), p. 62.

travelled—with effective leadership. Actually, of course, there are available more detailed "maps" or "blueprints" for each of the generalizations listed above.[9] The major problem at the present is in making the general public aware of the needs for the future and familiar with the knowledge which is available.

As this is written the Gruen Plan for the development of Fort Worth has been introduced.[10] This plan call for major changes in the central business district, and related planning for the entire city and metropolitan area. For the downtown business area the plan suggests:

1. A freeway loop around the district (along Henderson, Belknap, Pecan-Jones, and linking with freeway already planned along Lancaster).

2. Construction of tunnels under the present street system to handle freight, cargo and garbage services for the downtown stores, shops and buildings.

4. Elimination of all surface vehicular traffic inside the freeway loop, converting that area for parkways, pedestrian use, and additional commercial use.[11]

Whether the Gruen plan or some other is adopted, it does emphasize the necessity of planning. In the opinion of the writer the alternative (no plan) will lead inevitably to chaos. A part of such planning must recognize the interrelatedness of Fort Worth with its county of location; in addition, in this instance, no plan for Fort Worth and Tarrant County can succeed without recognition of the increasing interdependence between Fort

---

[9]For examples of fairly complete plans, the following are illustrative: Austin L. Porterfield, *Youth in Trouble* (Fort Worth: Leo Potishman Foundation, 1946) Ch. 6, "Why Not Organize the Community for the Benefit of Youth and Parents?"; Austin L. Porterfield and Robert H. Talbert, *Mid-Century Crime in Our Culture* (Fort Worth: Leo Potishman Foundation, 1954); Ch. 7 (by Porterfield) "Charter for Delinquents and Their Parents Versus the Tradition of Blame and Punishment."; Howard E. Jensen, "Juvenile Behavior, Its Background and Treatment," (available from the Fort Worth Community Council); and, Austin L. Porterfield, *Wait The Withering Rain?* (Fort Worth: Leo Potishman Foundation, 1953).

[10]Conceived by Victor Gruen and Associates. The study of Fort Worth and its future needs by Gruen and his associates was instigated and financed by the Texas Electric Service Company as a public service. See Fort Worth *Star-Telegram*, March 11, 1956 (Sunday edition) and Fort Worth *Press*, March 11, 1956 (Sunday edition).

[11]See Fort Worth *Star-Telegram*, (evening edition) April 3, 1956. This article is one of several appearing in both the morning and evening editions of the *Star-Telegram* dealing with the Gruen Plan.

Worth, Dallas, the other cities in the two counties, and the larger hinterland area.

The Fort Worth-Dallas Area. It must be apparent that Fort Worth, or any other city, as a political entity cannot develop adequately without close reference to its metropolitan area. As we have mentioned previously, the city and its hinterland are inter-dependently related.

In addition, Fort Worth is in the somewhat unique position of being physically close to a larger city in a region where cities of metropolitan status do not otherwise exist. That is, ignoring local pride and competition, the Fort Worth-Dallas (or, Dallas-Fort Worth) area is rapidly becoming, for all but political purposes, a common socio-economic fact. Although at the present there are many conditions restricting sincere cooperation between the two cities, it seems apparent that in the future the results of cooperative planning and united action will far outweigh the results that could be achieved through competition and conflict. The fact of this need for the future has been underscored in an editorial in the Fort Worth *Star-Telegram* under the title, "Intercounty Planning:"

> Says the Dallas Morning News editorially: 'Now that Dallas and Tarrant Counties have become so largely urban, planning for the two-county area has become imperative.' We concur, and we can cite a current example of the need.
>
> Grand Prairie officials appeared before the State Highway Commission this week to seek extension to their city of a proposed four-lane highway from Fort Worth to Arlington. On the basis of cursory judgment, the extension appears logical and useful. If there were adequate area planning, we would know for certain, because the traffic needs of the entire area would have been surveyed and charted, with the needs of one segment related to the needs of all others.
>
> Piecemeal planning, with one town or city looking only to its own shortrange interests, would be out. And if the extension of the proposed Fort Worth-Arlington highway to Grand Prairie was a meritorious project, fitting into the overall plan, the Grand Prairie plea to the Highway Commission would be presented and supported by a delegation representing the entire area. It would be presented as part of an integrated plan, carefully thought out, and not as an isolated project.
>
> A start toward forming a two-county planning body was made at a meeting at Grand Prairie early this week of representatives of a dozen Tarrant and Dallas County cities and towns. The body will be only unofficial and advisory, but it can serve a highly use-

ful purpose if it embraces all the municipalities in the two-county
area and is given proper support.[12]

In the past, competition between the two cities has probably been generally productive. In the future, however, because of the increasing socio-economic interrelatedness, there appears to be the requirement of cooperation. If this is a correct
analysis, then the effective leadership of the present in both
cities will begin to lay the foundations which could lead to a
metropolitan area of first-grade importance in the United States.
The alternative appears to be that if bitter competition should
continue the adversaries would destroy each other or seriously injure each other in the process.

It appears apparent, because of the nature of the situation, that in the future Fort Worth and Dallas will grow closer
together physically. Reference to the pattern of development in
Dallas and Tarrant Counties, as shown in Figure 50, emphasizes the increasing inter-dependence of the two metropolitan
areas. Already the Dallas city limits extend to the Tarrant
County line, while the Fort Worth city limits, at the Fort Worth
International Airport, touch the Dallas county line. Much of
the industrial growth of the future will likely be in between the
two cities. It seems essential that a two-county planning group,
as mentioned in the editorial, can be not only useful, but is absolutely essential if the area is to avoid the waste inherent in
haphazard development.

Summary. In presenting the material in this book the writer has had several purposes in mind. One has been that of
showing the process of community development, as well as the
process of development of particular community structures.
The second purpose has been to provide facts which will make
the community more meaningful to the average citizen. A third
purpose has been to emphasize the role of effective leadership, or
the lack of it, in the community's development. With regard
to this third purpose, it has been suggested that leadership functions on various levels. Apparent in this emphasis on the role
of leadership has been the conclusion that the people of a community can, within limits, affect the direction of community
change and development.

[12]Fort Worth *Star-Telegram* (morning edition), February 24, 1956.

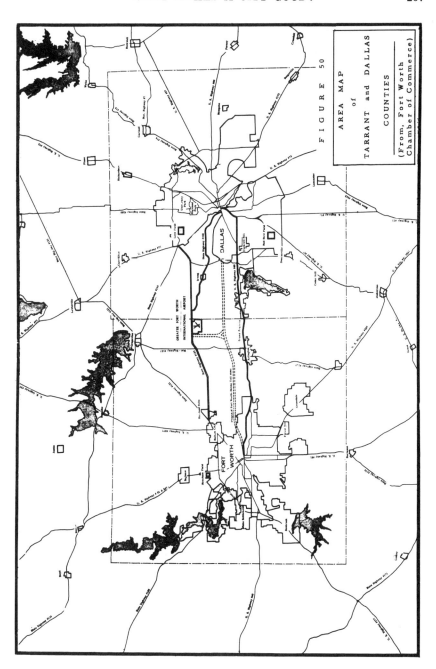

FIGURE 50

AREA MAP
of
TARRANT and DALLAS
COUNTIES

(From, Fort Worth
Chamber of Commerce)

Concerning effective leadership, Robert C. Angell's conclusions as to the nature of the "optimal leadership" group are pertinent. For him this group would include the following:

1. Composed of well-educated persons.
2. Composed of those whose original involvement in community affairs sprang from their own interest, the involvement of their friends, or the nature of their profession.
3. Widely representative of the socioeconomic groups within the city.
4. Made up in somewhat equal proportions of those who were born in the city, those who were born elsewhere but have lived in the community for a long time, and those who have lived in the community a decade or so.
5. Composed of those who have had enough contacts with other segments of the population to enable them to understand their points of view (social realism).
6. Marked by congeniality but not "cliquishness."
7. Composed of those who realize the importance of effort and informal organization in overcoming public apathy toward community problems.[13]

In emphasizing the role of effective leadership in the development of Fort Worth, there has been no intention to suggest that other factors were of no importance, or that leadership can accomplish miracles. Rather, the conclusion is that local action has been one of the forces in the growth of the city and in its internal development. Moreover, it should be emphasized, the effectiveness of leadership has varied with the situation, restricted or limited by the cultural context in which it has operated and by the abilities of the individuals involved. Included in the meaning of leadership as used herein would be the work of those individuals who were instrumental or had an influence in the addition of new primary economic activities; but, in addition, there would be the work of the hundreds of individuals who gave of their time and money to promote internal developments. Leadership, then, is the ability (within the limits of the cultural context) to translate ideas and goals into action— to arouse awareness of felt needs, to crystalize the required public opinion, to engender the necessary followship, and to carry through to the achievement of the desired ends. Later generations may conclude that past leadership was misdirected but such hindsight does not negate the role of leadership in socio-cultural change.

[13]Angell, *op. cit.*, pp. 108-109.

INDEX

ACTION (American Council to Improve Our Neighborhoods), 168.
Age-sex differentials, Fort Worth tract areas, 80-82.
Aircraft manufacture, importance of to Fort Worth, 132-133.
"All American Cities," 12.
Allen, Frances, 220.
Allen, Robert S., 260.
All-Saints Hospital, 195, 200.
American Medical Association, 198, 200.
American Red Cross, 219.
Anderson, C. Arnold, 222.
Anderson, Nels, 166.
Angell, Robert C., 13, 222, 262, 268.
Anti-hog law in Fort Worth, 31.
A. R. C. (Automotive Air Conditioning), 134.
Area differentials in Fort Worth (census tract areas): 75, ff.; agency board membership, 100; age-sex variations, 80-82; aid to dependent children, 100, 102; area stability, 95-97; composite indices of variations, 98, 104-107; education, 85-87; executive residences, 100; general welfare assistance, 100; income, 87-88; housing, 89-92; juvenile delinquency, 100, 102; natural areas, 72-74; occupations, 92-95; population and population per square mile, 79-80; population changes, 1950-1956, 108-112; race-ethnic variations, 83-85; tuberculosis morbidity, 100, 102.
Arlington Heights, 20.
Armour Packing Company, 34, 124, 150.

Baker, Robert E., 97.
Bell Aircraft Corporation, 134, 149.
Benbrook Dam, 17, 117.
Berrong, Verna Elizabeth, 25.
Bierstedt, Robert, xiii.
Billings, R. B., 179.
B'nai B'rith, Independent Order of, 210.

Board of Health, Fort Worth, 191.
Bogue, Donald J., 13.
Bond issues, Fort Worth municipal, 38.
Bradley, Charles E., 198.
Bradshaw, W. V., 189.
Brown, Daisy, 183.
Bunnell, James E., 113.
Bureau of Business Research, Texas Christian University, 137, 138-139, 153.
Burgess, Ernest W., 10-12, 13.
Burkburnett oil discoveries, 35, 36, 128.
Busby, Eldon, 108, 242, 243, 247.
Business and industry, growth of in Fort Worth, 3-7, 118-137.

Cain, L. B., 97.
Camp Bowie, 37.
Carpenter, David B., 12.
Carswell Airforce Base, 17, 41, 134, 151.
Carter, Amon G., 15-18.
Casaday, L. W., 114, 163.
Cattle industry, Fort Worth's importance in, 140, 161-162.
Census Tract Street Directory, Fort Worth, 98.
Census tracts: defined, 74-75; Fort Worth tract areas, 76; Fort Worth tract differentials, see Area differentials; Tarrant County tract areas, 77.
Chamber of Commerce, Fort Worth, 37, 38, 39, 98, 99, 108. 124, 150, 151, 258.
Charity, early city and county program, 210-211, 213, 214.
Chevrolet Motor Car Company, 38, 127.
Chicago Pneumatic Tool Company, 134.
City-County Hospital (John Peter Smith), 38, 195, 200.
Civil War, influence on Fort Worth, 2, 26-28.
Community Chest, see United Fund.